POPULISM AND ETHNICITY

McGill-Queen's Iberian and Latin American Cultures Series
SERIES EDITOR: NICOLÁS FERNÁNDEZ-MEDINA

The McGill-Queen's Iberian and Latin American Cultures Series is committed to publishing original scholarship that explores and re-evaluates Iberian and Latin American cultures, connections, and identities. Offering diverse perspectives on a range of regional and global histories from the early modern period to twenty-first-century contexts, the series cuts across disciplinary boundaries to consider how questions of authority, nation, revolution, gender, sexuality, science, epistemology, avant-gardism, aesthetics, travel, colonization, race relations, religious belief, and media technologies, among others, have shaped the rich and complex trajectories of modernity in the Iberian Peninsula and Latin America.

The McGill-Queen's Iberian and Latin American Cultures Series promotes rigorous scholarship and welcomes proposals for innovative and theoretically compelling monographs and edited collections.

1 Populism and Ethnicity
Peronism and the Jews of Argentina
Raanan Rein
Translated by Isis Sadek

Populism and Ethnicity

Peronism and the Jews of Argentina

RAANAN REIN

Translated by Isis Sadek

McGill-Queen's University Press
Montreal & Kingston • London • Chicago

Originally published in Spanish in 2015 as *Los muchachos peronistas judíos: Los argentines judíos y el apoyo al Justicialismo* by Sudamericana.

ISBN 978-0-2280-0166-9 (cloth)
ISBN 978-0-2280-0299-4 (ePDF)
ISBN 978-0-2280-0300-7 (ePUB)

Legal deposit second quarter 2020
Bibliothèque nationale du Québec

Printed in Canada on acid-free paper that is 100% ancient forest free (100% post-consumer recycled), processed chlorine free

Funded by the Government of Canada | Financé par le gouvernement du Canada | Canada | Canada Council for the Arts | Conseil des arts du Canada

We acknowledge the support of the Canada Council for the Arts.

Nous remercions le Conseil des arts du Canada de son soutien.

Library and Archives Canada Cataloguing in Publication

Title: Populism and ethnicity: Peronism and the Jews of Argentina / Raanan Rein; translated by Isis Sadek.

Other titles: Muchachos peronistas judíos. English

Names: Rein, Raanan, 1960– author. | Sadek, Isis, 1977– translator.

Description: Series statement: McGill-Queen's Iberian and Latin American cultures series; I [1] | Translation of: Los muchachos peronistas judíos. | Includes bibliographical references and index.

Identifiers: Canadiana (print) 20200176757 | Canadiana (eBOOK) 20200176765 | ISBN 9780228001669 (cloth) | ISBN 9780228002994 (ePDF) | ISBN 9780228003007 (ePUB)

Subjects: LCSH: Jews—Argentina—History—20th century. | LCSH: Jews—Argentina—Politics and government—20th century. | LCSH: Antisemitism—Argentina—History—20th century. | LCSH: Peronism. | LCSH: Argentina—Politics and government—1943–1955.

Classification: LCC F3021.J5 R45 2020 | DDC 982/.00492400904—dc23

This book was typeset by Marquis Interscript in 11/14 Sabon.

Contents

Figures vii

Acknowledgments ix

Abbreviations xi

Introduction: Deconstructing a Myth 3

1 The Other Promised Land: Jewish Immigration to Argentina 14

2 The Origins of the Stain of Fascism: Argentina's Neutrality in the Second World War and the Entry of Nazi War Criminals 45

3 The OIA, the Jewish Section of the Peronist Party 74

4 Peronism and the New Jewish State 114

5 Support from Jewish Intellectuals and Media 153

6 Support from Jewish Unionists and Businessmen 186

7 *Justicialismo* through Israeli Lenses, 1946–76 223

Epilogue 260

Notes 267

Bibliography 293

Index 311

Figures

1.1 The Italian ship *Giulio Cesare* bringing new immigrants to the port of Buenos Aires, 1928. Source: Archivo General de La Nación, Buenos Aires 16

1.2 A mosaic of identities: Jewish gaucho with a *tallit*, the shawl used in Jewish religious services, drinking mate, Entre Ríos, Argentina, 1984. Source: Beit Hatefutsot Photo Archive, Tel Aviv. Courtesy Gustavo Cohen, Argentina 20

1.3 Poster for Purim festival emphasizing the bond with Eretz Israel/Jewish Palestine, Buenos Aires, 1937. Source: Central Zionist Archives, Jerusalem. Courtesy Beit Hatefutsot Photo Archive, Tel Aviv 21

1.4 Jews in one of the Baron de Hirsch settlements in Entre Ríos, Argentina, 1922. Source: Beit Hatefutsot Photo Archive, Tel Aviv. Courtesy Louis and Shoshana Strauss, Israel 26

1.5 Jews working in the fields of Rivera, Buenos Aires, 1975. Source: Beit Hatefutsot Photo Archive, Tel Aviv. Courtesy WIZO, Buenos Aires 27

1.6 Hotel de Inmigrantes (Immigrants' Hotel), a complex of buildings constructed in the early twentieth century in the port of Buenos Aires to receive and assist mass European immigration, October 1905. Source: Archivo General de La Nación, Buenos Aires 29

2.1 False document, bearing the name of Zeev Zichroni, prepared for the abduction of Adolf Eichmann in 1960. Source: Catalog of the exhibition *Operation Finale*, Beit Hatefutsot, Tel Aviv, 2012 65

3.1 Pablo Manguel, leader of the OIA, next to Juan and Eva Perón at a Jewish support event for the Peronist government, early 1950s. Source: Archive of the Manguel Family, Buenos Aires 77

3.2 Eva Perón delivering a speech at an event organized by the OIA, early 1950s. Juan Perón and Pablo Manguel are sitting in the first row. Source: Archive of the Manguel Family, Buenos Aires 82

3.3 Shipments of garments and blankets sent by the Eva Perón Foundation for the residents of immigrant camps in the new state of Israel, received in the port of Haifa by Yitzhak Navon, future president of Israel, June 1955. Source: Government Press Office, Jerusalem. Photo by Teddy Brauner 83

3.4 Pablo Manguel, the first Argentine ambassador to Israel and leader of the OIA, with Juan Perón, early 1950s. Source: Archive of the Manguel Family, Buenos Aires 87

4.1 Chaim Weizmann, president of the state of Israel, during a conversation with the Argentine ambassador, Pablo Manguel, and the ambassador of Israel in Buenos Aires, Yaacov Tsur, August 1951. Source: Government Press Office, Jerusalem. Photo by David Eldan 132

4.2 Pablo Manguel, first Argentine ambassador to Israel and leader of the OIA (third from left), arriving at Lod Airport, August 1949. Source: Government Press Office, Jerusalem. Photo by David Eldan 134

5.1 José Ber Gelbard and his political archrival José Lopez Rega. Source: Archive of the Gelbard Family, Los Angeles 184

6.1 José Ber Gelbard, president of the Confederación General Económica, delivering a speech at the inauguration of the Confederation's headquarters in the presence of Argentine president Juan Perón, February 1955. Source: Archivo General de La Nación, Buenos Aires 197

Acknowledgments

This book is the culmination of a journey that began in 1995 at the meeting of the Latin American Jewish Studies Association, when I gave a talk on Israeli perceptions of the Peronism of the 1940s and 1950s. I am indebted to librarians and archivists, colleagues and students, friends and relatives, who each contributed in one way or another to this journey. They helped develop concepts, sought out unpublished materials, or contributed to an oral history project. I could not possibly name them all here.

I would like to begin by thanking the late Jorge Gelman, who encouraged me to write this book, originally titled *Los muchachos peronistas judíos: Los argentinos-judíos y el apoyo al justicialismo*, after publishing my *Los bohemios de Villa Crespo: Judíos y fútbol en la Argentina* in 2012 as part of the series *Nudos de la Historia Argentina*, which he edited for Sudamericana. Claudio Panella, of the Universidad Nacional de La Plata, has been a collaborator in various projects related to early Peronism. His support and collaboration in these projects has been invaluable.

I owe a particular debt of gratitude to Jeffrey Lesser of Emory University, David Sheinin of Trent University, Federico Finchelstein of the New School, and José Moya of Barnard College, for an inspiring and ongoing conversation on the topics of immigration, ethnicity, diaspora, and transnationalism. At various phases of this project, I have engaged in interesting conversations with Manuela Fingueret, Saul Sosnowski, Mirta Kupfermink, Adriana Brodsky, Edna Aizenberg,

Mariano Plotkin, Emmanuel Kahan, Alejandro Dujovne, Benjamin Bryce, and Nerina Visacovsky.

Susana Brauner, Fabián Bosoer, Santiago Senén González, Gustavo Nicolás Contereras, Adrián Krupnik, Diego Rosemberg, César Tcach, Andrea Matallana, Beatriz Gurevich, and Ariel Kocik facilitated important materials for this research. Julián Blejmar assisted me in preparing the section on Gelbard. I thank Rosalie Sitman of Tel Aviv University; she is a constant interlocutor in my studies on twentieth-century Argentina. My thanks also to many of my students, past and present: Efraim Davidi, Ariel Noyjovich, Tzvi Tal, Uri Rosenheck, Mollie Lewis Nouwen, Ariel Svarch, Ilan Diner, Maayan Nahari, and Omri Elmaleh, for their help in locating various sources used in this research.

I would also like to thank Richard Ratzlaff for his initiative to publish an English-language edition of my book, and Isis Sadek for her translation from Spanish to English. My thanks also to all those whom I have interviewed during all those years and who are mentioned in this book.

Last but not least, I thank my wife Mónica, who was born in Villa Crespo and has accompanied me in my scholarly trajectory for more than thirty years now, my sons Omer and Noa, my daughter-in-law Chen, and my granddaughter Lia, as well as the Walovnik, Frid, and Bichman families who always open their homes (and hearts) to me during my research-related stays in Buenos Aires.

I have benefitted from the support of the S. Daniel Abraham Center for International and Regional Studies and the Elías Sourasky Chair of Latin American and Spanish History, both at Tel Aviv University, as well as the Humboldt and Thyssen Foundations. I thank them all for having made this book possible.

Earlier discussions of several key issues related to Jewish-Argentine experiences in the first half of the twentieth century have appeared in my books *Argentina, Israel, and the Jews: Péron, the Eichmann Capture and After* (University Press of Maryland, 2003), *Argentine Jews or Jewish Argentines: Essays on Ethnicity, Identity, and Diaspora* (Brill, 2010), and *Fútbol, Jews, and the Making of Argentina* (Stanford University Press, 2015).

Abbreviations

ALN	Alianza Libertadora Nacionalista (Nationalist Liberation Alliance)
AMIA	Asociación Mutual Israelita Argentina (Jewish Mutual Association of Argentina)
CGE	Confederación General Económica (General Economic Confederation)
CGT	Confederación General del Trabajo (Trade Unions Confederation)
CPP	Comité Pro-Palestina (Pro-Palestine Committee)
DAIA	Delegación de Asociaciones Israelitas Argentinas (Delegation of Argentine Jewish Associations)
OIA	Organización Israelita Argentina (Argentine Jewish Organization)
UCR	Unión Cívica Radical (Civic Radical Union)
UD	Unión Democrática (Democratic Union)
UIA	Unión Industrial Argentina (Argentine Industrial Union)
UOM	Unión Obrera Metalúrgica (Metalworkers Union)

POPULISM AND ETHNICITY

INTRODUCTION

Deconstructing a Myth

In early August 2014, I was invited to take part in a debate on the figure of Juan Domingo Perón and his ties with the Jewish-Argentine community. The discussion took place in the main room of Tzavta, the progressive Zionist club aptly located on Perón Street, in Argentina's capital. In its coverage of the event, the newspaper *Nueva Sión* took note of the "unprecedented audience attendance."[1] It wasn't necessarily my talk that had drawn so many. Rather, what had summoned participants in such numbers was the possibility of debating whether the founder of the doctrine and movement known as *Justicialismo* (from the word "justice") and the members of his administrations were antisemitic or not. Even though the event was almost seventy years removed from Perón's entry into the presidential palace, this topic continues to generate lively controversies both within and outside of the Jewish community.

Many in the audience were surprised by the "ten commandments" (which were in fact eleven) that I presented that day. It was as though the audience members still had, fresh in their minds, the memory of the electoral campaign advertisements that the Unión Democrática (Democratic Union) ran between the final months of 1945 and the start of 1946, portraying Perón as a Nazi fascist. Since the regime that Perón established following his electoral victory was allegedly antisemitic, Argentines of Jewish descent were necessarily hostile to this government. Such myths are still deeply rooted in the collective consciousness of broad swaths of Argentine society. The present book seeks to challenge precisely these myths.

These were the arguments that I put forward: first, Perón was not a Nazi. This accusation is based on the neutral stance that the administration prior to Perón's (in which he held various posts) adopted during the Second World War. It is false. The Argentine government's delay in siding with the Allies was rooted in two features inherent to the country's diplomatic relations. On the one hand, Argentina had traditionally maintained a neutral stance in international conflicts, one largely supported by the Argentine population, as had been the case during the First World War. On the other hand, Argentina's neutrality was crucial for Great Britain – then Argentina's main trade partner – as a declaration of war on Germany would have greatly endangered the transatlantic shipments of wheat and beef, which were vital imports for Britons.

The second argument: Perón was not a fascist. He spent some time in Italy at the end of the 1930s, mountain climbing, far away from Rome and from the centre of political events. This is not to say that he had no contact with leading figures of fascism. His thinking certainly was nationalist and included authoritarian elements, but this does not make him a fascist. Further, in the post-Second World War context, when Perón was first elected to the presidency, it was not possible to give a fascist orientation to a new regime. This is where the third argument comes in: I emphasized the heterogeneous nature of Peronism by referring to the combination of political and ideological influences that shaped the movement. While extreme-right nationalism was one of those influences, it was not the only one. Peronism was also shaped by the Catholic Church's social doctrine, in addition to socialist currents of varying nuances. In order to characterize Peronism, I adopted a theoretical perspective by insisting on the concept of populism, which continues to be much more relevant than fascism for understanding Peronism.

The fourth argument stated that Perón was not an antisemite. Upon reading the numerous speeches that Perón pronounced against antisemitism during his first two presidencies, it immediately becomes clear that no other president before Perón had rejected discrimination against Jews so clearly and unambiguously. The same goes for Eva Duarte de Perón. In many of her speeches, Evita argued that it was the country's oligarchy that upheld antisemitic attitudes, but that Peronism did not.

Nor was the Peronist regime antisemitic. During its decade-long rule, there were fewer antisemitic incidents than during any other period in the twentieth century. Between the late 1940s and early 1950s, many Jews became public servants and secured more important posts than in any previous administration. My sixth argument therefore disproved the idea that the Jewish community was generally hostile to Peronism. This false portrayal of a homogeneous group must be challenged by recalling that, on the one hand, most Jews never affiliated with community institutions, and, on the other, that the positions adopted within the Jewish community on any matter, be it political, social, economic, or cultural, have always been varied.

Jews were some of the earliest supporters of nascent Peronism. This initial support grew as the new regime entrenched itself in power and even more so when Perón was re-elected in November 1951. Between those two events, the impact of the Second World War began to recede while Peronism lasted, proving to be more than a fleeting phenomenon. Although never a majority among Jewish-Argentines, it became equally clear that a considerable number of Jews changed their opinion upon seeing the social and economic policies that Peronism advanced and that benefitted many middle-class and lower-middle-class Jewish-Argentines as well. Support for Perón's government also stemmed from its ongoing struggle against antisemitism and its marginalization of extreme-right figures from important posts within the administration.

I then discussed the role of the Organización Israelita Argentina (OIA; Argentine Jewish Organization), which openly cultivated close ties with Peronism. The OIA is sometimes described as a group of marginalized persons within the Jewish community who eagerly awaited an opportunity to play a more prominent role. While some members of the OIA were indeed opportunists or marginal characters, many were motivated to join the OIA for other reasons: because they identified with Peronism's concept of social justice or with its economic and social policies, or because they wished to back and join a movement that enjoyed the support of a majority of Argentines.

The ties that the Argentine government maintained with the state of Israel have always been particularly important to Jewish-Argentines. The Peronist government forged excellent relations with the nascent Jewish state. While Argentina abstained from the United Nations vote on the partition of Palestine and the creation of the state of Israel, Argentina would be the first Latin American country to establish an embassy in Israel and to sign a trade agreement with the new country. In fact, Perón's decade-long presidency marked a peak in this bilateral relation.[2]

My tenth argument highlighted the attempts on the part of the leadership of Argentina's Jewish community to erase from collective memory the support that Peronism enjoyed among many Jews. This effort, which began with the overthrow of Perón in September 1955, was in line with the new political conditions at the time. Finally, in my eleventh argument, I posited that Perón was the first Argentine head of state to legitimate the idea of the nation as a mosaic of different ethnic groups. Perón saw no incompatibility between being a good Argentine, being a good Jew, and supporting Zionism or the state of Israel. For him, any Argentine of Spanish descent could support his or her motherland, Spain; any Argentine of Italian descent could support Italy; and any Argentine of Jewish origin could support the state of Israel. The speeches that Perón gave at the time included no references to a "double loyalty," a common accusation that the ranks of the extreme right in Argentina voiced throughout the twentieth century.

These arguments, discussed in detail in the following chapters, provoked a lively debate on that winter night in Buenos Aires. The audience brought diverse approaches to the forum, which included specialized researchers, historians, students, and people who had an interest in the topic, as well as participants who were alive at the time and were eager to contribute their testimony based on their personal experiences. The gathering had also summoned Peronist militants and members of Congress, even attracting the participation of Pablo Manguel's two sons – one of whom, Juan Domingo, was born in Tel Aviv. Manguel had been at the head of the OIA and became the first Argentine ambassador to Israel. Coverage of the event noted that my lecture "gave way to interesting counterpoints between perspectives focused on the autobiographical dimensions and those that were grounded in historiographic research. The debate was heated and passionate, as some portrayed Perón as a quasi-Nazi and fascist, while others agreed with Raanan Rein's perspective," according to *Nueva Sión*.

One week later, I was invited to the Círculo de Legisladores (Legislators' Club) to meet with a group of former senators and congresspersons of the first Peronist administration, which included some veterans such as Rodolfo Decker, leader of the Peronist majority in the national Congress from June 1946 onward, or Duilo Brunello, who collaborated closely with José Ber Gelbard in the Confederación General Económica (CGE; General Economic Confederation). The vice-president of the Congreso Metropolitano del Partido Justicialista (Metropolitan Congress of the Justicialist Party), Raquel Cecilia (Kelly) Kismer de Olmos, as well as a former member of Congress, Ana Kessler, also spoke at the meeting. The two of them had met during the mid-1980s when they were Justicialist militants, and they recalled the surprise that people (Jewish or not) expressed upon meeting a "Jewish Peronist," as if this were a rarity.

Indeed, traditional historiography holds that throughout the Peronist decade (1946–55), Juan D. Perón failed in his attempts at attracting the support of broad sectors of Argentina's Jewish community. Despite Perón's efforts to eradicate antisemitism and despite having cultivated close ties with the state of Israel, historians tell us that most Argentines of Jewish origin remained hostile to Perón. The leader's numerous initiatives to win the community over supposedly did not yield the expected results. Shortly after the end of the Second World War, when the magnitude of the decimation of the old continent's Jewish communities began to come into view, Argentine Jews, who mainly originated from the devastated areas of Central and Eastern Europe, were understandably sensitive toward a government that resembled in some respects the countries of the recently defeated Axis. This reaction was further strengthened by the support that Perón received from nationalist and antisemitic circles at the start of his political career, particularly the Alianza Libertadora Nacionalista (ALN; Nationalist Liberation Alliance), and by the pact that Perón made with the Catholic Church in the second half of the 1940s. The political identity of many Jews, who typically belonged to democratic liberal or leftist organizations, as well as their socioeconomic identity (many were part of Argentina's middle class), led them to express their reservations about this regime that was increasingly developing authoritarian tendencies while striving to improve the conditions of the Argentine working class. Perón's gradual incorporation of the fight against antisemitism into his political platform did not succeed in allaying the suspicions of many Jews about his government.

While this picture is not entirely false, it is largely one-dimensional and fails to accurately reflect a reality that was far more complex. In the August 1948 inauguration of the OIA headquarters, located at 2000 Corrientes, its president, Sujer Matrajt, stated that, "Perón is not only the careful promoter of our political sovereignty, he is also the head of state who, in a world dominated by intolerance, was able to raise the banner of consideration and of respect toward all of the communities that are part of the nation, chasing away from these lands the ghost of persecution and intolerance." Perón also spoke at the event: "How could antisemitism in Argentina be accepted or accounted for? There should only be one class of men in Argentina: men who work for the good of the nation, without distinctions … This is why … as long as I am President of the Republic, no person shall persecute another."[3] The newspaper *El Argentino* reported on the event with the following headline: "Argentine Jewish Organization Incorporated into Peronism."

Evita expressed similar notions during that same month of August: "In our country, the only ones who have distinguished between classes and religions have been the leaders of the baleful oligarchy who have governed our country for fifty years. Those in power are responsible for antisemitism, as they have poisoned the people with false theories, and they did this until Perón made it possible to proclaim us all equals."[4] The Peróns' shows of sympathy toward Jews were intended as a challenge to the traditional Argentine elites, who had not stood out for their openness toward Jews.

While the OIA was unable to challenge the leadership of the Delegación de Asociaciones Israelitas Argentinas (DAIA; Delegation of Argentine Jewish Associations), it was an important mediator between national authorities and the organized community, and it succeeded at negotiating with the government collective benefits for Jewish-Argentines, thus promoting the community's ethnic and religious interests. The majority of the OIA's leadership were first-generation Jewish immigrants from Eastern Europe. Some were strongly involved with the community, with Zionism and Israel, but their identity was that of Jewish-Argentines more than that of Argentine Jews. They advocated for the social integration of Jews through Peronism without renouncing the Jewish and Zionist components of their identity. Most of them continued to be loyal to Perón and to the

Justicialist movement even after Perón was overthrown, which further proves that their ties with Peronism were not merely opportunistic. During the self-designated Revolución Libertadora (Liberating Revolution) that followed the ouster of Perón, many of these supporters paid a high price for their loyalty to Peronism.

While most of the leaders of Jewish organizations had their reservations about the Peronist administration and the Peronist movement, some figures had a different stance. It is a little-known yet interesting fact that the president of the DAIA, Ricardo Dubrovsky, became a member of the Justicialist Party. In the middle of 1953, Dubrovsky was appointed professor in the Universidad de Buenos Aires's Chair of Obstetrics. The directors of the Hospital Israelita also supported the Peronist government and its social and economic policies. These examples illustrate support for or identification with the social and political movement that had a lasting impact on Argentine society. This support came from within the organized Jewish community and, especially and more importantly, from common people who were not affiliated to Jewish community institutions and whose case is less known. Peronism, which divided Argentine society between adherents and opponents, caused similar divisions among Argentines of Jewish origin, even if the government's supporters were never a majority among them.

The workers movement was the backbone of Peronism. Various Jewish leaders of trade unions not only identified with the nascent movement, but also played an important role in mobilizing popular support for Peronism. Ángel Perelman, who founded the Unión Obrera Metalúrgica (UOM; Metalworkers Union) in 1943 and was its first secretary, is recognized for his contribution to the workers' marches held on 17 October 1945, and for his instrumental role in shaping the political coalition that won the general elections in February 1946. A comparable contribution was that of Ángel Yampolsky, general secretary of the autonomous union of the "La Negra" meatpacking plant in Avellaneda and one of the founders of the Partido Laborista (Labour Party). Rafael Kogan, one of the founders of the Railworkers' Union and its managing secretary, deserves much of the credit for rallying support for Perón within that important union. Abraham Krislavin, who would become undersecretary in the Ministry of the Interior, and David Diskin, both from the Confederación General de Empleados de

Comercio de la República Argentina (General Confederation of Employees of Business of the Argentine Republic), would play an important role as links between the Peronist government and various Jewish persons or groups.

Argentine populism was a multi-class coalition whose membership included not only the organized workers' movement and sectors of the armed forces, but also incipient industrialists – particularly those who manufactured goods to substitute the imported products that satisfied local demand – in addition to provinces' commercial elites. This coalition also included businessmen and entrepreneurs of various immigrant communities (including Jews, Arabs, and Japanese) who had benefitted from Peronism and its protectionism of Argentine industry. This was especially the case in the textile and clothing industries, as well as those that produced leather goods, furniture, foodstuffs, and other consumer goods. José Ber Gelbard is a clear example of the social and economic mobility made possible by Peronist policies: he came to Argentina from Poland with his parents, prospered as a salesperson in the province of Catamarca, and then became the leading figure in the Peronist-leaning CGE for almost two decades. Julio Broner and Israel Dujovne are other examples of Jewish-Argentines whose trajectory was similar to, although less spectacular than, Gelbard's.

The support of businesspersons for Peronism is also clearly exemplified in the figure of the communications magnate Jaime Yankelevich. Yankelevich played a central part in the emergence and development of commercial radio in Argentina and also launched countrywide television broadcasts (the inauguration of television broadcasts in Argentina coincided with the 1951 celebrations of the Peronist Day of Popular Loyalty). Yankelevich's biography is that of a self-made man who went from being a poor immigrant to become a rich entrepreneur who owned Radio Belgrano, founded the first Argentine broadcasting channel, and was general director of the national state radio corporation during the first Perón administration. Some interpreted Evita's positive attitudes toward Jews as a way of showing her gratitude to the owner of Radio Belgrano, the platform from which she was catapulted to fame. It was from the airwaves of Radio Belgrano that, in 1943, Eva Perón began to broadcast a program on famous women in history.

The support of Peronism among Jewish-Argentine intellectuals is also noteworthy. The cultural supplement of the newspaper *La Prensa* illustrates this. After the Peronist government expropriated the newspaper and entrusted it to the Confederación General del Trabajo (CGT; Trade Unions Confederation),[5] the cultural supplement of *La Prensa* was directed by an editorial team composed of Argentine intellectuals of Jewish origin, beginning with its director Israel Zeitlin (known by the pseudonym César Tiempo), and its members Bernardo Ezequiel Koremblit, León Benarós, and Julia Prilutzky Farny. In its short span of publication, between 1952 and 1955, this iteration of *La Prensa* published more Jewish-Argentine authors than the prominent conservative newspaper *La Nación* did over the course of fifty years. Many other Jewish intellectuals showed their sympathy for Peronism, including Bernardo Kordon and Fernando Valentín (pseudonym for Abraham Valentín Schprejer), author of *El día de octubre* (That October Day), one of the few literary works to examine the deep underpinnings of 17 October 1945.

It should also be noted that, during the November 1951 presidential elections, the Justicialist Party won the majority of votes in the Jewish agricultural colonies of Santa Fe and Entre Ríos. Even cities or provinces like Córdoba that are not necessarily considered to be Peronist had Justicialist militants of Jewish origin, such as the congressperson José Alexencier or Raúl Bercovich Rodríguez. The Córdoba branch of the youth Zionist movement, known as "Lamerjav," changed its name to "Eva Perón" in 1954. Jewish public servants also occupied posts in various state organizations to which they had previously not had access, particularly in the realm of diplomacy: Pablo Manguel, the first Argentine ambassador to Israel, comes to mind, as do Ezequiel Zabotinsky, who would succeed Manguel in Tel Aviv, and Israel Jabbaz, member of Argentina's delegation at the United Nations when it held the vote on the partition of Palestine and the creation of the state of Israel. In this sense, these Peronist administrations marked a step forward for Jews' aspirations to break the glass ceiling in various spheres of public life.

The young rabbi Amram Blum, head of the community's rabbinical council, was identified by many anti-Peronists as a symbol of the ties between Perón and Jewish-Argentines. Perón designated him as his advisor on religious matters and, in 1952, during a ceremony held in the synagogue on Paso Street and sponsored by the OIA, Blum said a prayer for Evita's return to health. Blum successfully negotiated unprecedented gains for Jewish conscripts who were henceforth relieved of their obligation on religious holidays such as Rosh Hashana and Yom Kippur. Blum also launched the Chair of Hebraic Studies at the Universidad de Buenos Aires's Faculty of Philosophy and Letters as a "result of the inspiration from his Excellency, the Head of State."

And one of the most notable gestures of the Peronist administration toward the state of Israel – aside from a bilateral trade agreement that benefitted the latter – was sending clothing and medicine to the camps housing new immigrants to the Jewish state through the Fundación Eva Perón (Eva Perón Foundation). Israel's minister of labour, Golda Meir, personally thanked Evita for the donations during her visit to Argentina in April 1951.

Despite this varied and broad evidence, the leadership of Jewish community institutions has undertaken a systematic effort to erase a phenomenon that did not suit its narrative and political purposes. The first of these efforts was launched in September 1955, when the leadership used all the tools at its disposal to erase the memory of support for Peronism among various sectors of Jewish-Argentines. In fact, once the Peronist regime had been overthrown, the initiatives to "de-Peronize" the Jewish community were more successful than similar efforts in Argentine society at large. Jews may, as the saying goes, "have a long memory," but, like that of other social and ethnic groups, this memory is selective. The fact that a substantial number of Jews supported Perón and the Justicialist movement during the 1940s and 1950s was almost entirely erased from the collective memory of Jewish-Argentines and from the historical record.

This book aspires to recover the silenced voices of those Argentines of Jewish origin who supported early Peronism. It makes two additional contributions. The first, an analysis of the relations between Perón and the Jewish-Argentine community, proves that the power of the Peronist government to intervene in some areas and sectors of Argentine civil society was more limited than is typically acknowledged. Jewish organizations demonstrated their ability to defend their autonomy in the face of state actions to mobilize and "Peronize" them; this reveals the limit of the paradigm through which the ties between Peronism and Argentine civil society are typically viewed.

The second argument that I make here is that Jews, prior to the emergence of Peronism, were not considered to be a part of the "polis," the "civitas," or the "demos" of the Argentine nation, as imagined by governing elites, regardless of social and demographic realities. Furthermore, the influence of Catholicism played a part in the exclusion of specific social sectors and various non-Latin ethnic groups. That formal citizenship was granted to all the indigenous groups and immigrants was of little consequence in a society where electoral fraud was widespread and elites looked down upon popular culture or the cultural traditions of migrants. It was Peronism that, in part due to its socialist component, accelerated notably the processes that would give new social, political, and cultural meaning to citizenship. Peronism rehabilitated popular culture and gave folklore a place in Argentine culture, attempted to rewrite national history and included various ethnic minorities who, up until that point, had been relegated to the margins of the nation – as was the case for Arabs and Jews. In doing so, it transformed many of those "imaginary citizens" into an integral part of Argentine society. Perón's efforts to redefine the meaning of citizenship were reflected in his policies, designed to acknowledge the legitimate claim of multiple collective ethnic identities and to redistribute national wealth. It is precisely in this consideration of rights as collective – and not as individual – that, to a significant extent, Peronism paved the way for the multicultural Argentina that we know today.

1

The Other Promised Land

Jewish Immigration to Argentina

Between 1889 and 1930, nearly one hundred thousand Jews abandoned Central and Eastern Europe to settle permanently in Argentina. Their stories resemble in many aspects those of millions of other European immigrants who set sail for the New World, fleeing the privations of the Old World. These mass migrations were facilitated by technological advances in transportation and prompted by the migrants' home countries' uneven integration into the global economy. Pioneering emigrants were the first links in a chain migration of friends and relatives from the home country. The printed media that these immigrants produced and circulated, along with personal correspondence, disseminated information about lands that promised new opportunities, such as Argentina.

The late nineteenth and early twentieth centuries witnessed accelerated demographic growth in the South American nation, and the city of Buenos Aires mushroomed into the largest and most populous metropolis in Latin America. Its population of 180,000 in 1870 had by 1910 multiplied sevenfold to 1,300,000. Buenos Aires became a city of European immigrants hailing particularly from Italy and Spain. It came to be known as the "Paris of South America" due to its unique architecture and urban planning, as well as its cafés and cultural institutions.[1]

During the second half of the nineteenth century, Argentine elites and national authorities jointly espoused a policy grounded in positivist ideals and strategically designed to encourage immigration from Europe. Their aspiration was clear: they wished to increase the relatively small population and to "improve" (a euphemism for "whiten") the composition of this population by attracting immigrants, preferably originating from the northern parts of the Old Continent, who would bring in European "civilization" at the expense of the indigenous population and its "barbarism." That way, it was hoped, immigrants could improve the development of the Republic and its modernization. In 1853, the renowned liberal intellectual and politician Juan Bautista Alberdi coined the slogan *To govern is to populate*.

This slogan was put into action when, in the span of hardly three years (1888–90), Argentine delegates in Europe handed out 133,000 free tickets for ships to Buenos Aires. It should be noted that in 1810, at the outset of the process of independence from the yoke of Spanish colonialism, the nation's territory spanned an area of approximately 2,780,000 square kilometres – equivalent to almost the entirety of continental Europe – but this area had less than half a million inhabitants, that is, a quarter of the population of the small and mountainous Swiss confederation at the time, or a fifth of the population of the city of London. With this vast arable land, Argentina was destined to play an important role in the global economy by providing various foodstuffs. To that end, it required tens of thousands of working hands. The demographic revolution in European countries at that time fueled mass migrations to the New World, particularly to the United States and the region of the River Plate, which spanned eastern Argentina, Uruguay, and southern Brazil. Between 1880 and 1950, Argentina received more immigrants, both in relative and absolute terms, than any other Latin American country.[2]

Hopes of attracting Protestant immigrants from the industrialized European northeast would soon be dashed. Most of the recent arrivals in Argentina came from Southern and Eastern Europe and, to a lesser extent, from the eastern Mediterranean and the Balkans. Only a minority of migrants (including Muslims and Jews) were not Christian. Many did not even try to settle in the inland agricultural colonies – either because they were not motivated to do so or did not have the means to purchase land – and opted instead for the large urban agglomerations, particularly Buenos Aires, which quickly became a metropolis. By the 1920s, half (or more) of the city's inhabitants had not been born there. This provoked the ire of xenophobes and nationalists alike, and

Figure 1.1 The Italian ship *Giulio Cesare* bringing new immigrants to the port of Buenos Aires, 1928.

increased efforts to assimilate new immigrants into Argentina's melting pot of races, particularly through the state's educational system. Participation in sports and music also offered immigrants paths through which to integrate, with the additional advantage, for Jews, that these activities neutralized the accusations of cowardice or lack of manliness typically voiced by antisemites.

Argentina's Jewish community, the largest in Latin America, is basically a product of this sweeping wave of transatlantic migration from Central and Eastern Europe and, to a lesser extent, the Middle East and the Balkans to the Americas. With the migratory wave ensuing from the outbreak of the First World War in 1914, Eastern European Jews (Ashkenazim) became the third-largest group of immigrants and the largest of the non-Catholic minorities in Argentina. At its peak, toward the late 1950s and early 1960s, Ashkenazi Jews amounted to 310,000 out of a total population of twenty million.[3]

The community had far greater visibility than these numbers suggest, largely because most Ashkenazim lived in Buenos Aires and congregated in specific neighbourhoods within the city, such as El Once and Villa Crespo. Their speech patterns initially contributed to their visibility: many first-generation immigrants did not become fully fluent in Spanish and their accent sounded strange, almost as strange as the garb of Orthodox Jews with their headdresses, suits, and long side locks. The simultaneous accumulation of stereotypes about Jews, whether racist, class-based, or targeting religion, made the Ashkenazim even more visible. As these Jews aspired to integrate and to gain acceptance, they saw soccer, tango, and, later, work in the film industry as aspects of local culture through which they could become Argentine. Their social, economic, and cultural integration is a fascinating success story.

This introductory chapter offers the necessary context to understand some of the central topics addressed in this book. After analyzing the processes of immigration and settlement, as well as the characteristics of the Jewish community, the chapter emphasizes the rapid process through which Jews became Argentines. It also discusses the Jewish presence in the working class and lower middle class during the first half of the twentieth century. These processes account in part for the support that Peronism enjoyed among sectors of the Jewish community. The ties that Jewish-Argentines maintained with their European countries of origin, however, made them more distrustful of nationalist ideas, charismatic leadership, and mass movements. In the pages that follow, I question commonly held assumptions among historians of Jewish life and institutions in Argentina, premises that have led to an overstatement of antisemitism in Argentina in general and within Peronism in particular.

JEWISH IMMIGRANTS: "RUSOS" AND "TURCOS" BECOME CRIOLLOS

As with any immigrant group, understanding the migration of Jews requires an analysis of the factors that led them to leave their homes, of the appeal that other places held for them, and of the migration patterns adopted by that particular group. During the late nineteenth century, an increasing urgency to seek a better future outside of Europe was felt among the Jews of Eastern Europe, particularly those living in the "Pale of Settlement," an area located between present-day Poland and Russia, which was home to a large Jewish population. They were motivated to leave the region due to assaults on their persons, as well as social pressures and economic hardships.

1905 marked a watershed in the migration of Jews. That year, the Russian Empire lost its war against Japan and put down a revolution. Reactionary groups, with the collaboration of police forces loyal to the czar, launched a series of pogroms in more than 600 cities and villages of the Pale of Settlement. The economic downturn, fear of violence, and the feeling of being endangered prompted massive emigration. Simultaneously, beginning in the mid-nineteenth century, the Ottoman Empire was also in crisis: religious minorities were persecuted, Arab nationalism intensified, and mandatory conscription was enforced. A growing number of artisans and small traders found it harder to make a living due to economic changes. These shifts were at the root of a Syrian-Lebanese migratory wave in which Christians, Jews, and Muslims left their homelands due to a combination of political, economic, religious, and cultural factors.[4] During the first years of Arab immigration to the Americas, the overwhelming majority of immigrants were Christian (Catholic Maronite or Greek Orthodox), and, just as it was for Jews, Argentina was the most popular destination in Latin America. In any case, the percentage of Muslims also grew steadily, making them a sizeable minority within the Arabic-speaking community.

Both the northern and southern American continents seemed to promise prosperity and a better future to both Jewish and Arab immigrants (commonly referred to in Argentina as "rusos" and "turcos" respectively, due to their areas of origin). Hundreds of thousands of these immigrants made Argentina their home. Whereas a small quantity of Jews from Eastern Europe found refuge in Palestine – their real or imagined homeland – others sought to cross the Atlantic to make their lives in the New World. Various European-based Jewish organizations considered a gamut of proposals to settle Eastern European Jews outside the continent. One such proposal focused on a country in South America that was virtually unknown to most of them. Theodor Herzl, in his book *Judenstaat* (1896), described the choice faced by the Jewish masses of Eastern Europe as one between "Palestine or Argentina."

Those immigrants who chose the latter largely settled in the capital, Buenos Aires, and a significant minority became farmers. The latter are at the origin of the myth of the Jewish *gaucho* (horseman or cowboy), a typical characterization of immigrants who settled in the Argentine hinterland. These Jewish gauchos were brilliantly portrayed in Alberto Gerchunoff's novel, named after them and published in 1910 to coincide with the centennial anniversary of the Revolución de Mayo (May Revolution), which launched Argentina on the path to independence from Spain.[5] The emblematic figure of the Jewish gaucho appears repeatedly in subsequent works authored by Jewish-Argentine writers in ways that emphasize the authenticity of Jewish life in Argentina and the rootedness of Jews in, and their attachment to, the Argentine land.[6] The agricultural settlements that the Jewish philanthropist Baron de Hirsch established in Argentina and subsequently in neighbouring Brazil seemed to offer a partial solution to the Jewish national question at the turn of the century.[7]

In their determination to sever ties with the old colonial power, Spain, the members of Argentina's governing elite turned their gaze toward Republican France as a secular and progressive model to emulate. This cultural and political orientation, coupled with increasingly strong economic and commercial ties with Great Britain, contributed to the adoption of a liberal constitution in 1853, which guaranteed freedom of religion and was favourably disposed to welcoming immigrants. In 1876, a liberal-leaning migratory law that did not discriminate against non-Catholic immigrants was passed, in addition to legislation in 1884 enshrining the state's role in providing public education and keeping a register of births, marriages, and deaths. These measures limited the power and the influence of the Catholic Church.

Rumors about emigration to Argentina spread among Jews living in the urban agglomerations and rural villages of Central and Eastern Europe and the Ottoman Empire. They portrayed Argentina as a land of possibilities in which anyone could live free and prosper. The myth of "making it in America" spread quickly by way of transoceanic ethnic and family networks through which relatives, friends, and former

Figure 1.2 A mosaic of identities: Jewish gaucho with a *tallit*, the shawl used in Jewish religious services, drinking mate, Entre Ríos, Argentina, 1984.

neighbours exchanged in their letters news about new opportunities and advised on precautionary measures. In fact, for most Jewish immigrants, both Ashkenazim and Sephardim (Jews originating from northern Africa or the Ottoman Empire), Argentina proved to be a "promised land," a place in which they could establish themselves, live in safety, guarantee their children's education, and try to build a new home. In a brief lapse of time, these immigrants established community institutions and Jewish schools that satisfied their social, economic, and cultural needs. In doing so, they created a rich mosaic of social, cultural, political, and ideological life reflective of a wide variety of beliefs, identities, and social practices: communists and Zionists, religiously orthodox and secular, some emphasized their Jewish identity and others

Figure 1.3 Poster for Purim festival emphasizing the bond with Eretz Israel/Jewish Palestine, Buenos Aires, 1937.

preferred to highlight the Argentine components of their identity. Many of these immigrants came to occupy prominent posts in the social, economic, artistic, and political spheres.

This relative success does not mean that Jews, or any other ethnic group of immigrants, had always been welcomed by all. Like Arabs and other immigrants, Jews benefitted from Argentina's open immigration policy, but they also suffered, from the late nineteenth century onward, the disappointment of *criollo* elites (supposedly white, locally born people) upon seeing the tangible results of their own initiatives to "Europeanize" or "whiten" their country. Consequently, both of these ethnic groups experienced a general sentiment of hostility toward immigrants. Against the backdrop of growing nationalist, authoritarian, and xenophobic currents, particularly in the 1910s, 1920s, and 1930s, immigrants of "semitic" origin, whether Christian Arabs, Jews from Eastern Europe, Muslim Arabs, or Jewish Arabs – in sum, all those who were not always considered as "white" or were not Catholic – were criticized by those who viewed them as the most undesirable members of the migratory wave and were characterized by some Argentine positivists as racially inferior, dirty, and corrupting elements.

An 1898 article in the *Buenos Aires Herald* documents this attitude: "Are we becoming a Semitic republic? The immigration of Russian Jews is now the third largest [in the country], while Syrian Arabs (Turks) and Arabians are also flocking to these shores."[8] Similar concerns were voiced in the columns of several Spanish-language newspapers. For example, in 1910, the conservative daily *La Nación* stated that Syrian Lebanese peddlers' deplorable trafficking of cheaply made jewelry was a stain on the honour of the host country and that it was therefore necessary to restrict immigration from the Levant.[9] In addition to economic factors, arguments grounded in racial factors could also be adduced to oppose immigration. This is what Ernesto M. Aráoz, a politician from the province of Salta, did in defending his support for the exclusion of Jews from Argentina by alluding to the threat of dissolution and the challenge that recently arrived Jewish immigrants posed to the homogeneity of "our race."[10]

Among the country's liberal elites, even the most loyal advocates of immigration embraced the concept of the racial melting pot. It was expected that all those recently arrived, particularly those who were not Catholic, would abandon the customs and idiosyncrasies of their countries to adopt those of the new culture that migrants were shaping in Argentine society. This attitude, and the pressure to homogenize and assimilate, were particularly pronounced among those who upheld nationalist and xenophobic views. Although they were a minority within Argentine society, they had always existed and at times their influence was broader than their numbers, as their reach extended to political, military, and religious circles and seeped into the contemporary intellectual climate. This phenomenon caused permanent unease among Jewish-Argentines, whose European origins and family ties with the Old World predisposed them to view through a European lens Argentine episodes of increasing hostility toward their people.[11] Peronism would bring about a change in the multiple identities of these Jewish-Argentines.

There has been much debate about the size of the Jewish population in Argentina, throughout the twentieth century and still today.[12] Attempts to establish the exact number face several hurdles. Most studies tend to focus on Jews who were affiliated with community institutions, even if research has shown that most Jews, like most members of other ethnic communities, never affiliated with these institutions. Furthermore, in nationwide censuses, many Jews chose to not identify as such, whether out of fear of having an ethnic label next to their names in governmental records and databases, particularly during authoritarian regimes, or because the form offered no option to simultaneously select the various components that constituted one's identity or to unite, as if with a hyphen, the various components of one's identity. Respondents therefore avoided giving more weight to the Jewish component of their identity than to the Argentine one. The use of religious criteria in the census has created further obstacles to the compilation of data about a community that was known for the prevalence of secularism. The distorted, yet common, image of the negative attitude of Jewish-Argentines toward Peronism is attributable to the use, in many studies, of sources produced by the community institutions and their memberships at the expense of large numbers of non-affiliated Jews.

The demographer Sergio Della Pergola estimates that the Jewish population in Argentina grew from 14,700 in 1900 to 191,400 in 1930.

Jews from Romania, Poland, and Lithuania sought to make their homes in a new country and joined those who had come from Russia, after conditions in Eastern Europe worsened during the First World War and the interwar period. Argentina became more attractive to those seeking to immigrate as refugees, particularly after the United States instituted a very strict quota in 1921, which excluded most immigrants originating from Eastern Europe, and many potential host countries followed suit, adopting similar measures.

By the end of the Second World War, Argentina's Jewish population was at 273,400, and at the start of the 1960s it reached its peak of 310,000. Since then, the population has decreased in size due to migration to Israel, the United States, other Latin American countries, or to Europe. Exogamous marriages in which one of the parties was Jewish became more frequent, increasing from between 1 and 5 percent in the mid-1930s to 20 to 25 percent at the start of the 1960s, and 35 to 40 percent during the mid-1980s. Current estimates are that some 200,000 Jews live in Argentina today.[13]

Jewish immigrants to Argentina were mostly Ashkenazim, even if Jews from Morocco also emigrated to Argentina during the mid-nineteenth century. The decline of the Ottoman Empire also spurred Jews to emigrate, especially from Aleppo and Damascus, arriving in Argentina nearly at the same time as the waves of Jewish immigration from Central and Eastern Europe.[14]

The first Jewish immigrants to Argentina began to arrive during the 1840s (unlike in Brazil, very little evidence has been found in Argentina of the presence of *conversos*, Jewish converts to Catholicism, during the colonial period). These immigrants were a small number of highly assimilated German and French families. The first synagogue in Buenos Aires was established in 1862. The year 1881 marks the first watershed in this process, when a series of pogroms in czarist Russia prompted the Argentine government to send a special envoy tasked with inviting Jews to settle in Argentina if they wished to do so. The first organized group of immigrants was comprised of 820 Russian Jews and arrived in August 1889 on board the famed cargo ship *Wesser*, which Jewish-Argentine collective memory has transformed into its *Mayflower*.[15] These immigrants were sent to agricultural settlements and some founded the colonies of Moisesville (1889), Mauricio (1892), and Villa

Clara (1892), among others. Baron de Hirsch's Jewish Colonization Association (JCA) founded 26 agricultural settlements, though many of these were short-lived. When agricultural colonies reached their peak on the eve of the First World War, their population was never higher than 20,000 Jews in total. Many of these settlements were ephemeral, and by the 1930s they only accounted for 11 percent of the Jewish population.[16]

The state policy encouraging immigration substantially changed the composition of the country's population, as reflected in the 1914 census. In a span of twenty years, Argentina's population had nearly doubled, reaching approximately 7.9 million. Over a third of the total population, and over half of the population of the city of Buenos Aires, had been born in another country. The Jewish population grew at an even faster pace, from 6,000 in 1895 to 125,000 in 1919, a quarter century later.

Nevertheless, the original vision of attracting Jewish migrants through agricultural enterprise was short-lived. If, by the end of the nineteenth century, the majority of newly arrived immigrants settled in the JCA's colonies, by the end of the First World War most Jews lived in cities, predominantly Buenos Aires. In urban centres, Jews tended to favour specific neighbourhoods, which in turn increased their urban and social visibility.[17]

The immigration to Argentina of Jews and other populations continued apace, with the exception of a temporary halt during the First World War, when the country experienced a recession and unemployment rose due to fluctuations in commercial ties with Europe. In contrast to the restrictions imposed in the United States and other countries, Argentina's liberal immigration policy remained virtually unchanged but for minor amendments during the mid-1920s. The great economic recession that ensued worldwide, following the Wall Street crash of 1929, froze migratory flows. The subsequent political effervescence spurred the first military coup in Argentina's history (September 1930), which in turn strengthened nationalist, Catholic, and xenophobic tendencies that had until then remained latent in Argentine society.[18]

Argentina's Jewish population grew to 250,000 during the 1930s, when political and economic restrictions were imposed on immigration.

Figure 1.4 Jews in one of the Baron de Hirsch settlements in Entre Ríos, Argentina, 1922.

National elites were concerned that social and political turmoil in Europe would funnel "undesirables" into the country, which could potentially endanger the existing order. These restrictions caused a myriad of obstacles for Republicans and refugees fleeing the Spanish Civil War and the subsequent dictatorship of Francisco Franco in their quest for admission into Argentina. Authorities viewed them as carriers of a dangerous leftist or anarchist "virus,"[19] and often characterized Jews as "Bolsheviks." In light of the recession, precedence was given to professionals who could fit the needs of the national economy, and xenophobic attitudes posed further challenges to potential immigrants who were not Catholic or who were presumably less likely to adapt to Argentine society and culture.[20]

Jews hoping that Argentina would adopt a stance favourable to them at the Evian Conference in France were disillusioned. The conference was summoned in July 1938 by the League of Nations to debate viable solutions to the problem of refugees fleeing Nazi Germany and Austria.

Figure 1.5 Jews working in the fields of Rivera, Buenos Aires, 1975.

Argentina, like other participating countries (except for General Trujillo's Dominican Republic), did not genuinely wish to welcome these refugees and upheld this same restrictive policy until the end of the Second World War. This did not prevent the clandestine or legal arrival on Argentine shores of some 40,000 Jews between 1933 and

1945, a fifth of whom arrived at a time when Jews were being systematically annihilated in Europe.

Emigration to Argentina picked up again – though in smaller numbers than before – by the mid-1940s, after the defeat of fascism and the end of the war. In 1947, the populist president Juan D. Perón repealed most of the restrictions that had been imposed on immigration. In the three following years, some 300,000 immigrants came to the country, chiefly from Spain and Italy, the two main sources from which Argentina's population hailed. Even if only 1,500 Jews emigrated to Argentina during the second half of the 1940s, the Peronist regime's decision to offer amnesty to all residents whose status was irregular allowed some 10,000 Jews to normalize their situation.[21] Unfortunately, war criminals and collaborators with the Nazis were also among those who benefitted from this amnesty, as they had sought refuge in Argentina using false identities. Their presence in the country contributed greatly to the myth that Argentine society and its authorities were antisemitic and pro-Nazi.

The final wave of Jewish immigration to Argentina (and to Brazil) took place during the 1950s. Most of these immigrants were refugees fleeing communist repression in Hungary in 1956, Moroccan Jews who had arrived after the North African countries won their independence, or Jews fleeing Egypt due to the hostile policies adopted by Gamal A. Nasser's regime in the wake of the joint offensive to assure free passage in the Suez Canal on the part of Israel, the United Kingdom, and France. From that point on, Argentina's Jewish population began to diminish.

FROM THE IMMIGRANTS' HOTEL TO THE TENEMENT HOUSE, AND THEN THE UPPER MIDDLE CLASS

Like other newcomers, Jews who reached the Argentine coast in the ships that docked on the River Plate spent their first days in the capital of their new country at the Hotel de Inmigrantes (Immigrants' Hotel), the first stop on their journey to becoming Argentines. Many then lodged at *conventillos* – tenement houses typically two or three storeys tall with high ceilings. The one- or two-bedroom apartments on each floor could be accessed from the long hallways that lined one or

Figure 1.6 Hotel de Inmigrantes (Immigrants' Hotel), a complex of buildings constructed in the early twentieth century in the port of Buenos Aires to receive and assist mass European immigration, October 1905.

two interior patios. One or two immigrant families huddled together in a single, stuffy room. The kitchen, bathroom, and washtub were shared. In 1887, 2,885 such houses in the city of Buenos Aires housed 80,000 inhabitants. In other words, that year, more than a quarter of the city's population lived in tenement houses. By 1901 that proportion had decreased to 17 percent, and to 14 percent by 1904.

In 1877, doctor and hygienist Eduardo Wilde wrote about

> Those omnibus houses that are home to all, from the beggar to the small industrialist, have a single door that opens onto the patio and fulfills a variety of purposes: it is the bedroom of the husband, the wife, and their litter, as these people say in their expressive language; this litter includes five or six children who are appropriately dirty; it is dining room, kitchen, and pantry, it is a patio where the children play, the place where feces are disposed of, at least temporarily, the trash dump, the storage place for clothes both dirty and clean; it is a den for the dog and cat, a storage place for water and gas; a place that at night is lit by an oil lamp, a candle, or a lamp; in sum, each of these rooms is a pandemonium in which four, sometimes five, people breathe, against all hygienic rules, against the laws of common sense and good taste, and even against the very necessities of the organism.[22]

Though many contemporary descriptions of tenement houses focus on the dampness, filth, and overcrowding, those who shared this lifestyle recall it with nostalgia, contrasting it with accelerated changes that were taking place in Buenos Aires. In their recollections, they highlight the solidarity among the different immigrant groups, as well as the rapid socialization of those newly arrived. It was in those houses that they learned their first words of Spanish as well as some of the country's customs and cultural codes. Jevel Katz, the popular singer-songwriter who sang in Yiddish, was widely acclaimed among Jewish-Argentines for the songs he wrote in a language that was a cross between Yiddish and *lunfardo* – Buenos Aires's popular speech form – that he called "casteidish," thus coining a word that combines the names of the Spanish and Yiddish languages. These songs gave voice, with great wit and cunning, to the daily lives of Jewish immigrants in Argentina, including life in the conventillo and their initial efforts to learn Spanish.

To describe the urban and social history of Jews in Buenos Aires, it is useful to examine the patterns that emerge from their settlement in the city's neighbourhoods. Eugene Sofer maps the development of the organized Jewish community by outlining four phases during the period 1890–1947: the first corresponded to the immigrants' arrival and their subsequent effort to attain some institutional and spatial stability; the second was one of "ghettoization and unity" (a characterization from which I differ); the third was connected to a westward movement within the country and also reflected processes of "ghettoization"; and the fourth was one of dispersion and fragmentation of the community.[23]

Various factors influenced the decision to live in a specific neighbourhood. Important criteria included location in relation to one's place of work, cost of rent, availability of public transportation, commercial opportunities to open a business, and whether relatives or compatriots lived nearby. Many found it easier to integrate in an area where they could use their mother tongue as well as familiar cultural codes, and where they found the social and cultural institutions that could meet their needs. Such circumstances made it easier for one to develop a sense of belonging by adopting local identity traits while maintaining distinctive ethnic features.

In 1895, 62 percent of the city's Ashkenazi Jews lived near Plaza Lavalle, and only a minority of Ashkenazim were located in the western neighbourhoods. The plaza was the heart of the Jewish community. After completing the formalities of immigration at the port, many immigrants headed there to meet other Jews, find work, and become acquainted with the local reality. The religious institution known as the "Congregación Israelita" (Jewish Congregation) was built in that area, and in 1897 a synagogue was constructed on Libertad Street. For years, Lavalle Street would be the site of most of the commercial activities carried out among Jews in small shops or stands set up all along the sidewalks. It was also the centre of Jewish prostitution and of the infamous Zwi Midgal, an organization of Jewish procurers.[24] The area was not, however, a Jewish neighbourhood; rather, it was densely populated with immigrants of varied origins and had a high proportion of Jews.

Before long, Jews began to move from Plaza Lavalle to the Once neighbourhood (named after the local train station "11 de septiembre"). This westward move corresponds to the second phase, "ghettoization and unity," which Sofer situates between 1907 and 1925. The yellow fever epidemic that struck the city in 1871 modified the city's demographic distribution: the elites moved to the northern area of the capital, which was safer in terms of hygiene due to its elevation. Simultaneously, a series of factors spurred a dramatic increase in the cost of property in the downtown area: population growth due to ongoing migration, the construction of new buildings offering municipal services, and the development of the Avenida de Mayo area, which typically required the demolition of residences. In light of these factors, many Jews who could not afford the high rents chose to migrate westward from downtown and began to abandon the area to move to less trendy streets such as those of the Balvanera neighbourhood, generally known as "El Once."

El Once quickly became the most important centre of business and life for the city's Jews. It is the cradle of many of the institutions through which the community organized itself: the Asociación Mutual Israelita Argentina (AMIA; Jewish Mutual Association of Argentina) and DAIA, the clubs where social, sporting, and religious activities were carried out, and the editorial boards and offices of the most important Yiddish-language newspapers: *Di Presse* and *Di Idishe Tzaitung*. Symbols of Jewish ethnicity could be easily spotted in the neighbourhood: from Ashkenazi synagogues to shops and rotisseries whose displays featured the delights of Eastern European cuisine.[25] The synagogue that went up on Paso Street, between Corrientes and Lavalle, was a response of sorts on the part of Jewish immigrants from Russia, who fled the failed 1905 revolution, to the Libertad Street synagogue built by immigrants from France and Alsace. In sum, various features of the area – including affordable housing, cultural and language-based ties, accessibility from people's workplaces, and a range of educational, cultural, and commercial institutions – all contributed to the adaptation of Jews to Argentine realities while allowing them to maintain their ethnic characteristics.

When Sofer described El Once as a "ghetto," he was not using this term to imply that the area's geographical or physical boundaries confined Jews to live in it. He was, however, referring to the informal process through which the area was created – that is, based on economic motivations, on the choices voluntarily made by those who preferred to remain close to members of the same ethnic and cultural groups and to their own frameworks in educational, health-related, social, and cultural matters. Although, as José Moya indicates, Buenos Aires's Jewish community seemed to have been much more segregated at the start of the twentieth century than the communities of French, Spanish, or Italian immigrants, "Jews in Buenos Aires were less segregated than their coreligionists elsewhere in the diaspora. Moreover, Jewish residential segregation also dropped faster than in most other cities."[26]

The use of Yiddish as a spoken language as well as cultural production in that language formed an integral part of Once's distinctive landscape, at least until the 1940s. Jews nevertheless remained a minority in this new neighbourhood and accounted for less than 10 percent of its population, even if their presence on its streets was noticeable. In 1914, almost 40 percent of Jews originating from Eastern Europe and living in Buenos Aires resided in Once or an adjacent neighbourhood. It therefore comes as no surprise that the nationalist shock troops first set their sights on that area in 1919 and attacked Jewish immigrants during what would become known as the Tragic Week.[27]

Spanish-speaking Jews and some of those who spoke Judeo-Spanish (originating from North Africa, Turkey, or the Balkans) chose to move to the Constitución neighbourhood, and those who came from Syria (especially from Damascus) largely settled in Boca, Barracas, or Flores, but also in Once, Lanus, and Ciudadela. Jews from Turkey and from Aleppo nevertheless preferred to live in Once, near Eastern European Jews, and avoided contiguity with their Damascene counterparts.

Buenos Aires continued its westward expansion during the first three decades of the twentieth century. The population of the Vélez Sarsfield neighbourhood grew from 4,500 in 1895 to 100,000 in 1914; Belgrano, which became part of the city of Buenos Aires in 1887, went from a population of 15,000 in 1895 to nearly 230,000 in 1936. During that same period, the population of Flores, another neighbourhood that became part of the capital in 1887, grew tenfold. Villa Crespo expanded similarly, in part thanks to the subway line that served the neighbourhood with stops along Triunvirato and Corrientes streets, and brought commuters from Chacarita to downtown in a few minutes. By the mid-1930s, Villa Crespo was home to 30,000 Jews – that is, a quarter of the city's total Jewish population. This period corresponds to the third step of the urban history of Buenos Aires Jews: the westward move and the transformation of the neighbourhood of Villa Crespo into the largest concentration of Jews in the city.

Villa Crespo also had tenement houses in which Jews cohabited with other ethnic groups. The most famous such house was La Paloma. The 112-room dwelling had entrances on Serrano and Thames streets, and was immortalized in, among other works, Alberto Vaccarezza's well-known play *El conventillo de La Paloma*.[28] Tenants moved out, as they became part of a socioeconomic lower middle class. Unlike Once, La Paloma was home to a greater proportion of poor Jews but less to practising Jews. Shortly after the First World War, the look of Buenos Aires gradually changed. Trams replaced horse-drawn carriages and the first subway lines began to operate. New waves of Jewish immigrants mainly originating from Poland were drawn to Villa Crespo, just as migrants from the Russian Empire had been drawn to Plaza Lavalle and Once. By the late 1950s and early 1960s, the joke was heard time and again: "What's the capital of Israel? Villa Crespo!"

The final phase in Sofer's periodization describes the dispersion and atomization of the community that began in the mid-1930s, when Jews moved to Almagro and Caballito, Floresta, Villa Devoto, or Villa Urquiza, or northward to Belgrano and Palermo. After the Second World War, Jews within the city once again moved toward the outskirts to work, for example, in the textile industry that Polish Jews had established in Villa Lynch. By then, every neighbourhood in the city had some degree of Jewish presence. In spite of this, only Once and Villa Crespo became iconic "Jewish neighbourhoods." Though opportunities were countered by financial limitations, many of those who dwelled in these neighbourhoods became sufficiently integrated so as to be able to live without the local Jewish support network. Despite initial difficulties, these immigrants became *porteños*, as the inhabitants of Buenos Aires are known.

From the start of the twentieth century, Villa Crespo and its Jewish population stood out for their passion for football, practising the sport in many of its social, sport-related institutions. Most of these were unable to stay afloat as professional football clubs consolidated and thus failed to gain worldwide acclaim. Nevertheless, Villa Crespo is connected to the history of three major football clubs: Chacarita Juniors, Argentinos Juniors, and Atlanta. The latter settled in Villa Crespo in 1922 and, by the mid-1940s, when Atlanta drove Chacarita out to San Martín, it become emblematic of Villa Crespo. So many Jews affiliated with Atlanta that they became conspicuously present in the club's directorate. The "Peronization" of Atlanta contributed in turn to Peronizing many members of the popular classes among Jewish-Argentines.[29]

While it may be true that the Jewish presence in Argentina always spurred manifestations of antisemitism, it is important to distinguish the variants of this stance, the effects of which on the lives of Jews in South America have been widely examined. Haim Avni has differentiated between three levels of antisemitism in Argentina: one is popular, the other organized, and the third state-sponsored.[30] Popular antisemitism is difficult to measure. It is deeply rooted in Catholic teachings and has frequently been stoked by Nazi propaganda (during the 1930s and during the Second World War) or by propaganda from Arab countries (from the 1960s onward). Several polls over the years have nevertheless indicated that Jews in Argentina are not more hated than other ethnic or social groups (they are certainly less hated than Paraguayans or Bolivians), whereas many respondents considered that multinational corporations, banks, politicians, or the armed forces hold "too much power" – more than that of the Jews.

The first organized antisemitic groups emerged in 1910, the year of the ceremonies marking the centennial of Argentina's process of independence. In 1919, they took advantage of a workers' strike to attack Jewish neighbourhoods that they viewed as hubs of revolutionary ferment. At the start of the 1960s, they exploited the kidnapping in Buenos Aires of Nazi war criminal Adolf Eichmann by Mossad agents (May 1960) to accuse the country's Jews of "double loyalty" and to carry out a series of violent antisemitic attacks led by groups such as Tacuara and the Guardia Restauradora Nacionalista (Nationalist Restorationist Guard).[31] These incidents did not recur, but during the following decades, organizations frequently handed out antisemitic propaganda and even carried out isolated attacks against Jewish institutions. These groups were generally small but came to gain a degree of influence in military, ecclesiastical, and political circles. From the 1960s onward, some antisemitic propaganda also adopted elements of anti-Israel or anti-Zionist discourse.

State-sponsored antisemitism has been infrequent in Argentina. It manifested in the restrictions imposed on the immigration of Jews between 1930 and 1940, and was also present during the brutal military dictatorship that governed the country between 1976 and 1983. During that regime, the Jewish community disproportionately suffered the effects of the terrorism inflicted by the armed forces: even though Jews amounted to only 1 percent of the country's population, they accounted for up to 10 percent of those disappeared by the military regime.[32] The prominence of Jews among the disappeared also reveals their disproportionate weight in left-wing activism. Numerous first-person accounts still attest to the fact that Jews detained by the military were made to suffer more than those who were not Jewish. In spite of this, the community's institutions pursued their regular activities, antisemitic legislation was not penned, brought forward, or passed, and relations between national authorities and the state of Israel were excellent.[33]

IN THE SHADOW OF THE JUNE 1943 MILITARY COUP

Both the military coup led by General José Félix Uriburu on 6 September 1930, and the coup that inaugurated the (self-denominated) Revolution of 4 June 1943, which was led by, among others, Colonel Juan Perón, created auspicious conditions for the rise of the nationalist Right and the onset of a new antisemitic wave in Argentina. Internal documents of the Grupo de Oficiales Unidos (GOU; Group of United Officers), the young military men who devised the 1943 coup, point to judeophobic tendencies – at the least – among some of its members.[34] After the coup, multiple groups, among them the notorious ALN, began to openly attack Jews and their community institutions located in the country's capital and in many large cities in the provinces. Authorities did nothing to prevent or stem these attacks. The ALN caused concern to many *porteños*, with their squadron-like marches in which they gave the fascist salute with arm outstretched and wished death upon Jews, communists, and Anglo-Saxon imperialism. Antisemitic publications became increasingly frequent, as did *pintadas* – graffiti that, in this case, featured pejorative slogans about or against Jews. The reigning atmosphere lent itself well to such public manifestation of antisemitism. Many key personalities of the nationalist Right, a tendency that since the 1930s had carved a presence for itself in Argentine public debates, held office at various levels in the military government.

In October 1943, after various moderate members of the de facto government stepped down, the administration was reorganized. The leading figures of the new government were much more reactionary and nationalist. The new minister of the interior was Colonel Luis Perlinger, a Germanophile officer in favour of eliminating liberals and communists, whom he considered to be enemies of the nation's interests. A nationalist intellectual, Gustavo Martínez Zuviría, was in charge of justice and public education. Martínez Zuviría was one of the most renowned activists of Acción Católica (Catholic Action) and, up until his nomination in 1943, was director of the National Library, as the Uriburu administration had named him to that post in 1931. He was also known for the novels he wrote under the pseudonym Hugo Wast. Two of these, published during the mid-1930s, were viciously antisemitic: *El Kahal* (22 printings by 1955, with a total of 107,000 copies printed) and *Oro* ("Gold"; 21 printings, with 104,000 copies printed). These two novels drew inspiration from texts such as the *Protocols of the Elders of Zion* and circulated widely. This in turn caused great concern among the local Jewish community, which tried to prevent these novels from being sold. The German embassy in Buenos Aires purchased 40,000 copies of these novels to distribute among Argentine citizens in positions of power. The novels were also translated into a variety of languages.

In 1943, during the first months of the military government, authorities in federal and provincial administrations adopted various antisemitic measures. Some regulations or decrees limited butchers' ability to observe kosher rules. These restrictions were rolled back when community leaders intervened to denounce them to provincial governors and the minister of the interior. Similarly, Jewish teachers were frequently singled out to authorities and then fired from their positions at educational institutions or city hospitals in Buenos Aires, which prevented newly graduating Jewish doctors from carrying out their residencies there.[35] At the time, the use of foreign languages, including Yiddish, continued to be prohibited. The Yiddish-language printing press was closed down on 11 October 1943, with the justification that censors could not read material that was not printed in Spanish. US president Franklin Roosevelt criticized this measure, expressing in a White House communiqué that he could not refrain from manifesting his concerns regarding the adoption in the Western hemisphere of a clearly antisemitic action, which borrowed from the most repellent facets of the Nazi doctrine. The pressure exercised by the United States was effective as the prohibition was voided after a few days and the Jewish newspapers, including the important *Di Idishe Tzaitung* and *Di Presse*, were returned to kiosks. The leadership of the DAIA – an organization formed in 1935 to bring together community representatives and give them a voice vis-à-vis political authorities – met with Colonel Alberto Gilbert in July and September 1943 to raise its concerns about antisemitic activities. On those occasions, community leaders highlighted the contributions of Jewish people to the country and its development, and portrayed antisemitism as an imported evil that was not intrinsic to the national way of being.[36]

While the DAIA's portrayal of antisemitism as foreign to Argentine society (a strategy that the organization would maintain for many years) may have been driven by a political logic, it was also fuelled by a lack of understanding and by self-delusion, which, to some extent, contributed to exonerating governmental authorities from their responsibility in stoking these manifestations of judeophobia. Antisemitism in Argentina drew from various sources. While Nazi Germany undeniably deployed efforts to disseminate racist propaganda in Argentina, these seeds were sown on fertile ground where these hateful stereotypes had already taken root. Local factors included the perception that viewed the country's Catholic heritage as a primordial component of the national being, as well as the close-knit bonds between extreme right-wing nationalists and the Catholic Church, which were much stronger than in Chile or Brazil.[37] As Argentina was a country with a high proportion of immigrants, nationalists adopted a discourse that was hostile to newcomers in general and to Jews in particular – who stood out because of their religious, ethnic, cultural, and linguistic differences – characterizing them as carriers of "noxious" influences. One of the first expressions of this stance was the novel *La Bolsa* (The Stock Market), by Julián Martel (pseudonym for José María Miró), published in Buenos Aires in 1891 and considered a classic of Argentine literature. The novel is set in the capital's stock market and emphasizes the stereotype of the corrupt Jew active in the financial sphere. It was written at the height of a national economic crisis and it imitated, in some aspects, the style of Edouard Drumont, the French antisemitic novelist.

To this initial overview of the national roots of antisemitism we can add the existence of a sizable and visible Jewish community, mainly in Buenos Aires, and the identification of Jews as Bolsheviks, whether because some were workers or because most of them originated from Eastern Europe, earning them the nickname of "rusos" (Russians). These factors provoked hostility whenever fears of communist influence were disseminated. The most notorious such attacks occurred after the revolution of October 1917 in Russia, which prompted fears that the Argentine working class would radicalize itself. This led to the Tragic Week, a pogrom against the Jews of Buenos Aires in January 1919. These conditions were optimal for the introduction of antisemitic content into nationalist agendas.

Yet, outside influences also played a part in shaping xenophobic and antisemitic currents in nationalism. As Argentine society was mainly composed of Southern European immigrants, it turned its gaze toward the Old World and eagerly absorbed a wide range of cultural and ideological influences. The influence of the fascist and semi-fascist Right developing on the other side of the ocean, particularly in countries with Latin cultural roots, could be felt in the daily lives of many Argentines: Charles Maurras and the Action Française, the dictatorial regimes of Benito Mussolini and Miguel Primo de Rivera, the Falange, the Spanish Civil War, and the subsequent dictatorship of Generalissimo Franco, as well as German National Socialism, all marked the political and intellectual life of the Southern Cone nation, generating an atmosphere of hostility toward Jews.

The above description of the string of antisemitic incidents that resulted from the military revolt of June 1943 should not mislead us, however: most Jews in Argentina conducted their day-to-day tasks without interference. Readers of studies on antisemitic publications or activities could infer that the lives of Jews became unbearable during the entirety of the twentieth century. The reality was otherwise. Public figures on the Left and Centre of the political spectrum were involved in the struggles against racism and antisemitism, and thereby countered the influences of nationalist elements on governmental policies. In spite of this, the military dictatorship prompted palpable uneasiness in Jews, many of whom viewed it as fascist and pro-Axis. This unease, also shared by many non-Jews, can also be explained by the arrival of news about the extermination of European Jews. In 1943, the leadership of DAIA declared that commemorations would take place between 21 June and 20 July to honour the memory of the victims of the Nazi regime. The institution contacted authorities in Franco's Spain, which had formally adopted a neutral stance during the Second World War, to ask their help in saving Jewish lives in the Old Continent.[38]

Even though Perón gradually became the strongman of the military government, it is only from October 1945 onward that he began to have public ties with antisemitic nationalism. Political rivals attempted to stain Perón by casting him as the author of an antisemitic speech, presumably given to an audience of officers, in March 1944; but this accusation apparently proved to be baseless.[39] During the political crisis of October 1945, Perón obtained the support not only of the masses of workers who banded together behind the leader – who, for them, symbolized the promise of economic and social reforms – but also from nationalist groups. Members of these latter groups would voice their support for the leader with "¡Vivas!" which they coupled with antisemitic slogans ("death to the Jews"). The day after the landmark events of 17 October 1945, when the masses of workers had gathered on the Plaza de Mayo opposite the presidential palace to demand that authorities liberate the "People's Colonel" from prison,[40] nationalist groups in favour of Perón provoked riots in those neighbourhoods of Buenos Aires with the largest Jewish populations. Passers-by were beaten, stones were thrown at the centrally located great synagogue, and, strikingly, those Jews who were inside the building were arrested. The rioters targeted other Jewish institutions as well, and painted numerous graffiti instigating violence against Jews. Over the course of the following years, opponents of the regime referred to these events to identify Peronism with antisemitism. This is the case in the short story "La fiesta del monstruo" ("Monsterfest"), co-authored by Jorge Luis Borges and Adolfo Bioy Casares, which describes a group of Peronist workers lynching a young Jew during the mass gatherings of 17 October.

In the city of Córdoba, a gang desecrated a synagogue and damaged a building housing a community organization. Nationalists marched on the streets the entire day, stirring considerable fear among Jews. Similar episodes occurred in the following weeks, involving members of the ALN.[41] Arnaldo Cortesi, the *New York Times* correspondent in Buenos Aires, wrote with some exaggeration about the terror and panic that took hold among local Jews and about the antisemitic notes that were passed about at every mass gathering in support of Colonel Perón. As Cortesi had been transferred to Buenos Aires after some years covering events in Mussolini's Italy, he tended to see current events in Argentina as a South American version of Italian fascism.[42]

The organized community was nevertheless firm in its resolve to react. The DAIA prepared and handed a memorandum to the president, General Edelmiro Farrell, to express the pain and perplexity caused by the explosion of racially motivated hatred against the community, adding that its members felt deeply connected to the nation and that this phenomenon was severely detrimental to Argentine civilization. They decried the racism that they experienced as Argentines and as Jews, and, in the purest Argentine tradition, invoked their inalienable human and civic rights to denounce and protest these attempts to disseminate this venom and to poison the nation's life.[43]

The wave of antisemitic episodes of October–November 1945 also caused concern among members of Jewish institutions in the United States. The *American Jewish Year Book* compared these events to a pogrom. The fact that Jewish youths organized to fend off nationalist attacks carried out by Perón's supporters was likened to "the tragic parallel of the defense of the Warsaw ghetto." Perón's campaign for the presidency, leading a movement that was generally interpreted as fascist, "stirred memories of Germany in the final days of the Republic of Weimar."[44] It should come as no surprise, then, that in late 1945 the American Jewish Committee enjoined the US State

Department to launch initiatives aiming to eradicate "Nazi anti-Semitism" from Argentina.[45]

During the electoral campaign of late 1945 and early 1946, the loud antisemitic minority within the ranks of Perón's supporters did indeed make itself heard on more than one occasion. But the Partido Laborista (Labour Party), a central component of the Peronist coalition and one whose leadership included various Jews, denounced in no uncertain terms the attacks waged against Jews in the federal capital. In November 1945, the party's secretariat in La Plata, capital of the province of Buenos Aires, demanded that its members put their bodies on the line and even risk their lives when necessary to defend Jews from the attacks of Nazi/fascist gangs and that they show no tolerance for displays of hostility. This particular order aimed to show the truth of a workers' doctrine that expressed its sympathy toward a people unjustly persecuted across the world.[46] In a statement that Colonel Perón wrote and published in *La Época* in late November, he sought to reject the categorical accusation that his camp was antisemitic by vigorously condemning attacks against Jews: "They attribute racist and Nazi ideas to me because some disoriented individuals shout out my name with '¡Vivas!' while they attack those people and principles that they oppose. I de-authorize and deny that those who act thusly can support my principles and my ideas." In that column, Perón accused some of his opponents of having incited the deplorable episode, which should have warranted the police's intervention. In the name of his training and his conscience, and acknowledging the painful experience of other peoples and of the motherland, the Colonel condemned those who used violence as a means to attract supporters and expressed the hope that Argentina's future would be characterized by tolerance and mutual respect.[47]

In fact, from December 1944 onward and in several instances during 1945, Perón made statements in which he condemned antisemitism, a gesture that he would repeat throughout the decade-long span of his two presidencies. The newspapers *Democracia* and *El Laborista*, which supported Perón's candidacy, published even stronger condemnations when they declared themselves to be anti-Nazi and free of racial or religious prejudices, which were foreign to them as free and Argentine human beings.[48] Indeed, the antisemitic nationalist groups' propaganda waned during the final weeks of the campaign.

Doubts persisted among many Jews in regard to the "Nazi-fascist" candidate, Perón. Perón's opponents, grouped in the Unión Democrática (UD; Democratic Union), also attempted to convince the Jewry that the Colonel posed a danger to Argentina and to their ethnic group. In light of this, it is understandable that, shortly after the conclusion of the Second World War, Jews were hesitant to embrace a charismatic leader and a movement that had the support of, among others, groups that exhibited some fascist traits and nuances. While many Jewish-Argentines accordingly supported the Democratic Union, a significant number of them cast their votes for Perón. According to various sources, Perón obtained several thousands of votes in Once and in the province of Entre Ríos, in an area with a sizeable Jewish population. Nevertheless, it is difficult to calculate the exact number of Jews who voted for Perón as Jews were spread out across the districts of Buenos Aires and its greater metropolitan area. In May 1947, the representative of the American Jewish Committee in Buenos Aires, Máximo Yagupsky, wrote that in retrospect it seemed like the community institutions had made a mistake in manifesting their support for of Perón's opponents in the election prior to voting day. The candidate of the Unión Cívica Radical (UCR; Civic Radical Union), José Tamborini, was invited to attend a reception hosted by the Sociedad Hebraica (Jewish Society), but Perón, who had expressed hopes of receiving a similar invitation, was not.[49]

Perón's identification with the rising working class also pushed away Jews, the majority of whom were by now middle-class. The rapid economic growth and social mobility that Argentina enjoyed for many decades allowed these Jews to climb the social ladder and become integrated into the urban middle classes.[50] The disproportionate presence of Jews among Argentina's intellectual circles and university students, many of whom opposed Perón, partly accounts for the particularities of the Jewish vote. In spite of this, the DAIA, which was helmed by Doctor Moisés Goldman (a famous doctor whose grandparents had been agricultural settlers in the colonies that the Baron de Hirsch founded in the province of Entre Ríos), abstained from expressing a clear political posture so as to maintain its neutral stance vis-à-vis party politics. In the DAIA's condemnations of antisemitic acts, it avoided linking these unfortunate actions to Perón.

The federal elections held on 24 February 1946 are considered the most transparent and fair in the country's democratic life up until then. As the results trickled in, the charismatic colonel's triumph was in sight. His supporters began to celebrate. Among the celebrants the number of Jews was still small. During his first two presidencies, however, Perón would gradually win over the support of a growing number of groups and individuals in the Jewish community, as will be seen in the following chapters.

2

The Origins of the Stain of Fascism

Argentina's Neutrality in the Second World War and the Entry of Nazi War Criminals

The portrayal of Perón as a fascist is rooted in the challenge that Argentina posed to US hegemony across the continent by adopting a neutral position during the Second World War and maintaining it even after the United States became involved in the conflict. This image was subsequently strengthened with the revelations that many Nazi war criminals were living in Argentina and, later, with the kidnapping of Adolf Eichmann, the SS's "expert on the Jewish question," by agents of the Israeli Mossad in Buenos Aires in May 1960.[1] Whether in movies, novels, or media, the stereotype of Perón as a fascist leader continues to circulate in the US popular imagination and, with it, the portrayal of Argentina as the primary haven for Nazi war criminals.[2]

In an article published in the *New York Times* in 1997, Ann Louise Bardach posited that Argentina still refused to acknowledge the most glaring flaw of Peronism: "The complicity of the European neutrals, however, paled in comparison with the treachery of a country that deserves greater scrutiny: Argentina. Whereas the Swiss-Nazi relationship was entirely mercenary, that between Juan Peron's Argentina and Hitler's Germany was seamless and symbiotic, an ideological marriage of caudillismo [a political system led by a local strongman] and Fascism."[3]

Any debate about Argentina's stance during the Second World War must begin by emphasizing that, from 1939 to 1945, neutrality was successively upheld by four different presidents, two of them military men and the other two civilians. It would therefore be misleading to identify neutrality exclusively with the figure of Juan Perón.

Furthermore, a majority of Argentines supported this policy. This neutral position therefore originated in reasons of national interest and in the recognition of the geographical distance that separated Argentina from the battlefields,[4] in addition to the clear difference between the attitudes that Argentina's successive governments adopted respectively toward Great Britain and the United States.[5] Whereas Argentina's reservations about strengthening its ties and cooperation with Washington were palpable, its collaboration with Her Majesty's government was assiduous. Argentina sold a large volume of foodstuffs and other staples to the British, which ultimately contributed to their war effort and helped both the troops and the civilian population resist the Germans' attacks.

Argentina's neutrality also resulted from its longstanding economic and cultural ties with Europe and its equally longstanding doubts regarding US hegemonic aspirations over the American continent, which the northern nation voiced clearly in successive panamerican conferences.[6] Frictions between Argentina and the United States were also rooted in the impossibility of their becoming trade partners, as their economies were competitors and not, as those of England and Argentina, complementary. For many years, Argentine grains and beef – the country's main sources of revenue – were blocked from the United States. The historical neutral stance adopted during the First World War, a period that stood out as one of prosperity and development in Argentines' collective memory, should also be taken into consideration, as well as Argentina's neutrality during the Spanish Civil War (1936–39).

In assessing Argentina's position during the Second World War, we should not ignore the existence in the country of nationalist groups that were sympathetic to the Axis countries. Although these groups were a minority, they influenced the intellectual and political climate at the time.[7] The authoritarian and anticommunist attitudes prevalent within the Catholic Church and the governing oligarchy were not uncommon in contemporary Europe and the Americas, and members of the military also exhibited Germanophile tendencies. It is useful to recall that, from the late nineteenth century up until the Second World War, Germany was the country that most strongly influenced the Argentine army, but this influence did not extend to the navy or to the nascent air force.[8] The German embassy in Buenos Aires also did its part by investing considerable sums in financing and bribing politicians and journalists to ensure that the country maintained its neutral position.

When war broke out, all the New World countries (except Canada) had declared their neutrality. Yet, as Franklin Roosevelt's administration started to show signs of siding with the Allies, tensions between the United States and Argentina increased. Prior to the war, Cordell Hull, then Roosevelt's secretary of state, had developed a plan to coordinate panamerican military forces in a joint action under US leadership in the event of a threat to the continent's security. This plan was to be agreed upon at the Inter-American Conference for the Maintenance of Peace, held in Buenos Aires in 1936, but by the end of the gathering, the United States and Argentina were in total disagreement, the latter wary of Hull's efforts to secure US hegemony across the continent. As a result, Hull felt thoroughly alienated from Argentina and developed a great animosity toward this country, which he perceived as obstructionist.

In subsequent years, Hull would exercise great pressure for the Argentine government to adopt a more amicable position toward US interests. Roberto Ortiz's presidency, beginning in 1938, was marked by a growing polarization in society regarding the position that Argentina should adopt vis-à-vis Germany and Great Britain. The newly minted president insisted on the need to once again hold open elections in Argentina, thus rejecting the more restrictive structure ushered in by the military coup of 1930, a regime that the United States had legitimated in exchange for maintaining the panamericanism fostered and promoted by the northern nation. Ortiz's expressed preference for open elections allowed the UCR to triumph in the following election. The return to power of this party – marginalized from political activity since 1930 – also marked a pro-British orientation in keeping with the UCR's preference.

Consequently, the sectors of the country that sympathized with Germany, particularly those within the army, joined forces to mount a conservative opposition to Ortiz. Thus, when the world war broke out, the Argentine government seemed to favour the Allied cause, despite the strong pressure coming from groups that saw Germany in a favourable light. This position was also guided by a sentiment widely shared among Argentines that the country's stance in the war had to protect its commercial interests.

In this context, Ortiz also had to grapple with a dramatic worsening of the country's economic situation. As part of an effort to achieve a balance between internal opposition and international pressures, while attempting to obtain improved commercial and financial terms from the United States, Ortiz proposed the possibility of coordinated action involving those countries of the American continent willing to shift from their neutral stance to one of non-belligerence. Although this push could have benefitted the Allies, the United States did not pursue it, in part out of fear that it could strengthen Argentine hegemony in South America. Shortly after Ortiz's proposal for non-belligerence was dropped, the president was relieved of his duties due to health reasons and was replaced by his vice-president, Ramón Castillo, a staunch supporter of neutrality.

Even prior to the invasion of Poland, Argentina had firmly refused to participate in the Pan-American Defense Agreement. In January 1941, the United States began to provide armaments to Latin American countries, as stipulated under the Lend-Lease agreement. Argentina did not receive any of these supplies, while neighbouring Brazil was the main beneficiary of this military help, which caused concern and anxiety in Buenos Aires. Relations between Argentina and the United States reached a crisis point following the Japanese attack on Pearl Harbor in December 1941, which in turn precipitated US participation in the world war. Although Washington expected solidarity from the entire continent, the United States preferred that the countries of the Americas express this solidarity by severing their diplomatic ties with the Axis and that they avoid declaring themselves in a state of hostility. This preference was justified for reasons related to defence, as it would spare the United States the effort of sending ships to defend coastal areas across the continent.

As a result of the US's involvement in the war, that country developed a quasi-paranoid obsession with the presence of pro-Nazi elements in Argentina. Secretary of State Hull increasingly applied pressure on Argentina for it to follow the US strategy so that the latter could play a leading role in defining the position of Latin American nations in the conflict. Argentina was steadfast in its neutral stance, as became clear in the gathering of foreign ministers from across the Americas in Rio de Janeiro in January 1942.[9] On that occasion, due to the reluctance of the Argentine army to sever ties with any of the countries involved in the conflict, the Argentine delegation rejected the US condition that all countries receiving military aid were required to sever relations with the Axis countries. By the close of the summit, Argentina and Chile were the only countries that had not severed ties with the Axis countries. When Chile abandoned its policy of neutrality to side with the other nations of the Americas in early 1943, Argentina stood alone, lacking a policy that could unite it with its neighbours. An inglorious isolation resulted from these events.

Argentina's refusal to side with the Allies unleashed a series of painful diplomatic and economic sanctions designed to force Argentina to adopt a position similar to that of the countries of the Western Hemisphere. An embargo was imposed on arms sales to Argentina. The country was denied credit, and shipments of heavy machinery and crude oil were interrupted. President Castillo's regime – Castillo became *de jure* president after Ortiz died in 1942 – was characterized as fascist and pro-Nazi. Great Britain intervened to sway the United States to temper its pressure on Argentina for a variety of reasons. London did not perceive Argentina's neutral stance as a possible hindrance to its interests, as regular shipments from Argentina of beef, grains, and other agricultural foodstuffs so crucial for Britons, both civilians and military personnel, were thereby safe from German submarines. The British were also careful to avoid endangering their considerable investments in Argentina or jeopardizing a future market of consumers for exported British manufactured goods once the war had ended. From the British perspective, neutrality was therefore not tantamount to support for the Axis.[10]

Argentina's isolation generated ever-greater pressure by the army for the government to request armaments from the Germans. Castillo finally launched negotiations with the Germans, resulting in the paradox of a president who was accused by the United States of being a Nazi sympathizer but perceived by his own country's army as weak in his commitment to the nation and insufficiently involved in meeting the country's military needs. Castillo was deposed in the 1943 military coup.

The question of how to orient foreign policy became a source of conflict within the military government that took shape following the June 1943 "Revolución de junio" (June Revolution).[11] In August of that year, the foreign minister, Admiral Segundo Storni, addressed a letter to his US colleague, Cordell Hull, asking him to understand Argentina's position and to cancel the embargo on US armaments. The letter infuriated Hull, who rejected the request and demanded that Buenos Aires sever its diplomatic ties with the fascist powers before asking him to consider any request. Once this exchange became public, Storni was ousted from the administration and the nationalists strengthened their position within the government. Relations with the United States continued to deteriorate. Argentina's perseverance in its policy of neutrality and the dictatorial nature of the military government were the target of constant criticism from political circles in Washington.

When, in late 1943, a coup in Bolivia swept to power a neutral regime that supported Argentina, Washington accused Buenos Aires of having stoked the revolt and of backing similar conspiracies in other Southern Cone countries.[12] At that point, the already limited trade and economic relations were further restricted, and the United States pressured other countries to follow suit. Within that effort, they increased shipments of armaments to the Brazilian regime of Getúlio Vargas, who governed through means that were far from democratic, since the country's foreign policy was already aligned with that of the northern power.

Argentina's increasing disadvantage vis-à-vis its neighbour Brazil caused alarm among the upper echelons of the Argentine military, who tried to remedy the effects of the embargo by acquiring weapons and equipment from the armed forces of Nazi Germany and Generalissimo Franco's Spain (whose neutral stance benefitted the Axis).[13] Although these plans did not come to fruition, they caused an increase in Washington's pressure on the Argentine government that, this time, was backed by the British. President Pedro Pablo Ramírez faltered when the war in Europe reached what would be its final stage: on 26 January 1944, he announced that Argentina was severing its diplomatic ties with Germany and Japan (Italy had already been liberated). After a few weeks, Ramírez was overthrown for his "betrayal" of Argentine neutrality. General Edelmiro Farrell took power as president. Colonel Perón was this government's strongman and was promptly named minister of war. Only a few months later, in June 1944, he would become vice-president.

The United States refused to recognize the new government and went so far as to organize a diplomatic boycott. They withdrew the US ambassador in Buenos Aires, and many other countries in Europe and the Americas followed suit. After this, Argentina maintained regular diplomatic relations with only twelve countries. Hull then accused the Argentine government of sheltering Nazi fugitives from Europe and harbouring expansionist designs in South America.[14] Access to the Argentine gold deposited in US banks was frozen in August; in September, the embargo over exports was expanded to prohibit the export to Argentina of railroad machinery that was necessary for the crude oil industry, as well as auto parts. It was only thanks to the stance of the British, who privately criticized Hull's irrational attitude and valued immensely the shipments of Argentine beef, that a total and absolute boycott of Argentina was averted.

The US position relaxed in early 1945, thanks to changes in the State Department. After Cordell Hull's resignation, Edward Stettinius became secretary of state and Nelson Rockefeller was in charge of Latin American affairs. Between mid-1943 and mid-1947, Washington had four successive secretaries of state who worked with five different sub-secretaries for Latin America and four different ambassadors in Argentina. This accounts for the frequent swings in relations between the two countries during such a brief period.

In Argentina, Perón became influential within the army and publicly expressed his support for re-establishing relations with the United States. It was, in that sense, Argentina that promoted the creation of a new panamerican union of cooperation, presenting this initiative at the Chapultepec Conference of February 1945, where the United States attempted to gain the support of Latin America for the creation of the United Nations. In exchange for this support (and prior to granting it), the other participating nations requested the normalization of US relations with Argentina. In late March of 1945, Argentina signed the Pan-American Agreement adopted in the Chapultepec Conference, and declared war against Germany, which was on the edge of defeat, and against Japan. In thanks for this gesture, the United States recognized the Farrell administration. In Cordell Hull's memoirs, he describes with great hyperbole the decision to recognize the Farrell administration and Argentina's consent to be part of the nascent United Nations, characterizing it as the most severe blow to the panamericanist movement in all its history and revealing his emotional investment when it came to the topic of Argentina.[15]

Reconciliation was short-lived. After Roosevelt died and Truman was sworn in as president, bilateral relations once again became tense. Washington again began to apply commercial sanctions, which it only agreed to lift if free elections were held. The new US ambassador to Argentina, Spruille Braden, was a fierce advocate of this hard line, having defined the policy that the United States would adopt toward the South American country even before setting foot in it. Braden was known as an enemy of fascism from his tenures as US ambassador in Colombia and Cuba during the Second World War. He brought US intervention in Argentine domestic affairs to a climax. It became clear that the US State Department was straying from its efforts at pacification when Braden encouraged the US press in its criticisms of the rigorous measures adopted by the Farrell-Perón administration in April vis-à-vis elements of the political opposition. Washington announced that arms shipments would not resume until the Argentine government expelled Nazi agents and liquidated German interests in its territory.[16] The British criticized Braden's attitude toward Argentina – reminiscent of the Hull era – in which they saw only paranoia, particularly in the United States's insistence on linking the South American country with Nazis. Braden unequivocally violated the rules of diplomacy, both written and unspoken, as he made numerous public speeches and frequent public appearances with leaders of the Argentine opposition. According to David Kelly, the British ambassador to Buenos Aires at the time, Braden's work in Buenos Aires was guided by his firm belief that Providence had designated him to overthrow the Farrell-Perón regime.[17] International and domestic pressures on the regime forced Farrell to call general elections for February 1946.

In the months leading up to the elections, Braden, in keeping with his attitude since the start of his term as ambassador, made one more attempt to tip the scales against Perón and in favour of the opposition parties by assembling the UD. The US diplomat, who had been promoted to undersecretary of state for inter-American affairs in August 1945, was successful in his efforts to convince the State Department to publish the *Blue Book* in Washington, DC. The *Blue Book* was a detailed document prepared from a variety of sources, including German archives appropriated by the Allies as well as the official testimonies of former prisoners of war, and it included accusations that the leadership of the outgoing de facto administration, including Perón, had cooperated with the Axis countries during the war. Although the very title of the book described it as *A Consultation among the American Republics with Respect to the Argentine Situation*, none of the countries south of the Río Bravo were consulted in its preparation and the document was published exclusively in English.[18]

When John Cabot, counsellor at the US embassy in Buenos Aires, heard of the State Department's intention to publish this document shortly before the Argentine elections, he warned that "to throw 'atomic bomb' [*sic*] directly at the Argentine government in present supercharged atmosphere is to court incalculable result" and added that "opinion will be universal that we are trying to influence election results."[19] But his warnings could not stop Braden in his anti-Peronist crusade, which Joseph Tulchin described as a truly pathological obsession.[20]

The Argentine press, for the most part hostile to Perón, dedicated more space to the *Blue Book* than to any other event since the end of the war. The day after the *Blue Book* was released excerpts were published in translation in newspapers, with accompanying op-eds and columns. But, as they were published two weeks before the elections, they had the opposite effect from that intended. Perón was clever enough to turn in his favour this clumsy intervention in the nation's affairs. He rejected the arguments in the *Blue Book* in a book that he authored and published under the title of *The Blue and White Book* (referring to the colours of the Argentine flag), exhorting his compatriots to choose whom they preferred to entrust with the country's destiny: "Braden or Perón." Perón portrayed the elections as a choice between voting for the candidate who represented the nation's sovereignty and the interests of the Republic or submitting to the dictates of the United States. Perón's electoral victory was interpreted as a response, via the ballot box, to US policies across the South American continent and its economic and military might and dominance during the postwar period, and fired up the imaginations of nationalists across Latin America.

When voting stations closed on 24 February 1946, the leaders of the UD, anticipating a victory, announced that these elections had been the fairest in the country's history up until then.[21] The Unión's candidate for president, veteran UCR politician José Tamborini, congratulated the Army for having upheld the transparency of the political process and having renewed the fraternal bonds between the people and the armed forces. A few days later, after the slow and suspenseful recount of votes, Perón emerged as the winner, with the support of 52.4 percent of the 2,839,507 valid ballots cast. Perón's triumph was dramatic: Perón and his running mate, former Radical Hortensio Quijano, had won by only 280,806 votes over the UD's candidates José P. Tamborini and Enrique Mosca.

The United States had failed in its attempt to prevent Perón from being elected to the presidency. This bitter pill was made even bitterer by the necessity of recognizing the new administration, which had been brought to power through democratic means. Perón was able to use the hardening of the opposition from the United States, and the years of accumulated pressure on Argentine governments, to develop a policy partly premised on the rejection of a reviled US imperialism, a position that was in keeping with the new regime's populist rhetoric and which enjoyed the support of many Argentines. The image of the new president would continue to be perceived negatively in Washington. The efforts of the Argentine president to modify this situation would shape his relations with the local Jewish community and the state of Israel.

IMMIGRANTS AND CATHOLIC EDUCATION: THE CHALLENGES FACED BY JEWISH-ARGENTINES

Throughout the 1940s, the agenda of Jewish community organizations focused on two main topics: the restrictions imposed upon the immigration of Jews to Argentina and the implementation in Argentina's public schools of mandatory classes in catechism. In both of these matters, Perón's administration inherited its predecessor's policy orientation, which discriminated against Argentines of Jewish origin. Perón gradually shifted toward policies that recognized Argentina's pluralism and multiculturalism. As early as 1947, he began to rectify the policy regulating the immigration of Jews. A few years later, he abolished mandatory Catholic education.

One infamous episode exemplifies the restrictive policy toward Jewish immigrants: the failed effort to bring to Argentina twenty German-Jewish children and young persons who had found refuge in Great Britain and wanted to be reunited with their relatives in the South American country. Haim Avni analyzes a meeting with the Argentine ambassador in London, Tomás Le Bretón, held during the second half of 1941. Le Bretón denied these young people's request for visas, alleging that "there were too many Jews in Argentina" and that "their population had considerably increased in the last two or three years" thanks to clandestine immigration. The official argued that, "the resident Jewish population was very alarmed by the growth of the general Jewish population, and feared that this could spur severe antisemitism." At one point, Le Bretón told his British interlocutor that, "he was willing to grant them visas on the condition that they accept forced sterilization prior to their departure."[22]

Santiago Peralta, director of immigration since late 1945, also embodied the administration's rejection of Jewish people. Leonardo Senkman characterizes Peralta as a "reputed anthropologist, affiliated with pro-fascist nationalism and author of discriminatory books such as *La acción del pueblo judío en la Argentina* [Actions of the Jewish People in Argentina]."[23] Peralta's book was published in 1943, when news of the extermination of Jews in Europe was beginning to reach Argentina; it was an attack on the avaricious and wily "owners of the world," the traders and lenders who also found their way into Argentina from the colonial period onward. The Argentine people are characterized as victims of the Jewish people: "Opposite this defenceless people stands the Jewish colossus; solid, organized, guided by a single idea and a hand that executes it; this giant is master of all lives, managing finances and agricultural wealth, which is the main source of national wealth."[24]

In his tract, Peralta laments the Argentine condition and reaches the following conclusion: "A home, destroyed. A people physically and morally corrupted by the effects of the traffic of women and degraded by gambling. This tragedy is orchestrated by the Jews who obey the orders of the Northern colonizer [the United States]."[25] Peralta also alleged that a Jewish conspiracy was responsible for the general decrease in immigration to Argentina at the time: "The Department of Immigration has been in their [the Jews'] hands for a good while … They advised ignorant and barbaric governments to cease accepting immigrants from Europe so that they could remain as the only possible settlers … This strange relation coincided with the fall of the Jews' regime in Germany … Those 'persecuted' in Germany needed a new homeland and our country would be that place … the slow and silent swarm of poor Jewish immigrants continues to arrive, slowly, while Argentines are under the spell of black music [jazz], tropical dance, and American movies.[26]

From the beginning of his tenure at the head of the Department of Immigration, Peralta suggested that, in developing an immigration policy, anthropological criteria should be taken into consideration as they were allegedly scientific. Peralta's preferences and his ethnic prejudices were on full display in an internal pamphlet prepared in 1946 by the immigration department and titled *Conceptos sobre inmigración. (Instrucciones de difusión al personal)* (Notions on Immigration: Instructions for Staff). The text emphasized the importance of defending Argentina's population from the risk posed by an incoming avalanche of immigrants following the Second World War, while outlining the goal of establishing which "human types" would most seamlessly integrate into the Argentine population. The leaflet characterized the restrictions imposed in the 1930s and the decrees issued during the war as a defence mechanism in the face of a potential invasion of large masses of immigrants fleeing postwar Europe. In addition to these restrictions, Peralta characterized the measures as a form of racial protectionism. Peralta suggested that immigrants should be classified according to nationality of origin under a new immigration policy guided by criteria that are in accordance with the "laws that govern peoples, based solely on the concept of man and people, that, is, on blood."[27]

Peralta insisted on establishing the ethnic profile of each population of immigrants so as to adjust the distribution, transplantation, and absorption of the cultural and somatic features of these incoming populations. The aim of Peralta's obsession was to "perpetuate the native people, defending their culture in all of its manifestations:

language, art, sciences, moral and religious ethic, institutions, justice, history, traditions ... [to perpetuate] that culture that is inherited from its lineage and that is the source of its national pride." Peralta distinguished between two categories of immigrants: one was good, rural in nature, and came to Argentina to work the land; the other was nefarious, dominantly urban, and thrived on the exploitation of man. The latter was typified in immigrants whose professions were in commerce or industry, which Argentina supposedly did not need. For Peralta, only immigration from one rural area to another could guarantee a genuine mixing between farmers and the aboriginal population due to the affinity of their racial features.

It should therefore come as no surprise that Jewish community organizations protested this policy and used all available means to exercise pressure on the new president for him to remove Peralta from his post at the Department of Immigration. Indeed, in July 1947, Perón removed the public servant from his post due to accusations that he had exercised discriminatory practices while in public office. While this measure was partially a response to international pressure, it also reflected a change in the government's attitude toward Jewish-Argentines and their place in Argentine society.

The leadership of Jewish community organizations was also concerned with the decree that instituted religious education and was issued upon the initiative of the military government's minister of education, Gustavo Martínez Zuviría. This decree represented a pact between military officials and clergymen. It was signed on 31 December 1943 – the same day as the signing of another decree that dissolved political parties and banned their activities – and instituted catechism classes as mandatory in all schools operated by the state. The Argentine clergy had fought toward this goal for over half a century, since Law 1420 was passed in 1884. This famous law had established that education in Argentina would be secular and that religious schooling could only be taught outside of the official schedule for study and by members of religious orders. Regular educators were prohibited from teaching religion. This law reflected Argentina's process of secularization during the second half of the nineteenth century, when the liberal elites had adopted positions influenced by the separation between church and state implemented at the outset of the French Third Republic. From the moment that this separation was sanctioned in Argentina, the Church fought to recuperate its place in the public educational system and to participate in the spiritual molding of children and youth.

Some decades after the milestone of Law 1420, the clergy's efforts would begin to bear fruit. During the 1930s, against the backdrop of the economic difficulties experienced across the world during the Great Depression, and in addition to the restrictions on political freedoms implemented by the regime that overthrew President Yrigoyen and to the rise of conservative trends, the Church was able to solidify its position and strengthen its influence. This success manifested in various forms. In the city of Buenos Aires, the number of religious associations rose from 39 in 1929 to 105 a decade later. Acción Católica, an organization of Catholic laypersons founded in 1928, was proud that its membership had increased to 80,000. A massive audience of more than a million people participated in the International Eucharistic Congress when it was held in Buenos Aires in 1934. Many provinces then decided to institute catechism classes in the schools under their jurisdiction – a shift that nevertheless affected only a small percentage of students, since most pupils were enrolled in schools run by the federal government.

The abrogation of Law 1420 and the imposition of catechism classes in December 1943 therefore represented an unquestionable triumph for the Church. The new decree instituted mandatory religion classes in every student's program of study. Official documentation in the decree explained that the law passed sixty years prior was absurd as it ran contrary to the Catholic nature of the republic. This step was part of the military government's broader attack on liberalism and involved the legitimation of the military government by the Church's most powerful representatives. A series of ties were thus forged in which military officials and clergymen mutually relied upon one another. This interdependence gave shape to the alliance that would bring Perón to power in the February 1946 elections. It also in part motivated the understandable suspicions on the part of many Jews toward the incipient movement called Justicialismo.

The decree supposedly respected freedom of religion and conscience, as it exempted from the mandatory classes those students whose parents had explicitly voiced their opposition to catechism because they were not Catholic. Those children nevertheless had to take another course on "morals." Other articles in the decree authorized Church authorities to determine the contents of study programs and to select school textbooks, as well as to participate in the Ministry's special section in charge of organizing and supervising how religion and morals were taught.

Catholic circles greeted the decree with fitting enthusiasm. The central council of Acción Católica immediately thanked President Ramírez for having given to the children of Argentina their ancestors' authentic legacy by reinstituting Jesus Christ in the schools and the schools in Jesus Christ. The Argentine Council of Bishops also praised the decree in February 1944 for strengthening the spiritual unity of the motherland by harmoniously linking its present to its past. As might be expected, Protestants and Jews expressed their reservations; while these populations – which each accounted for only 2 percent of the general population – were not obligated to receive education on Catholicism, they felt slighted by the equation of Argentine identity with Catholicism.[28] Organizations representing teachers who were secular, liberal, Socialist, and Communist also opposed the decree. It is relevant to observe that whereas Protestant communities organized public protests to manifest their discontent, Jewish community organizations and their memberships preferred to avoid publicly stating their displeasure. The DAIA's leadership simply approved the text of an announcement, issued on 23 March 1944, which stated that the nation's executive branch upheld the constitutional principle that unequivocally granted freedom of conscience, in light of which every Jewish parent was required to express to the director of their child's school their will that their child be exempted from the catechism course. For the DAIA, parents who did not observe this requirement were acting immorally as their conduct amounted to either an intolerable hypocrisy or an obvious lie.[29]

In the following months, the DAIA launched a campaign aiming to convince Jewish parents to defend their rights. Many of these parents refrained from exercising this right, shying away from conflict with school authorities so as to ensure that their children did not feel isolated from the majority of their classmates, or simply out of indifference.[30]

Nationalist and Catholic militants also began to be hired as staff in the various departments of the Ministry of Education under the directorship of Martínez Zuviría, and then his successor, Alberto Baldrich, who was even more vocal in his nationalism. A similar shift occurred in universities and teachers' colleges. The military government also took it upon itself to increase the salaries of those working in ecclesial institutions, transferring considerable sums of money to various Catholic organizations.

Within the framework of his electoral campaign, Perón made statements from which the audience could infer that if he were voted into office, he would turn into law the provisional decree that guaranteed religious education in schools. While this was music to the ears of ecclesial authorities, it displeased many Jewish-Argentines. The Catholic hierarchy saw Perón as the least distasteful alternative to challenge the UD bloc that had joined forces against the candidate.

In the context of the electoral campaign and shortly before election day, ecclesial authorities published a pastoral letter calling upon the faithful to refrain from casting their votes for parties that supported the separation of church and state, the elimination of religious teaching in public schools, and divorce. In sum, this letter demanded from voters that they oppose the UD, which included, among others, Radicals (UCR supporters), Socialists, and Communists whose ideas on these topics were well defined and well known.[31] Years later, the authors of this letter would maintain that it had been a mistake to interpret the pastoral as an expression of support for Perón, noting that similar letters had been written and published in the 1930s during the presidential electoral campaign in which General Agustín P. Justo ran against the leader of the Partido Demócrata Progresista (Democratic Progressive Party), Lisandro de la Torre. In the turbulent political atmosphere of late 1945 in Argentina, the pastoral was nonetheless received as a call on the part of Catholic authorities to vote for Perón.

Perón, for his part, relied on the Church to mobilize votes and support. As the Peronist doctrine had not yet taken shape, Perón also used Catholic messages to draw in potential supporters. In his election campaign, he portrayed himself as the "Catholic candidate" and added that his social message was based on the social doctrine of the "authentic Church" as manifested in several encyclicals, particularly those of Leo XIII and Pius XI, which had a marked emphasis on social issues and attempted to forge a third path situated between Marxism and liberalism.[32]

Following Perón's electoral victory, the president and his wife made certain gestures toward the Church: for example, they attended official religious ceremonies and included (and attended) a mass as part of the celebrations for the Day of Peronist Loyalty (17 October) in 1947. The Day of the Virgin of Luján (devotion to which saint goes back to the colonial period) was declared a statutory holiday. The extent to which these gestures were an expression of Perón's personal beliefs is unclear as they were likely deployed out of political necessity. Ecclesial authorities repaid Perón in kind by silencing priests critical of the regime and by participating, as Cardinal Santiago Luis Copello did, in public events and gatherings that had a clear political orientation toward or otherwise supported Perón's party. To account for these relations, Argentine historian Lila Caimari has referred to the span 1946–49 as Peronism's "Catholic period" and as the Church's "Peronist period."

In March 1947, nine months after Perón was sworn in, the president fulfilled his campaign promise and Congress approved the law instituting religious education in all public schools. Although the representatives of the Justicialist movement held the majority of seats in Congress, getting the bill passed into law was a complex process in which Perón had to exercise pressure through all available means to convince the congressional representatives from his own movement to overcome their reservations about the bill, attributable to their clear left-wing and unionist backgrounds.[33] Perón supported the bill, as he was eager to win over the Church's support and believed that Catholic education could function as a crucial tool to promote national unity. On one occasion, he stated: "One cannot properly speak of an Argentine home that is not also a Christian home … It is under the cross that we have conceived offspring. Under the cross that we have recited our aaa-bee-cees … All of what can be highlighted in our customs is Christian and Catholic."[34] This constituted a blatant attempt to transform religion into one of the pillars of national identity and to portray communism – the ideology that, at the time, competed for the support of the working class – as an imported atheism foreign to the spirit of Argentina.[35] The Jewish community and other non-Catholic groups found this definition of national identity problematic as it marginalized them from society.

In October 1946, when one of the congressional commissions was debating a proposal brought forward by the Radical Party (UCR) – the opposition at the time – to cancel the 1943 decree instituting religious education, the DAIA sent a memorandum to Ricardo Guardo, president of the Lower Chamber, asking him that the decree not be passed into law. The memorandum's authors, Moisés Goldman and Benjamín Rinsky, asserted that this measure harmed, in spirit and in letter, the equality of Jewish-Argentines enshrined in law, as it segregated Catholic from non-Catholic students and limited the freedom of religion guaranteed in the nation's constitution. The leadership of the Jewish community emphasized that, as Law 1420 excluded religious studies from classrooms, it contributed to forming a sense of unity and belonging to the motherland among all students.[36] In spite of these reservations, and unlike various Protestant organizations, the Jewish community's leadership remained silent during the months-long debates, both in the public sphere and in Congress. This silence was likely motivated by a fear among Jewish community organizations that, if they took an active stance, they might be further identified with the opposition to the government and that, in turn, their dealings with the government might be hampered.

Following intense debate that broached basic questions about the Argentine character and national identity, the representatives of the majority bloc in Congress abided by their leader's decision and, in 1947, transformed the 1943 decree into law.[37] The Radical Party congressman Luis Mac Kay advised supporters of the resolution to oppose it so as to avoid creating divisions among Argentines, adding that, as Argentines originated from such a diversity of racial, religious, and philosophical backgrounds and regimes, they had to solve their differences with respect and mutual tolerance in order to bring about unity and harmony in their country.[38] His words had little effect and the law was approved. Perón could finally address a letter to Pius XII in which he highlighted the importance of the new law and the Christian facets of his social policy.[39]

During the first years of Perón's administration, the Church abstained from publicly voicing criticisms of the regime. This attitude was motivated by its perception of Peronism as an effective means of containing communism and also by its expectation that Perón would contribute to strengthening acceptance of the Church among the working classes. This was a clear attempt at a quid pro quo within which each party sought to take advantage of the other in order to further its own interests. Within this exchange, the government assigned an annual subsidy for Catholic institutions and continued to emphasize Peronism's Christian character. The Constitutive Assembly of 1949 upheld the article that established the support of the government for the Roman Catholic apostolic faith.

The reciprocity between Perón and the Church cannot, however, be described as a strong pact. Each of the parties involved was suspicious of the other, in addition to being aware of opposition to close cooperation within its ranks. The clergymen took issue with the state's interventions in their typical areas of activity, such as charity, relief during emergencies, and education, as well as with Perón's arrogation of the ability to interpret "true Christianity." In one of his 1948 speeches, Perón proposed an equation according to which a good Christian was necessarily a good Peronist, and in 1950 he announced in a speech to an audience of Catholic educators that the 2,000-year-old doctrine that was Christianity could stand to be adapted to modern times. These statements provoked great discomfort and fear in ecclesial circles. At this stage, it also became clear that Peronist leaders had not reached a consensus as to the bishops' requirement that Catholicism be granted a preferential position. At no point did the government express the will to restrict the rights or activities of those who professed other faiths. Furthermore, public officials increasingly began to speak about tolerance and respect for other religions as one of the distinctive characteristics of Peronism. The regime viewed loyalty to Perón as more important than loyalty to any other framework.[40]

This posture was a transposition to the religious sphere of the movement's broader aspiration to protect the rights of minorities and groups that were marginalized in comparison to dominant sectors. Peronism sought to portray itself as a movement in which all decent Argentines who supported its project could find their place. Within this vision, ethnic identities became less of a threat to the concept of Argentine identity. Instead of espousing the traditional idea of the racial melting pot, the regime increasingly legitimated hyphenated identities or multiple identities, emphasizing the breadth and diversity of the cultural wellsprings from which Argentine society took shape. This new attitude made it easier to mobilize several sectors of the Jewish-Argentine community to support Perón, especially during his second presidency.

WAS ARGENTINA A "HAVEN FOR NAZI FUGITIVES"?

In his 1989 book *Justice, Not Vengeance*, Simon Wiesenthal wrote that, "in Perón's Argentina the Nazis exercised considerable power, they were the organizers of the Argentinian army, experts in Argentinian industrialization, their money added to the liquidity of Argentinian banks," adding that "Eichmann could feel secure in Argentina."[41] Wiesenthal's words expressed the widely held and longstanding opinion that Argentina in general, and the Peronist regime in particular, was the main refuge for Nazi war criminals after the defeat of the Third Reich. Various sources – overwhelmingly those of the written press – alleged that tens of thousands of Nazi war criminals found refuge in the southern republic.[42]

For decades, supporters of Perón reacted similarly to these exaggerated descriptions: they consistently denied the fact that, during the second half of the twentieth century, their country had sheltered figures who, in one way or another, had been connected with the extermination of Jews in Europe, whether through German war operations or Nazi propaganda. For example, historian Fermín Chavez was cited in a 1992 newspaper as having stated that Adolf Eichmann had been the only war criminal to find refuge in Argentina.[43] It has been said that, as the former president of Argentina "never spoke out publicly against the excesses of Adolf Hitler and his followers, the most precise way to qualify his attitude about Nazism is to say that he did not voice an opinion on it."[44]

Although a number of questions about the presence of leading Nazis in Argentina remain unresolved and many relevant documents have not been found or published, the extent of this phenomena has been better illuminated in a series of studies conducted during the 1990s as well as the results of the investigations conducted by the Comisión para el Esclarecimiento de Actividades Nazi en Argentina (CEANA; Commission of Enquiry into the Activities of Nazism in Argentina) formed and appointed by President Carlos Saúl Menem. Four starting points must be considered when examining such a delicate topic. The first is that, at that time, Argentina sought, as did many other countries, to recruit scientists, technicians, and military experts trained in Germany and

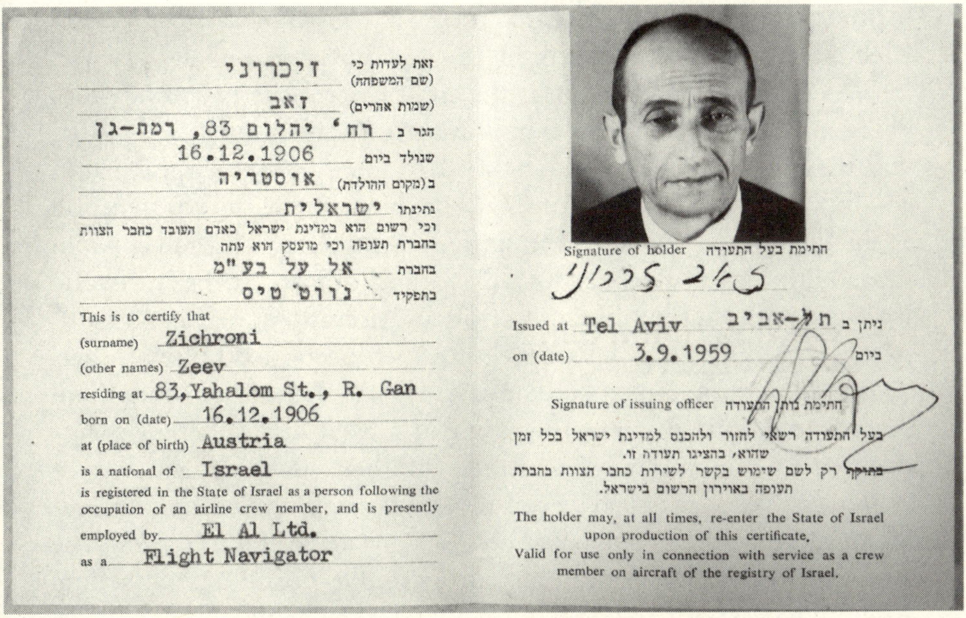
זאת לעדות כי זיכרוני
(שם המשפחה)
(שמות אחרים) זאב
הגר ב רח' יהלום 83, רמת-גן
שנולד ביום 16.12.1906
ב(מקום ההולדה) אוסטריה
נתינתו ישראלית
וכי רשום הוא במדינת ישראל כאדם העובד כחבר הצוות בחברת תעופה וכי מועסק הוא עתה
בחברת אל על בע"מ
בתפקיד נווט טיס

This is to certify that
(surname) Zichroni
(other names) Zeev
residing at 83, Yahalom St., R. Gan
born on (date) 16.12.1906
at (place of birth) Austria
is a national of Israel
is registered in the State of Israel as a person following the occupation of an airline crew member, and is presently
employed by El Al Ltd.
as a Flight Navigator

Signature of holder חתימת בעל התעודה

Issued at Tel Aviv ניתן ב תל-אביב
on (date) 3.9.1959 ביום

Signature of issuing officer חתימת נותן התעודה

בעל התעודה רשאי לחזור ולהכנס למדינת ישראל בכל זמן שהוא, בהציגו תעודה זו.
תקפה רק לשם שימוש בקשר לשירות כחבר הצוות בחברת תעופה באוירון הרשום בישראל.

The holder may, at all times, re-enter the State of Israel upon production of this certificate.
Valid for use only in connection with service as a crew member on aircraft of the registry of Israel.

Figure 2.1 False document, bearing the name of Zeev Zichroni, prepared for the abduction of Adolf Eichmann in 1960.

employed in that country until 1945, hoping that they might contribute their expertise to programs designed to enhance the development, industrialization, and modernization of Argentina. After the war, many countries made efforts to attract the best German scientists. The two main powers in the Cold War developed operations to this effect under the code names "Paperclip" (US) and "Osvakim" (USSR).[45] In his memoirs, Perón refers openly to these efforts without moral ambiguity: "What a deal it would be for the Republic of Argentina to attract scientists and technicians? We would only have to pay for their airfare, after Germany invested thousands of Marks to train these experts."[46]

Perón's administration opened offices in Europe to recruit such professionals.[47] Not surprisingly, some of these experts had been Nazis and had supported Hitler's regime. German scientists and technicians were quickly integrated into the industries that supplied the military and into research institutions, where they were involved in the development and production of weaponry and in developing infrastructure for the country's nuclear research program. Austrian scientist Ronald Richter, who arrived in Argentina in 1948, initiated a nuclear project located on Huemul Island near the city of Bariloche in southeastern Patagonia.[48] Kurt Tank, an expert in aerodynamics at the Luftwaffe, was the most famous of the scientists to immigrate to Argentina. In collaboration with the city of Córdoba, he oversaw the construction of the Institute for Aviation and staffed it with those who had collaborated with him in Europe.[49] Many former officers of the Luftwaffe were test pilots at the Military Factory of Aircraft.[50] The most famous of these was Hans Ulrich Rudel,[51] the much-decorated Luftwaffe ace.

Second, it should also be emphasized that the arrival of many of these immigrants was not the result of a clear and coherent policy dictated by the national government. Rather, visas were either purchased or they were issued by consuls and immigration officials according to varying criteria and based on decisions made at lower levels. The Argentine consul in Barcelona, for example, profited from selling Argentine passports to German agents after the war.

Third, many of the Germans who entered Argentina did so under false identities using falsified travel documents issued either by highly placed members of the Catholic Church in Europe, such as the German bishop Alois Hudal, who was the rector of Rome's Pontifical Colegio Teutonico (German College) and a fervent believer in the greatness of the German nation as well as a fervent antisemite and anti-Zionist; or by the Red Cross's International Committee, which kept no records of these documents.[52] Germans who feared for their future in post-Second World War Germany often fled by finding shelter in a network of monastic houses stretching from northern Bavaria to Austria and thereby reaching to Genoa, Rome, and Naples. A number of international institutions regularly pressured Argentine authorities to accept specific immigrants, even when they had been supporters of Hitler, arguing that their lives were in danger in Western and Central Europe, or the Balkans, within reach of the occupying Red Army troops. From 1947 onward, US political leaders were more focused on the reconstruction of Europe and on halting the communist threat than on locating war criminals and Nazi collaborators.[53]

The fourth and final factor that should be taken into consideration is the Argentine elites' preference, as early as the nineteenth century, for immigrants from northern Europe in the hope that they would "improve" the national population.[54] In this respect, Argentine immigration policy of the nineteenth and twentieth centuries exhibits more continuity than it does change.

The detailed studies conducted by German historian Holger Meding estimate that some 80,000 Germans and Austrians arrived in Argentina during the decade of consecutive Peronist administrations (1946–51 and 1951–55), which coincided with the first decade following the end of the war. Approximately three quarters of these migrants continued on to other destinations across the South American continent, such as Bolivia, Chile, or Paraguay, while others returned to Europe, dissatisfied with the prospect of settling in South America. The remaining 19,000 Germans and Austrians settled in Argentina. The latter number increases to 30,000–40,000 if we include Germans who arrived from other Western or Central European countries that had fallen into the hands of the Red Army. Many of these immigrants were able to adapt to life in their new homeland thanks to the longstanding resident German population, which was 250,000 persons strong before the Second World War broke out and enjoyed prestige and influence upon social circles related to industry, trade, the military, and the universities.[55] While the war raged in Europe, some members of this German community supported the Nazi regime and some opposed it, while others showed little interest in politics. These German-Argentines were also targeted by Nazi propaganda and funds sent either directly from Germany or through the German embassy in Buenos Aires, which succeeded in garnering the support of many, particularly during the early years of the war when the Axis countries seemed to have a chance at victory.[56]

In considering these migrants, it is crucial to differentiate between war criminals and supporters of the Third Reich or members of the National-Socialist Party. The CEANA has identified 180 Nazis, or collaborators with Hitler's regime, who emigrated to Argentina, and more recent research indicates that some 50 war criminals were among the first group of immigrants to Argentina. The highest-ranking individual in the Nazi hierarchy to emigrate to Argentina was Albert Gazenmueller, who had been vice-minister of transport. Other immigrants were lower-ranking members in the Nazi decision-making process, the most famous of whom were Adolf Eichmann and Josef Mengele (Auschwitz's "angel of death," who carried out medical experiments on children, twins, and midgets). Eichmann arrived in Buenos Aires in July 1950 with false documents, registered as a bachelor named Ricardo Klement. His wife, Vera, and his children joined him two years later. In May 1960, he was kidnapped by Mossad agents and taken to Israel to be put on trial. Mengele arrived in Argentina in June 1949 under the name of Helmut Gregor and emigrated to Paraguay during the late 1950s.[57]

The macabre list of these sinister figures includes Walter Kutschmann, an SS official and member of the Gestapo secret police in the occupied area of Galitzia, who in January 1948 presented Argentine immigration officials with a Spanish passport issued to Andrés Ricardo Olmo; Eduard Roschmann, known by the nickname "the executioner of Riga" after the city where he was in charge of the ghetto, arrived on Argentine shores in October 1948 and was admitted under the name of Federico Wegner; Erich Priebke, the SS official involved in the massacre of 335 Italians in the Ardeatine Caves near Rome in 1944, arrived in Argentina in November 1948; Josef Schwammberger, head of the Przemysl ghetto, arrived in March 1949;[58] Gerhard Bohne, who was involved in the euthanasia of mentally ill and disabled persons, entered Argentina in 1949; and Klaus Barbie, the "butcher of Lyon," was admitted into Buenos Aires on his way to Bolivia in 1951.[59] Nazi hunters spent years searching for these figures up until their extraditions to Germany, France, or Italy, where they were put on trial for crimes against humanity. Either under Juan Perón's presidency or in subsequent administrations over the following decades, Argentine authorities made little effort to locate these men and bring them to trial. In some cases, they went so far as to hamper or thwart extradition.[60]

Germans were not the only ones to immigrate to Argentina following the defeat of the Axis.[61] Thousands of Ukrainians, Croatians, and Yugoslavs headed for Italy, fleeing the inexorably advancing Russian tanks. With the help of their compatriots who were already settled in South America, along with the support of the Vatican and, in some cases, US or UK intervention, more than 20,000 such migrants headed to Argentina, then governed by Perón's anticommunist regime. Many of these immigrants had collaborated with Nazi occupying forces, but in the new international framework, particularly in the context of the quickly escalating Cold War, the binary opposition between fascism and democracy dominant during the Second World War receded, making way for the opposition between democracy and communism. In these circumstances, many were willing to forget the past sins of those who had collaborated with the Third Reich. Some 10,000 Yugoslavs (over half of whom were Croatian), 6,000 Poles, and a similar number of Russians and Ukrainians are estimated to have immigrated to Argentina. Unlike the German refugees, these migrants from collaborationist countries did include some of the top fascist figures. Ante Pavelić, and the rest of the leadership of the Ustaše, Croatia's fascist organization, docked on the banks of the River Plate in 1948; Jan Ďurčanský, the Slovak leader responsible for the massacre of Czech citizens from November 1944 onward, and Radasłaŭ Astroŭski, leader of the puppet regime that the Nazis installed in Belarus, also emigrated to Argentina.[62] In 1970, while Perón was in exile in Franco's Spain, the former president admitted that he had granted asylum to thousands: "moved by a humanitarian sentiment," he had authorized the entry into the country of "5,000 Croatians whose lives were threatened by Tito's regime."[63] Italian fascists also chose Argentina as a postwar destination. Among others, the Italian refugees included Vittorio Mussolini, the Duce's son, as well as high-ranking party figures such as Carlo Scorza and Dino Grandi, as well as General Mario Roatta, who had been in charge of the Italian "volunteers" who fought alongside the nationalists during the Spanish Civil War.[64]

Argentina was first accused of harbouring Nazis while the Second World War was still underway. The US involvement in the Allied war effort following the attack on Pearl Harbor unleashed in that country an obsession with the Nazi presence in Argentina. Although some of these exaggerations often verged on fantasy and wove conspiracy theories around how Argentina allegedly began to support Nazi refugees as soon as the war's balance of power leaned toward the Allies, they benefitted from the efforts of the Argentine opposition, then in exile, to delegitimize the military government. Some of these theories even argued that the Führer himself landed in Argentina. These exaggerations of the presence of Nazi fugitives in the country would be taken up in the 1980s in a new group of revisionist texts, which, having been written with little scholarly rigour, hampered the possibility of clarifying the facts that would be crucial to developing a more nuanced perspective on the topic.

The first in a series of legends about the flight of Nazi authorities to Argentina emerged as a result of the disinformation produced within wartime propaganda. In an attempt to undermine the morale of the German population, the British reproduced information that they knew to be false, circulating a narrative according to which Hitler and his personal secretary, Martin Bormann, had fled Germany in a submarine filled with riches. Stalin and the Soviet marshal, Georgi Zhukov, made that version credible by propagating it further, unaware that it was a falsehood but nonetheless receptive to it as it favoured their war plans. These two Soviet leaders found an eager audience in the Argentine community exiled in Uruguay, whose members validated their reports. The British misinformation campaign was only brought to light in the 1980s as a result of the investigations of historian Ronald Newton.

Many such myths and legends narrating similar stories persisted after the end of the war and were reformulated successively in the following decade. In the 1980s, a series of texts was written that attempted to prove the veracity of these murky narratives emerging in the postwar period. One of the central arguments woven through these texts sought to prove that top Nazi authorities colluded with the Reich's most prominent businessmen, bankers, and industrialists to design a plan for them to flee the defeated Germany and recuperate their wealth, salvaged from the country so as to lay the basis for a rebirth of the Nazi regime. These revisionist papers and books speculated that an underground organization – the famous ODESSA – was created with the aim of coordinating these actions. As the literature speculates, this plan took shape in a conference held in Strasbourg in August 1944 and was later discovered in a secret US intelligence report. In 1961, Simon Wiesenthal qualified this report as very important. The Stasi, the secret service of the German Democratic Republic, went so far as to launch a (truncated) investigation on the subject. The existing documentation does not offer conclusive evidence that top Nazi officials participated in the 1944 meeting or that a detailed plan was made to oversee the flight of capital. In any case, as these revisionist historians were not diligent in their evaluation of the documentation on the Strasbourg meeting, their interpretation can accurately be characterized as "nonsense, that has its place alongside legends and concocted narratives."[65]

The arguments on which these revisionist texts focused most consistently were those that aspired to prove that Hitler and Bormann had fled to Argentina and thus to challenge the investigations of US judge Michael Musmanno, who, toward the end of the 1940s, confirmed the veracity of narratives maintaining that Hitler had committed suicide, a conclusion first reached by British historian Hugh Trevor-Roper in late 1945.[66] Hypotheses about the flight of the two figures were based on hearsay that circulated following the Allied victory and was not backed by evidence or documentation. One of these stories hinged on the alleged Ultramar Sur operation in which a fleet of submarines – varying in number from one story to another – was said to have evacuated Hitler, Bormann, and other German Nazi leaders to Argentina, carrying loads of gold and with the cooperation of the United States and Great Britain. These conspiracies were rooted in the fact that the bodies of the missing Nazi leaders were never found. But although revisionist historians suggested that Bormann might have died in Paraguay, the fact is that his body was found in Berlin in the 1970s. Even Wiesenthal, who had previously voiced doubts about the circumstances of Bormann's death, ultimately signed on to the official version of his demise. The FBI qualified rumours about Bormann's flight through Spain, which had been disseminated by the opposition to Perón in exile, as part of a "fantastical story."[67]

As for the fate of the Führer, during the late 1980s Argentine writer Manuel Monasterio published, under the pseudonym Jeff Kristenssen, an account alleging that Hitler had died in Argentina. The exclusive source for this hypothesis was a crewmember of the ship in which Hitler is presumed to have fled. This text does not reveal the identity of this crucial source, preventing anyone from verifying not so much the story's veracity as whether or not the informant actually existed. Other, similar publications saw the light of day, also relying on shoddy evidence. It may seem paradoxical that Georgi Zhukov was the one who finally demystified doubts about the Führer's death, as the Soviet marshal had previously helped to disseminate the false British information about Hitler's flight from Germany during the war's final battles. As Zhukov's memoirs had been translated into English in the 1970s, they were available to the same revisionist historians who, a decade later, would insist that Hitler had fled to Argentina. Zhukov acknowledged that, despite the veracity that he had initially ascribed to the hypothesis according to which Hitler had fled Germany, subsequent Soviet investigations had confirmed that Hitler had died in Germany in the war's final phase.

Speculations as to the participation of the Argentine government in the fate of Nazi war criminals revolve around the issuance of Argentine passports and visas to these figures with the aim of expediting their flight and granting them shelter. Wiesenthal initially calculated that approximately 7,500 such travel documents had been issued – a number he subsequently revised to 2,000 in 1993. Other accounts, primarily based on information provided by revisionist historians, speculated that a much greater volume of documents had been issued but did not back these estimates with tangible proof. Although it is difficult to estimate the number of passports issued, sources from Argentine diplomacy have confirmed that consulates and embassies did issue many such documents. Father José Silva in Genoa may have been responsible for issuing these travel documents. Silva had been handpicked by the Peronist administration to distribute passports to a potentially large group of recipients, which mainly included Nazis and their collaborators, according to his own ideological preferences. The government abandoned this strategy following the arrest in Copenhagen of one of Kurt Tank's collaborators in possession of one such passport. From that point on, the majority of Nazi war criminals and their collaborators entered into Argentina using documents issued by the Red Cross.

Ambassador Braden's hostile attitude toward Argentine authorities would mobilize the United States in exaggerating Argentina's involvement in the fate of Nazi authorities. Specifically, US media focused strongly on the whereabouts of Nazi authorities and circulated tales about them. The publication of the *Blue Book* was also a part of this effort. Due to its need to secure the cooperation of potential allies, including Argentina, against the Soviet bloc, the US attitude gradually softened. From that point on, the exiled opposition to Perón would be responsible for the bulk of the initiatives to discredit Peronist administrations by emphasizing its ties with the former Axis countries.

The capture of Adolf Eichmann in May 1960 by Israel's Mossad spurred international interest in the topic of how Nazi war criminals had entered Argentina in general, and in the policy of the Peronist administrations in particular. The former SS officer became a symbol of the atrocities committed by the bureaucratic machinery that was in charge of executing the "final solution to the Jewish question." In the eyes of many, Perón's image as a Nazi sympathizer was strengthened when they found out that Eichmann had entered Argentina in July 1950. The detractors of Peronism saw in Eichmann's presence one more piece of evidence of the regime's supposedly fascist character and were undeterred by the fact that Eichmann had entered the country as an unmarried person, with travel documents issued by the International Red Cross to one Ricardo Klement, or that he had spent the next ten years far away from political and social life in a state of relative poverty.

3

The OIA, the Jewish Section of the Peronist Party

The Peronist regime deployed considerable effort to mobilize the support of Argentina's Jewish community. Despite the administration's excellent ties with the state of Israel and Perón's numerous gestures toward this community, debate continues about the effects that these policies had, if any.

In February 1947, a group of Jewish activists showed up at the office of the minister of the interior, Ángel Borlenghi, to express their support for Perón's regime and its policies. Borlenghi's vice-minister, Abraham Krislavin, had encouraged the group to visit the minister. Krislavin was born in Buenos Aires in 1914 to a wealthy family of Jewish-Polish immigrants and had been classmates with Borlenghi in high school. The two had started their political activism in the Socialist Party, and became close friends. They both supported Perón's work as head of the Secretariat of Labour and Welfare and were rewarded with positions in the Ministry of the Interior.[1] Krislavin's position in the public service was unprecedented for a Jewish-Argentine: the scope of the files assigned to him was much broader than questions pertaining strictly to the Jewish community and he participated actively in designing policies across various areas.

Borlenghi would become an important link between the Jewish community and the government. On that occasion, he hosted the activists enthusiastically and accompanied them to the president's office for an interview. Perón congratulated the group on their initiative and repeated notions that he had previously expressed, stating his rejection of any discrimination toward Jews and of prejudices against them:

"My only wish is that all those who live here feel that they are Argentines, that they are truly Argentine, independently of their origin or where they came from, because, in this country, we are too mixed to discriminate in that manner."[2]

The president was uneasy at having been unfairly accused by his political rivals of being hostile toward Jews. He added: "It is my impression that many members of the community who have opposed us have done so, just as half of Argentines, largely under the erroneous impression generated by the newspapers that have spared no expense to defame us … I will prove with deeds that this is not true."[3] He then emphasized that people were free to have differing opinions, so long as they contributed to the development of the nation and to its prosperity. As a gesture toward the community, and wishing to encourage initiatives capable of shattering the wall of opposition to his regime raised by Jewish community institutions, Perón told them that, just a few hours prior to the meeting, he had signed an order to allow the entry into the country and the residency of forty-seven Jews embarked on the ship *Campana*. These Jewish immigrants had come to Argentina without proper papers after Brazil had denied them entry.[4] The DAIA promptly thanked Perón for this "wonderful gesture in granting our request that the immigrants on board the *Campana* be allowed to enter freely, as this will allow the integration into the country of men, women, and children who, for years, have suffered between life and death and who are eager to begin new lives in our Republic, in an atmosphere of productive work, in peace, justice, and fraternity."[5]

Two days after this meeting, the Organización Israelita Argentina (OIA; Argentine Jewish Organization) was founded. According to a secret memorandum of the World Jewish Congress, the "first cautious moves to create a Jewish Peronist organization were taken in mid-1945," but this attempt failed due to the lack of support among community organizations. The immediate precursor to the OIA was the Organización Nacional Israelita Argentina (ONIA; National Jewish Argentine Organization). As Alberto Woscoff recounts, his father, Salvador, founded that precursor organization. The epithet "nacional," Woscoff holds, would subsequently be omitted from the title due to its negative connotations for Jewish people.[6]

Little is known about the OIA due to the unfortunate lack of relevant documentation. The OIA's first president seems to have been one of the Cortés brothers, either Eduardo or Natalio, who changed their family name from Schejtman and originated from the Santa Fe agricultural colony of Moisesville.[7] At the time, Natalio was also the first president of the Ezrah Jewish hospital in Buenos Aires. Other founding members of the OIA included Samuel Rozenstein and the popular sports reporter Luis Elías Sojit, as well as Salvador Woscoff, Mauricio Nikiprovesky, Julio Jorge Schneider, J. Krasbutch, Samuel Buerdman, Carlos Lokman, Jaime Weitzman, Gregorio Perlmuter, Manuel Grinstein, José Kafia, and Jaime Rozovsky.[8] Other figures, such as textile industry entrepreneur Sujer Matrajt and young lawyer Pablo Manguel, also played a key role in the organization shortly after it was launched.[9] The OIA was therefore the result of the initiatives of a group of merchants, businessmen, and middle-class professionals. The nephew of Manuel Scheinsohn recalls how his uncle was, in his eyes, "the rich uncle."[10] It is clear that, at least in its infancy, the organization competed with the DAIA in its efforts to represent the community vis-à-vis national authorities.

An excerpt from the OIA's statement of purpose outlines the positions of the Cortés brothers and the organization over which they presided: "We Argentines of Jewish origin have only one motherland, Argentina, and are (appropriately) loyal only to our leader Juan Domingo Perón. Toward Israel, we express admiration, we support its existence, and maintain affectionate bonds, similar to those that bind the [Argentine-born] sons of Italian parents to Italy or the sons of Spanish parents to Spain. We do not feel for Israel the loyalty that we profess to our country, as we do not feel that we have dual nationalities. All of our compatriots should understand this very clearly."[11] In other words, they advocated for the social and political integration of Jews via Peronism while putting forward a conception of identity that had at its centre their Argentine nationality and also integrated the Jewish and Zionist components of their identity.

The OIA developed a clear political identity as a Peronist organization.[12] In that regard, it differed from the DAIA, which claimed to maintain its neutrality vis-à-vis party politics, particularly during that rocky period, which ensured its longevity from 1935 to the present day. It is an interesting yet little-known fact that one of the DAIA's presidents, Ricardo Dubrovsky, joined the Peronist party. Halfway

Figure 3.1 Pablo Manguel, leader of the OIA, next to Juan and Eva Perón at a Jewish support event for the Peronist government, early 1950s.

through 1953, during Perón's second presidency, Dubrovsky was named professor at the Chair of Obstetrics of the Universidad de Buenos Aires. It is telling that once he found out about this nomination, he sent letters to thank the OIA's leaders, Pablo Manguel and Ezequiel Zabotinsky. Manguel, in turn, congratulated him on "such a remarkable nomination, which illustrates once again how highly our most esteemed president values Jewish-Argentines."[13]

The initiative of the OIA's leaders in creating a "parallel" organization was reminiscent of Perón's strategy during the military dictatorship of 1943–45, when he was at the head of the Secretariat of Labour and Welfare and encouraged the creation of new trade unions that would back him so as to counter the influence of those who opposed his policies. Such efforts were also made to coopt other sectors of

Argentine society. Nevertheless, even after support for Perón began to grow among Jewish-Argentines, he did not exercise pressure on the organized Jewish community to join the OIA, and the community maintained a high degree of autonomy. In this regard, relations between the government and Jewish community organizations demonstrate that the Peronist administration was less capable of intervening in specific areas of civil society than is typically acknowledged. The leaders of Jewish organizations that were not aligned with Peronism demonstrated their ability to defend their autonomy in the face of state actions to keep them in check; this reveals the limits of common interpretations of the ties between Peronism and the different social and ethnic groups within Argentine civil society. In this regard, we support the argument put forward by historian Omar Acha, according to which "it is a conceptual error to see only a manipulative and totalitarian purpose in the 'associationism' favoured by Peronism. This error hinders the understanding of one of the crucial logics of Peronist power. Associations were not pretexts or empty tools for the subordination of entire groups or social classes to Perón's political ambitions."[14]

Despite the suspicions that many community leaders harboured toward the president, the DAIA maintained its status as the community's official representative and its leaders forged good working relations with the government. From the outset, the DAIA, particularly leaders like Moisés Goldman, perceived that it would have to adapt to the "codes" expected by the governing regime and that doing so would ensure its survival.

The OIA offered Perón a public platform from which to voice statements of sympathy toward Jews and toward the state of Israel. Members of the OIA had easy access to governing figures. For example, a few days after the organization was launched, two of its leaders, Salvador Woscoff and Mauricio Nikiprovesky, met with the minister of the interior and the secretary of public health, Ramón Carrillo, after which the representatives announced that solutions were forthcoming to address the restrictions on the killing of animals according to kosher laws, as well as the discrimination against Jews in the medical faculty of the Universidad de Buenos Aires. The OIA could not similarly boast about the results of its March 1947 meeting with the chief of the federal police, General Juan Filomeno Velazco, in which the organization requested of him to take all possible measures to halt antisemitic violence. Perón, however, removed Velazco from the directorship shortly after the meeting. In June 1948, the OIA's leadership clearly showed its ambition to become intermediaries between the Jewish community and the regime, when they accompanied the leadership of the DAIA to the presidential palace to request that Perón admit twenty-seven undocumented Jewish refugees – a request that the president granted.[15]

Perón and his wife Evita spoke in the ceremony to mark the inauguration of the OIA headquarters in August 1948, and other dignitaries, such as Foreign Minister Juan Atilio Bramuglia, were also present. Numerous community leaders and community members who did not necessarily identify with the regime also participated in the ceremony, which was the first visit of an Argentine head of state to a Jewish community institution. On that occasion he asserted: "How could antisemitism in Argentina be accepted or accounted for? There should only be one class of men in Argentina: men who work for the good of the nation, without distinctions ... This is why ... as long as I am President of the Republic, no person shall persecute another."[16] In that same meeting, Perón also described the OIA's leaders as "comrades from this admirable Peronist organization."

The OIA's leadership made efforts to mobilize Jewish public opinion in favour of the government. One such effort was a manifesto titled "Why are we with the government?" This manifesto was a call to potential supporters: "We write these words for the members of our hardworking community: workers, academics, intellectuals, business owners, industrialists, as well as thousands of Argentine Jews whose effort and dedication has contributed to bettering this noble motherland, which is also ours."[17] The authors' interpellation of their audience appealed to both the patriotism of Argentines and the interests specific to Jews, the majority of whom were members of the middle class. Indeed, Perón promoted commerce and industry and a sizable number of Jewish-Argentines benefitted from credits granted by the Central Bank. These beneficiaries included the Teubal family, for example, a Jewish family that originated from Syria and owned textile businesses.

The OIA issued communiqués mentioning Perón's gestures with regard to immigration, as well as his condemnations of antisemitism and pronouncements in support of the state of Israel. The leadership also undertook considerable efforts to transmit these messages to US Jews. Pablo Manguel, minister plenipotentiary to Israel – an assignment that, in the words of a witness, he received as "a treat"[18] to thank him for his cooperation with the regime – often visited New York on his trips between Buenos Aires and Tel Aviv, holding meetings in the US metropolis to tell journalists about Perón's gestures of sympathy toward Jews. Sujer Matrajt and Manuel Scheinsohn also visited the United States with the aim of stating that antisemitism did not exist in Argentina, in large part thanks to Perón's active participation in countering this ill. Scheinsohn was sent to the United States with the specific aim of forging and strengthening trade ties with the northern country and attracting tourists to Argentina, as this would, in turn, signify an influx of cash for the southern republic.[19]

Perón, in turn, held various meetings with Sujer Matrajt, the OIA's director, who, it seems, was close to the president as he also sold goods to the army. These meetings played a crucial role in the resolution that Perón put forward to include a clause in the new constitution, approved in 1949, which would broaden the article from the 1853 Constitution enshrining the equality of all citizens regardless of race or creed.[20] Prior to the election of representatives to the Constituent Assembly in charge of reforming the 1853 Constitution, the OIA called upon Jewish-Argentines to support this clause and thus also the new constitution. The OIA designed a poster that it plastered on downtown streets and that the newspaper *Crítica* reproduced in its issue of 4 December 1948, stating: "The OIA recommends that you vote for the reform of the constitution, and support the entire list of the candidates for the people and for Peronism. *Viva* General Perón." The poster displayed the Justicialist emblem and, next to it, a list of the names of the twenty-two Peronist candidates to the Constituent Assembly.

Both Perón and Evita gave speeches in which they vigorously rejected antisemitism. The first lady went as far as to identify antisemitism with the enemies of the regime, when she claimed in an August 1948 speech: "In our country, the only ones who have separated between classes and religions have been the leaders of the baleful oligarchy who have governed our country for fifty years. Those in power were responsible for antisemitism, as they have poisoned the people with false theories, and they did this until Perón made it possible to proclaim us all equals."[21] In the following years, the Peróns characterized Jews as those who were most capable of understanding the meaning of Justicialismo due to their history as victims of oppression and injustice. Evita characterized the Jewish people as exemplary of those who had long upheld a national conscience and fought a tenacious struggle for the lost motherland.[22] The governor of the province of Buenos Aires, Carlos Aloé, praised the figure of Theodor Herzl in 1954, highlighting the moral courage and the example for humanity embodied in that founding father of Zionism. Aloé went as far as to name a street in the city of La Plata after the Zionist figure.[23] A year later, following the visit of Israeli finance minister Levi Eshkol, President Weizmann Park was inaugurated in the district of Ezeiza, named after Israel's first president.

Once Argentina established diplomatic relations with Israel, the OIA attempted to mediate between delegates of the Middle Eastern country and the Peronist administration. The OIA's attempts initially caused discomfort and divergences of opinion among the Israeli governing elite, but the country's diplomats quickly understood that the goodwill and services of the OIA's leaders could contribute to strengthening ties between the two countries.

Curiously enough, we have no records documenting female participation in the OIA's activities. It is nevertheless likely, as Nerina Visacovsky asserts, that many women, such as Clara Maguidovich, the wife of Minister of the Interior Borlenghi, or Frida de Woscoff, the wife of Salvador Woscoff, director of the OIA, accompanied their husbands and encouraged other women to support the actions undertaken by the government.[24] We do know for certain, however, that the Organización Sionista Femenina Argentina (OSFA; Argentine Organization of Zionist Women), founded in 1926 in the province of Mendoza, voiced its support for the Fundación Eva Perón. Sandra McGee Deutsch recounts, in her book on the history of Jewish women in Argentina, how the leader of the OSFA, Berta Guerchunoff, negotiated with Evita Perón so that shipments of clothing and medicine could be sent to Israel through the foundation as the OSFA could not send assistance directly to the fledgling country.[25] The shipments bore the foundation's logo.

Figure 3.2 Eva Perón delivering a speech at an event organized by the OIA, early 1950s. Juan Perón and Pablo Manguel are sitting in the first row.

The first such shipment included ten boxes of secondhand clothing gathered by the OSFA, placed in a larger container along with a donation from the foundation of clothing and foodstuffs for newcomers to Israel. On another occasion, Evita facilitated the shipment to Israel of a large volume of new clothing items. The first lady played a similar role for other Zionist organizations, such as the Central Committee of Sephardi Women and the Sephardi Friends of the Histadrut (the latter being the confederation of Israeli trade unions).

Gradually, the gestures of the Peronist administration toward Jewish-Argentines and the state of Israel, as well as the philanthropic efforts of Zionist women in Argentina, complemented one another and enhanced the image of the government among the members of the OSFA. The Israeli branch of the Women's International Zionist Organization sent its thanks and greetings to Evita on behalf of the Jewish state. When Minister of Labour Golda Meir visited Argentina in April 1951, she personally thanked Evita for the donations received from and via the foundation. The following year, Ambassador Manguel

Figure 3.3 Shipments of garments and blankets sent by the Eva Perón Foundation for the residents of immigrant camps in the new state of Israel, received in the port of Haifa by Yitzhak Navon, future president of Israel, June 1955.

bestowed upon Meir a Peronist medal recognizing her as a "loyal friend." After Evita's death in 1952, the OSFA sent its condolences to Perón in a telegram. It also praised the first lady on the front cover of its bulletin, emphasizing her commitment to the workers and the elderly, her leadership of the women's Peronist movement, and her contribution to securing for women the right to vote.[26]

The expectations that Perón and Evita harboured of effecting a rapid change among the majority of the Jewish population did not materialize. In the March 1948 legislative elections and in the elections for the Constituent Assembly in December of the same year, the OIA failed in its attempts to obtain substantial support for Peronist candidates from Jewish voters. In July 1950, Abraham Krislavin recognized in a conversation with the heads of the Israeli diplomatic delegation that the organization had not succeeded in its goal of attracting a large proportion of Jewish-Argentines to Perón's party.[27] The OIA nevertheless persevered in its campaign to win over the community's hearts and ballots. In an April 1951 meeting between Natalio Cortés and Perón, the former informed the president that the OIA, over which he presided at the time, was poised to open offices in various locations in the country's hinterland and that these offices would include women's centres.[28]

In early July that same year, a delegation headed by the OIA visited Perón in his office at the Casa Rosada (the seat of government) to ask the president to run for a second term. In this regard, the OIA was one group among other organizations advocating for ethnic groups, trade unions, or cultural and social causes. This particular delegation represented the near totality of Jewish community organizations in Argentina. The event was widely covered. It featured the participation of the presidential couple, as well as ministers, the president of the Congress, and other renowned leaders. Key leaders of Jewish community organizations spoke, among them José Ventura, president of Keren Hayesod (United Israel Appeal), and Moisés Slinin, president of the AMIA. The ceremony was an achievement for the OIA – a formal acknowledgment that a firm stance opposing antisemitism occupied a central place in Peronist policy. Given the DAIA's customary neutrality, some community members criticized the organization for joining the OIA at this event, thus supposedly "surrendering to blackmail from the OIA."[29]

PABLO MANGUEL: A KEY FIGURE IN THE OIA

Ahead of the presidential election, the OIA would spare no effort in its propaganda through newspaper ads, advertisements, meetings, and rallies. To that end, Pablo Manguel returned to Buenos Aires from Israel to further the president's electoral campaign vis-à-vis the Jewish population. The president and Eva Perón participated in a homage to Manguel, marking the two years of his tenure as ambassador to Israel, held early in August 1951 at the fancy Les Ambassadeurs hall and organized by delegates of the OIA's Buenos Aires branch together with OIA delegates from the branches in the country's hinterland and Uruguay. Manguel praised the presidential couple for demonstrating their "keen awareness of problems facing the Jewish people." As a report in the newspaper *La Nación* registers, when "one of the guests expressed that the entire Jewish community wished for General Perón to be re-elected and for his wife to run as vice president, the room stood up and cheered them both." Perón subsequently praised the OIA leader and diplomat to Israel for his work: "Dr. Manguel is more than worthy of the trust that I have placed in him. His intelligence and his hard work have been crucial to the success of his endeavors." The affinity between Manguel and Perón comes across clearly in the photos from the event, which are held in Argentina's national archives and which capture the familiarity between them.

Within this context, Manguel is emblematic of the bond of Jewish-Argentines to their South American homeland. He was born in Buenos Aires on 18 November 1912 to immigrants from Europe. The family of his father Adolfo originated in Innsbruck, Tyrol, in eastern Austria, while that of his mother, Elsa Elijovich, came from the Kamenetz-Podolsky region in Russia. Manguel was one of four children who grew up in a family of modest means. He had to look for work at a young age, to contribute to the household's income. At age 15, he worked in the union of bread bakers of Buenos Aires, an experience that instilled in him an awareness of social issues and led him to identify with Justicialismo. He had published a book about this topic when he was 20 years old and working toward a law degree. He then worked as a lawyer for the union of newspaper and magazine delivery persons. By the mid-1940s, Manguel was therefore well aware of the ties between unions and nascent Peronism.

Despite these efforts, Jewish Peronist candidates were defeated in the November 1951 elections. One of these candidates was a leading figure of the OIA, lawyer Ezequiel Zabotinsky, who was running for office in the Once neighbourhood.[30] By contrast, the opposition party UCR succeeded in electing three Jewish candidates to Congress, Santiago L. Nudelman, Manuel Belnicoff, and Rodolfo Weidman, thanks in part to the votes of members of the Jewish community. Only one Peronist Jewish candidate was elected to Congress: David

Diskin, of the Confederación General de Empleados de Comercio de la República Argentina, headed by Borlenghi. To account for Zabotinsky's loss, Manguel explained to Perón that the riding in which he ran had a Jewish population of only 10 percent, and that this small Jewish population was therefore not responsible for the candidate's electoral loss.[31]

In the aftermath of the failure to capture the Jewish vote, leaders of Jewish community organizations and Israeli diplomats in Argentina alike began to fear that Perón would be less welcoming toward them or that he might retaliate.[32] Yet none of this came to pass, possibly due in part to Perón's overwhelming victory and the little weight of Jewish voters. This restrained reaction may have also been motivated by the government's concern that any action that could be perceived as antisemitic might negatively affect relations with the United States. Perón upheld his positive policy toward Israel and Jews, and continued to trust in the OIA. Manguel was promoted within the Ministry of Foreign Affairs and designated to supervise all the Argentine embassies and delegations in the Middle East. Evita's death in July 1952 also prompted similar fears that the regime's attitude toward the Jews might change, as the young first lady was considered to have been behind the foundation of the OIA and played an important part in mediating Argentina's relations with Israel. These fears once again proved to be unfounded.[33]

In these new circumstances, Israeli diplomats perceived that Borlenghi, the minister of the interior, had strengthened his position and, in turn, collaborated with his close friend Krislavin to further the OIA's activities. Under Zabotinsky, the OIA restructured its leadership in 1953, after a number of its leaders were involved in dubious episodes; this time, it seemed, the OIA would grow stronger.[34] In this new phase, the OIA also seemed to be more open to cooperating with the DAIA on questions such as Jewish immigration, Zionism, and the struggle against antisemitism.

In November 1953, nearly 6,000 Jews attended a ceremony that was the culmination of an OIA initiative to inscribe Perón's name in the Golden Book of the Jewish National Fund (Keren Kayemeth Leisrael). Tuvia Arazi, an advisor in the Israeli embassy, described the president's speech on that occasion as a "psalm of praise for Israel

Figure 3.4 Pablo Manguel, the first Argentine ambassador to Israel and leader of the OIA, with Juan Perón, early 1950s.

and the Jewish people." A year later, the OIA gave Perón a book, compiled and published by the DAIA, that contained the president's speeches and statements against antisemitism, and asserted the right of Jewish-Argentines to have ties with the state of Israel.[35] The latter ceremony was attended by the leaderships of the DAIA, the OIA, Keren Hayesod, the Organización Sionista Argentina (OSA; Argentine Zionist

Organization), and dignitaries from other organizations. As attested to in an internal report prepared by the OIA, the organization had the support of over 120 institutions, including a number of banks (the Banco Israelita del Río de la Plata, Banco Comercial de Buenos Aires, and Banco Mercantil Argentina), newspapers (*Diario Israelita*, *Di Presse*, *Mundo Israelita*, *Israel*, *La Luz*, and *Semana Israelita*), schools, and cultural and social institutions (Macabbi, Hacoaj), whether they were Ashkenazi or Sephardi, Zionist or non-Zionist, or grouped together women or men. The show of support was impressive.

Borlenghi also succeeded at winning Socialists over to Peronism, including Enrique Dickmann as well as the group of pro-Peronist dissidents in the Socialist Party. In 1948, Dickmann, one of the most respected and veteran Socialist leaders, had expressed doubts about the marked hostility that his party had shown toward Peronism. Following the failed coup led by General Benjamín Menéndez and Perón's crushing electoral victory in the 1951 elections, the crisis within the Socialist Party deepened. This tension culminated when Dickmann met with Perón in February 1952. As a result of this meeting, various political prisoners and union leaders were released from prison and the newspaper *La Vanguardia* was reopened. Acting upon Borlenghi's suggestion, Perón honoured Dickmann with a merit medal in recognition of his academic achievements at the university, an award he should have received forty years earlier but had been denied him due to his Jewish origins.[36]

The cadres of Jewish community organizations nevertheless lived in constant fear and harboured suspicions. They shared a sense that Peronism was a populist regime with a charismatic leader who could abruptly change direction at any time. They also felt that the internal distribution of power among the forces that made up the heterogeneous Peronist movement was prone to shift, creating the possibility that the antisemitic elements present within this group could, under varying circumstances, become more influential. None of this came to pass – at least up until Perón's overthrow in September 1955.

OPPOSING VIEWS OF THE OIA

While Emilio Corbière likely overstates the support that the OIA had among Jewish-Argentines,[37] statements such as those of Kurt J. Riegner, among others, according to which the organization had little clout among members of the community, seem similarly exaggerated.[38] As mentioned earlier, statistics documenting the size of the OIA's membership are not available and little is known about the activities of the organization's provincial branches. It is clear, however, that the OIA enjoyed support in several provinces. Various press reports from that period mention "OIA delegates from the interior provinces." For example, *Mundo Israelita* reported that in late December 1950, the leaders of the OIA's Córdoba branch sent a donation by cheque of 40,000 pesos to the Fundación Eva Perón. It is also known that delegates from the provinces were present at a meeting with Perón held in the Casa Rosada in March 1952. During the following month, Pablo Manguel, along with the leadership of the OIA's Buenos Aires headquarters, undertook a tour in the country's provinces as one of the Peronist party's candidates for Congress. In addition, a letter dated July 1954, which we found in Argentina's national archives, is signed by Benzión Guzmán of the OIA's branch in Paraná, and a press clipping describes the participation of an OIA delegation from one of the first Jewish colonies in Argentina, Basavilbaso in the province of Entre Ríos, at the inauguration of a train station named after the noted Jewish-Argentine author Alberto Gerchunoff.

The cabinet of Domingo Mercante, governor of the province of Buenos Aires, included various Jewish-Argentines who collaborated with Peronism, particularly Jaime Glattstein, Jaime Bernstein, and Bernardo Serebrinsky, all of whom worked in education. Glattstein was general inspector of preschool education. He oversaw the project that culminated in the passing into law of public kindergartens in the province. Bernstein and Serebrinsky participated in the creation and development in 1949 of the provincial education ministry's Department of Psychology, with Bernstein working in vocational psychology and psychometrics, and Serebrinsky in psychiatry and professional orientation. Mercante's administration also hired Dino Jarach as an advisor. Jarach was an Italian Jew who had moved to Argentina in 1941, escaping war, persecution by the Nazis, and racial laws. He held a doctorate in jurisprudence and was specialized in fiscal sociology. Jarach worked as an advisor to Mercante and to the Ministry of Interior, Economics, and Planning, at that time headed by Dr. Miguel López Francés. Jarach drafted the project proposal for the province's Fiscal Code, which was then approved in the provincial legislature and became the template for similar codes subsequently adopted in various provinces across the country. Journalist Eduardo Chernizki has told us about the cooperative bank Caja Popular of San Fernando, which funded the Jewish school and the local synagogue, and, in the mid-1980s, attracted the participation of former members of the OIA.

In considering Jewish public servants at the time, Salomón Chichilinsky, doctor and employee of the Ministry of Public Health, should be recalled. Historian Fermín Chávez recounts the story of the cultural circle known as Peña Eva Perón: "This [initiative] came about to satisfy a need among workers in the cultural spheres to know more about the [Eva Perón] Foundation's activities."[39] In meetings, especially when dessert was served, someone would usually make a short speech. During one such meeting, Dr Chichilinsky, who was also a writer, stood up and asked for Evita's permission to read from a speech that he had given that afternoon in a public OIA event.

It thus becomes clear that many Jews sincerely believed, as did many other Argentines, that Peronism would enact reforms to lead the country toward a better future, one of development and modernization, with a promise of social justice; they therefore joined the OIA, motivated by the belief that the Jewish community, as such, should not alienate itself from the wishes of the majority of people, who supported Perón. Due to the lack of reliable data, we can only estimate that these new members were not a massive contingent. At the same time, as the OIA's leaders received support from the Peronist regime they also wielded considerable influence among Jewish-Argentines.

The depiction of the OIA in the memoirs of the Israeli ambassador, Jacob Tsur, is the polar opposite of Corbière's cited characterization. Tsur evokes them as a handful of contemptible Jews who were close to authorities and executed their instructions in Jewish spheres. He also describes them as an organization of Jewish climbers, to whom the community was opposed. In a similar vein, I. Schwartzbart of the World Jewish Congress viewed the leaders of the OIA as little more than petty criminals and fraudsters.[40] Some Congress officials used an alarmist tone in their reports discussing the OIA. In reporting on the OIA's initiative of collecting monetary donations to build a new Jewish hospital in the province of Entre Ríos sponsored by the Fundación Eva

Perón, Jacob Hellman wrote about the "terror campaign" that the OIA led against the DAIA, and characterized the request for donations as a "thieving demand of the OIA to defraud [the community of] three million [pesos] to construct a hospital with the name of the First Lady."[41] Hellman used a similarly alarmist tone to describe the atmosphere in which Jews in Argentina lived: "men live here as marranos, under a ghastly coercion and outwardly it will be said that the Jews of Argentina are free and do not experience any anti-Semitism."[42]

Numerous interviews that I have carried out challenge Tsur's depiction of the OIA's status – a depiction echoed, in some ways, in the works of historians Haim Avni, Leonardo Senkman, and Jeffrey Marder, and in the doctoral theses of Joseph Goldstein and Lawrence Bell. These studies are based on sources such as community newspapers (which typically ignored the OIA), the documentation of other Jewish institutions that competed with the OIA, or the archives of Israel's foreign ministry, part of which was hostile toward the Justicialist Party's Jewish contingent. Portrayals of the OIA's leaders as charlatans and fraudsters were also based on a long report published by the Comisión Nacional de Investigación (CNI; National Investigation Commission) convened by the Revolución Libertadora (Liberating Revolution) – the military regime that took power after deposing Perón – to document the "authors and accomplices to the irregularities [committed] during the Second Tyranny."[43] The report, in a chapter about illicit self-enrichment among "the dictatorship's legislators," singles out Pablo Manguel, the OIA's most prominent figure, among other "corrupt persons," for the "accrual of his wealth."[44] Our oral history initiative, in contrast, has led us to interview, from August 2008 onward, relatives of OIA leaders, including Salvador Woscoff, Adolfo Minyevsky, Sujer Matrajt, Luis Elías Sojit, Pablo Manguel, Natalio Cortés, and Ezequiel Zabotinsky. These interviews yield nuances crucial to countering this negative portrayal of the OIA, so frequent in the work of historians.

The majority of OIA leaders were first-generation Jewish immigrants from Eastern Europe. Some, such as Sujer Matrajt or Salvador Woscoff – who kept their original family names – were very active in the organized Jewish community and were dedicated to Zionism and Israel. Others did not have a strong Jewish identity, as can sometimes be seen in their adapted last names. This was the case for sports journalist Luis Elías Sojit (whose original family name was Shoijet).[45] Sojit coined the often-used phrase "Today is a Peronist day!" which he typically reserved for sunny days; he frequently omitted from his sportscasts the names of athletes who were considered hostile to the regime. Sojit was born in 1910 to a modest family, one of five children of a tailor. He launched his career as a journalist when he was 13 years old, working as a reporter in the newspaper *La Argentina*. Sojit began studies in engineering in La Plata when he was 17 years old, yet still reported on matches for *El Mundo*, a newspaper helmed at the time by the famous Jewish writer Alberto Gerchunoff. In 1933, journalist Julio César Marini welcomed Sojit to radio broadcasting. Almost accidentally, Sojit began to broadcast automobile races, and was greatly acclaimed for his commentary despite being a novice to the sport. While he was still young, Sojit was the official broadcaster of Radio Splendid, the rival station to Radio Belgrano. Radio Splendid was then headed by Jaime Yankelevich, another Jewish-Argentine, who convinced the young star to work for his station. Sojit later became affiliated with Peronism and would become a notorious voice within the movement. He was president of the Círculo de Periodistas Deportivos (Circle of Sports Journalists) between 1950 and 1951. During the latter year, he began to host the television show *Visiones deportivas*, the first sport program to appear on Argentine television.

Our interviews also yielded another insight: none of the OIA leaders regularly practiced their religion. Manuel Scheinsohn's nephew told us that his uncle "may have had ties with the Jewish community, but wasn't a Zionist." The OIA's leaders found common ground around a vision of identity that emphasized the Argentine facet common to the mosaic of their collective and individual identities. They were Jewish-Argentines rather than Argentine Jews. Many, such as Adolfo Minyevski or Sujer Matrajt, became prosperous business owners and, as such, benefitted from Peronist economic policies. Most of them remained loyal to Perón and to the Peronist movement after Perón was overthrown in 1955 – additional proof that their ties with Peronism were not solely opportunistic. As we will later see, many of them paid a high price for continuing to support Peronism during the Revolución Libertadora that followed the 1955 coup.

The support that Perón enjoyed among many fútbol (soccer) clubs also acquainted a sizeable number of Jews with Peronism, bringing them into the movement's fold. The Club Atlético Atlanta, located in the neighbourhood of Villa Crespo, was one such club. As the government invested in fútbol through various avenues, many fans of the sport were particularly exposed to Peronist rhetoric and thus learned about the policies aimed at redistributing the nation's wealth to society's poorest. If some members of Atlanta supported Peronism out of pragmatism despite not fully identifying with the regime's aspirations, others found their way into the movement through fútbol. Leopoldo Bard's convergence with Peronism was even more interesting. An Argentine of Jewish origin, Bard was the captain and first president of the Club Atlético River Plate (CARP). He was always at the side of Hipólito Yrigoyen, the UCR's president. Bard was elected to the national Congress and was president, between 1922 and 1930, of the congressional majority bloc led at that time by the UCR. In 1947, when Bard was a member of the executive board of CARP and in charge of the club's cultural activities, he was named by the Perón administration to the post of general director of hygiene and workplace safety. In 1951, he published an article in the CARP's magazine in which he praised the sport-related initiatives undertaken by Perón's government.

Final assessments show that the OIA succeeded at negotiating with the government collective benefits for Jewish-Argentines by promoting the community's ethnic and religious interests. While the lack of data makes it difficult to estimate the extent of the OIA's influence upon the voting patterns of Jewish-Argentines in presidential and congressional elections, the organization did offer Perón a loyal Jewish tribune via which to disseminate his anti-racist and pro-Zionist discourse to important international audiences, such as the United States. The OIA influenced Perón's decision to include in the constitution an article opposing racial discrimination and to declare amnesty for clandestine Jewish immigrants. The OIA also succeeded at securing the nomination of Pablo Manguel, its secretary, as Argentina's minister plenipotentiary in Israel, despite the reservations expressed by the Argentine Ministry of Foreign Affairs.

In fact, up until Perón was overthrown, the OIA was in charge of Argentina's diplomatic representation in Israel: the first emissary that

Perón sent to the newly created state, in March 1949, was Sujer Matrajt.[46] Matrajt spent one month in Israel and delivered a letter from Perón to President Weizmann. On his way back to Argentina, Matrajt and his wife, Berta Gleizer de Matrajt, visited Rome, and Pope Pius XII hosted the couple in a special meeting. When the two countries formally established ties, Pablo Manguel became Argentina's first plenipotentiary delegate. When Manguel's term came to an end, another key OIA figure, Ezequiel Zabotinsky, was to be his substitute. The latter would see his diplomatic career come to an abrupt end prior to taking on this post, however, as Perón was overthrown and Zabotinsky's nomination rescinded. Manguel contributed to successfully negotiate a bilateral commercial agreement between the two countries from which Israel benefitted in various ways.[47] The OIA leaders also convinced Evita to facilitate a shipment of blankets and medicines to Israel.

It should therefore come as no surprise that Jews, even those who did not find it politically correct to support the Peronist movement, did not look down upon the OIA's leaders.[48] The DAIA abstained from boycotting the OIA, which it used as an intermediary to communicate with the government. In spite of this, the DAIA did put obstacles in the OIA's way to prevent it from broadening its support within Jewish public opinion. Ezequiel Zabotinsky, the OIA's last president, was generally respected in community circles. As Bell posits on the basis of reports in Jewish newspapers, Zabotinsky was viewed as "an honest man ... a good Argentine and a loyal Jew," who "hailed from a well-esteemed family."[49] As Bell also brings to light, Zabotinsky's father had been president of the AMIA in 1925, and Ezequiel had joined Jewish self-defence groups in his youth.[50] When it was made public that Zabotinsky had been named to the post of ambassador, the first round of congratulations that Manguel and Zabotinsky received came from Dr. Abraham Mibashan, the representative of the Jewish Agency in Buenos Aires since 1944, who had been director of the Pro-Palestine Committee that sought to mobilize political and popular support for the creation of a Jewish state in Palestine. For all these reasons, it seems to us that historians' dramatic verdict that the OIA had been a failure must be reconsidered or, at least, understood in a more nuanced light.

AMRAM BLUM: THE PERONIST RABBI

In 1948, Perón chose the young rabbi Amram Blum to be his advisor on religious matters. At the time, Blum was head the of the Jewish community's rabbinical council. Eli Eliachar, one of the foremost leaders of Sephardi Jews in Jerusalem who travelled to Buenos Aires as part of a mission on behalf of community leaders in Jewish Palestine, would write in his memoirs: "Amram Blum was the main Sephardi rabbi in Buenos Aires. He was beloved, handsome, and approachable. He was an enthusiastic Zionist who had previously fulfilled various functions in important institutions in Jerusalem. He is equally accepted by Ashkenazi and Sephardi [Jews] and by the Peronist administration."[51]

Blum was an interesting figure. The rabbi originated from Hungary and was recognized for his theological training, having obtained his doctorate at Jerusalem's Hebrew University. He was a charismatic leader who arrived in Argentina in 1946 as the representative of a Zionist orthodox religious party. In 1947, he was named Great Rabbi of the community of Syrians from Aleppo. It isn't clear how Blum developed ties with Peronism, but he seemed to look favourably upon the government's social policies. He supported demands for better working conditions among teachers in Jewish religious schools that fell under his purview, and voiced this support to the schools' governing body, which was opposed to negotiating with teachers. It is therefore likely that his sensibility to social questions brought him closer to the Peronist project. In 1948, he was named advisor to Perón on religious matters, and in 1952 he said a prayer for Evita's health in a ceremony hosted by the OIA in the Paso Street synagogue.[52] Máximo Yagupsky, of the American Jewish Committee, described how, by August 1953, Blum had become the spirit that guided Perón in matters concerning Jews.[53] Blum's influence, however, does not seem to have extended to other facets of the relationship between the state and religion, as Blum was not involved in the conflict between Perón and the Catholic Church that unfolded during the mid-1950s.

In a recent interview, Miguel Teitelbaum, Blum's private secretary, sheds new light on this figure. Teitelbaum describes Blum's imposing presence: "When Blum walked in the room, everyone noticed him and looked with admiration at the unique way in which he carried himself. He was tall (at 1.8 metres, he was taller than most Jews), bearded, wore a broad-brimmed hat and, under it, a kippah. He also walked with a stick, holding its gold-plated handle, and had a car, which was, at the time, a mark of importance."[54] Sephardi and Ashkenazi Jews evidently saw Blum as a prestigious figure. When Blum accepted the position of chief rabbi of the Jewish community and ceased to be the rabbi of the community of Syrian Jews from Aleppo, many Syrian Jews began to frequent the Ashkenazi synagogue on Paso Street to hear his sermons and so that he could officiate over their children's bar mitzvahs. This was not typical in relations between Sephardi Jews and their Ashkenazi counterparts at the time.

Upon recalling the first meeting between Blum and Perón, Teitelbaum mentions that "the rabbi's kippah fell and Perón bent over to pick it up and handed it back to Blum for him to put it on. Blum was very touched by this. Perón always hosted him with the greatest respect and, as far as I know, he never denied [Blum] any request he made in person."[55] It does indeed seem that Blum had direct access to the president's private secretary; he always requested appointments through Captain Alfredo Máximo Renner. Blum was in regular contact with all of the administration's ministers. The rabbi invited the ministers of public health and foreign affairs, among others, to dinner at his home. Teitelbaum recalls: "when we went to a ministry, we spent very little time waiting."[56] Blum met with Minister Borlenghi and his vice-minister, Krislavin, every fifteen to twenty days with the aim of helping Jewish-Argentine individuals solve specific issues. Teitelbaum rejects the idea that Perón was antisemitic: "Quite the contrary; Perón always took actions that benefited the Jewish community."[57]

Blum and Perón addressed a variety of topics in their meetings: whether Jewish-Argentines could have days off from work or study on their holy days, the designation of Blum as the army's chaplain – a measure that had a symbolic value for Jewish and non-Jewish army personnel – or the benefits that the government could grant the network of Jewish schools. Indeed, it was thanks to Amram Blum's mediation that Jewish conscripts could, for the first time in Argentina's history, be granted a holiday to mark the religious festivities for the New Year (Rosh Hashanah) and the Day of Atonement (Yom Kippur). Blum's designation as army chaplain set a precedent for the spiritual assistance that Jewish soldiers would receive decades later during the Falklands/Malvinas War in 1982.[58] Blum typically put forward various requests on behalf of the Jewish community. As Teitelbaum explains, when Blum met with Perón, "he was the spokesperson for the DAIA and the AMIA. They all used him [as an intermediary], they came and lined up to meet with him; when they wanted to request things from Perón, they asked the rabbi."

Blum's mediation made it possible for the candy factory Mu Mu to reopen its doors following its shuttering in 1949 due to a conflict between its Jewish owners (the Groismans) and Evita. In 1953, Blum made the case that his openness mirrored General Perón's "quest for justice" evident in his policies, which were "opposed all forms of racial discrimination."[59] The following year, Blum inaugurated the Chair in Jewish Studies at the Universidad de Buenos Aires's Faculty of Philosophy and Letters, characterizing it as "the result of the inspiration of His Excellency, the head of state."[60] As might be expected, these close ties between the president and Blum (dubbed "the syndicalist rabbi" by some members of the community) caused unease among Jews opposed to Peronism.

PERÓN'S CONFRONTATION WITH THE CHURCH AND FREEDOM OF WORSHIP

In a manner that paralleled his ascent, the fall of Perón's regime was largely a result of his relations with the country's Catholic Church. In each of these two phases, albeit for different reasons, Perón's alliance with the Church, and his conflict with it, were respectively the cause of much concern among various Jewish sectors of society. From 1950 onward, differences began to emerge that put a strain on relations between national authorities and the ecclesial establishment.[61] The death of Eva Perón in mid-1952 marked a turning point in the deterioration of these relations. Although the first lady had described her husband as "an emissary of God" in various speeches, it was her own figure that inspired a popular myth during the final months of her life, and even more so in the immediate aftermath of her passing. Many began to refer to her as the "Virgin of America" or "Our Lady of

Hope," going so far as to ask that she be beatified. In early August 1952, hardly a week after her passing, the morning paper *La Época* published a front-page story about the halo of sanctity that surrounded the "martyr" Evita and about the thousands of improvised altars and sanctuaries that popped up across the country to worship her. The union representing food industry workers wrote a letter to the Pope to request the immediate beatification and canonization of the deceased first lady. The letter asked that the Vatican take action to ratify what the hearts and minds of the people had already decided. The CGT's general secretary, José Espejo, went so far as to compare Evita to Jesus Christ in an interview he gave to the newspaper *La Prensa*, which had been expropriated from its owners that same year and placed into the union confederation's hands.[62]

As might be expected, the Church, both in Argentina and the Vatican, was less than thrilled with this new saint informally canonized by the masses and the *descamisados* ("the shirtless," a term used to describe Perón's working-class supporters). Prelates in Buenos Aires grew more dismayed when Perón decided where the first lady's cadaver was to be buried. Shortly before her death, Evita had asked her husband to bury her in the church of San Francisco, in Buenos Aires, and requested that a mausoleum be built on the site. Ecclesial authorities accepted, but the president changed his mind, deciding that the body would remain in the CGT's headquarters, where it was being embalmed, and that the monument would be built at that location. This decision was interpreted as a victory of the civil and lay strands within Peronism over the religious elements.

In October 1952, Perón convened a meeting with his designated provincial administrators. In the speech he gave, he compared the Peronist movement to Christianity in its early phases. He accordingly portrayed himself as the leader of a movement that wished to attract millions of faithful so that they could disseminate the Justicialist doctrine.[63] At that stage it was clear, at least to some sectors of the ecclesial authorities, that Peronism had become a competitor that the Church could not brook and that the Church's prior cooperation with Peronism might paradoxically lead to its marginalization from any meaningful function in Argentine society. The moment of Evita's death also marked an acceleration of the process of "Peronization" of the educational system. In no uncertain terms, Peronism had become the "national doctrine" that served as a model for youth and for the entire nation. In the struggle for the souls of Argentines, Catholicism began to fade into the background.[64]

This crisis reached its peak in late 1954, when rumours began to circulate that the Church intended to create Catholic organizations for workers, as well as a Christian Democratic party that would, it was thought, undermine the strength of the governing party by combining a progressive social platform with a religious worldview. Within this context, it should be recalled that various priests participated in activities that specifically opposed the regime. There is a lack of consensus among researchers about whether these intentions were the true reasons behind Perón's confrontation with the Church.[65] Some suggest that the president was led to this path due to his megalomania, coupled with his belief that no one could challenge his power. Others argued that the tenets of the Peronist political vision were essentially totalitarian and that it could therefore not tolerate competition of any sort or accept the long-term existence of an independent institution that had power and influence, as it constituted an obstacle to the leader's aspiration to subjugate and dominate all of Argentine society.

Another group of researchers emphasize that, after nine years as head of state and now without Evita at his side, Perón was exhausted, and they attributed responsibility for these shifts to the influence of some of the members of his entourage. Some were content with the explanation that the president had no patience for attempts on the part of Acción Católica to compete with the Unión de Estudiantes Secundarios (Union of Secondary School Students), a Peronist youth organization, in trying to garner youth support, particularly in the province of Córdoba. Some opponents of the regime suggested that the conflict with the Church was a smokescreen to divert the public's attention away from the agreement that the government had signed with the US Standard Oil Company, allowing it to prospect in the Patagonia region and exploit the mineral resources, a move the opposition denounced for handing over the country's resources to foreign owners and betraying the values of Argentine nationhood.[66]

Without invalidating the partial contribution that each of these explanations may offer, I contend that Perón's confrontation with the

Church also marked the start of a new step in Peronism's evolution toward a multicultural society. Instead of sustaining the traditional model of the racial melting pot, with its emphasis on Catholicism, the regime bestowed increasing legitimacy to multiple identities and, in so doing, recognized the wide array of cultural sources that were at the root of Argentine society. In this new phase, those ethnic and religious identities that were not Catholic became less threatening to the concept of Argentine identity. Jewish-Argentines found in this shift the full confirmation of their place in Argentine society.

Perón's overt attack on the Church was launched in a speech he gave to an audience of provincial governors on 10 November 1954. The speech's tone surprised many, as it was stern and suffused with anger. Perón attacked many priests, despite specifying that he did not intend to confront the Church in its totality but aimed to clarify a political question. He accused specific priests of participating in anti-Peronist activities and mentioned attempts to infiltrate trade unions, employers' organizations, and associations of the liberal professions, as well as student organizations. He targeted Acción Católica with a strong accusation by portraying it as an international organization that was hostile to the regime.[67]

From that point onward, the struggle for power heightened. In mid-November 1954, it was resolved that all primary and secondary schools would have secular "spiritual counsellors" to inculcate the youth with moral values and, of course, Peronist values. Shortly thereafter, the Ministry of Education eliminated from its staff the positions of those who were in charge of organizing religious education. These measures deepened the Peronization of the educational system, diminishing the Church's influence in schools. A number of Catholic education institutions were shuttered and priests who taught in schools were laid off.

At the same time, the government was beginning to emphasize that the respect of all religions and all ethnic groups was one of the distinguishing features of Peronism. The regime considered that loyalty to Perón and his movement took precedence over loyalty to any other institution.[68] It also aspired to implement in the religious sphere the Peronist ambition to protect the rights of minorities and of groups that were marginalized and defenceless in the face of abuses committed by those most privileged. Peronism sought to portray itself as a conglomerate in which all decent Argentines who supported its project could find their place.

The fact that within the public educational system the dichotomy between Catholicism and other religions was substituted for one between Peronists and anti-Peronists simplified the lives of many Jewish students. It was often easier to conceal their parents' lack of support for Peronism than to hide their Jewish identities. At the start of the 1950s, teachers were encouraged to respect the principle of freedom of worship instead of pressuring non-Catholic students into participating in catechism classes. The new Peronist textbooks published between 1953 and 1955 were equally informed by the defence of this principle.[69]

In December 1954, the confrontation came to a head when Perón gave a speech at the CGT's general assembly meeting, encouraging his supporters to take to the streets and punish those "clerical puppets" who were the enemies of the people. He also referred to a religious scheme to overthrow the regime and its enemies, who now shielded themselves behind the priests' robes. The op-eds published in *La Prensa* and *Época* the following day warned that the patience of the people was wearing thin when faced with reiterated political-religious provocations. Those priests whose homilies attacked the government were detained and Catholic militants were dismissed from their functions in the public sphere.[70]

The next step in this direction was the passage, in both chambers of Congress, of legislation that legalized divorce and allowed divorced persons to remarry, assured equal status to children born to unmarried couples, and decriminalized prostitution. These laws resulted from initiatives undertaken in various Peronist groups during Perón's first presidency, particularly trade unions, whose members were largely opposed to the law instituting religious education. The Argentine Church published a pastoral letter that condemned the legalization of divorce, and the Catholic newspaper *El Pueblo* – shuttered by authorities shortly thereafter – decried the passage of these laws, adducing that prior debate had not been held and that the laws had been too hastily voted upon. The changes also met with sharp criticism in the Vatican's official newspaper, *L'Osservatore Romano*, which characterized the new situation as one of "oppression toward Catholicism and freedom of worship, as well as the faithful's moral values and the rights of the Church."[71]

In April 1955, Peronist media outlets launched a campaign to promote the separation of church and state through a constitutional reform. Newspaper columns were published arguing that the only way to ensure true freedom of religion and genuine equality in Argentina was to follow the example of the United States, which held all religions as equal and did not privilege one over the others.[72] During the massive May Day gathering held on the Plaza de Mayo, across from the Casa Rosada, Perón announced that if the people wanted to separate church from state, they had the right to do so. In the following days, the men's and women's branches of the Peronist party, along with many of the party's senators and congresspersons – most of them through speeches in Parliament – expressed their support for "the people's will" as it had been manifested on Workers' Day.

Congress therefore resolved that elections be held within six months to vote for a constituent assembly that would reform the constitution and guarantee total and absolute freedom of worship and the equality of all religions. A wave of layoffs of catechism teachers in public schools anticipated the resolution that officially repealed the law instituting religious teaching. The congressional session in which this decision was reached lasted less than five hours, demonstrating a hastiness that contrasted with the lengthy and polemical debate held eight years earlier about whether to pass into law the decree that had instituted the mandatory teaching of catechism in public schools.[73] That the law was repealed following a relatively brief debate indicates that the regime did not view an agreement with the Church as necessary and that it felt that spiritual and cultural hegemony over the nation was within reach. The law was indeed repealed by both chambers after a few days.

PRIESTS, NATIONALISTS, AND THE ANTISEMITIC CAMPAIGN

It would seem that Jews should have welcomed Perón's measures to separate church from state, as some of these could potentially benefit the situation of Jewish people in Argentina. Some of the laws passed in 1954 brought an end to the subordination of various non-Catholic citizens to the religious norms upheld among the majority, in addition to diminishing the Catholic features of the state. Jewish community institutions nevertheless maintained the same low profile as in the 1940s, when Catholic education became mandatory. Even if these institutions' leaders viewed the changes as positive, they avoided expressing their opinions publicly.[74] As these measures were considered to be part of the government's confrontation with the Church and with opponents of the regime, the DAIA preferred to stay out of the conflict. It is likely, as well, that the government's abrupt change of direction in its policies caused fear among some, as did its condoning of attacks on churches, some of which it may have secretly encouraged. Given the current shift, it seemed plausible that, under different circumstances, the government might turn against Jews and synagogues (not only churches) could become legitimate targets.[75]

The cautious attitude of the community leaders should also be understood in relation to the distribution of antisemitic pamphlets that included accusations against Jews and freemasons, who were supposedly part of the president's inner circle and were perceived as the architects of the attempt to separate church from state. These pamphlets laid the blame on "Borlenghi the Jew" and added that, "rumors have it that his name isn't Borlenghi, but Borlenski."[76] These accusations were false and baseless, as Borlenghi was a Catholic married to a Jewish woman, and he seems to have opposed the confrontation with the Church.[77] One such pamphlet portrayed Perón as a freemason and a puppet whose strings were pulled by secret Jewish lodges.[78] In the city of Córdoba, traditionally viewed as a stronghold of Catholic activists, the police intervened in 1954 to disperse a protest of Catholics holding posters with the slogan "Out with Perón and his Jewish friends."[79] Many Catholic activists were particularly irritated at the constant presence of Rabbi Amram Blum in the president's inner circle. The rabbi had made even more enemies when he said a prayer for Evita's health. In the atmosphere generated around the confrontation with the Church, many Jews began to perceive that it wasn't Perón's government that posed an antisemitic threat but, rather, the regime's Catholic and conservative opponents. They feared that, as in other periods and places, the Jews would become a scapegoat and the victims of a war between cultures.[80]

In an attempt to stem the antisemitic tendencies that became palpable in the context of the crisis and to adjust misperceptions that identified Jews with the regime, the Instituto Judío Argentino de Cultura e Información (Jewish-Argentine Institute of Culture and Information, a local delegation of the American Jewish Committee) took the initiative of addressing the Catholic authorities to clarify that the Jewish community was concerned about the situation and that it opposed the attacks on the Church, which it respected as a religious group. On behalf of the institute, Máximo Yagupsky and Rabbi Guillermo Schlesinger met with the secretary to Cardinal Santiago Luis Copello – even as, at that time, the police watched closely the activities of Church authorities. The secretary thanked the visitors for their expressions of solidarity and clarified that, following Perón's overthrow, Jews would have nothing to fear, as the Church would protect them from any harm. The institute's delegates held similar meetings with, among others, Cardinal Antonio Caggiano, Monsignor Miguel De Andrea, and Father Carlos Cucciti, the Vatican's cultural attaché in Buenos Aires. To shield participants from the authorities' scrutiny, these meetings were held in various, sometimes unusual, places. In every one of these meetings, the institute's emissaries asked the prelates to put an end to the distribution of antisemitic pamphlets. Diplomats of Israel's legation, which became a full-fledged embassy in 1955,[81] also met with Church authorities.[82]

The leaders of Jewish community organizations preferred to avoid making superfluous statements. Nevertheless, specific gestures were interpreted by the regime's opponents as a show of support for Peronism, including the publication by the DAIA, precisely at that moment, of an anthology of Perón's speeches under the title *El pensamiento del Presidente Perón sobre el pueblo judío* (President Perón's Thinking on the Jewish People), as well as Moshé Tov's characterization of the book as outlining "the anti-discriminatory doctrine and the Argentine president's constructive approach to the Jewish people."[83]

Various Jewish organizations were uneasy about the gestures that Perón made toward non-Catholic faiths from late 1954 onward. In letters that Máximo Yagupsky addressed to the American Jewish Committee from Chile (concerned that authorities might open and censor them), he wrote that, "as of late, Perón has been 'overly' friendly with Jews, Evangelists, Protestants, and Spiritualists."[84] Yagupsky added that, "as regards any manifestation of friendship toward Jews, I must acknowledge that we were never particularly thrilled with this and, throughout, we maintained our awareness that this would not end well."[85] In later letters Yagupsky accused the DAIA of being short-sighted. He also exaggerated in his depiction of DAIA as having undergone a process of "Peronization" and of the embassy of Israel as unequivocally sympathizing with Perón.

For approximately six months, Perón seemed to have succeeded at passing measures that diminished the role of the Catholic Church, without stirring strong opposition. In fact, this shift turned the Church into a symbol of anti-Peronist struggle by giving the scattered opposition a topic around which to join forces. This very same topic gradually generated differences and discord within the Peronist band as well. Perón's campaign against the Church also lessened the loyalty of the armed forces, one of the pillars of the regime. Malaise began to be felt beyond the ranks of the navy, which had manifested its reluctance to accept Perón from the outset.[86]

On 11 June, the opposition held a massive anti-Peronist protest within the frame of the traditional Corpus Christi procession, which had been prohibited by authorities. Most participants joined not out of religious fervour but to repudiate the regime. The government accused the protesters of having hoisted a foreign flag, that of the Vatican, outside the nation's Congress on masts reserved for the nation's flag; of having set fire to an Argentine flag (in fact, this was more likely the result of an action undertaken by police forces); and of having damaged a plaque, also located outside the Congress, commemorating the "martyr of workers," Eva Perón. Hundreds were arrested. Perón expelled two bishops from Buenos Aires, Manuel Tato and Ramón Novoa, a measure that the Vatican saw as outside of the president's purview. In response, Rome excommunicated all those who had harmed the rights of the Church or used violence against one of the Church's men. Perón's name was not mentioned in the latter category but it was understood to include the president and the members of his cabinet.[87]

A few days later, a failed coup took place. On 16 June, the army's planes dropped bombs on the Plaza de Mayo area in an attempt to depose Perón and destroy the neighbouring presidential palace.[88] Although no Jews or Jewish institutions were harmed, the community's leaders began to feel anxious and to panic. Many were afraid to maintain contact with the embassy of Israel while these events were unfolding. Ambassador Kubovy, who had been a senior official in the World Jewish Congress and was acutely aware of the issues that preoccupied the local Jewish population, ceased to send reports to Jerusalem and began to meet with community leaders, and with official authorities and opposition members alike.

Some explained the fact that the Jewish community was not harmed during these events by pointing, alternately, to the favourable treatment of Jews by Perón, the ties that the Israeli embassy had forged with the ALN, and Ambassador Kubovy's ongoing dialogue with Catholic groups (the embassy sheltered Catholic nuns during the events in an attempt to garner the sympathy of Church authorities). The initiatives that Pablo Manguel energetically undertook in acting as an intermediary between the regime and the Church helped to lessen the antisemitic propaganda originating in Catholic circles.[89] Manguel submitted to Turkow an account of his meeting with Perón in which he reported that the president had stated that the stifling of the failed rebellion, as well as the regime's positive treatment of Jewish-Argentines, had been instrumental in preventing a dramatic antisemitic outburst.[90] Manguel was also in touch with Catholic leaders, as he attempted to defuse tensions between the Church and Jewish institutions. Under the circumstances, Jewish newspapers, though far from identifying with Peronism, published articles defending Perón's regime and condemning those who had conspired against a constitutional government as well as other critics from Catholic groups who were responsible for disseminating antisemitic propaganda.[91]

Between the 16 June rebellion and the 16 September coup, Perón adopted a series of measures, some of them contradictory, which bespeak his lack of certainty as to how to orient his policies.[92] After a new rebellion in mid-September, Perón had no choice but to resign from government. He found refuge on a Paraguayan gunboat docked at the port of Buenos Aires. Two weeks later, a naval airplane flew him to the neighbouring country. This was the first destination on an exile that would last eighteen years.

DE-PERONIZING A COMMUNITY: THE SHADOW OF THE REVOLUCIÓN LIBERTADORA

The final insurrection against Perón took place on 16 September. The new president, General Eduardo Lonardi, was a militant Catholic who had the support of the Argentine Church. The day Lonardi was sworn in, he stepped onto the balcony of the Casa Rosada with the archbishop of Buenos Aires, Cardinal Copello, at his side. This was the most eloquent testimony of the Church's role in the anti-Peronist revolution.

Jewish community institutions received positively the overthrow of Perón in September 1955 and the military regime's takeover of power, because, among other reasons, they hoped for political stability after a particularly rocky year. Jewish newspapers such as *Di Idishe Tzaitung* and *Mundo Israelita* praised the new government. The DAIA published a prayer of rest for all those who fell during the self-named Revolución Libertadora and manifested its hope that peace would reign, as it was vital to guaranteeing freedom and democracy.[93]

But this satisfaction was undercut by fears among the wider Jewish population. As in the earlier military coups of September 1930 and June 1943, the regime that took power in September 1955 installed nationalists of the Catholic extreme right in the government's highest echelons. Lonardi surrounded himself with nationalists identified with the Catholic ultranationalist current that had emerged in Argentina during the 1920s and which was influenced by Charles Maurras and his *Action Française*, Italian fascism, Primo de Rivera's dictatorship in Spain, and that country's Falange.

The ultranationalist Juan Carlos Goyeneche was the new cabinet member responsible for information and the press. Goyeneche had been the editor-in-chief of the prestigious magazine *Sol y Luna*, which had supported the Spanish nationalists' rebellion in 1936. He lived in Europe between 1942 and 1946, and had been a guest of Francisco Franco's dictatorship. During the Second World War he sided with the Axis and, as correspondent for the nationalist newspaper *Cabildo*, he interviewed some of the most notorious fascist leaders, such as Adolf Hitler, Heinrich Himmler, and Galeazzo Ciano. His duties as a journalist included accompanying the División Azul (Blue Division) that Franco's regime sent to fight alongside the Wehrmacht against Soviet troops on the Eastern Front. Even when the Allied victory seemed imminent, Goyeneche remained loyal to Germany.[94]

Lonardi designated Mario Amadeo as minister of foreign relations and worship; Amadeo had been supportive of German interests during the 1930s and the Second World War, and saw Franco's regime as a model to emulate.[95] At the head of the Ministry of Education, Lonardi named the ultra-Catholic Atilio Dell'Oro Maini, who at the end of the 1920s had founded the right-wing magazine *Criterio*. Lonardi named his own brother-in-law, Clemente Villada Achával, as his private secretary. Villada Achával came from a respectable Catholic family in the province of Córdoba and was a nationalist sympathizer. These members of cabinet aspired to shape a regime similar to the military government of 1943–45, prior to the coalescing of the Peronist movement and the populist government of the past decade.

The composition of this governing elite did not bode well for the Jews. When it came to religion, particularly the teaching and learning of catechism in public schools, it was expected that the new leaders would cancel the secular or anti-clerical legislation passed during the last months of Perón's regime. Indeed, the new regime restored to the Church all of the rights that the Peronist government had repealed. In spite of this, in the first press conference that Lonardi and his second-in-command Admiral Isaac Rojas gave, they expressed their commitment to respecting the religious freedoms of all the groups that comprised the citizenry. Lonardi abstained from instituting mandatory catechism so as to avoid antagonizing broad swaths of supporters of his Revolución Libertadora who were completely secular.

In the meetings of the DAIA's leadership, participants discussed the organization's position vis-à-vis the overthrown regime. The dominant tone was one of expiation of sins, of self-justification in attempts to explain why Jewish institutions had not criticized the regime of "terror and subjugation." Participants mentioned Perón's positive attitude toward the Jewish people, his support for the state of Israel, and his condemnations of antisemitism both within Argentina and internationally. One of the participants attempted to highlight that "a majority of Jews refused to become Peronists, and [that] the DAIA did not become a tool for Perón." Participants agreed to draw conclusions from the foregone experience and, as much as possible, to return to a policy of non-alignment with the powers-that-be. To this end, participants agreed to marginalize those who had helped to identify the Jewish community with the overthrown regime. It should be observed that authorities at the embassy of Israel requested that such a "purge" in the leadership of Jewish community institutions be limited in scope, considering that the leaders of the OIA in general, and Pablo Manguel in particular, had made all possible efforts to promote relations between the two countries.

The DAIA's leadership deliberated extensively about how the organization should situate itself vis-à-vis the new regime and also consulted with the Israeli embassy on this matter.[96] It would seem that many members of the community organizations felt that the DAIA and other Jewish institutions had gone too far in manifesting their support for Perón. Many of them feared that many non-Jewish Argentines might end up viewing the Jewish community as committed to the Peronist state. This seemed to be, according to Máximo Yagupsky, "a truly serious question," as the contemporary political climate had forced Jewish organizations to "periodically voice statements in praise of Perón, to show up at his office, to make speeches honoring him or to participate in meetings also designed to honour the leader," which, in turn, posed the "challenge of what to do to erase this record."[97]

In these debates, Moisés Goldman expressed the hope that the DAIA could outline the path forward and smooth the rough edges and discrepancies, as this would undoubtedly favour the interests of the community, to whose well-being all the leaders aspired.[98] Other speakers blamed the current situation on the pressures exerted by the OIA, referring to some of its leaders as a small faction that had "betrayed" the community. At the end of the meeting, Goldman addressed various community institutions to request that they strip of their main duties any leaders who had adhered to the previous regime.[99] Although this meeting was held behind closed doors, Jewish media outlets found out about it.

The statement issued was signed by the DAIA's president, Goldman, and its secretary general, León Lapacó, both of whom expressed the organization's identification with the liberal values espoused by General Lonardi in his first speech as president. The DAIA, which had earlier shown itself capable of adapting to the "codes" that the Peronist regime had expected of it, now adapted itself to the "codes" of the Revolución Libertadora. Once again, leaders such as Goldman were outlining that path. A delegation of the DAIA met with Amadeo, then minister of foreign relations and worship, who promised to uphold the treatment that the previous regime had afforded to the Jewish community and to Israel.[100] Similar promises were made to Ambassador Kubovy.[101] After all, the authorities of the Revolución Libertadora aimed to forge closer ties with Washington and, like their predecessors, perceived in exaggerated terms the power and the influence of US Jews.

AMRAM BLUM: THE MAIN VICTIM

The Lonardi administration was short-lived. On 13 November 1955, an internal coup was declared and General Pedro Eugenio Aramburu took power. The most emblematic Catholic nationalists were also removed from their posts in the cabinet. Aramburu launched a campaign to dismantle all of the "expressions of totalitarianism" that Peronism had installed in Argentine society. Public servants named by the overthrown government were ousted from their posts. The constitution sanctioned under the Peronist administration was repealed and the country reverted to the prior constitution of 1853. The dissemination of Peronist propaganda, as well as the use of slogans and symbols associated with the movement, was prohibited.

The victims of this "de-Peronization" campaign included the leaders of the OIA, beginning with Pablo Manguel, in whose home authorities found "highly valuable documentation, alcoholic beverages, and US cigarettes." His wife recalls how "they openly went into the house, they came to search the house, to see if they found anything. Of course they did. They found a little wine, a coffee with milk, a bit of this and that … things like that. We had lived abroad for six years, of course we brought some things with us."[102] In my archival research into the documents of the Revolución Libertadora's National Investigation Commission, I found more material on Manguel than on any other Peronist member of Congress. Manguel and Zabotinsky were arrested and held for a brief period in the Las Heras prison.

Alongside Borlenghi, former vice-minister of the interior Abraham Krislavin sought refuge in neighbouring Uruguay, and Argentina demanded that he be extradited.[103] From Montevideo, using false documents, Krislavin relocated to New York. Later on he resided in Brazil and returned to Argentina only in the mid-1960s. Krislavin's brother-in-law Jacobo Bajraj, former head of the Tax Administration Department, also paid dearly for his service to the Peronist government.[104] The popular sportscaster Luis Elías Sojit exiled himself to Brazil and only returned to Argentina in 1958 with the end of the military regime.

Parallel to the efforts by the military regime's authorities to "de-Peronize" Argentine society and eradicate any element that bore the stain of identification or cooperation with the overthrown regime, the Jewish community also began to "put its ducks in a row" so as to align itself with the new government. Because the leaders of the DAIA feared that the Jewish community had been too closely identified with Peronism, they acted swiftly to remove from duty any public officials of community organizations who had, in Máximo Yagupsky's graphic expression, "licked Perón's boots."

The removal of Peronist Jews from their functions also affected community organizations with economic or philanthropic missions, such as the Ezrah hospital or psychiatric asylums. The hospital's removal of Salvador Woscoff, one of the OIA's founding members, caused a considerable stir and yielded embarrassing situations for Jewish institutions and individuals alike. In mid-October 1955, Goldman asked Woscoff to resign from his position. The latter responded vigorously to the request.[105] After all, he was not the only member of the hospital's steering committee to have supported Peronism. It should come as no surprise that the members of this committee protested the DAIA's intervention in its internal affairs. The DAIA did not budge from its position, which it explained publicly in Jewish newspapers. Woscoff had to give in to the pressure, but did so only after publishing a spirited letter in which he argued that under Goldman's presidency, the DAIA had "failed to act impartially, as the situation required," perhaps because Dr Goldman had appointed members to the committee who, in turn, should apologize "for their direct or indirect collaboration with the Peronist regime."[106]

As part of this confrontation, on 4 October 1955 the position, within the AMIA, of president of the rabbinical tribunal was annulled so as to eject Rabbi Amram Blum from the post. As mentioned earlier, Blum had been Perón's advisor in religious matters and, standing next to the president, had pronounced the Kaddish funeral prayer upon Evita's death.[107] Blum had numerous enemies within the Jewish community. The Sephardi weekly *La Luz* began to attack this "protégé of the tyrant" in late 1954, stating that, "Rabbi Blum has done nothing positive to benefit Argentine Judaism."[108] With Perón's fall from power, the newspaper grew louder in its criticisms of those who, like Blum, had supported "the politics and conduct of the overthrown dictator." According to *La Luz*, "the triumphant revolution has shaken the consciousness of the citizens of this nation out of its state of torpor ... Suddenly, as if by miracle, the Argentine people stood up and shouted in unison: Freedom!"[109] *La Luz* named these Jewish supporters of Perón to demand that they be removed from their positions.

At first, Blum, like Woscoff, clarified that he would not resign from his position without a fight, and promised to publicly state that he would henceforth limit his opinions to internal religious questions. He also threatened legal action against the AMIA. Blum maintained that his removal from the position of head of the rabbinical tribunal had been illegal, as only a religious organization comprised of other rabbis was authorized to implement such a disciplinary measure. This was in vain and Blum had no choice but to resign.[110] It should come as no surprise that, after his removal from this position, the rabbi decided to go into exile in December 1955. He moved to the United States where, in the following years, he officiated over religious ceremonies in the Jewish communities in Los Angeles and Cleveland. He died in the latter city in 1970 at the age of 57.[111]

Decades later, Miguel Teitelbaum, Blum's private secretary during Perón's mandate, spoke with bitterness of the Jewish leadership's self-serving attitude toward Blum, "because immediately after Perón was overthrown, they used him as a scapegoat, and abandoned him in an ugly way due to which he had to leave the country. He couldn't stand having fallen from the important place he occupied and being snubbed."[112] The authorities of the AMIA and the DAIA, who "were regulars at the rabbi's home ... and who constantly asked him for favours," now turned their backs on him. "He was very angry when he left. He did not deserve that fate. The truth is that the community's treatment toward him was very, very unjust."[113]

The position of the weekly newspaper *Mundo Israelita* attested most eloquently to the shift among community leaders. A few months prior to the coup, the weekly had published articles and reports favourable to the OIA and the Peronist regime.[114] On 17 September, the day after the coup, it still published Perón's wishes to Jewish-Argentines and the state of Israel on the occasion of the Jewish holidays. Shortly after that, however, the newspaper adhered to the broader effort toward the "de-Peronization" undertaken across the country. In its issue dated 1 October 1955, it praised the new regime and the freedoms that it preached. Three weeks later, in the 22 October issue, it referred to Perón's "totalitarian regime" that had oppressed human and civil rights, imitating the regimes of Hitler and Mussolini. It is no coincidence, the newspaper wrote, that the "overthrown tyrant" surrounded himself with Nazi advisors. The directors of *Mundo Israelita* attempted to justify to their readers and to the new authorities their previous support of Perón in the pages of the newspaper, alluding to their fears that the publication of any criticisms might endanger the publication of the weekly. It was out of terror of the dictatorship's possible reaction, so they alleged, that they had published columns sympathetic toward the overthrown president.

4

Peronism and the New Jewish State

In early 1947, Great Britain's minister of foreign affairs, Ernest Bevin, announced that his country was to transfer the problem of Palestine to the United Nations. The institutions of the British Mandate felt that they had reached an impasse as to Palestine's future, as time and again they were confronted with the conflicting demands of Jews and Arabs.

In early May of that year, the UN General Assembly agreed to send a special fact-finding committee to Palestine, the United Nations Special Committee on Palestine (UNSCOP), comprised of representatives from eleven member states. The delegation travelled to the Middle East in June and published its conclusions at the end of August, following weeks-long deliberations. Most members of the committee were impressed by the Jewish struggle against Mandate authorities and accordingly recommended that the British withdraw and that the territory be partitioned into three sections: a Jewish state, an Arab state, and the Jerusalem area, which would be under international administration. The representatives from Uruguay (Enrique Rodríguez Fabregat), Guatemala (Jorge García Granados), and Peru (Arturo García Salazar) left their imprint on the UNSCOP's proceedings by fulfilling an important role, both in bringing about the recommendation to partition the area and in ensuring that the committee adopt this recommendation.[1]

The UN General Assembly's ad hoc committee adopted a similar plan, which it submitted to a plenary vote in late November. When the votes were counted, thirty-three states had supported the partition, thirteen had opposed it, ten had abstained from voting, and one was absent. The British did not await the final decision. In mid-November, they announced the timeline for the termination of the Mandate and the withdrawal of their forces.

The Latin American nations accounted for twenty of the UN's fifty-five members and were therefore a central element of this newly created organization. Some measure of support from the Latin American states played a vital part in the adoption of every important resolution, which required a two-thirds majority.[2] In fact, most studies examining the resolution emphasize the decisive role of the support of Latin American states for the resolution that paved the way for the creation of the state of Israel, which was adopted by the General Assembly on 29 November 1947 under the presidency of Brazilian Oswaldo Aranha. Thirteen of the twenty Latin American member countries voted in favour of the resolution (accounting for nearly 40 percent of the total votes), six abstained, and one, Cuba, opposed the resolution. It is difficult to obviate the fact that three of the most influential countries of the Spanish-speaking bloc – Argentina, Chile, and Mexico – chose to abstain from voting on the resolution.

CONFLICTING PRESSURES AND ARGENTINA'S ABSTENTION

A number of factors shaped the Perón administration's policy approach to Palestine between 1946 and 1948. The most ponderous of these was Argentina's relations with the United States as a hegemonic power in the continent. In that regard, the administration wished to demonstrate a degree of autonomy in its foreign policy – a crucial goal, considering Argentina's diplomatic tradition and Perón's nationalist rhetoric. As the question of Palestine was not a central one within Argentine foreign affairs, adopting an independent position on the matter could allow the country more room to manoeuvre and increase its leverage in negotiating relevant points of Perón's agenda for development and modernization.

From the outset of his presidency, Perón introduced his socioeconomic policy as one that would be equidistant from the two extremes of a cruel capitalism devoid of a social conscience and an oppressive, soulless communism. The country's foreign policy was, at least in principle, in keeping with this third position. In that regard, it sought to demonstrate that

Argentina was not the backyard of the United States and that it could not be subordinated to the diktats of any power. The administration's international policies would henceforth exclusively benefit Argentina. In spite of this aspiration, Perón's government made all possible efforts to avoid unnecessary confrontations with the United States. At the end of the 1940s, Perón, similarly to his minister of foreign affairs and minister of war, repeatedly stressed in conversations with US diplomats that the "third position" was "a bit of political demagogy for home consumption" and that this should not be taken to mean that Argentina would be neutral in the event of a conflict involving the two main blocs.[3]

Argentina adopted a similarly cautious stance vis-à-vis Great Britain, its main trading partner since Argentina became an independent republic. Although it had become clear after the Second World War that Great Britain could no longer play such a preponderant role in the country's economy, no alternative had yet emerged. Among other reasons, this explained Argentina's reluctance to adopt an intransigent posture on the subject of Palestine, which was such a ponderous issue for the British.

Another key motive that justified the abstention from the UN vote was Argentina's desire to maintain the support given to it by Arab countries in the international arena in general and within the United Nations in particular. Argentina's entry into the United Nations had been the result of a complicated process due to the country's late timing in declaring war to Germany and Japan. This considerably weakened its position within the organization. Most of the Arab states – which had also attained full political independence during the late 1940s – also sought to increase their international legitimacy by developing a network of diplomatic relations that included as many countries as possible. This ambition led to the establishment of diplomatic relations throughout 1947 between Argentina and Lebanon, Syria, Saudi Arabia, Iraq, and Egypt.

Those in charge of implementing Argentina's foreign policy viewed as crucial the support of these six Arab countries – already UN members at that point – and of other predominantly Muslim countries such as Iran, Pakistan, and Afghanistan. The Arab countries did indeed support Argentina's failed attempts at winning election to the United Nations International Court of Justice and to join its Economic and Social Council. In September 1947, Argentina's bid to become a member of the Security Council was successful, in part thanks to the support of the Arab nations. Argentina reciprocated by supporting the election of candidates from these countries to key UN posts. This dynamic made the architects of Argentine diplomacy wary of adopting a position that ran contrary to that of most of the Arab states. Perón's fear of upsetting Arab leaders by supporting the Zionist position comes across in an anecdote involving the Argentine-born Israeli diplomat Moshé Tov. When Tov asked Perón why Argentina was delaying its recognition of Israel, the president replied with his typical humour: "Look, my friend, you know the Arabs very well. They can become irrational. If I were to recognize Israel today, it's possible that on the next day we might find the Argentine ambassador hung from a lamppost or a tree on a Cairo street."[4]

Although Perón had expressed sympathy with Zionist aspirations in a 1945 meeting with the Jewish journalist and diplomat Benno Weiser Varon,[5] the confidential instructions that Argentina's Ministry of Foreign Affairs sent to the country's UN delegation in October 1946 explicitly stated that, "Jewish institutions have tried in various ways to gain our country's support if the question of Palestine comes up for debate [in the UN]. In this most delicate of matters, the following should guide you: *Argentina does not want for its relations with the Arab League to suffer, in any respect whatsoever. Argentina has not committed to supporting the Jews*."[6] The same document suggested, further on, that, despite this instruction, if circumstances forced Argentina to vote in a way favourable to Jews, efforts should be made to do so without offending Arab sensibilities.

Ten months later, in August 1947, the Ministry of Foreign Affairs sent new instructions, in a somewhat different tone, to its UN delegation:

> Argentina is sympathetic to the creation of a Jewish homeland in Palestine. This support is assisted by reasons of humanity. We cannot forget the Balfour Declaration, ratified by the League of Nations upon agreeing on the mandate, and the hopes that the principles enshrined in said declaration fomented in the Jewish people, as well as their efforts to make the desert fertile and to build villages.
>
> Argentina is not directly involved in this problem and its intervention must not be primordial. It will nevertheless make efforts to reach the most suitable formula so that the solution voted

> upon is the most equitable and humanitarian. Argentina does not wish to alter its good relations with the Arab states, with which it has established diplomatic ties. It does not forget the beneficial contribution that sons of these countries have made to Argentina's progress. Argentina deems that the Arabs should be decent in considering the situation of the Jews, with whom they have coexisted since antiquity.

As Argentina was primarily a land of immigrants, its approach to foreign relations was necessarily influenced by the multiple minority communities that inhabited its territory. The creation of a Jewish state involved two of these communities: the Jewish one, which was the most numerous in Latin America (Brazil's much smaller Jewish community was the second-largest), and the Arab community, largely comprised of Syrio-Lebanese who had migrated during the waning years of the Ottoman Empire, estimated at the time at 400,000 persons. It is relevant to point out here that, unlike Perón's relative lack of success among Argentina's Jewish community – the majority of which had voted for the UD in the 1946 presidential elections – the Arab community is considered to have been favourable to Perón's candidacy, which, to some extent, committed the president toward that group.[7] In late December 1945, the newspaper *Democracia* published a series of articles authored by Enrique de Marenz under the title "Why is the Jewish community opposed to General Perón?"[8] On the other hand, once the election results were officially published, the Arab-Argentine periodical *Azzaman: La Época. Órgano Libanés* could boast of the political achievements of the Arab community, from whose ranks one deputy governor (in the province of Córdoba), one national senator, and five national congressmen were elected.[9]

As the instructions of the Ministry of Foreign Affairs suggest, as early as the second half of 1946, the Zionist lobby was engaged in vigorous efforts to win the sympathy and support of public opinion and members of government. Key public figures took part in that initiative. Avraham Mibashán represented the Jewish Agency in Buenos Aires from 1944 onward. There, he collaborated with the DAIA and the Consejo Central Sionista (Central Zionist Council), the umbrella group founded one year earlier to gather together all the Zionist groups in Argentina in organizing a series of protest meetings against the British policy in Palestine and to disseminate information through media channels about the Zionist movement and the Jewish people, with the additional aim of reaching politicians and other public figures.[10]

In August 1946, the Comité pro-Palestina (CPP; Pro-Palestine Committee) was created in Argentina. The organization included gentile intellectuals and representatives from all political parties and was helmed by the renowned poet Arturo Capdevila and the Peronist Leonardo Benítez Piriz (originally from the UCR's Junta Renovadora, the union radical-dissident section, which supported Perón).[11] The committee was in charge of organizing meetings and receptions, which it did in collaboration with Mibashán, the DAIA, and the Zionist Council. Mibashán even succeeded at uniting several Peronist congressmen, whom he convinced to join forces with members of the opposition – then in the hands of the UCR – to write and submit a letter to the government enjoining it to support the creation of a national Jewish homeland in the land of Israel. This was a rare example of cooperation between parties in the strife-ridden and polarized Argentine political scene of that period.[12]

Under the guidance of Moshé Tov, the CPP's president collaborated with Mibashán and the DAIA's president, Dr. Moisés Goldman – who had developed good relations with Perón – to obtain Argentina's support for the Zionists' bid at the United Nations through the minister of foreign affairs, Juan Atilio Bramuglia. Tov, an Argentine-born Zionist Jew who had presided over the Organización Hebrea Macabi (Jewish Maccabee Organization) and had been secretary of the DAIA, visited Argentina in August 1946, and again in September 1947 after completing his duties in New York as the official in charge of liaison with the members of the UNSCOP.[13] As the date of the UN vote neared, Zionist activity in Buenos Aires intensified.[14] Rallies, press conferences, and open letters in newspapers decried the British policy in Palestine and expressed support for the "just demands of the Jewish people." The DAIA and other organizations acted on the request made by Tov and Stephen Wise, president of the World Jewish Congress, that they send telegrams to US president Harry Truman and to Perón asking the two heads of state to give their delegations the necessary instructions to vote in favour of the partition.[15]

Two meetings between Jewish community leaders and Minister of Foreign Affairs Bramuglia were made possible thanks to the mediation of Diego Luis Molinari, then president of the Senate's Committee for Foreign Relations. Molinari had expressed solidarity with Zionist activities already in the late 1920s. Bramuglia promised to prepare instructions for the delegates to the UN that could bring about "a comprehensive solution to the Jewish problem"; he emphasized that Argentina would vote in the same way as the two superpowers, the United States and the USSR – that is, in favour of the partition of Palestine and the creation of a Jewish state.[16] In an attempt to engage Argentina into adopting a pro-Zionist stance, a telegram was sent to thank the minister of foreign affairs, and Mibashán made the minister's statement public in an event that was held in early November to mark the thirtieth anniversary of the Balfour Declaration.[17] Benítez Piriz and the CPP also put pressure on the minister. But, as will be seen, Bramuglia was not the only player in the decision-making process within the Ministry of Foreign Affairs. In November, Molinari, originally of the UCR, once again wrote to the vice-president, Hortensio Quijano – also of the UCR – and to Bramuglia, attempting to convince them to add Argentina's vote in support of the majority proposal put forward by the UNSCOP.

The Arab countries launched their own lobbying efforts in Argentina after diplomatic relations were established with newly independent Lebanon and Syria. In May 1946, for example, delegates of the Arab League met with the outgoing president, General Edelmiro Farrell. They exited that meeting feeling that they had won over Argentina's support in their struggle for Palestine – an impression that was quickly denied by the foreign minister at the time, Juan Cooke.[18] A Lebanese diplomat, who would shortly undertake the first public relations tour of Latin America on behalf of the Arab countries, met with president-elect Perón in Buenos Aires and demanded that Argentina support the position of the Arab nations in an eventual UN debate on the future of Palestine. Perón implied that the decision had already been made, and that Argentina sympathized with the diplomat's cause. Moshé Tov, however, reported having had a different impression in the meeting that he held with the president. In response to these contradictory perceptions, a member of Argentina's UN delegation cynically observed that presidents, Perón in this case, always tried to give their interlocutors the impression that their wishes or requests would be granted. A month prior to the vote, Argentina's minister of foreign affairs told the Spanish ambassador in Buenos Aires that his country did not wish to adopt a stance that could provoke the ire of either the Arab or Jewish communities in Argentina.[19]

Akram Zuaytir, a key Palestinian activist since the 1930s, headed an Arab League delegation that visited Argentina in 1947, aiming to mobilize the support of the local Arab community in favour of the struggle for a Palestinian nation-state. This visit led to the creation of the Comité Argentino Árabe de Defensa de Palestina (Arab-Argentine Committee for the Defence of Palestine) and to a flood of letters and telegrams to the Casa Rosada and the Ministry of Foreign Affairs, asking that the government adopt a stance hostile to the Zionist demands. It is worth noting that, even if a number of the Arab community's press outlets in Argentina, such as *Istiklal* and *La Bandera Árabe*, adopted anti-Jewish and anti-Zionist stances in 1946 and 1947, the community's main newspaper, *El Diario Sirio-Libanés* (The Syrio-Lebanese Newspaper), upheld a moderate line, in a possible echo of the healthy relations that Jews from Syria and Lebanon maintained with Muslims and Christians originating from the same lands.[20]

The impact of the Jewish lobby, both in Argentina and in the UN's New York headquarters, is difficult to estimate. This group was evidently neither the sole nor the main influence in Perón's considerations. Yet, as the president was making efforts to improve his image on the international stage in general, and in the eyes of US officials in particular, the Jewish lobby's pressures were effective, even more so considering that the Justicialist leader was at pains to counter perceptions that he was antisemitic. As examined in the first chapter, following the end of the Second World War, due to Argentina's neutral stance in the war, Western countries and Eastern European nations manifested in multiple forms their suspicions that Perón's regime was fascist and totalitarian.

PERSONAL CONFLICTS AND IDEOLOGICAL STRUGGLES

In surveying Argentina's position regarding the question of Palestine, historians have seldom examined the debates between the key cadres of the Ministry of Foreign Affairs and their influence in orienting Argentina's UN vote. The protagonists of these debates were Minister of Foreign Affairs Bramuglia, José Arce, who was head of Argentina's

UN delegation and ambassador to the United Nations, and Enrique Corominas, the vice-president of the Argentine delegation. Documents from Bramuglia's personal archive (presently in possession of the Hoover Institution at Stanford University) illuminate various facets of the debate, involving ideological, personal, and intergenerational aspects, and illustrate its impact in shaping Argentina's stance vis-à-vis Palestine, which it adopted at the last minute. Among other aspects, these documents illustrate that, despite Perón's personalist and charismatic leadership, internal struggles within the Peronist bureaucratic apparatus did play a part in orienting the administration. They also shed light on how the political decision-making process was neither homogeneous nor smooth. At that phase of the Arab-Israeli conflict, when the situation in the Middle East was not yet clearly defined, Perón's attitude contrasted with his visible participation in shaping and implementing various facets of Argentina's international relations. Here, he preferred to avoid the limelight and left his subordinates in charge of this diplomatic challenge.

Arce was a prestigious surgeon who had previously been rector of the Universidad de Buenos Aires and dean of that university's medical faculty. He was also an experienced politician, having been a congressman for many years. He belonged to one of the most conservative groups in the heterogeneous coalition that united under Perón's leadership in 1945. Following Perón's victory in the February 1946 elections, Arce was named ambassador to the United Nations. Arce's nomination to this post, like that of Oscar Ivanissevich to the post of ambassador in Washington, was intended to project the image of Argentina as a respectable nation in the international arena. Arce was staunchly opposed to communism and expressed great sympathy for Franco's regime and, in equal measure, aversion for the Jewish people and their ambition to establish a sovereign state. Arce refused to defer to the authority of the Ministry of Foreign Affairs or its minister, Bramuglia. This has implications for our thesis about the multiple factors that played into Argentina's vote. Arce often told his friends that "all ambassadors have to abide by the instructions of the Ministry of Foreign Affairs, but for the ambassador to the UN," emphasizing that he was accountable only to the president of the republic.[21] This attitude inevitably spawned a conflict between Arce and Bramuglia regarding numerous questions, among them Argentina's position vis-à-vis Israel and the Jews.

Bramuglia was undoubtedly the most respected and talented of all the ministers who held posts during Perón's first presidency.[22] Moshé Tov described him as "an intelligent and studious man, skilled in handling matters, sober in his manners, and discrete in social contexts." The minister was a self-made man, born to a family of Italian immigrants of modest means. He was orphaned early in his life. Bramuglia began to work at a young age while studying toward a doctorate in law. Having specialized in workers' rights from the 1920s onward, he became a legal advisor to various trade unions. In the 1930s, Bramuglia joined the Socialist Party; shortly after the 1943 military coup, he became one of Perón's supporters. In the numerous posts that he filled in Perón's service, he had been one of the main architects of the nascent Peronist coalition – as director of social planning in the Secretariat of Labour and Welfare, as the designated official responsible for the province of Buenos Aires, and as president of the National Grouping for the Coordination of the Revolutionary Political Parties during the presidential campaign held between late 1945 and 1946. Bramuglia was very effective as minister of foreign affairs, but this success may have turned against him, as it caused unease among the Peronist leadership.[23]

Bramuglia named his trusted friend Enrique Corominas as the UN delegation's second-in-charge in an attempt to keep Arce in check and to ensure that he received complete and detailed information about all of Arce's words and deeds in the UN's New York headquarters. Bramuglia and Corominas were of the same generation; they had worked together in political life for more than twenty years, from the beginning of the 1940s up until Bramuglia's death in 1962. Like Bramuglia, Corominas had also commenced his activism among left-wing organizations, and he shared Bramuglia's sympathy toward the Zionist ambition of establishing a national Jewish homeland in Palestine. Between September and November 1947, Corominas sent lengthy and detailed reports on a near daily basis from New York to Bramuglia's private residence (not his office) in Buenos Aires. These letters are an invaluable primary source, as they reveal the debates within the delegation between its head and his first advisor, as well as the differing perceptions of Jews and of Zionism among the different figures in the Peronist milieu. These letters constituted an alternative, unofficial channel of communication separate from the letters and telegrams exchanged between the minister and the delegation head.

As the vote on the resolution about Palestine neared, Corominas's criticisms intensified. Pointing at Arce, he complained bitterly about the behaviour of "these men who lived abroad and act as if they owned the country," arrogantly imposing their personal wills on those around them. From these missives, it can be surmised that the conflict between Corominas and Arce involved generational differences. Corominas viewed Arce as a representative of the old guard, unable to grasp the changes that had occurred in the world, or in Argentina, since the end of the war, and equally incapable of understanding the very nature of Peronism. For Corominas, the ambassador stubbornly held on to bygone conservative notions that were outdated, and he therefore could not properly represent the "new Argentina" or the "Third Position."

In fact, during Arce's tenure as head of Argentina's UN delegation, his behaviour exhibited some of the traditional trends in his country's foreign policy, namely a sort of isolationism and a propensity to turn historical or political issues into legal questions. His dogmatic attitude and refusal to commit to a stance in, for example, any matter related to the principle of non-intervention in the affairs of a sovereign state led the delegation to cast its votes in a manner that was, if not surprising, at least polemical, projecting a conservative image of Perón's regime as well. As the voting record shows, to Corominas's great dismay, Argentina did not support the motion to censor South Africa for racial discrimination against its Hindu minority; it also opposed efforts for South Africa to grant independence to Southwest Africa (Namibia). Argentina also opposed proposed resolutions for any revision of France's colonialist policy in Morocco and did not support criticisms of Dutch imperialism in the Far East. Argentina's ties with Spanish strongman Francisco Franco also harmed efforts to counter perceptions of the regime as pro-fascist.[24] In 1950, when Arce was removed from his post as head of the UN delegation, this policy orientation changed considerably due to the official's departure and other factors. Argentina began to show more flexibility in its stances in the UN, working to find political solutions instead of resorting to legal or doctrinaire means.

In debates on the question of Palestine, Arce justified his position using legal arguments as well as political and moral ones. He emphatically reminded Bramuglia that the plan for partition contradicted the specifications of the Charter of the United Nations as to peoples' rights to self-determination.[25] He insisted that the General Assembly was not *authorized* to impose a solution upon one of the parties involved in the conflict, and did not have the *ability* to do this, as it lacked a military branch. Arce's proposal that the inhabitants of the disputed territory be allowed to vote on their own destiny under the UN's supervision was, in fact, a recommendation to adopt the point of view of the Arabs, who constituted the majority of the population.

Corominas responded to this by arguing that the legal interpretations of the UN Charter were inadequate to the situation, as they "lacked emotional life. The coldness of law no longer exists. It always loses to emotional law ... which wins over the conscience of peoples ... Men do not win over popular emotions by being wiser or by exhibiting a greater command of juridical science; they do so through the goodness of their souls ... through the tenderness of their actions."[26] Corominas was in essence calling upon his superiors to consider affective factors and moral values.

JEWISH NATIONAL DEMANDS AND THE "THIRD POSITION"

Arce expressed his reservations about the plan for partition in the debates held by the ad hoc committee on how to formulate its recommendations to the General Assembly. On one occasion, he declared: "the Argentine delegation, in its wish to support the establishment of not one, but of many Jewish homelands as are necessary to put an end to the situation of precariousness of [Jewish] men, women, and children, persecuted without reason in Europe, must, for racial motivations, avoid elevating this aspiration to such an extent that it would violate the Charter by forcibly imposing the creation of a Jewish state in Palestine."[27]

The Jewish Agency's representatives found out that Corominas, unlike Arce, supported the plan that the majority of the UNSCOP had recommended, as well as the Jewish people's historical right to establish a sovereign state in Palestine. Corominas's stance was based on humanist principles, on principles of international law, and on universal and Christian principles. In a letter addressed to Bramuglia dated 22 November, he stated his position as follows:

> Jewish people represent some of our country's 400,000 citizens who move, act, and circulate in relation to Jews around the world, whom, if they add up to three, four, or five million people, or more, according to statistics, can potentially involve 50 [million people], as we do not know the extent of this group's influence. If they have succeeded in touching the entire world with this problem and in putting it before the United Nations, despite lacking a state or a homeland, or even a land in which to reside ... this is because they are aided by some right or because their leadership is extraordinary. If they have leadership, then they deserve to have a home, and if they are aided by justice, then it must, without a doubt, be abided by, even at the expense of the resistance, the staunch resistance of the Arabs.

Consequently, the representatives of the Arab countries and the Higher Committee of Arabs in Palestine were in close and constant contact with Arce, whereas Corominas was in regular contact with the representatives of the Jewish Agency and became an important source of information for Moshé Tov in his attempts to win over the support of the Latin American member states of the UN. Corominas relayed to Tov information about his conversations with his colleagues from other Latin American countries and about how delegates from the Arab League also approached these countries' diplomats. When he visited Buenos Aires, Corominas met with Mibashán, the representative of the Jewish Agency, who organized a reception hosted by the CPP to honour the Argentine diplomat and recognize his support of the Zionist cause. The president of the CPP, Leonardo Benítez Piriz, a member of the Peronist party, also met with Corominas to encourage him to maintain his stance.[28]

Corominas accused Arce of failing to grasp this facet of human sensibility and to consider that which is "well known, that displaced

Jews, who do not wish to build their homes upon the graves where their relatives are buried, do wish to go to Palestine and nowhere else."[29] In another letter to Bramuglia, he described the issue of displaced Jews and explained the necessity of finding solutions so as to "avoid the martyrdom of these groups of men."[30] The disagreement between Corominas and Arce also hinged on the very essence and meaning of the Third Position. As both of the superpowers involved agreed that the creation of a Jewish state was necessary, what consequences would abstention have in the context of the escalating Cold War? Corominas understood the consensus on the question of Palestine between the two powers as precisely reflecting a third position, when he said:

> Doctor Arce has strayed from the Third Position, veering toward a place where he should not venture, or rather, led to that place by his racism, his antisemitism, his strongly conservative and classist spirit, and what's more, his forgetting of the moral premises and of the instructions that the Foreign Ministry has imparted upon us.
>
> When Arabs in Argentina hold public events to celebrate Ambassador Arce's name and Argentina's pro-Arab policy, this is because the ambassador has sided with the Arab faction. In doing this, he has gone against the ministry's instructions.[31]

Corominas warned that opponents of Peronism, national or internationally, would interpret as racist or antisemitic any action on the part of the regime that wounded the sensibilities of those who supported a national Jewish homeland. In making this comment, he was mainly thinking of Jews in the United States who, just as the members of Jewish-Argentine community organizations, still harboured suspicions, if not some hostility, toward Perón. He also explained that if Argentina voted "no" in the General Assembly's vote on partition, it would become a satellite of the Arab world, whereas both Arabs and Jews would view abstention as an expression of Argentina's support for Arabs. Abstention would also be seen, he warned, as an evasion of Argentina's responsibility, as a failure to show up or to participate in the vote to determine the outcome of the unfolding historical drama, since abstentions would not be taken into account to establish the relative size of the majority in the vote. An abstention would accordingly amount to a failure to grasp the historical meaning of the resolution, and to trample upon Argentina's "true sentiments, as it aspires to be, in this worldwide political moment, a country that leads and guides."[32] He would later add: "This reminds me, in passing, that our president, and those of us who adhere to his doctrine, have always said that we would fight for the great causes. I have maintained the belief that this cause [the desire to establish a national homeland for Jews] is one of the great human causes. This is why I have fought for it."[33]

Corominas qualified his statements with various types of warnings, adducing that the Arabs would soon forget the abstention but that Jews would not forget those who had not supported them at such a crucial juncture in their national history. He further warned that the opposition in Argentina would exploit the country's abstention to harass the regime and accuse it of having an anti-Jewish and racist attitude, one "that members of the government do not feel, and that they don't even dream" of adopting.[34] Finally, he enjoined his reader to recall that international media and banks were in Jewish hands. At least in this regard, it seems that anti- and philosemites often coincided.

When the ad hoc committee held its vote, on 25 November, Argentina abstained. Out of the twenty Latin American member states, a majority of twelve voted in favour; six, including Argentina, abstained; and one was absent. Arce thought that his country should also abstain when the General Assembly held its vote. He telephoned the Ministry of Foreign Affairs in Buenos Aires and, as Bramuglia was not in, spoke with the vice-minister, Doctor Carlos Desmarás. According to Desmarás, Arce explained the situation with "his typical pro-Arab tone and lacking the impartial tone corresponding to Argentina's position." Upon hearing his arguments, Desmarás instructed him to also abstain in the General Assembly's vote.

Argentina did indeed abstain in the General Assembly vote of 29 November. This stance was interpreted in a variety of ways by different observers. Some saw it as an expression of hostility toward Jews dictated by the influence of significant right-wing nationalist elements within the Peronist coalition and by the Church's influence – at the time, it was still a strong ally of the regime. These interpretations concluded that "a regime that exhibited fascist characteristics" had to be treated with suspicion. Others focused on Argentina's refusal to oppose the resolution and saw in this an achievement on the part of Corominas and supporters of the partition plan.

Perón was conspicuously absent from the confrontation of forces around this vote. When the president's position was clear regarding a specific matter, he ensured that his point of view prevailed and that his delegates abided by the instructions issued from the Casa Rosada, which took precedence over their own particular opinions. In regard to the vote of partition, Perón preferred to avoid adopting a clear stance as a result of the contradictory pressures to which he was subjected. In response to his national and international critics, he let the responsibility fall on the country's diplomats. Abstention, after all, was conducive to his goals and would allow him a wide margin of action in defining and implementing his country's Middle East policy according to changing international circumstances.

This episode is equally illustrative of how the Peronist movement harboured a variety of positions. Its members held conflicting points of view about a variety of political topics, both domestic and international, including the Jewish question and Zionism. Arce continued to demonstrate hostility toward the nascent state of Israel after the 1947 vote, for example, when Israel presented its candidacy to become a UN member state.[35] Arce's star gradually extinguished itself, however, as did his influence on Argentina's diplomacy. Despite having reservations, Argentina supported Israel's bid to become a UN member in votes held in December 1948 and May 1949.[36] Unsurprisingly, Argentina's vote was met with criticism from Arab countries.

Argentine diplomat Rodolfo Muñoz recalled that the representatives of the Arab countries had "on various occasions, expressed their feelings of displeasure at our vote in Paris – a vote that we explained as resulting from a reality that we have not shaped." As evidenced in this vote, Argentina's foreign policy began to be guided by the central necessity of improving Peronism's image on the international stage and of forging closer ties with the United States. This new priority also shaped Argentina's attitude toward the state of Israel, once it became clear that the state would exist.

CELEBRATING THE ESTABLISHMENT OF THE JEWISH STATE

Despite the ongoing competition between the OIA and the DAIA to represent the Jewish community vis-à-vis national authorities, both organizations approached the government to ask that it support the proposal to partition Palestine, and then that it promptly recognize the new state of Israel and, finally, that it build bilateral ties with Israel. Although many Jewish-Argentines felt disappointed at their country's abstention in the UN vote held on 29 November 1947, once Argentina recognized the new state in February 1949, Jewish-Argentines – whether supporters or detractors of Peronism – could find satisfaction in the relations that the two countries forged.

On 14 May 1948, as the news spread that a new Jewish state was created, tens of thousands of exalted Jews gathered in the neighbourhood of Retiro. In a festive atmosphere, seven community leaders gave speeches as did five representatives of Jewish Palestine and veteran Socialist Party leader Enrique Dickmann, who did not want to miss this celebration despite his precarious health. The speeches were met with ovations and, once the event concluded, participants walked the main streets of Villa Crespo. The march grew as Jews and gentiles joined, and many greeted the marchers and threw flowers from their windows. At that time, it didn't cross anyone's mind to incite hatred toward Jews for their presumed "dual identity."

As for Perón, the president clearly understood that his efforts to win the support of the Jewish community required that he establish ties with the state of Israel. Furthermore, he was convinced that maintaining fruitful relations with Israel would improve Argentina's relations with the United States. This convergence of criteria involving both domestic and foreign policy, which in turn took into account Argentina's position on the international arena as well as the country's image in Western public opinion, led Argentina to publicly express its sympathy toward Israel, from the establishment of diplomatic relations in May 1949 up until the overthrow of Perón's second administration in September 1955.

When Israel declared its independence, the architects of the country's foreign policy had no particular reason to hope that Argentina would establish strong ties with the new nation, despite having the largest Jewish community in Latin America. Many, both in Argentina and abroad, viewed General Perón as a fascist and as sympathetic to Nazism. Nevertheless, once the 1948 War of Independence concluded, the existence of the state of Israel became a given, and after the United States, Great Britain, France, and other Latin American countries recognized the new country *de jure*, Argentina followed suit.[37] Upon the initiative of the OIA and the leadership of the Jewish community organizations, an event was organized for 19 March to thank the president and the first lady for this important measure. In their speeches, community leaders praised this move and Perón saluted "the new dawn for the people of Israel," also expressing hopes that peace would reign between Arabs and Jews in the Middle East.[38]

In May of that year, after the Jewish state, legitimated and supported by a range of countries, was accepted as a member state of the United Nations, Argentina established bilateral diplomatic relations with the country. Through Sujer Matrajt, one of the OIA's leaders, Perón sent a letter addressed to his Israeli counterpart, Chaim Weizmann.[39] Shortly afterward, Argentina became the first Latin American country to open a diplomatic legation in Tel Aviv (similarly to other Catholic countries, Argentina supported the Vatican's position on the internationalization of Jerusalem, which was aimed at protecting the Christian holy sites). An additional gesture within that initiative was to name a Jewish-Argentine as minister plenipotentiary to the legation. This was none other than the notable OIA leader Pablo Manguel.[40] Manguel was installed into this post in 1949 and returned to Argentina in March 1955. When Manguel returned to Buenos Aires, he was national congressman and secretary of the Congress's Comisión de Relaciones Exteriores y Culto (Committee for Foreign Relations and Worship).

Israel conversely designated Jacob Tsur, its representative in the neighbouring republic of Uruguay, as its minister in Buenos Aires.[41] Tsur was speechless upon witnessing the intense emotion with which the Jews of Buenos Aires greeted him. When his ship anchored at the port, so many came to welcome the new minister that he had difficulty walking through the crowd. Similar scenes occurred on the day that he presented his credential letters. Masses of Jewish-Argentines waved

Figure 4.1 Chaim Weizmann, president of the state of Israel, during a conversation with the Argentine ambassador, Pablo Manguel, and the ambassador of Israel in Buenos Aires, Yaacov Tsur, August 1951.

the flags of the two countries and manifested their enthusiasm on either side of the path that the diplomat's carriage would cross on its way to the Casa Rosada. Once the official ceremony was completed, Perón and Tsur stepped onto the palace's iconic balcony and the thousands of Jews gathered in the Plaza de Mayo cheered them at length.[42]

Jewish community organizations expressed their identification with Israel and with Zionism. Their members were second- and third-generation immigrants, mostly Ashkenazim, whose connection with religion had weakened and for whom, to some extent, identifying with Zionism was a central component of their identity. By the mid-1950s, the city of Buenos Aires had only four rabbis to offer services to its 300,000 Jews. Jews living in the country's provinces had no access to a rabbi.[43]

The designation of Manguel to the legation caused some malaise within the Israeli Ministry of Foreign Affairs, as the minister plenipotentiary was a member of an organization that did not have the support of the organized Jewish community. The Israeli officials feared that the OIA might become a mediator of relations between the Jewish state and Perón's regime, and that the young nation might consequently be dragged into the internal struggles of the Jewish community or the differences between the community and national authorities. These fears quickly subsided. Indeed, as Tsur subsequently recognized, "Manguel made numerous, sincere efforts – to the best of his knowledge and understanding – to strengthen relations between Argentina and Israel," and, as he had direct access by telephone to General Perón, he could bypass the Ministry.[44]

Manguel's designation also met with obstacles in Argentina due to his Jewish origins. He had the support of Perón and Evita, but there were indications of opposition and resistance from various spheres, particularly in the Ministry of Foreign Affairs, traditionally controlled by Catholic nationalists and hermetically closed off to Jews. Attempts were made to impose upon the president the designation of a Catholic diplomat who would have the blessing of the Vatican and show interest in the situation of the Christian holy sites. Manguel told Tsur that, among the pressures exercised, the apostolic nunciature had mentioned that the pope had demanded that Argentina name a Catholic to the post in Israel. Perón was steadfast in his decision and Evita also intervened and, finally, Manguel became Argentina's first representative in Tel Aviv.[45] In September 1949, Tsur and the legation's first advisor, Arieh Eshel, met with the vice-minister of interior, Abraham Krislavin. The vice-minister explained to the Israelis that, "from the point of view of publicity," it was very important to Perón to name precisely a Jewish person as minister in Israel, and that he did this "to put an end to accusations that his regime was antisemitic."[46]

In the following years, Perón and Evita participated, sometimes in person, in relations with Israel. Manguel, as ambassador, was in direct

Figure 4.2 Pablo Manguel, first Argentine ambassador to Israel and leader of the OIA (third from left), arriving at Lod Airport, August 1949.

contact with the presidential couple. As part of his numerous efforts to shake off depictions of him and his government as Nazi/fascist, the populist leader made multiple overtures to establish good relations with the local community and with the state of Israel. One of his main objectives was to touch the hearts of US Jews – whose influence on the media, politics, and unions Perón perceived, in exaggerated terms, as powerful – in the hope that they could improve Argentina's image in the eyes of the general public and those in charge of US foreign relations.

This attitude was in evidence in a speech that the president gave on 21 June 1949:

> I feel deep affection and great respect for the state of Israel. And this, ladies and gentlemen, is because I am an Argentine patriot, and I deeply respect the patriotism of other regions of the world. [The nation of] Israel, in the mighty struggle that it waged during

> hundreds of years, set, for the world to see, the example of a nation that is one of the most patriotic on the face of the Earth. Hence my deep affection and great respect for this people who, for centuries, have maintained intact their virtues, the strength of their race, their perseverance in their cause, and the integrity that has distinguished them as a people of honest workers all over the world.[47]

Two elements should be highlighted here. The first is that, for Perón, the loyalty of Jewish-Argentines toward Argentina did not contradict their support for Israel, which they called "their motherland," similarly to how each immigrant community also had such a motherland. Just as the "tanos" (from the Spanish: "italianos") had close ties with Italy, or the "gallegos" with Spain, it was natural that Jews maintained such bonds with their country. Perón's statement thus fully legitimated the manifest identification of the Jewish-Argentine community organizations with Zionism and Israel. As a result, Jewish-Argentines' relations with each of the two countries during the Peronist mandates was not interpreted as the expression of a dual loyalty – as extreme right-wing nationalists would suggest following the capture of Adolf Eichmann in mid-1960. On one occasion, Perón stated, "an Argentine Jew who abstains from helping Israel is not a good Argentine." Additionally, Perón often publicized his administration's gestures toward Israel or his expressions of sympathy toward the cause of the young state to or through leaders of the OIA with the aim of strengthening this organization's influence in the local Jewish community.

DISAGREEMENTS IN THE ISRAELI MINISTRY OF FOREIGN AFFAIRS

Some members of the Israeli Ministry of Foreign Affairs, such as Moshé Tov, and some of the leaders of Argentina's Jewish community were wary of the good relations that Tsur was able to cultivate with both the Peronist authorities and the OIA. On one occasion, Tsur received a memorandum from his superiors at the Department for Latin America warning him to be careful of overly identifying with Peronism. On another occasion, he hosted a delegation of community leaders who criticized him for having agreed to participate in an assembly organized by the OIA at which Perón was also present, and for having made a proposal to plant a bush in Israel in tribute to Argentina's liberator, General José de San Martín. Tsur recalled that "one community leader after another recommended that I keep some distance vis-à-vis Perón – this person that, to them, was the embodiment of reaction and fascism; they added that despite Perón's attentiveness toward the Jewish community, there was no doubt that he was an antisemite." Tsur replied to these arguments: "As I am the representative of a foreign country, to me, General Perón isn't the leader of the Peronist party, but the president of the nation, to whom I owe respect. It is not my task or concern to criticize his behaviour. When I participated in the meeting to pay homage to Perón, I was not taking part in a Peronist event or expressing preference for him over his political adversaries. I was showing respect to the person who is the head of state of the country in which the legation is located."[48]

Tsur, who had the support of Walter Eytan, the director general of the Ministry of Foreign Affairs, and of Abraham Darom (formerly Drapkin),[49] the director of the Ministry's Department for Latin America, was not taken aback by these criticisms. He continued to observe the regime with objectivity, expressing reservations toward certain aspects and support for other ones, all the while trying to benefit as much as possible from this regime in his efforts to promote the interests of Israel and of the local Jewish community.

Early in 1950, Tsur submitted a report to the ministry in Jerusalem in which he praised Perón's attitude toward Israel and Argentina's Jews, and expressed his esteem for several facets of the regime and its aspiration toward social justice.[50] At the same time, his report included criticisms of the regime, for repressing various freedoms in Argentina, and enumerated the defects of the OIA at a time when several of the organization's leaders were involved in questionable episodes. Still, Moshé Tov, who by then was a member of Israel's UN delegation in New York, was furious when he read this report, which he took to be a defence of the Peronist regime. Tov had been critical of Tsur's policy for many months on the grounds that it was harmful to the DAIA and to Jewish community leaders, who for their part continued to send to Tov partial, negative information about the Argentine government. Tov acted as if he was still in charge of questions pertaining to Latin America even though that was now Darom's dossier.[51] He deemed it necessary to boycott the OIA, whose members he had nicknamed "Quislingian" Jews (after the Norwegian leader who had collaborated with the Nazis).

In a lengthy and detailed memorandum to the ministry, Tov asserted that the OIA turned Jews into second-class citizens as it made them dependent upon the mediation of a political organization named by the government to guarantee their basic rights. He argued that Perón's sympathy toward Jews was conditional upon their adherence to Peronism and that his aspiration to support Jewish-Argentines would guarantee the failure of all independent Jewish activity. He qualified OIA leaders as opportunists and alleged that they were motivated by selfish criteria and individual corruption. Tov warned that the Jewish community's identification with the government would affect its relations with the opposition parties and that it constituted a hidden threat to Jews, one that would become manifest as soon as the government changed. Tov's conclusion, in light of the factors adduced, was that the OIA was "a terrible and dangerous force of antisemitism."[52]

Tov's reaction, in turn, infuriated Tsur. The diplomat stationed in Buenos Aires deemed that, if Tov's suggestions were put into effect, Israel would be at odds with the presidential couple. In fact, Tov's actions undermined the footing of the legation and its activities. Tsur marginalized Tov by diminishing his ability to intervene in questions concerning the representation that he led. Tsur wrote to the general director of the Ministry of Foreign Affairs, Eytan, stating that, "it was impossible to ascertain whether [Tov] was a representative of Israel's Ministry of Foreign Affairs or an Argentine Jew eager to win over the hearts of the Jewish general public."[53] The confrontation between the two figures culminated in March–April 1950. The OIA had organized a big party to be attended by Perón and Evita as well as a broad swath of representatives of most Jewish community organizations. During the event, Perón gave a speech that was markedly pro-Israel and pro-Jewish, in which he chastised any expression of discrimination in Argentina: "our policy promotes rapprochement and brotherhood among all Argentines, and I do not and will not ever understand why some should be considered to be less Argentine than others because of their faith or because they originate from another country or place."[54]

The president also announced to those present that the two countries had decided to sign a trade agreement that gave Israel discounts on the purchase of Argentine products and raw materials.[55]

Tov then accused Tsur of "flirting with the OIA." At that point, and no longer able to withstand Tov's systematic campaign against him, Tsur told Abraham Darom that he was severing his ties with Tov due to drastic differences between their worldviews. Tsur firmly defended his position that Israel should develop the strongest ties possible with the Peronist regime in order to promote the interests of the young nation and that the legation should maintain contact with the OIA, just as it did with all other Jewish organizations.[56]

In his speeches, Perón often highlighted the fact that Jewish-Argentines enjoyed the same rights as all citizens, and expressed his appreciation of the Jewish community's contribution to the development of the Argentine Republic. He put these statements into practice by making the struggle against antisemitism into an integral part of his policies. In his memoirs, Tsur acknowledged the "regime's ardent interest in expressing publicly its sympathy toward Israel."[57] Indeed, in retrospect, Perón's multiple efforts to satisfy the Israeli diplomat stand out – as in the time, for example, when Tsur wanted to travel to Israel to participate in the twenty-third Zionist Congress held in Jerusalem but had his request denied by the ministry due to lack of available funding. When Perón found out about this, he requested that the state-run airline reserve seats for the Israeli diplomat and covered the fees for round-trip travel. When Tsur's mandate in Argentina came to an end, Perón ordered that Tsur be lodged in the best suite of a luxury Argentine ship upon which the diplomat would travel from Buenos Aires to New York, and that the ship's mast fly the Israeli flag every time it made a stop at a port.[58]

In mid-1951, Perón received an ancient Bible from Chaim Weizmann, by then president of Israel. On this occasion, Perón made a speech in which he mentioned the persecution that the Jewish people had experienced in the flesh and their clear victory after centuries of struggle.[59] When President Weizmann died in 1952, Argentina reacted most vocally to the event.[60] It is no surprise that the Jewish press published numerous obituaries for the veteran Zionist head of state, or that community organizations postponed their festivities until the end of the week of mourning prescribed in the Jewish faith. Other spheres of public life were also involved. The day Weizmann was buried, authorities declared a nationwide day of mourning, and flags on all government buildings in Buenos Aires, the city's military barracks, and ships docked in the port were flown at half-mast. The city's largest synagogue officiated a service in his memory and, for the first time in the life of the Jewish-Argentine community, national authorities were invited to participate in ceremony held in a Jewish synagogue.

Perón's preferential treatment of Israel was evident to many different visitors to Buenos Aires from the fledgling state. The Israeli dignitaries who visited Argentina included the president of the Knesset (Israel's parliament), Yosef Sprinzak, Minister of Labour Golda Meir, and Minister of Foreign Affairs Moshe Sharett. They were all welcomed as official guests of Argentina and were greeted with ceremonial protocol, even though the purpose of their visits was to collect invited funds for the United Jewish Appeal.

SUPPORT FOR ISRAEL IN THE FACE OF ANTISEMITISM IN THE USSR

In the first two years of its existence as an independent state, Israel, somewhat like Perón's Argentina, took pains to adopt a policy of nonalignment with regard to the two Cold War superpowers and avoid involvement in the growing polarization between the two. The minister of foreign affairs, Moshe Sharett, considered this policy to be very important. Israel made every possible effort to avoid alienating the Soviet Bloc. Indeed, the USSR's influence had been decisive in shaping and bringing about the November 1947 UN resolution to partition Palestine. The Soviet Union was also the first country to fully and officially recognize the state of Israel and, using Czechoslovakia as an intermediary, it provided indispensable military aid during Israel's War of Independence. The intensification of the Cold War weakened Israel's ability to maintain this neutral stance. With the creation of NATO in 1949, Europe became explicitly divided into two blocs. The United States saw the communists' victory in China in September of the same year as one step further in the confrontation between the "free world" and the "red menace." Eastward, the Korean War took the Cold War to a new climax in which Washington and Moscow pressured their friends across the world to align with one or the other. From mid-1950, Israel abandoned its efforts to maintain a neutral or semi-neutral stance, and began to support the cause of the United States.

This shift in Israel's official policy was prompted by the "Prague trials" and the trials of Jewish doctors, held in Moscow and made public in January 1953. Israel confronted Moscow, which in February 1953 temporarily suspended relations with the "Zionist state." Israel launched an international campaign against the Kremlin's antisemitic policy. Within this framework, Israel's embassy in Buenos Aires also made efforts to mobilize public opinion, Jewish and general, against the agitation against Jews being carried out in USSR. The OIA, particularly Pablo Manguel, assisted the embassy in that campaign.[61] The president of Argentina was the first to support Israel in this conflict. Just a few days after relations between Jerusalem and Moscow were severed, Perón published a vigorous condemnation of Soviet antisemitism, despite the fears of various Peronist figures that this position could damage relations between Argentina and the communist countries.[62]

During this period, Perón publicly emphasized his determination to sever at the root all expression of antisemitism in Argentina and expressed his regrets that the confrontation between the two powers had generated an atmosphere in which the Jews became a convenient target. In these circumstances, Jews residing in the Soviet bloc had to be allowed to seek refuge in Israel or in the countries of the free world. Insofar as it was necessary, he added, Argentina would also open its doors to those who suffered persecution.[63] Israelis welcomed the president's statements and many spokespersons praised Perón for what Minister Sharett referred to as a "noble and humanitarian" gesture.[64] Abraham Darom wrote to Manguel: "I know that you are one of the main architects of President Perón's policy," which he described as a policy that strengthened "the admiration and affection that Israelis have felt toward the General for years."

The leaders of Argentina's Jewish community institutions also praised these speeches and the representatives of the American Jewish Committee visited Argentina's ambassador in Washington, DC, Hipólito Jesús Paz, to thank him for his government's stance once they had ensured that the State Department did not oppose this. When the Israeli government asked Argentina to represent its interests in Bucharest in the event that Romania decided to take measures similar to those of Moscow by severing its ties with the Jewish state, Argentina responded affirmatively in less than a day. In the end, Israel did not take Argentina up on that request since Romania did not suspend relations.

In this context, Tsur made all possible efforts to improve the negative image of Perón in New York and Washington, but US Jewish organizations, such as the World Jewish Congress and the American Jewish Committee, rejected similar attempts by the Israeli embassy in Washington. Tsur persevered in his efforts, even after the end of his mandate, during his journey from Buenos Aires to Europe. In a lunch with the leaders of the American Jewish Committee, Tsur encouraged them to make specific gestures toward Perón. He explained that, "in Argentina, the [Peronist] regime is the only one to represent a stance of opposition to antisemitism and of sympathy toward Israel, whereas the opposition to Perón, whether on the Left or the Right, is more susceptible to antisemitic stances than the regime."[65]

A few weeks later and in relation to the antisemitic campaign unleashed in Eastern Europe, Tsur sharpened his arguments:

> Jewish public opinion in the US must understand that Argentina is a friend of Israel and the Jews, both in theory and practice. It must put an end to the constant distrust, typical of the World Jewish Congress, and to its inflation of news about antisemitism in Argentina. In today's situation, we can't afford to lose the friendship of a country on the basis of suspicions or assumptions alone. We should adopt a position of esteem and respect for Argentina and its regime, as they have courageously driven out antisemitism in all the years of its existence. In this spirit – and referring only to the Jewish element – the leaders of the US Jewry must speak up, as must the spokespersons and the ministers of the Israeli government.[66]

This time, Israel's diplomats in the United States also expressed their reservations about Tsur's initiative, arguing that the Jewish and liberal publics were fervently opposed to Perón's regime and that any further such attempts would only harm the Israeli embassy's diplomatic activities.[67]

Moshe Sharett's visit to Buenos Aires in April 1952 revealed the close ties between Argentina and Israel.[68] It also coincided with the climax of Tsur's activity in South America before he became Israel's ambassador in Paris. In September 1953, Arieh (formerly León) Kubovy became Israel's ambassador in Argentina.[69] Kubovy's first meeting with Perón, as well as the massively attended ceremony that the OIA had organized to mark the inscription of the president's name in the Golden Book of the Jewish National Fund, strengthened in Kubovy the impression that he had formed in conversations with Tsur: that Perón demonstrated with clarity and cohesiveness his favourable attitude toward the Jews of Argentina and toward the state of Israel.

During this ceremony, Perón addressed an audience of 6,000 that included representatives from 120 community organizations. He expressed admiration for the ties that Jewish-Argentines maintained with their homeland, the state of Israel. It should be noted that the president used the word "homeland" in a symbolic sense, not a geographical one, which in turn accounts for the lack of contradiction, in his view, between the loyalty of Jews toward the republic of Argentina and their support for Israel.

The president's words were received enthusiastically in Israel. President Yitzhak Ben-Zvi, as well as the former (and future) prime minister, Ben Gurion, the minister of police, Bekhor Shitrit, and others, all publicly praised Perón's speech.[70] The vice-director general of the Ministry of Foreign Affairs in Jerusalem, Arieh Levavi, wrote to Kubovy that, "the development of matters with Perón is convincing proof that Perón's approach to issues specific to Jews is in all facets positive and committed, in that Perón does not stop at making statements or adopting stances circumstantially, but shows his willingness to go much further."[71] In September 1954, the Argentine Congress ratified the agreement on culture that the two countries had signed a year earlier. Peronists and Radicals (members of the UCR) joined forces to vote unanimously on the accord and praise Israel and the Jewish people.[72]

COMPLEMENTARY ECONOMIC INTERESTS

In May 1950, the US bank of imports and exports, Eximbank, approved a loan of $125 million to the government of Argentina. Four weeks earlier, Argentina had signed its first trade agreement with Israel. At the time, the consecutive timing of these actions was not viewed as a coincidence. Argentine officials saw the strengthening of ties with Israel as a means to neutralize obstacles to improving relations with Washington and to benefit the image of the Peronist regime in US public opinion. Whereas Israel looked to the South American nation in the hope that a trade agreement could alleviate to some extent the hardships and shortages that characterized the economy of the fledgling nation, political criteria – in addition to the economic ones – were the primary factors guiding the decisions that led to the trade agreement that the Perón administration signed with Israel on 21 April 1950.

This trade agreement with Israel also reflected the economic difficulties that Argentina had begun to experience in 1949, as well as Perón's aspirations to diversify his country's export markets and import sources. Perón sought to reduce Argentina's economic dependence on the United States and Great Britain, and to remedy the problem of dwindling dollar reserves, which limited his country's ability to purchase machinery, raw materials, and manufactured goods from the United States.

The two countries began to discuss the possibility of establishing commercial ties immediately after diplomatic ties were established. To that end, Arpalsa – the Compañía Argentino-Palestinense para el Intercambio y Turismo (Argentine-Palestinian Company for Trade and Tourism), then representing Israel's economic interests in Buenos Aires – requested a meeting with officials at Argentina's Ministry of Foreign Affairs.[73] The meeting included the participation of Carlos M. Grünberg, the temporary official representative of Israel's interests in Argentina. Arpalsa had been founded by a group of Jewish Latin American investors in 1946 as a result of the initiative of José Mirelman, who had travelled to Jewish Palestine that same year, when it was under British Mandate, to identify areas worthy of investment and that showed potential for trade growth.[74]

In their meeting with officials of Argentina's Ministry of Foreign Affairs, the Jewish-Argentine entrepreneurs requested a large loan, which Israel would reimburse partly through the goods that it would ship to Argentina and via cash payments. To back these conditions, the members of Arpalsa offered to immediately ship from Israel a variety of goods: cement, dentures, diamonds, citrus fruit, wines, chemical products, books, and art and religious objects.

Perón's intervention, with that of his wife Eva, ensured the success of later economic negotiations.[75] The president also sought to benefit as much as possible from the agreement. Pablo Manguel, who had assisted Tsur in negotiating this trade agreement, publicly admitted that Perón hoped that the relations he was forging with Israel would generate a more favourable disposition among Jews toward his regime. Evita also played an important part in the process leading up to the signing of the agreement; the first lady also expected that the process would strengthen the OIA's standing in the Jewish community. To that end, the president's office wanted to publicize the signing of the agreement; officials accordingly decided to hold a formal ceremony, with key members of the administration as well as the OIA leaders present, to be broadcast on radio airwaves. Perón's speech on that occasion highlighted the bonds of friendship between the two nations.

Israeli officials were also very satisfied with the agreement, as can be gauged in the contemporary local press coverage.[76] *Haaretz* mentioned the participation of the presidential couple in its description of the ceremony and also emphasized that "this agreement is not philanthropy and both parties will benefit from it." *Davar*, a vehicle for the viewpoints of Israel's governing MAPAI party, provided the details of the agreement and described its scope, adding that Israel was the first Middle Eastern country to have signed a trade agreement with Argentina. *Herut*, an organ of the right-wing opposition party, quoted the words of Argentine senator Diego Luis Molinari, who stated that, "Israel [would become] Argentina's headquarters for trade in the Middle East." Across the economic pages of these newspapers, many speculated with great optimism that this agreement – the only one to have been signed with a Latin American country up until then – would usher in a growth in exports to South America.[77]

Although the volume of this trade agreement – $10 million – was relatively small against the whole of Argentina's trade relations, it was significant for Israel. The agreement offered conditions that were generous toward the fledgling country, including a secret clause that gave Israel and the United Jewish Appeal many concessions for the purpose of buying goods in Argentina.[78] This was particularly crucial considering that, as Israel experienced great financial need during its first years of existence, the government implemented a program of austerity measures. The arrival of immigrants on a massive scale between 1948 and 1951 doubled the Jewish population, and these new citizens needed food, medical care, housing, and employment. Additionally, the War of Independence, which lasted over a year, entailed human and economic losses, dramatically altering the system of production. These factors account for the scarcity of foreign currency, which was required for the purchase of basic foodstuffs, such as flour and wheat, or fuel, among other items, and required the government to adopt measures such as price controls and the rationing of basic goods and staples when they were in short supply.

Shortly after independence was declared, the first of many large shipments of beef arrived from Argentina. During the transition period between the adoption in the United Nations of the resolution for partition and the withdrawal of the last British soldiers, the imperial administration prevented ships from the British Commonwealth from unloading goods on the shores of Palestine. This put a halt to large shipments of beef from South Africa. The arrival of a ship from the Argentine merchant marine was the first of many such vital shipments for Israel.[79]

The inclusion in the trade agreement of conditions beneficial to Israel also reflected Argentina's reduced power in matters of trade at that time. In 1949, the country's situation changed dramatically. The exceptional set of circumstances that Argentina had enjoyed since the end of the Second World War – large gold and currency reserves, as well as the fact of finding itself in the midst of a process of industrialization – and which were at the root of Peronism's success, vanished completely. Argentina's ability to accumulate reserves during the Second World War thanks to reduced imports and increased export profits had created a false sense of security among authorities. Furthermore, the visible growth in revenue from the export of foodstuffs to a starved Europe between 1946 and 1948 produced an exaggerated optimism among the Peronist leadership, which failed to assess that this situation was temporary and liable to change at any time.

On the basis of this erroneous perception, the government crafted its ambitious Five-Year Plan and, with great ritual, pronounced its

Declaración de Independencia Económica (Declaration of Economic Independence) in July 1947. Within that framework, the size of the merchant marine's fleet was significantly increased and public services owned by foreign investors were nationalized or purchased. The most famous of these nationalizations involved the railway services, which were owned by British companies. This period also saw a notable increase in imports of raw materials, fuel, capital goods, and various manufactured goods.

Currency reserves, however, were weakened from running deficits for two fiscal years, and most of the remaining reserves were held in funds in European currencies that could not be converted to US dollars. In January 1949, the nation's coffers were nearly empty of US dollars and Argentina owed the United States $150 million. Authorities had to confront galloping inflation. The cost of living also increased dramatically as industrial and food production decreased, leading to concern among the working class, a fundamental pillar of Peronism, upon seeing its purchasing power decline.

Fierce opponents of Perón chalked up the crisis to his irresponsible economic policy, his social demagogy, and his supposedly obsessive attempts to industrialize the country at all costs, even at the expense of agriculture, the longstanding source of the country's wealth and monetary reserves. Although the government was at least partially responsible for this crisis, other, external factors beyond their control also did the economy great harm. For example, in August 1947, the British decided that they would no longer allow for the British pounds that they paid to Argentina to be converted to US dollars. As Great Britain was the main client for Argentina's exports, this measure deprived the country of the currency that it used to purchase imports from the United States.

The main challenge posed by trade relations between Argentina and the United States stemmed from the fact that the two countries' economies were competitors in the export of agricultural commodities – unlike the complementarity between economies which was at the root of the bilateral trade relations that Britain and Argentine had shared since the mid-nineteenth century. This challenge came into view when the Marshall Plan was implemented. The Plan could have saved Argentina's economy, but ended up sinking it. As is well known, the economies of the European countries were in tatters at the end of the Second World War. Most were unable to feed their populations and had to purchase foodstuffs from markets across the ocean. As the United States feared that this economic scarcity could become fertile ground for the growth of communist movements in Western Europe, it adopted a program to help these countries rebuild. The United States committed to funding the loans, trade concessions, machinery, capital, raw materials, and foodstuffs that European reconstruction required.

Argentina pinned its hopes on the Marshall Plan. The country's agriculture was in great shape and capable of producing large excess quantities of grains and beef for export. Politicians in Buenos Aires were convinced that the countries of Western Europe could buy large quantities of their products and that this would replenish the country's weakened US currency reserves. Perón and Minister Bramuglia claimed several times that various officials – among them Howard Bruce, who was in charge of administering the Marshall Plan, and US Ambassador to Argentina James Bruce – had led them to believe that Argentina could export its excess agricultural production to Europe within the Plan's framework.[80]

Disappointment was directly proportional to the hopes that had preceded it, as Argentina's access to the European markets that were beneficiaries of the plan was blocked based upon the argument that South American grains were too costly. The US agricultural lobby was clearly behind this decision. Argentina was thus marginalized from the Marshall Plan and deprived of a golden opportunity for economic growth, which dislodged it from its position as the primary provider of grains on the world market.[81]

These conditions explain Argentina's efforts to identify new export markets and to obtain loans from the United States. In February 1950, Edward Miller, the US assistant secretary of state for Latin American affairs, addressed the topic of loans in meetings held in Buenos Aires. In March of that year, Ramón Cereijo, Argentina's minister of the treasury, travelled to Washington to negotiate a $125 million credit from Eximbank for a group of Argentine banks so as to pay off debts to US creditors.[82]

The Perón administration was uneasy about having to request credit from the United States as it wished to keep up the appearance that its economic and diplomatic policies were independent, unaligned with either of the two major powers. Those in charge of orienting the economy nevertheless understood that assistance from the United States was inevitable. Both parties agreed that the assistance would be granted in the form of a credit rather than a loan with the aim of simplifying things for Perón, who had previously stated that he preferred to lose his right hand rather than ask the United States for a loan. The Argentine Congress took a measure that was interpreted as an effort to secure a credit from the United States when, against the wishes of the UCR opposition, it ratified the inter-American military treaty that had been drafted and put forward during the 1947 Pan-American Conference held in Rio de Janeiro. These two shifts – the search for new markets and the request for credit from the United States – provided the framework for the trade agreement struck with Israel. With this conjunction of factors as a backdrop, Ambassador Manguel paid Cereijo a visit – coincidental or not – during his stay in Washington to inform him about the possibility of commercial trade with Israel.

Some of the terms that Argentina granted Israel in the trade accord were indeed generous, particularly in regard to the payment arrangements. Israel was allowed to pay for 10 percent of its purchases in Argentine pesos, with funds originating from the United Jewish Appeal and raised among the local Jewish community, while the remaining amount could be paid in dollars. This made it possible for Israel to conserve precious foreign currency and to purchase Argentine beef at a price lower than the normal rate on the world market.

Even before the agreement was signed, permits had been granted to use donations collected in Argentina by the Jewish National Fund to pay for shipments of meat, hides, and light industry products. These permits had been negotiated by the OIA's president, Sujer Matrajt, after 15 percent of the funds collected by the JNF were transferred to the Fundación Eva Perón, the charity and welfare institution operated by the first lady. The April 1950 accord also contemplated the possibility of granting permits for private capital investments in Israel, so long as these furthered trade relations between the two nations. Businessman Benno Gitter writes in his memoirs that, "Argentina's export laws, on the authorization of General Perón, were bent to benefit us."[83]

Even if the scope of the agreement was relatively modest, it was visibly designed to benefit Israel, particularly considering that the Argentine government tended to prohibit funds transfers to other countries. Spanish and Italian immigrants, for example, could not transfer money to help their relatives in a devastated Europe. Relations with the United States hit another snag when, in late 1948, officials in Buenos Aires decided to restrict foreign investors from withdrawing their profits from the country.

The collections of funds from Jews in the diaspora, including Argentina, must be contextualized in relation to the small volume of foreign aid granted to Israel between 1949 and 1951. The first significant aid from the United States was granted in 1952 and the money from German reparations, which only began to arrive in 1953. During its first years of existence as an independent nation, the help that Israel obtained from Jewish sources was between two and three times greater than that which it obtained from foreign governments.

The United Jewish Appeal was a major channel for Jewish-Argentines to express their solidarity toward the Jewish state during the latter's first decade. Donations to the campaign were encouraged in the Jewish-Argentine media and by community leaders. These donations were sometimes viewed as a mandatory tax and a condition for membership in community organizations. The campaign carried out in Argentina in 1948 raised 44 million pesos (approximately USD $5.3 million). Donations were received from 44,000 individuals of varying economic means. Donations collected in 1949 were dramatically lower as a result of the division between the United Jewish Appeal's efforts and the broader efforts of the communists. In 1950, $1.25 million were raised and, the year after that some $1.1 million.[84] Israel paid in dollars for the products and goods that it acquired from Argentina, as well as the cost for their transportation aboard the ships of the Merchant Marine.

The original trade agreement was to last eighteen months, but its duration was extended three more years in late 1951. In May 1953 and January 1954, an additional extension was agreed upon. On 29 April 1955, a new agreement governing trade and payments was signed that had similar features as its predecessor.[85] An analysis of bilateral trade evidences a considerable increase in the volume of trade after 1950. Argentine exports soared between 1950 and 1953, peaking in the latter year. Israeli exports to Argentina were almost non-existent in 1949–50. Although they did increase thanks to the trade agreement, the balance of trade was in Argentina's favour in each year of that period except 1955. An example of the gestures that Argentina made to benefit Israel was to import citrus fruit, which it might have obtained from Brazil or Spain for a lower price.[86] In any case, the 1950 agreement marked the point when Argentina became Israel's main trading partner in Latin America: it was Israel's main client, except in 1953, and the largest source of Israel's imports. In 1955, 87 percent of Israel's exports to South America were sold to Argentina and 60 percent of its imports came from Argentina.

Within Argentina's trade relations with Middle Eastern countries, Israel also became the main market for Argentine exports to the region during that period. In 1953, Israel received no less than 86 percent of Argentina's sales to the Middle East. Nevertheless, Israel supplied an insignificant proportion of Argentina's imports except in 1950. In later years, when Argentina began to import oil from the Middle East, Israel was relegated to a place of lower importance, competing with Arab countries to be Argentina's main provider.

In the early 1950s, shipments of beef were primordial for Israel, as the country was still under conditions of austerity and suffered scarcity in various areas. When Tsur visited Israel, the country's minister of agriculture, Pinhas Lavon, reminded him that Argentina was the source of the meagre ration of meat received by the new state's citizens: "[Lavon] asked me to redouble my efforts in Argentina and Uruguay to guarantee that the freezer ships carrying meat depart regularly. Back then, this was not such an easy task, as the demand for meat was great in all European countries, which all vied for these exports. We had to appeal to all of our contacts in the president's office in Buenos Aires and in the Uruguayan government so that the inhabitants of Israel could get a taste of meat; as the holidays neared, telephone calls between Tel Aviv and Buenos Aires became more frequent."[87] Perón's Argentina continued to sell meat to Israel even during months-long droughts that severely affected the availability of meat for internal consumption, leading to a prohibition on the sale of meat on Fridays.

Aid from the first lady through the Fundación Eva Perón, whose budget she managed as she saw fit, was not economically substantial but it played a crucial symbolic role. As the economic difficulties that Argentina faced in 1949 forced the government to dramatically slash the budget for public services, the foundation, in theory a private fund, became the only state institution that was able to continue supporting various projects to improve the living conditions of the working class. As the real wages of workers began to lose their purchasing power, the foundation's social initiatives became of utmost importance. Seeking to improve Peronism's image abroad, the foundation sent aid shipments to Europe and other Latin American countries to support victims of disasters and other people in need. The shipments of food and clothing to the immigrants housed in transit camps in Israel were also part of this policy.[88]

In Tsur's first conversation with Evita, he told the first lady about the thousands of immigrants who had arrived during the first years of the nation's life and about the many difficulties that awaited them in the transit camps where they were lodged until permanent housing was ready. Between 1948 and 1951, Israel received some 690,000 immigrants, which duplicated the country's Jewish population. In light of the new country's economic hardships during that period, Tsur asked that the first lady ship specific commodities and products that he would pay in the local currency (pesos), in addition to shipments of meat that could be paid for in dollars. He also asked the first lady to authorize a shipment of wool blankets for the immigrants housed in tents. Evita replied to his request as follows: "Yes, of course I will give you that permission, even if this contradicts Argentina's currency regulations. I will go further by allowing for the shipment of clothing as well, so long as you don't use this authorization to send secondhand clothing, only good, new clothing, because it does not do honour to the Fundación Eva Perón to send shipments of clothing inferior to the best clothing that can be bought in this country … Mr. Minister, I will send all these goods free of charge in Argentine boats."[89]

If further proof were needed of the Perón regime's desire to publicly demonstrate its sympathetic attitude toward Israel, it could certainly be found in Eva Perón's gesture. The first lady made good on her promise by dispatching an Argentine cargo ship carrying 400 tonnes of blankets, an important item at a time of mass immigration to Israel. When the first lady died in July 1952, the DAIA published a message of condolence emphasizing how Evita had taken every opportunity to show her friendship toward the Jewish community and send generous help from the foundation to those in need in Israel.

Israeli diplomats made sure to emphasize that, "the shipments [from the Foundation] ... whose value can be estimated at hundreds of thousands of dollars, exceed comparable shipments to other countries (Lebanon, Italy, Greece...). The Argentine ship carried them free of charge, as the government covered these fees and took responsibility for the shipment."[90] After Evita's death, and due to the economic hardships that Argentina was experiencing at the time, fears spread in the Israeli legation that bilateral relations might cool off and that this would harm the successes of the economic agreements and modify the arrangements made for the use of funds collected by the United Jewish Appeal. To the relief of Israelis and of the Jewish community leaders, ties nevertheless continued to be strong so long as the Peronist regime was in power.

In November 1953, OIA leaders asked Perón to authorize the export to Israel of one thousand tonnes of commodities and goods to be paid in local currency – from the funds collected among the community – and to be shipped through the Fundación Eva Perón. This request originated from an earlier application that the United Jewish Appeal made to Manguel in mid-June, expressing thanks for "the generous assistance, both historic and humanitarian, to help us reach our goal, offered to us by the president of Argentina, and particularly from his beloved spouse, the deceased Eva Duarte de Perón, whose memory will be eternally blessed." Perón also approved that shipment.[91]

5

Support from Jewish Intellectuals and Media

Toward the end of the 1960s, Jacobo Kovadloff, then president of the Sociedad Hebraica Argentina (Argentine Jewish Association), decided to invite writer César Tiempo to give a talk to the club's members. Kovadloff's initiative spurred an intense debate among the institution's leadership, as some members argued against hosting an intellectual who had "sold out to Peronism." Tiempo did indeed give a talk at the Hebraica, but many in the establishment of the Jewish-Argentine community did not view his social and political identity as politically correct. A glance at the catalogue of César Tiempo's correspondence, held in the archives of Argentina's national library, reveals that the Hebraica sent the writer a large volume of letters and invitations throughout the 1930s but only one letter during the decade of Peronist administrations (1946–55).[1]

Some years later, in the 1970s, intellectual Samuel Rollansky invited various Jewish scholars to a gathering held in the library of the Instituto Científico Judío (IWO). During the conversation that took place, Rollansky mentioned the fact that this library's holdings did not include any of César Tiempo's books. The very same Jewish writer who, during the 1930s, had spearheaded the campaign against Gustavo Martínez Zuviría, the antisemitic writer and director of the national library who wrote under the pseudonym of Hugo Wast, was by now not worthy of having his books grace the shelves of the IWO.[2]

These anecdotes illustrate this book's central arguments, as it aspires to challenge, or at least to add nuance to, three commonplaces in historical studies and in popular images of Peronism: that all Jews were opposed to Perón, that all prestigious or influential intellectuals kept a distance from Peronism, and that the cultural supplement of the newspaper *La Prensa*, once the newspaper was entrusted to the CGT workers' confederation, was worthless and had little cultural significance due to its propagandistic nature.[3]

INTELLECTUALS AND PERONISM

Whether in literature or popular imagination, Peronism is most commonly characterized as a movement that is markedly "plebeian" and anti-intellectual. As many historians don't bother to differentiate between the birth and emergence of this popular movement and the subsequent phases of Peronist administrations, they paint a simplistic picture of "the divorce between the intellectual classes and Peronism during the decade spanning from 1945 to 1955."[4] According to this portrayal of Peronism, the only intellectuals who supported Peronism were extreme-right Catholic nationalists. As these intellectuals had adopted anti-liberal reactionary stances, they hoped that the charismatic colonel, with his statist and semi-corporatist ideas, would also espouse the defence of Catholicism and of more traditional cultural values so as to strengthen the national consciousness even as it was marred by foreign and external ideas. This stance is most frequently associated with Mario Amadeo, Gustavo Martínez Zuviría, Ernesto Palacio, Manuel Gálvez, and Delfina Bunge (Gálvez's wife, who was a writer), and Carlos Ibarguren.[5] Other members of the intelligentsia viewed Perón with distrust or, more typically, with a combination of horror and stupor, as if the identities of intellectual and Peronist were incompatible.

Recent studies nevertheless show that a good number of intellectuals, albeit a minority, had high hopes for Perón and the movement that bore his name, whereas nationalists, many of whom were part of the established oligarchy, began first to distance themselves from Peronism and then openly break ranks with him during his conflict with the Catholic Church. Some nationalists who clearly focused their attention on the masses and their needs and aspirations, such as Arturo Jauretche, Raúl Scalabrini Ortiz, and Atilio García Mellid, also sided with Peronism. The less consecrated Elías Castelnuevo, Nicolás Olivari, and César Tiempo belonged to a group of intellectuals who also supported

Peronism. During the 1920s, these three writers had belonged to the Boedo literary group, which ascribed a social function to literature. Their relations with Peronism therefore reflected their constant concern with social and working-class topics.

These intellectuals (some of whom had previously been active in the Argentine Communist Party), among others, were marginalized from Argentina's cultural scene – the majority of which opposed Perón – and were belittled by established intellectuals and the literary journals that they directed, as was the case with *Sur*, whose founder and director was Victoria Ocampo.[6] Similar scorn was expressed by the cultural supplements of prestigious newspapers or by organizations such as the Sociedad Argentina de Escritores (SADE; Argentine Society of Writers). As Flavia Fiorucci posits, these elite intellectuals considered that "being a Peronist was a crime against intellectual activity."[7] Faced with this hostility, Peronist intellectuals attempted to create a space of their own for their publications and intellectual activities. Several smaller-scaled initiatives were part of this broader effort: the establishment, as early as 1945, of the Asociación de Escritores Argentinos (Association of Argentine Writers), an organization representing nationalist writers; the launch of the cultural journal *Sexto Continente*; or the political magazine *Hechos e Ideas*, which was originally founded during the mid-1930s as a publication of the UCR and which ceased its activities in 1941 until it was launched anew in 1947 by a group of national popular intellectuals who supported Perón.[8] One could perhaps add to this list the magazine *Argentina de Hoy*, published by the Instituto de Estudios Económicos y Sociales (Institute for Economic and Social Studies). Many of this magazine's contributors had been Socialists and supported Peronism to a greater or lesser extent. This group included Juan Unamuno, Rodolfo Puiggrós, Eduardo Astesano, Isaac Libenson, Joaquín Coca, and many others. In addition to Olivari and Castelnuovo, the writers who contributed to this magazine included the Jewish-Argentines César Tiempo and Bernardo Ezequiel Koremblit.[9] The cultural supplement of *La Prensa*, under the CGT's leadership, must also be understood as part of that effort.[10]

All these literary and cultural publications indeed became increasingly partisan. They underwent a Peronization that left little room for voices that did not support Peronism or could not be tuned to the official line. It should come as no surprise that Scalabrini Ortiz complained in 1951 that Peronist intellectuals did not have "a crack, a trench from which to continue indoctrinating,"[11] as many of them had in fact become official spokespersons of sorts. Months before Perón was ousted, Tiempo faced increasing pressure, as can be deduced in the letter he sent to the Jewish-Argentine intellectual Máximo Yagupsky. When Tiempo was contemplating inclusion in the cultural supplement that he directed of an unpublished text authored by Cansinos Assens in which the author compared the Bible and the Iliad, the Odyssey, and the Aeneid, he wrote: "You wonder why I am reluctant to publish it in [the *La Prensa*] cultural supplement. The reason for this is very simple. This is because we no longer analyze 'parallel books' or 'parallel lives.' We are content with publishing articles and short stories for the least discerning readership … Sic transit."[12] Changes in the cultural milieu shine through in this quotation. Yet, as Tiempo clarified, he was never pressured to join the Justicialist Party.[13]

CÉSAR TIEMPO: THE PORTEÑO JEW

César Tiempo was born Israel Zeitlin in 1906 in Ukraine. His pseudonym is based on this name, as *Zeit* is "time" (*tiempo*) in Yiddish and German, and *lin* is the Yiddish verb "to cease" (*cesar*).[14] Before his first birthday, Zeitlin was already living in Argentina with his parents who had fled the pogroms and antisemitism in Tsarist Russia. His father gave him a pluralist education that sought to bridge his attachment to the Jewish tradition with his desire to integrate into the new host country's society. He took on the pseudonym César Tiempo early, as a teenager. From the age of 18, Tiempo participated in literary cafés and wrote his first poems. Two years later, he began to publish columns on Jewish issues in *La Nación*. Similarly to Alberto Gerchunoff, Tiempo's Jewish identity did not exclude him from publishing in a consecrated Buenos Aires newspaper. The words of Eliahú Toker convey eloquently how prolific Tiempo was in his writings and creative works: "hundreds of poems, six, seven tomes of news stories, real or imagined, nearly a dozen plays, some fifty film scripts, thousands of press columns in newspapers across the world."[15] Literature thus seemed to offer possibilities for integrating into Argentine society and, conversely, for bringing about a pluralist society in Argentina.

From the outset, Tiempo collaborated with the two main literary groups in the 1920s, the writers of Boedo and those of Florida (known for its slogan "art for art's sake"), exhibiting a clear preference for the former.[16] This group clearly manifested a greater awareness of the suffering of the masses. Its greatest virtue has been characterized as "that of disturbing, in a way that was iconoclast but not anarchic, the neat bookshelves that had been populated with the works of individuals that dominated the local cultural scene."[17] Tiempo's engagement with social causes brought him ever closer to marginalized social groups, leading him to collaborate with Peronism decades later. This context partly accounts for the focus of his first book-length poem "Versos de una…" (Verses of a…), published in 1926 under the feminine pseudonym of Clara Beter and written as the diary, in verse, of a Jewish sex worker with a social consciousness.[18] In the 1920s, prostitution was not yet illegal in Buenos Aires, and a good number of sex workers were known as *rusas* (Russian women) or *polacas* (Polish women) as they originated from those communities of Jewish immigrants. Tiempo's identification with this character of modest means led him to include in the poems an element drawn from his family history. The Boedo writers loved this type of socially oriented literature, authored by a Clara who stood apart from both her society of origin (Ukraine) and her host country's society (Argentina):

> To all, I give myself, but belong to no one;
> To win my daily bread, I sell my body
> What can I sell to keep whole
> My heart, my sorrows and my dreams? … At times
> I am even ashamed of crying
> When I realize how small my sorrows are
> Next to the world's immense sorrow.[19]

When Tiempo published *Libro para la pausa del sábado* (Book for the Saturday Break) in 1930 at the press owned by the Jewish editor Manuel Gleizer,[20] he won Buenos Aires's first municipal prize. Other books followed, also using Saturday as a metaphor for the weekly homage that porteño Jews offer to an Argentina that becomes, in these texts, a genuine Promised Land: *Sabatión argentino* (Argentine Sabbath, 1933), *Sábadomingo* (SaturdaySunday, 1938), and *Sábado pleno* (Full

Saturday, 1955). In his books as in his plays, Tiempo attempted to root Jewish immigrants in national life. *Sábadomingo*, according to Leonardo Senkman, represented a combination of the Jewish day of rest on Saturday and Argentines' traditional day of rest on Sunday.[21] All of Tiempo's work exalts the confluence between the Jewish and Argentine identities. Each of these was equally important for him and he was unwilling to sacrifice one in favour of the other.

Tiempo's exaltation of Saturday as a metaphor of his Jewish identity expressed this writer's style – "so porteño and so Jewish at once," in the words of Abrasha Rotenberg – one that would turn him into a literary symbol of Jewish urban immigration in Buenos Aires and was representative of a generation of Jewish-Argentine writers whose "Jewishness surged from them like a spring."[22] Tiempo's texts also aimed to reclaim pluralism, to infuse poetry into the everyday, and to sketch the lives of everyday people with compassion and tenderness. Many of his books' pages are peppered with phrases from Yiddish or lunfardo, Buenos Aires's slang.

As he reiterated time and again in characterizing his identity and expressing his opposition to xenophobic nationalists:

> Thousands of examples show us that the land in which one grows roots and finds fulfillment is much more influential than one's race ... The fact of being born Argentine, Ukrainian, or Guatemalan does not involve will or confer upon the beneficiary other prerogatives than those that can be obtained in function of one's talent, if one has some, or their work, if they fulfill it. The former act involves one's birth – this is linked to physiology – and the latter pertains to one's spirit or to reason. One of these involves outward growth, like that of a skyscraper, and the other, inward growth, like the metaphysical growth of a soul. One, in sum, is the fact of being, and the other, of becoming.[23]

By the mid-1930s, Tiempo had no more patience for the antisemitic offensive helmed by Hugo Wast and his fellow nationalists. In 1935, he published *La campaña antisemita y el director de la Biblioteca Nacional* (The Antisemitic Campaign and the Director of the National Library), in which he denounced Martínez Zuviría's books *Kahal* and

Oro, which offered fictionalized versions of the *Protocols of the Elders of Zion* and were typically set in Buenos Aires. This unequivocal condemnation of the racism of the most xenophobic wing of Argentine nationalism led Tiempo to engage in harsh polemics with nationalist groups such as the National Restorationist Guard and with writers such as Leopoldo Lugones, whom Tiempo identified with fascism.

During the period in which xenophobic nationalism peaked, Tiempo wrote two plays crystalizing his vision of the integration of Jews into Argentine society: *El teatro y yo* (The Theatre and I, 1931) and *Pan criollo* (Criollo Bread, 1937). In the latter, a character declares that, "Jewish blood and Argentine heart will sweeten the land that gives us our bread and elevate the love high above the grain stacks." This play won the national theatre prize awarded by the Comisión Nacional de Cultura (National Committee for Culture). In a curious twist, this committee was presided over by none other than the Catholic nationalist and fascist sympathizer Senator Matías Sánchez Sorondo, who had been minister of the interior during the administration of General José Félix Uriburu. Audiences and newspapers of all sorts, including nationalist ones, applauded this symbol of the "union of two races," the Jewish and the criollo. In this sense, Tiempo was firmly opposed to the idea of the racial melting pot, as he understood it not as an effort to integrate but, rather, an attempt to make difference disappear by denying it. Tiempo was a vocal critic of a sector of the Jewish bourgeoisie who, as their economic situation improved, embraced the idea of a racial melting pot in the hope of gaining acceptance from the country's elites and renounced their Jewish identity.

His work as an editor of journals is also worth mentioning. Tiempo was only 17 years old when he began to direct *Sancho Panza*. At 31, he became editor-in-chief of the literary magazine *Columna*, whose contributors were renowned Argentine writers – Alberto Gerchunoff, Macedonio Fernández, Arturo Capdevila, Luis Franco – and international writers such as Cansinos Assens, Stefan Zweig, Waldo Frank, and Jacques Maritain. One of the magazine's slogans was: "Prepared to make all sacrifices, except the sacrifice of truth." This maxim expressed Tiempo's vision of the editor's job and of the engaged intellectual. These understandings accounted for the decision of this Jewish-Argentine intellectual to take the reins of *La Prensa*'s literary supplement, once the Peronist government had expropriated this conservative newspaper (printed each morning) from the hands of the Gainza Paz family and entrusted it to the CGT.

LA PRENSA'S EDITORIAL TEAM: IN FAVOUR OF INCLUSION AND PLURALISM

Tiempo's decision to assume the role of editor-in-chief of the *La Prensa* cultural supplement spurred considerable polemic at the time and continues to do so. Some maintain, allegedly in "defence" of this intellectual, that his acceptance of this position was not driven by ideological motives but was motivated by personal interest, by questions of money or prestige. Yet Tiempo's identification with Justicialismo was congruent with his intellectual trajectory both before and after the 1950s, as reconstructed here. His awareness of social issues and the attention his work paid to subaltern social sectors, which led him to side with the Boedo writers in the 1920s, seem also to have been his motives for supporting Peronism in the 1940s and 1950s. Some traits of the Peronist movement were compatible with Tiempo's social awareness and his notion of culture – which was sufficiently broad to encompass both the intellectual production of the lettered elites and the manifestations of the people's sentiments – as well as with his identification with those most marginalized in society and their forms of cultural expression. Despite the rejection of Peronism by a good part of the organized Jewish community and among writers of that period, Tiempo seemed to see in the movement an opportunity to include marginalized groups in the citizenry.

The *La Prensa* cultural supplement offered Tiempo the possibility of opening the door to new voices or to those who had been relegated to the margins of Buenos Aires's cultural scene. As Tiempo recalled in a conversation with journalist and writer Osvaldo Soriano, published in *La Opinión*:

> I returned to Buenos Aires in 1951 and reported for various newspapers until 1952, when I began to direct the cultural supplement of *La Prensa* that had become the responsibility of the CGT. I remained in that post until 1955. I put up with

the resentment and hatred coming from all of the liberal forces, but I did give myself the pleasure of making a good supplement. I was not forced to become a member [of the Peronist party] and I hired a Communist as a layout artist. I published Quasimodo, Neruda, Gabriela Mistral, Amaro Villanueva, who was the Communist Party's candidate for governor of Entre Ríos. One day, [Colonel Jorge] Osinde, the director of the [police's] department of federal coordination, called me to tell me that I had turned *La Prensa* into a Communist organ. In response, I told him that this was the work I had agreed to do with General Perón, as he wanted to welcome all ideological tendencies and what-have-you. Of course, this was a lie.

In 1952, Perón travelled to Chile and I accompanied him on behalf of *La Prensa*. I went to visit Neruda, who was hospitalized, and he asked me to set up an interview with Perón for him. The two met and, on that occasion, Neruda gave me the poems of his *Odas elementales* [Elemental Odes] so that I could publish them. These poems stirred quite a hubbub. I remember that once I had to stop the presses at 3:00 a.m. due to one of Neruda's poems. The president of the board of directors came to speak to me in person. I told him that the general had given the order [to publish the poems] and abracadabra. At that time, an expression was in vogue among Peronists: "No corre" [it's a no-go], which had capriciously been attributed to the general. To me, it sounded like a hoax, so I began to use the opposite expression, "Corre por orden del general" [it's a go, ordered by the general], and everything went smoothly. No one even thought of questioning this. At the time, I was approached by a lot of people, by workers and trade union members, who brought me poems that paid tribute to Perón, but I never ran them.[24]

This quote eloquently attests to Tiempo's determination to pursue an editorial policy true to his ideological affinities when faced with pressures to conform to party lines. This independent positioning caused conflicts with some groups within Peronism, as Tiempo "did not behave as one who was strictly a militant. Indeed, he was not."[25] Not only did he reject apologists for Perón, he made a conscious effort to publish columns by collaborators originating from the leftist spectrum and from diverse ethnic groups, among them a lengthy list of Jewish writers.

In an article published in the US journal *Hispania* in early 1952 about Alberto Gerchunoff, author of the masterfully written novel *Los gauchos judíos* (The Jewish Gauchos), Tiempo wrote: "Enrique Méndez Calzada, the highly perceptive author of *El tonel de Diógenes* (The Barrel of Diogenes), often said that the best Argentine writers were Russians by birth or by background."[26] Tiempo followed this somewhat exaggerated and humoristic statement with a long list of Jewish-Argentine fiction writers, poets, playwrights, philosophers, sociologists, erudite scholars, exegetes, historians, and literary critics. The list included: Samuel Eichelbaum, Enrique Espinosa (the literary pseudonym of Samuel Glusberg), León Dujovne, José Rabinovich, Julia Prilutzky Farny, Lázaro Liacho, Bernardo Kordon, Luisa Sofovich, Samuel Tarnopolsky, Gregorio Berman, Lázaro Schallman, Carlos M. Grünberg, and others. It could be expected that Tiempo would invite some of these writers to contribute to the cultural supplement of *La Prensa*.

The index of the supplement's published collaborators does indeed reveal a high proportion of Jewish-Argentines – among them: Blackie (Paloma Efron), Nelly Kaplan, David José Kohon, Bernardo Kordon, José Rabinovich, Luisa Sofovich, Raquel Zipris, Enrique Dickman, José Isaacson, Sergio Leonardo, Lázaro Liacho, José Liberman, and Raquel Tibol. After Perón's ouster, Tiempo invited some of these writers to contribute to the literary page of the newspaper that he now directed, which was titled *Amanecer* and published every Saturday. Among them were Bernardo Ezequiel Koremblit, Germán Rozenmacher, and Sergio Leonardo.

As new voices were welcome in the *La Prensa* supplement, so were new topics. In addition to the typical columns on literature, poetry, theatre, film, philosophy, and music, the supplement included commentaries and reports on tango, sport, painting, short stories for children, photography, science and technology, and even fashion. In this regard, they echoed Tiempo's broader vision of culture in the second half of the twentieth century. This perspective, which combined canonical cultural forms with popular ones, constituted an alternative to the elitist approach of intellectuals such as Ocampo, Borges, or other great names of Argentine literary life at the time.

Tiempo's closest collaborators in the *La Prensa* cultural supplement included León Benarós, Julia Prilutzky Farny, and Bernardo Ezequiel Koremblit. Each of these three Jewish intellectuals who joined this Peronist cultural venture merits a brief biographical sketch.

León Benarós was born in 1915 in Villa Mercedes, in the province of San Luis, but grew up in Lomas de Zamora outside Buenos Aires. He then lived in La Pampa and Mendoza before settling down in the federal capital. His rich and varied work includes books of existential poetry such as *Décimas encadenadas* (Chained Tenths, 1962), *Memorias ardientes* (Burning Memories, 1970) and *El bello mundo* (The Beautiful World, 1981). He based his verse on popular speech when writing criollo "romances," which were praised by the future Nobel Prize for Literature laureate Pablo Neruda and Argentine novelist and essayist Manuel Mujica Láinez.[27] Benarós's social and national concerns came across in his song lyrics, which were featured on LPs aimed at broad audiences such as *15 canciones escolares* (Fifteen Songs for Schoolchildren), *Flores argentinas* (Flowers of Argentina), and *La independencia* (Independence). In addition, his folkloric song "La tempranera" was made famous by Mercedes Sosa when she sang it at the stately Teatro Colón. Some of his works were published under a variety of pseudonyms, one of them a woman's name, Sonia Bernal, as César Tiempo had done as well. Throughout his career, Benarós contributed to various journals such as *Sur*, *Nosotros*, *Lyra*, *Anales de Buenos Aires* (edited by Borges), *Conducta*, *Columna*, and *Continente*, among others. He died in 2012.

It is worth noting that he was a member of the "Tarja" group of poets, which, during the 1950s, developed a style of poetry that aspired to be "universal" while integrating "regional" elements from the Argentine northeast. Contrasting with the cosmopolitanism of Buenos Aires, these poets sought to reclaim regional poetry, elevating it to such a height that it transcended geographic boundaries. Contributors to the journal *Tarja* (1955–60) also expressed their interest in social topics.

Benarós's identification with Peronism became most explicit when he wrote the three tomes of *Cultura Ciudadana* (Citizen Culture), respectively titled *La sociedad argentina* (Argentine Society), *La cultura argentina* (Argentine Culture), and *La política argentina* (Politics in Argentina), textbooks intended to explain the meaning of Peronism to high school students.[28] Despite Benarós's involvement with the Peronist administration when it selected him to write these books, intellectuals and academics across the country did not boycott him in the years that followed. Quite the contrary. Historian Félix Luna, for example, welcomed him in the pages of the magazine *Todo es Historia* (Everything is History) from its inaugural May 1967 issue onward. For many decades, he prepared all the contents for a section titled "Cleo's Attic" in which he recounted historical anecdotes, or micro-histories, of the Argentine people.

In 1964, Benarós appeared with Borges in a documentary, directed by Solly Schroder, titled *Carlos Gardel, historia de un ídolo* (Carlos Gardel: The Story of an Idol). In this documentary, Benarós recalled: "There was one of my poems that Borges loved and knew by heart: it was the one about the life and death of the [caudillo] Chacho Peñaloza. I also dedicated a milonga to him and I am still a part of Vaccaro's excellent undertaking, the Asociación Borgeseana [Borgesian society]." His poem "Muerte de Juan Lavalle" (Death of Juan Lavalle) was published in the literary journal *Sur* (no. 149), to which Borges had close ties.

Benarós and Koremblit, unlike Tiempo, did not occupy prominent posts such as that of editor-in-chief of the cultural supplement of *La Prensa*; this may account for the fact that, unlike Tiempo, they had not been marginalized from or punished by their literary peers. Like Tiempo, they were already established writers before Perón's presidency. In November 1944, for example, a jury of the Club del libro (Book Club), which accepted works by these authors, included as members Jorge Luis Borges, Adolfo Bioy Casares, and Victoria Ocampo – three writers who would become notorious opponents to Peronism – in addition to Pedro Henríquez Ureña and Ezequiel Martínez Estrada.

Furthermore, when Benarós and Koremblit subsequently discussed their lives in interviews, or, more recently, in the biographies on their websites, they omitted any reference to their time at the Peronist *La Prensa*. Benarós, Koremblit, and Prilutzky Farny also differentiated themselves from Tiempo in that they never referred to Judaism or Jews in their literary works. A relative of Prilutzky Farny's speculated as follows: "It seems that Julia – for reasons unknown to me – did not like to talk about her Jewish identity. I don't know if she did this to avoid discrimination (for being a woman, Jewish, and a socialist) or for a more philosophical reason."[29]

Julia Prilutzky Farny was born in 1912 in Kiev, Ukraine, to a doctor (her mother) and an engineer (her father). Argentina became her home when she was still very young. Family friends included Spanish exile Miguel de Unamuno, the Socialist leader Alfredo Palacios (her godfather), and the painter Benito Quinquela Martín.

Prilutzky Farny is considered one of the most representative figures of the generation of poets active during the 1940s. She founded the cultural journal *Vértice* and, in 1941, her book *Intervalo* was awarded the Premio Municipal de Poesía (Municipal Prize for Poetry). In her literary works, she exalts love and deeply felt sentiments. As she had ties with Justicialismo, her book *El Escudo* (The Shield) compiled her poems about Juan and Eva Perón, and included the poem "Oración" (Prayer), which was read to mark the second anniversary of Evita's passing, at a massive public gathering held on 26 July 1954 along the 9 de Julio thoroughfare.

Prilutzky Farny was a contributor and theatre critic with a long list of Argentine and Latin American newspapers that included, among others: *La Prensa*, *La Nación*, *El Hogar*, *El Mundo*, and *Clarín*. In 1978, when Alberto Migré included poems from her *Antología del amor* (Anthology of Love) in the television series *Pablo en nuestra piel* (Pablo in our Skin), the book became a bestseller.[30] The writer passed away in 2002 at 90 years of age.

Bernardo Ezequiel Koremblit was born in 1917 in Buenos Aires (in a library, as he loved to add). At only 17 years of age, he was hired at the widely circulated newspaper *Crítica*, helmed by Natalio Botana. He continued to work at this daily until 1943, writing in the literary section during the final years. His comrades included Nicolás Olivari, Raúl González Tuñón, César Tiempo, Roberto Arlt, and Jorge Luis Borges.[31] During those years, he was also active in the Fuerza de Orientación Radical de la Joven Argentina (FORJA), an organization of young, progressive activists affiliated with the UCR, alongside Luis Dellepiane, Arturo Jauretche, Gabriel del Mazo, and Raúl Scalabrini Ortiz.[32]

After his departure from *Crítica*, Koremblit began to work at the Sociedad Hebraica Argentina in 1944. He strengthened his ties with

Borges, who wound up working in an office at the Hebraica for eighteen months. Borges had been employed at the Biblioteca Municipal Miguel Cané, located in the Almagro neighbourhood, from 1938 until 1946, when his anti-Peronist stance won him the designation of "Inspector of Caged Birds" from the municipal administration. Forced in this way to resign from his post, he found new employment at this Jewish-Argentine institution. During the 1960s, Koremblit directed the famous literary journal *Davar* and was also head of the cultural department of the Sociedad Hebraica Argentina.

Koremblit was a prolific writer who penned essays on humanistic topics as well as critical texts and political philosophy. He published, among other books, *La torre de marfil y la política* (Politics and the Ivory Tower), *Romain Rolland: humanismo, combate y soledad* (Romain Rolland: Humanism, Struggle, and Solitude), *Nicolás Olivari, poeta unicaule* (Nicolás Olivari: Single-Stemmed Poet); *Ensayo sobre Alejandra Pizarnik* (Essay on Alejandra Pizarnik), and *Eva o los infortunios del Paraíso* (Eva, or the Misfortunes of Paradise).[33] During the 1940s and 1950s, Koremblit had friends on the Left and friends on the Right, Peronist and anti-Peronist. César Tiempo, his "gran amigo del alma" (beloved friend and soulmate), wrote the prologue to his first book, *Ben-Ami, el actor abismal* (Ben-Ami, Terrible Actor).[34]

Yet, despite his friendships with socially engaged people, Koremblit was an elitist whose stance was closer to the Florida writers than the Boedo group, as he maintained that writers should not intervene in politics. Perhaps this played a role in the numerous prizes awarded him, including the Premio Nacional de Literatura (National Literary Award), the Premio Municipal (Municipal Prize), and awards from the Fondo Nacional de las Artes (National Arts Fund). In 1993, he was named director of the national library's cultural office. He was president of the Sociedad Argentina de Escritores and, briefly, of the Academia Nacional de Periodismo (National Academy of Journalism). He died in 2010.

AWAITING THE RETURN OF PERONISM

I was born in Dniepropetrovsk!
I care not when destiny

Rebuffs me
Argentine until the end!
I was born in Dniepropetrovsk.

Tiempo penned these verses in an attempt to challenge the xenophobia that was the hallmark of extreme-right Catholic nationalism. Like Alberto Gerchunoff and Carlos M. Grünberg, Tiempo was thoroughly Jewish, both in his education and in his beliefs. These three intellectuals also shared their explicit choice to become a part of Argentina's life as a nation. Their works emphasize the need for a pluralism that is generous and tolerant in a land mainly inhabited by immigrants. In this sense, and similarly to other Jewish-Argentine intellectuals or to the leaders of the OIA, Tiempo made efforts to offer to Jews in Argentina an approach to identity that valued Jewish and Argentine traits equally. Tiempo's espousal of Hispanic signifiers, such as his pseudonym, to express his identity was never tantamount to relinquishing his Jewish identity. He wrote on this matter in a letter addressed to journalist and writer Jacobo Timerman and explained that: "I'm not ashamed of my origins. On the contrary. My forebears are rabbis, tradition keepers, Talmudists, and exegetes. But my name is César Tiempo, a name that I adopted at the age of 15 and have continued to use all my life, against the preferences of Nazis and resentful people."[35]

The figure of Tiempo, and his work as director of the cultural supplement of *La Prensa* after the Peronist authorities expropriated it, are useful for adding nuance to some of the commonplaces that permeate historians' accounts and popular perceptions of Peronism alike, particularly the assumptions that all Jews were opposed to Perón, that all prestigious or important intellectuals had sought to distance themselves from Peronism, and that the cultural supplement of *La Prensa* had little value or cultural significance as it had been an organ for propaganda. In the 1940s and 1950s, a sizable number of Jews supported Peronism and paid a high price for that support, both during the decade of Peronist administrations and after Perón's ouster in September 1955. Tiempo was one such intellectual who was marked with the stigma of Peronism and saw the anti-subversive law applied to him by the military regime that followed Perón's. This barred him from nearly any possibility of participating in journalism or of continuing his activities as a writer.

This may account for why Tiempo has not received the recognition that he surely deserves in the Argentine cultural scene. People of letters, like the Jewish establishment, never forgave him for sympathizing with Peronism. This stance, in the words of writer and critic David Viñas, "cast a negative light upon him in the eyes of many colleagues and friends. Tiempo's wager was almost one for heterodoxy."[36] The main literary journals ignored Tiempo when he helmed the *La Prensa* cultural supplement. In his letter to Máximo Yagupsky, mentioned above, Tiempo wrote: "In a separate envelope, you will find a great book that I published with Argos and that was not commented on in *Davar*, or *Sur*, or in any other respectable journal. Fear of contamination." He followed this by asking Yagupsky whether the book could be reviewed in the journal *Comentario*.[37]

Once Perón was ousted, and as part of the persecution carried out by the Revolución Libertadora, the intellectuals who had collaborated with the "fugitive tyrant" became the target of attack and ridicule. One of these was César Tiempo:

Distorting his name,
As time is immutable,
César Tiempo, miserable,
Rests here, half rotting
On his tombstone: Peace, people think
But true peace: he of "La Prensa"[38]

In the years that followed, many doors were closed to Tiempo in cultural institutions, in newspapers and publishing houses, in film and theatre. "I withstood all the resentment and hatred from all the liberal forces," recounted Tiempo with bitterness.[39] It was only in the 1970s that he was able to return from this kind of forced exile. The newspaper *La Opinión* invited him to contribute reports and commentaries, and *Clarín* invited him into the columns of its supplement on "Cultura y Nación" (Culture and Nation). From the latter position, in June 1973, Tiempo reiterated his support for Peronism, which had just returned to power with the administration of Héctor José Cámpora: "Against the two giants' will to domination, with their aspiration to fragment man, to impose a single vision of their world and with the same horrific will to destroy everything, our land rises as the last bastion for freedom of conscience, for the respect of creative individuality, for the unequivocal rejection of the covetousness of imperialism."[40]

One month later, Tiempo was named by the third Peronist administration to the post of director of the Teatro Nacional Cervantes (National Cervantes Theatre). At that stage, the Jewish establishment's attitude toward Peronism was less hostile and the Sociedad Hebraica Argentina was among those who congratulated him on the new post.[41] He began to write and publish anew but his health was poor. His last book, *Manos de obra* (Working Hands), which portrayed the contemporary literary scene, was published posthumously in 1980, shortly after his death.

TELEVISION IN THE SERVICE OF PERONISM

The 1951 Peronist commemoration day known as Loyalty Day coincided with the launch of television in Argentina. This was a new medium that Peronism would use as a tool, as it already had done, at times to excess, with print media, radio airwaves, and cinema. The small screen also exemplified the progress and modernization of Peronism's new Argentina. The broadcasts of the newly launched Canal 7 (Channel 7) were linked to another Jewish-Argentine personality.

Jaime Yankelevich had played a central role in the emergence and development of commercial radio in Argentina and now became a trailblazer of television broadcasting in the country. His story is that of a self-made man who went from being a poor immigrant to a rich entrepreneur as owner of Radio Belgrano, founder of Argentina's first broadcasting chain, and director general of the state-owned radio channel during the first two Peronist administrations. Despite the weight of his contribution, little has been written about his life or his ties with the Peróns. Two pioneering works by Andrea Matallana compare Yankelevich with David Sarnoff and William Paley, respectively the creators of the NBC and CBS channels, and help us to understand this protagonist of Argentine history.[42]

It was between the two world wars that radio developed the fastest. Its trajectory in Argentina was very similar to that of radio in Europe and the United States. In the early 1920s, a radio set was a luxury good available only to a small market, but by the 1930s it was the most purchased of household appliances, becoming massively popular during the 1940s.[43] As the radio became increasingly popular, it shaped audiences of listeners who could potentially be transformed through the experience of listening to the radio. Yankelevich was not solely a businessman but a leader capable of launching associations and collaborations tied to the national radio industry and of establishing international ties. He organized conferences in Latin America on radio broadcasting and established a network of radio stations across Argentina. In 1937, he successfully organized the first Argentine radio channel, which stood out both for its size and its featuring of different musical, artistic, and religious genres. As Yankelevich understood Argentine popular culture, he contributed to its development and creation. His entrepreneurial and leadership skills turned him into a key player in the Perón government, which promptly recognized the power of radio as an element capable of generating political unity. Additionally, Yankelevich's profile as a national entrepreneur and his Jewish identity were broadly compatible with the head of state's ideas and projects.

FIRST STEPS IN ARGENTINA

As with so many other Jews who immigrated to Argentina during the late nineteenth century, the family of Jaime Yankelevich fled the murders and arbitrary impositions of Russian czarism. His parents, Felipe and Emilia, were from Sofia, Bulgaria, where six of their seven children were born. The family faced economic hardships and religious persecution, as they were a minority. This prompted Jaime's parents to immigrate to Argentina in search of a better future. The third of seven brothers, Jaime was just shy of 3 years old when his family arrived in Buenos Aires in 1899. They first stayed at the Hotel de Inmigrantes in Retiro, known at the time as the "hotel with the rotunda." They subsequently settled in Paraná, Entre Ríos, where they opened a family-run general store in which each member of the family had a role. Their clientele mainly came from the nearby small agricultural settlements.

It was in Paraná that Jaime learned to speak Spanish as if it was his mother tongue, sometimes interspersing words of Yiddish or Bulgarian.

While he attended primary school, he helped out in the family business. In 1914, he was the first of his family to move to Buenos Aires. His brother Jacobo would follow shortly afterward. Jaime first lived in a tenement house in the downtown area. At the time, the downtown core was home to a broad range of cinemas, theatres, bars, and the first dancehalls. Within this context of cultural and commercial effervescence, Yankelevich got his first job at the La Perla movie house on Independencia Avenue. He was tasked with spinning the projector handle. He also worked as electrician at the Teatro Nacional.

For a period of two years, he seemed to have been in charge of various tasks in cinemas and theatres of the downtown area. In 1918, once he had saved up enough money, he partnered with his brother Jacobo to open an electric equipment shop on Callao Street. In 1920, he opened a business selling electrical parts and appliances – Casa Yankelevich, on Entre Ríos Avenue – as the sole proprietor. As he got married that same year, he turned the rear section of the shop into his family home. Prior to this, he had always lived in more modest quarters.

Yankelevich married Carolina Chichilnisky. On their wedding day, Jaime couldn't afford to have their names engraved on the wedding bands. Carolina had come to Argentina from Odessa at only 17 years of age and was a seamstress who worked on commission. She lived in a boarding house in the heart of Villa Crespo, at the corner of Acevedo and Corrientes. Three of the couple's children were born in the home they had made behind the shop floor of 940 Entre Ríos: Paulina, Samuel, and Raquel. In keeping with the family-run business model, Jaime's wife helped make lampshades.

As Jaime continued to sell electrical products, he began to sell more and more items linked to radio broadcasting. Toward 1922, Casa Yankelevich ran advertisements in the magazine *Caras y Caretas*. When it became clear to Yankelevich that it was quite profitable for him to manufacture his own parts for sale, he made it his focus, requesting credit for twenty-four hours and repaying it once the parts were sold. He quickly became Latin America's main importer of parts for radio broadcasting. His shop sold electrical wiring and parts, lightbulbs, phonographs, gramophones, telephones, and radios.

His commercial acumen led him to take advantage of the "fight of the century" in 1923, between Luis Ángel Firpo and Jack Dempsey: to promote the sale of radios in his business, he place a radio in the entrance of Entre Ríos Avenue to broadcast the fight publicly. By 1926, Yankelevich was a prosperous business owner. In 1930, his family moved to a larger house nearby, where his fourth son Miguel was born.

INITIATION INTO BROADCASTING

Although the Yankelevich family lore recounts that Jaime set up the purchase of Radio Nacional on the very same day that he visited the broadcaster's office to repair a transmitter, this anecdote does not match the facts. Yankelevich had become interested in radio advertisements as early as 1926 when he bought advertising slots with Radio Nacional, Grand Splendid, and (Radio) Cultura. The ads proved surprisingly successful. On the basis of this success, he bought a daily thirty-minute slot. When he advertised in the *Revista Telegráfica* (Telegraphic magazine), the one-page ad prompted a turnout so massive that it forced him to close the shop the next day.

The prosperity of Yankelevich's business coincided with an offer from the owner of Radio Nacional, who, as he needed to sell off the station, made Yankelevich an offer of which the latter took full advantage. A sum for the purchase was agreed upon, as was a schedule of payments. On 5 February 1927, Yankelevich became the owner of Radio Nacional and promptly implemented changes that increased the broadcaster's impact: he opted for transmissions of live musical performances over pre-recorded music, he created a system of economic incentives for artists, thus eliminating ad honorem participation and making radio a part of these artists' professional development. In 1928, he moved the studios from Flores to the downtown area on Estados Unidos Street.

During the 1930s, Yankelevich updated the station's broadcasting equipment by travelling to Europe to purchase the most suitable parts. He also allowed provincial radio broadcasters to air his programs free of charge as a strategy to expand the broadcaster. Germany was his main source for up-to-date equipment, and after Hitler's rise to power in 1933 he turned instead to the Netherlands, Belgium, the United States, and France.

Upon the initiative of Yankelevich, construction began on the building known as "the Palace," a new complex that occupied an entire block on Belgrano Avenue. Four sixty-five-metre-tall transmitter towers soared above and the complex also included two diesel motors and alternators to generate electricity. Studios were rented out to other broadcasters. In 1931, Yankelevich organized the first Cadena Argentina de Broadcasting (Argentine Broadcasting Network) when he purchased several other broadcasters in the capital, as well as Córdoba, Rosario, Mendoza, and Bahía Blanca. In 1933, the broadcaster changed its name to Radio Belgrano after a decree prohibited the use of the word "national" for private activities.

The new name was chosen after an innovative contest in which Yankelevich summoned listeners to submit their ideas and win a prize. Yankelevich deployed a similar commercial acumen when he organized a raffle of radios among his listeners. Radio became competitive and dynamic market. Radio El Mundo, owned by the British Haynes publishing group, began broadcasting in 1935. Different radio channels had distinctive features. Radio Belgrano had some "high culture" traits but was inherently geared toward a large audience, and tango was predominant in its musical programing. Radio El Mundo catered to the consumer tastes and needs of a listener market oriented more soberly toward high culture.[44] The Haynes group's broadcaster nevertheless represented an important rival and an industry benchmark due to its use of recent technologies.

The Haynes group also purchased the newspaper *El Mundo* (The World) and several magazines such as *El Hogar* (The Home). But this media conglomerate was to suffer a fate very different than that of Yankelevich's emporium. As the owners of the Haynes group opposed Peronism, they were incapable of resisting the restrictions imposed on the media by the new political movement. The companies they owned weakened and disappeared. The Haynes group had criticized Yankelevich in its publications, questioning his business model and techniques. Natalio Botana, in his newspaper *Crítica*, also voiced criticisms of the businessman, and Radio del Estado, launched in 1937, became another of Yankelevich's competitors. In response to such competition, that same year Yankelevich retooled his broadcaster's programming, adding a variety of content including political speeches, listener contests, stock-market grain quotes, and live theatre sketches.

As Yankelevich had done in the past, the broadcaster's new building was connected to its owner's family home. His in-laws also resided there and his brothers visited regularly. Although these family members had no connection to the station, they partook in the prosperity ensuing from it and celebrated Jewish holidays and family occasions together. Yankelevich had no formal schooling; he was self-taught and persistent. He loved to listen to classical music, jazz, and tango. He showed his employees solidarity by granting them loans so they could buy their own homes. At the same time, he was demanding in regard to their performance in the workplace.

EXPANSION AND INTEGRATION

When Yankelevich was but an ordinary radio listener, he had already identified the commercial potential of this innovative means of communication. This intuition led him to buy airtime to advertise his businesses. Once he became a radio entrepreneur with his own broadcaster, he made efforts to expand the technology's commercial potential by targeting a mass audience.

Throughout the 1930s, his broadcaster's programs featured performances by international artists as well as national stars. He founded the Productora Cinematográfica Argentina Río de la Plata (Argentina Río de la Plata Movie Production Company), which produced movies and plays, and also founded the magazine *Antena*, which covered the entertainment world and used a format similar to magazines like *Radiolandia* or *Sintonía* but with most of its pages devoted to the radio world – in particular its owner's commercial universe. Yankelevich thus promptly achieved the vertical integration of the radiophonic industry, from the manufacture and sale of radios to the production of radio programming, by developing his operations on both ends of the industry (production and dissemination) into a continuum of businesses that shaped the artistic scene as well as the realm of commercial and entertainment content. In the 1940s, Yankelevich incorporated an advertising agency that produced jingles to meet the needs of companies that advertised on his broadcaster's airwaves.

During the 1930s, Yankelevich owned one of the largest broadcasters in Argentina as well as fourteen relay stations across the country. He also forged agreements with the main international news agencies. By the 1940s, he had become a central player in every sector of the radio industry and also had considerable influence in the artistic world.

Yankelevich's broadcaster was eminently geared toward working- and middle-class audiences and deployed great flexibility in showcasing varied musical forms, whether artistic or religious. The artists he featured had large and loyal followings. He broadcast radio theatre to great success after the genre's emergence in the 1930s and attracted wide audiences, with plays generally broadcast in multiple episodes. In Argentina, radio theatre initially drew from *gauchesca*, a genre that portrayed the gaucho as a heroic character representing national traits and which drew criticisms from liberals who considered this stance to be romanticized and unrealistic. Radio theatre became the stage upon which Yankelevich and Evita formed a bond, which in turn contributed to Evita's positive attitude toward Jewish-Argentines.

Yankelevich pioneered live radio (and later television) broadcasts of fútbol matches, as well as broadcasts of voices from the Catholic Church, which were featured in the program of Monsignor Dionisio Napal, a controversial figure who was not at all friendly to Jews. To rival this star host netted by Radio Belgrano, Radio Splendid hired the anticommunist priest Gustavo Franceschi of Acción Católica. Industry magazines often featured photos of the radio magnate signing contracts, meeting with other Argentine businessmen, or stepping off a boat upon returning from a trip abroad, thus turning him into a celebrity. His style of programming was the matrix that guided Argentine radio broadcasting until the late 1950s.

BETWEEN STATE AND RADIO

Until 1940, the state-owned Radio del Estado could only broadcast within the bounds of the country's capital. As had been the case in Europe and in the United States, since the 1920s the Argentine government acknowledged that radio broadcasting in general, and the content being broadcast in particular, should be subject to state legislation. The administration of President Hipólito Yrigoyen had drafted such legislation in 1929, instituting a system of licences that owners of broadcasters could purchase for a fee of 5,000 pesos per year. This system nevertheless had some legal shortcomings. In 1933, the government sanctioned the Reglamento de Radiocomunicaciones (Radio Communications Rulebook) as a temporary measure until legislation could be passed to regulate the system in its entirety. Under the framework laid out in the Reglamento, the licences granted to radio broadcasters were considered to be "precarious,"[45] and in 1938 the government made efforts to draft legislation that would restrict the private interests of radio broadcasters. This is when Yankelevich met with other owners of radio stations in an attempt to forge ties with President Roberto Ortiz, in order to protect his own situation.

In 1940, the government issued a decree mandating the creation of new broadcasters in the cities of the country's hinterland. A call for bids was issued as part of a contest to award the various licences. This effort aimed at slotting the system of broadcasters into the nation's agenda. In 1941, in the midst of the Second World War, the Castillo administration decreed that businesses that operated networks of radio broadcasters had to be "clearly Argentine." This went against two of the main players in radio broadcasting at the time: the Bulgaria-born Yankelevich, of Radio Belgrano, and Emilio Karstulovic, of the Haynes group. Ultimately, this measure was reversed due to opposition from the radio broadcasters. Toward the end of 1941, the government's interference in the selection of content for broadcast via radio became manifest when it denied Yankelevich's request to broadcast speeches from the United States supporting the anti-Nazi war effort. Yankelevich's name appeared in the *New York Times* in a report that mentioned the fact that the Ministry of the Interior had prohibited him from broadcasting the words of President Franklin D. Roosevelt.[46]

Following the June 1943 military coup, the government tightened its grip on media by passing a decree mandating the creation of a new Secretariat for Press and News to be housed in the Ministry of War. This department's mandate included a prohibition on broadcasts of such content that it judged to be inadequate – a measure it exercised, for example, when it censored broadcasts from the Allied forces in mid-1944. Yankelevich made efforts to adapt to this new situation by looking for ways to foster communication with the government.

Eva Duarte played a crucial role in this. The future first lady, then a singer and actress, had launched her artistic collaboration with Radio Belgrano in 1937 and, after a brief period working at the rival Radio El Mundo, she returned to Yankelevich's station to star in the radio drama "La amazona del destino" (The Amazon of Destiny). Yankelevich sought to build political capital based on Evita's connections with members of the military government, beginning with her friendship with Colonel Aníbal Imbert, a notable member of the GOU who was named by the military government to oversee and control radio, and subsequently through her romantic liaison with Juan Perón.[47] In late 1943, Perón was treated as a guest of honour when he visited the studios of Radio Belgrano.

In 1944, during the administration of Edelmiro Farrell and in the aftermath of the earthquake that severely affected the province of San Juan, Perón launched, from his post at the head of the Secretariat of Labour and Welfare, a solidarity campaign in which he enjoined artists to participate. Jaime Yankelevich actively supported this campaign, through which Perón gained a high degree of visibility across the nation.[48] From that point on, the future president became a regular on the broadcaster's airwaves through which he communicated his ideas. Yankelevich supported the government out of a desire to protect his interests. This motivated his inclusion on Radio Belgrano's airwaves of the radio drama "Hacia un futuro mejor" (Toward a Better Future), which praised the accomplishments of the Secretariat of Labour and Welfare.[49]

At least three factors are crucial for understanding how Jaime Yankelevich became a key figure in furthering Peronism's media policy. The first was his thorough knowledge of the radio industry, which the owner of Argentina's first nationwide radio station had earned through experience. This knowledge had enabled him to enter into exchanges with earlier administrations. President Pedro Pablo Ramírez used the microphones of Radio Belgrano in 1942 to address Argentines on the holiday of 12 October. Members of the military government paid frequent visits to Radio Belgrano's studios. To gauge radio's reach and the government's interest in this medium, it should be recalled that by 1940 Argentina had thirteen million inhabitants, with one million radios in use at the time and another 200,000 sold every year. Purchases of radios increased from one year to the next, to such an extent that estimates suggest that one out of every two Argentine homes had one.[50] In addition to Yankelevich's industry knowledge, he had proven himself capable of adapting to changing political contexts.

Second, Yankelevich had had the opportunity of dealing personally with both Perón and actress Eva Duarte, the colonel's future wife who worked at Radio Belgrano. The young actress began her activities at Radio Belgrano in 1937 as part of the musical group Remembranzas, and subsequently hosted a film contest sponsored by the broadcaster. After a brief period away from radio, Eva Duarte returned to Radio Belgrano in 1943 with her own company to write, produce, and voice radio dramas. Her works dramatized the life stories of women who had made a significant contribution to history. In 1944, Eva would play a protagonist in the aforementioned radio drama, "Hacia un futuro mejor."

In 1944, Radio Belgrano paid tribute to Evita for her career with the broadcaster. In early June of that year, she was featured on the cover of *Antena*, the publication showcasing the Yankelevich group's radio programming. Furthermore, the secretariat that Perón helmed lent its support to the Asociación Radial Argentina (Argentine Radio Association), over which Eva presided.[51] Perón's mother, who did not live in the federal capital, rented a suite from Yankelevich in an apartment building that he had built and opened in 1944. The entrepreneur and his family lived on one of the building's floors, and their daughter Raquel, by then married, lived on another floor. When Perón's mother stayed in that apartment during her visits to Buenos Aires, the media and onlookers followed her as though she were a celebrity. Yankelevich made sure that the doorman donned a uniform during her stay. These facts are fundamentally important in light of the high degree of personalism characteristic of Argentine political culture. Yankelevich and Perón mutually respected one another.

Third, Yankelevich was a successful Argentine entrepreneur whose skills in organization and leadership were crucial to the success of joint ventures. In this regard, he may be compared to the figure of Jewish-Argentine José Ber Gelbard, examined in the next chapter. General Perón also valued the fact that Yankelevich was Jewish and had international visibility. After all, for Perón, ties with Israel and with the local

Jewish community were a means to boost the legitimacy of Argentina as a democracy in the postwar world.

Yankelevich's circle of professional collaborators included a minority of Jewish-Argentines. Julio Korn was one such Jewish-Argentine collaborator. It was no secret that Yankelevich was Jewish. He was not a practising Jew and did not observe Sabbath, instead spending all day Saturday at the broadcaster – but he did feel nevertheless that he was part of the Jewish-Argentine community. He supported the Hospital Israelita with a monthly donation, along with various other Jewish community institutions and non-Jewish Argentine institutions. He made monetary contributions to these organizations and broadcast their events free of charge.[52] It seems that he used his direct access to Perón to promote the interests of the Jewish community on numerous occasions. Similarly to Rabbi Amram Blum, he discussed the necessity of granting a leave from military service to Jewish recruits on Yom Kippur.

PERONISM, THE MEDIA, AND RADIO

The first couple of years of Perón's administration, 1946–48, coincided with the largest expansion of the cultural industry in Argentina's history. Statistically, this growth was even greater than that of the 1960s.[53] In this context, Peronism imposed its own style, not only in Argentine politics but also in the media system that developed during that period. Paradoxically, the media opposed Perón when he came to power in 1946, but he had their support when he was overthrown in 1955.[54]

Mirtha Varela has identified three basic means through which Peronism used mass media: the expropriation of newspapers (as we saw in the case of *La Prensa*), the economic and political concentration of radio broadcasting, and the permanent presence of the figures of Perón and Evita.[55] These measures were implemented simultaneously and strengthened political control over the media during the last phase of the Peronist administration. During Perón's first administration (1946–51), the media system took shape. During his second administration (1952–55), this system was standardized and configured in accordance with Peronist ideology. In order to achieve its objectives, the government created two organizations: the Secretaría de Prensa y Difusión de la Presidencia (Press and News Secretariat), housed in the president's office and in charge of handling all aspects of political propaganda, and the Ministerio de Communicaciones (Communications Ministry), in charge of technical aspects.[56] Very little content was actually broadcast without having been subjected to regulations.

Perón had taken interest in the mass media from the time of his directorship of the Secretariat of Labour and Welfare (1944–46), when he pushed forward the professional code for journalists. In 1945, the Farrell administration created the Telenoticiosa Americana (TELAM) news agency as an alternative to US agencies and, a few days before handing the presidency over to Perón, it also approved the "Manual de Instrucciones para las Estaciones de Radiodifusión" (Instruction Manual for Radio Broadcasters). These guidelines provided specifications on how programming content should be broadcast so as to maintain the state's and nation's interests over commercial and private ones. Seeking to mould the mass media system as he had done with the unions, Perón simultaneously implemented certain measures to restrict the system and others to strengthen it. Restrictive measures included censorship and the concentration of media and capital goods related to media. A classic form of this concentration was the transfer of broadcaster-owned shares via the purchase of 51 percent of them by an individual close to the government. This process involved various actions: putting pressure on owners of media companies, threats, closures, and union strikes. The measures that strengthened the system involved credits and other incentives.[57] In this context of government-led media concentration, *La Prensa* (up until its expropriation) and *La Nación* became firm opponents of the government.

The government's strategy vis-à-vis the mass media also affected radio and, therefore, Yankelevich. By 1945, Argentina had three large radio broadcasters that could reach the entirety of the nation's territory. Each of these brands – Radio Belgrano, Radio El Mundo, and Radio Splendid – had separate owners. As businesses, these broadcasters had adopted a business model based on the sale of advertisements, and this allowed them to consolidate a circuit of artists that included Carlos Gardel (signed to Radio Belgrano until his tragic death in June 1935) and whose popularity ensured high audience quotas during prime time. This situation changed when Peronism came to power, as the private and commercial strategy was substituted with an expansion of radio in the service of the state and its political interests.[58]

The government required that broadcasters transmit from the national channel, Radio del Estado, during prime time schedules. In 1947, it used the strike of the Federación de Trabajadores del Espectáculo Público (Federation of Live Entertainment Workers) to force radio broadcasters to suspend all their activities until they agreed to rebroadcast the national channel. Although the strike was subsequently declared illegal, it allowed the government to make progress in its takeover of the majority of private enterprises. The broadcasters' owners thus came to be state employees entrusted with the leadership and administration of the firm.[59] This is precisely what happened to Jaime Yankelevich. His broadcaster was the most popular with Argentine listeners when it was suspended, intervened, and finally sold to the state. Yankelevich's situation was exceptional, as in 1948 he became Director General Coordinador (Director General), employed by the government and in charge of coordinating all broadcaster licences.

CONFLICT AND ADAPTATION

The scholarly research undertaken by Arribá asserts that Radio Belgrano was suspended because it hosted on its airwaves criticisms of the government; yet Arribá does not put forward evidence that would allow us to evaluate this statement.[60] Most of the available literature typically emphasizes a specific event as the catalyst for this process, which ultimately led to the transfer of Radio Belgrano to the state. In 1947, Perón gave a speech on national radio during which he took a moment to wish his wife well on her upcoming trip to Europe. The Radio Belgrano broadcast of this speech was interrupted, and someone said, "I don't believe a thing, it's all lies." As a result, the government shuttered the broadcaster and suspended its activities for a month. Following the suspension, the licences granted to the broadcaster were declared expired. For a year, Yankelevich contended with challenges to the legitimacy of his licences. At the same time, lawsuits were launched against him for tax evasion, threatening his financial stability. This situation led Yankelevich to sell his network of broadcasters to the state.

The broadcaster appealed the lawsuit before the Supreme Court but the case would only be resolved in 1953, after Yankelevich's death.

The pressure on Yankelevich began as the Peronist administration decided to take over the country's broadcasters. His offer to the state for purchase of the channel was compatible with the strategy adopted by the Ministry of Communications helmed by Oscar Nicolini, who preferred purchasing broadcasters' physical premises to shuttering them for political reasons. Nicolini's strategy allowed the government to continue to use these facilities. The transfer of Radio Belgrano to the state occurred on 14 October 1947, and Yankelevich was made Director General not long after. In this new position, he had to abide by the government's programming preferences and run the content it provided. A relative of Minister Nicolini sat as president of the company's board.

Not long after the Radio Belgrano sale, Radio El Mundo and Radio Splendid each underwent a similar process. Pointing to their monopolistic aims, the government denounced the companies' licences as expired, and the transfer to the state (via the sale of the companies' facilities) took place shortly afterward. Some accounts of these expropriations adopt a more apologetic or militant tone, arguing that the owners freely decided to sell.[61]

After having sold his broadcaster's installations to the state in 1947, Yankelevich was elected president of the Interamerican Association of Broadcasters (IAB). This position brought him international visibility. In 1949, for example, he met with the US director of the Office of Foreign Relations, who was interested in reversing the prohibition instituted by Perón on tourism advertisements on national broadcasters. His duties as IAB president conflicted with the position of the Asociación de Radiodifusoras Argentinas (ADRA; Argentine Association of Radio Broadcasters), over which he also presided. The tension stemmed from the IAB's criticisms of the Peronist government's approach to mass media and freedom of expression. In September 1948, the conservative Congress member Reynaldo Pastor asked the government to explain the lack of freedom in mass media and mentioned a statement from the IAB denouncing the de facto annulment of freedom of expression in the country.[62] Yankelevich opposed the IAB's attitude and, as a result, both ADRA and he himself left the interamerican association.

BRINGING TELEVISION TO ARGENTINA

While the beginnings of radio in Argentina were the result of private initiatives, the state was responsible for bringing television to the country.[63] In 1951, the government tasked Yankelevich with analyzing the potential cost of launching television broadcasts in Argentina. Earlier initiatives, such as one led by shoe entrepreneur Martin Tow in 1945, had proved futile, but Yankelevich promised that he could generate a network of thirty broadcasters.

In 1951, a portable transmitter arrived in Buenos Aires. It was located inside a truck, upon the exterior of which was printed the slogan "The Voice of Hope." The cost of the broadcasts was covered by Radio Belgrano, and the transmitting antenna was installed in the building of the Ministry of Public Works. That same year, on 17 October, the celebrations in the Plaza de Mayo to mark the Day of Peronist Loyalty were broadcast on television. On 18 November 1951, a fútbol match was broadcast for the first time on Argentine television. The match, between San Lorenzo and River Plate, ended in a 1-1 draw, and was broadcast from the Gasómetro Stadium by LR3 Canal 7 under the oversight of Jaime Yankelevich. Under the slogan "Everpresent in the Manifestation of Argentine Sport," the state-run petroleum company Yacimientos Petrolíferos Fiscales (YPF) sponsored the broadcast. The camera following the action was directed by Samuel Yankelevich and overseen by Max Koelble.[64] There had been no match the previous Sunday, 11 November, due to the presidential elections in which Perón was re-elected (again running with Juan Hortensio Quijano as vice-president, he bested the UCR's Ricardo Balbín and Arturo Frondizi). That election day, Argentine women exercised their right to vote for the first time in the country's history – including Eva Perón, from her hospital bed in Lanús.

The first television channel was operated from the facilities of the radio broadcasters and was initially called LR3 Radio Belgrano TV Canal 7. It is estimated that, at the time, Yankelevich imported into Argentina some 2,500 television sets.[65] Two years after the launch of television in Argentina, the country boasted 33,000 sets, a number that by 1957 had more than doubled to 75,000.[66] In the early years, the few available receivers had been placed in selected bars and businesses,

Figure 5.1 José Ber Gelbard and his political archrival José Lopez Rega.

where audiences would gather to watch. In 1954, Copehard Argentina, the country's first factory dedicated to manufacturing television sets, opened its doors.[67]

Only a few months after the first television broadcast in Argentina, Jaime Yankelevich died at the age of 58 in the city that had witnessed his impressive rise. His passing was acknowledged in the *New York Times*. In the process of distributing the estate to his inheritors, his properties were divided up and the empire he had built was taken apart. From that point on, television developed gradually in Argentina and, up until 1960, the state-owned Canal 7 was the only television broadcaster. A street in the Canal 7 complex is named after Yankelevich, as is a plaza in the neighbourhood of La Boca.

After the fall of Peronism in 1955, the new government launched a restructuring of mass media in order to dismantle the system that Peronism had created. Licences were revoked and the broadcasters once again changed ownership. The Junta Consultiva Nacional (National Consultative Junta) was convened in order to investigate the activities of private broadcasters. This junta prepared a report in which it levied criticisms against Yankelevich (who obviously could not defend himself from the grave). Even in the absence of convincing evidence, he was accused of tax evasion and portrayed as an "employee on Perón's payroll."[68]

6

Support from Jewish Unionists and Businessmen

When telling the story of Jewish experiences in Latin America in general, and in Argentina in particular, historians typically characterize the Jewish community as homogeneously middle- or upper-class. The focus on a people's history of highly successful social and economic integration only bolsters this social positioning. Jewish Argentines are typically portrayed as a social group that swiftly climbed the social ladder in a manner that eluded other ethnic groups. This portrayal is premised on an exaggeration that obscures certain actual phenomena and diverges from the socioeconomic realities that marked the lives of most Jewish-Argentines during the first half of the twentieth century. Just as this dominant assumption has led historians to presume that the lives of working-class Jews and poor Jews hold no interest for them, historians have also failed to notice the thousands of working-class Jews that supported Peronism during the mid-1940s, when the movement was in its infancy.

Furthermore, although the leadership of the organized Jewish community remained largely ambivalent toward the Peronist administration and the Justicialist movement, Jewish leaders from various workers' organizations identified with Peronism and came to occupy an important role in mobilizing popular support for this new political project. Ángel Perelman is the best known of these leaders. Perelman, who founded the Unión Obrera Metalúrgica (Metalworkers' Union) in 1943 and served as its first secretary, famously contributed to the marches that workers held on 17 October 1945, which were instrumental in shaping the political coalition that won the general elections in 1946.

The little we know about Perelman comes from his own memoirs, *Cómo hicimos el 17 de octubre* (How We Staged October 17), first published in 1962.[1] A self-identified worker-activist, Perelman followed in the footsteps of a family tradition of political activism. His father had been a member of the Communist Party up until 1935 when, according to his son, he abandoned the discipline of party activism, disappointed by the new "reformist and antinational" strategy that the party had adopted in line with the "popular front" politics of international pro-Soviet communism. Ángel's negative view of this antinational orientation of Argentine communism would be crucial to shaping his perception of how the Argentine working class might most effectively fulfill its aspirations.

Ángel Perelman was 10 years old when he began work in a metal factory. He had no choice but to give up his studies and begin an apprenticeship at the factory when his father lost his job due to the impact of the worldwide economic depression of 1929–30. In *Cómo hicimos el 17 de octubre* – his defence of Peronism – Perelman described the misery that permeated the "villas desocupación" (early shantytowns) throughout the country's capital in the early 1930s. He evokes how the families of unemployed workers lived in very close quarters and how boys his age lined up at the doors of factories that had advertised openings in *La Prensa*. Ángel first engaged in union activism at age 14, during the so-called "Década infame" (Infamous Decade) of 1930–43 (so named, in part, for being marked by undemocratic government). Ángel recalled particularly the actions of the special section of the security forces that had been ordered to repress communism. Perelman nevertheless acknowledged that socialism and communism had, at that time, sold out to an alliance of international capitalists and local barons, shedding their revolutionary, class-based goals.

According to Perelman's vision, which adopts various clichés commonly held among Peronist activists at the time, these left-wing parties responded to the interests of a working class composed mainly of European immigrants. Their militants were therefore incapable of distancing themselves from their European working-class worldview. This, in turn, limited their ability to fully understand the needs of Argentine-born workers in the country's current circumstances. Yet, as Perelman argues, the economic constraints of the 1930s made the development of national industry – still weak at the time – a necessity, as Argentina sought to satisfy the demand for manufactured goods and to cope with its decreased capacity to import such goods. This process spurred a new migratory wave from the rural provinces to the capital, generating a new, homegrown working class, which played a crucial role in the events that culminated in the explosion of widespread enthusiasm in favour of Perón in October 1945.

The "popular front" politics adopted in Argentina by the established Left had led to cooperation among syndicalists, Socialists, and Communists, which crystallized most visibly in the leadership of the CGT, the country's confederation of trade unions, and resulted, in Perelman's words, in a policy orientation that, within the context of the Second World War, was "ultra-reformist and conservative." The apolitical unions of the Unión Sindical Argentina grouping, all of which opposed the "imperialist war" (as Perelman described the Second World War), were excluded from this conservatism. Perelman's opposition to the leftist union leadership peaked during the metalworkers' protest in June 1942, in which he actively participated as a worker in a subdivision of the plant of the Compañía de Talleres Industriales de Transportes y Afines (Company of Industrial Workshops in Transport and Related Activities). Perelman was opposed to the subordination of the interests of Argentine workers to the necessities of the Allies. This stance led him to understand that the Communists, in their support of the Allies – indeed, they tried to interrupt the metalworkers' protest on the grounds that a halt in production might affect the British war effort – were betraying both their own class and the Argentine nation. Despite opposition from Communists, the metalworkers went on strike for seventeen days until the strike was suspended in an assembly meeting in which the police had to intervene to prevent the metalworkers, who wished to continue striking, from lynching the Communists. By then, workers disaffected with the union's leadership had begun to ponder the possibility of shifting the metalworkers' union away from the Communists.

The opportunity to break ranks with this leadership emerged in early 1943, when workers dissatisfied with the Communists and Socialists at the Fontanares factory met with Perelman to form a new metalworkers' union, the UOM, which would be founded in April and in which

Perelman would be secretary general. In June, the army led its coup against the government and, in November, Perón would be appointed head of the newly created Secretariat of Labour and Welfare. According to Perelman, Argentine Communists had been most complicit with British imperialism during the presidency of Roberto Ortiz. When the latter died, Socialists and Communists, allies of foreign imperialists, attacked the measures taken by his successor Ramón Castillo, measures which, Perelman observes, were destined to strengthen national industry. As the emerging national bourgeoisie had little political clout, the army became the political force that stood up for the national interest, acting as the Argentine bourgeoisie's champion. Perón played a crucial role in this context by ensuring that this movement harboured a progressive strand, one that made it possible for Argentine workers to defend their interests within the new national project: "The working class's political and union-based awakening ... was taking off at great speed."[2]

By mid-1944, Perelman suggested to the UOM's leaders that they request a meeting with Perón to ask him to support a host of salary-related requests. When faced with the opposition of a large part of the union's leadership, Perelman decided to visit Perón independently, accompanied by one of the few union members who had supported his request and not speaking on behalf of the union. This meeting convinced Perelman that the interests of the UOM were compatible with Perón's designs. After Perelman insisted that the UOM approve his request for an official meeting with the Secretariat of Labour and Welfare, the leadership finally gave its approval. To Perelman's surprise, the meeting with Perón drew a whopping 20,000 metalworkers, which convinced him that this meeting marked the triumph of the "national Left." According to the Jewish-Argentine, when workers understood that the established unions' leaderships would not pursue the takeover of power by the working class, the Argentine proletariat gave its support to Perón's capitalism, which was, at least, "national," and defended, at least in part, their class's interests. This new project would, under the leadership of Perón, yield an alliance between unions, the bourgeoisie, and the army.

In his narrative, Perelman observes that the new national project was dulled from the outset by the local oligarchy's resistance, which became manifest in proportion to Perón's growing success in politics.

This oligarchy, according to the typical Peronist narrative, joined forces in a heterogeneous alliance that included Soviet bureaucrats and was followed blindly by Argentine Communists and US imperialists. Protected by the established Argentine political parties, this alliance grew stronger with every statement made by US ambassador Braden. Perón's arrest in early October 1945 was thus perceived by UOM members as an attack on all workers. Perelman recounts the debate in which workers discussed how to proceed in this context, explaining that a majority of participants supported Perón and were determined to fight, but were waiting to see how events would unfold. Given the longstanding tradition of political activism among workers, the speeches that Perón made that month about "the government of the people" amounted to "the recuperation of an old, lost language."[3]

Although the Communists supported Perón's expulsion from the Farrell administration, during the debates that took place in the CGT a majority of workers finally decided to call a strike in support of Perón, with sixteen votes for and eleven against. This decision had the support of the masses, which decided, Perelman writes, to head toward the Plaza de Mayo. On this day, 17 October 1945, Perón's alliance with the working class was sealed, a development that positioned the workers at the vanguard of the national movement. Jewish-Argentines also participated in this massive gathering, as attested in an anecdote recounted by Israel Jabbaz. Jabbaz, a lower-middle-class Argentine, was originally from Aleppo. He had finished high school by attending night classes so that he could work during the day. Jabbaz recounts that he had his first romantic date with his future wife on 17 October, when he took her to the protest in support of Perón.

Ángel Yampolsky was another Jewish-Argentine leader, who played an important part in mobilizing workers on 17 October 1945. An anarchist, Yampolsky was secretary general of the autonomous union of the meatpacking plant La Negra in the neighbourhood of Avellaneda. He participated in the struggles of the meatpacking industry workers in 1944 and 1945, but realized early on that it would be necessary to take action outside of the union's "sectarian communism" and accordingly opposed the Communist leadership of the Federación Obrera de la Industria de la Carne (Federation of Meatpacking Industry Workers), led by José Peter. Yampolsky then joined his fellow meatpackers' union leader Cipriano Reyes in collaborating with the new policy of the Secretariat of Labour and Welfare in 1944–45. It is no surprise that Yampolsky was among the union leaders of the Avellaneda-Dock Sud area of Buenos Aires, whom the Communists called "thugs" or "lumpen." Reyes described Yampolsky's role in the workers' mobilization that took place on 17 October: "During the first hours of the afternoon, several columns converged in Avellaneda at the start of the bridge located at the juncture of Pavón and Mitre Streets. Fifty thousand people were thus gathered. There were large groups coming from the La Negra meatpacking plant, marching behind their secretary general, Ángel Yampolsky, from the Papini glass factories, and from other factories of Temperley, Lomas, Lanús, etc., mobilized by comrades Vicente Garófalo, José Calverio, Raúl Pedrera, Helio Mutis, and Juan Rodríguez."[4]

Yampolsky was part of the Comité de Enlace Intersindical (Committee for Inter-Union Relations) during those October days and became a founding member of the Partido Laborista (Labour Party). This party emerged in the aftermath of 17 October and had a strong pull during the emergence of the Peronist coalition, helping to secure the movement's electoral victory. Together with José María Argaña, Vicente Garófalo, Alcides Montiel, and Antonio Sánchez, Yampolsky was part of the committee in charge of preparing the Partido Laborista's declaration of principles. He also encouraged the new party to publicly repudiate the antisemitic activities of the ALN, which it did. In a broad consensus, it was decided that Yampolsky would stand for a congressional seat in the province of Buenos Aires on the Partido Laborista's ticket, headed by Cipriano Reyes and Ernesto Cleve.[5] After Yampolsky was elected, relations between him and Reyes grew distant as the latter challenged Perón's leadership. Still, Reyes held Yampolsky in high esteem for his ability to fight for the workers' cause. Yampolsky died before the end of his term.

Rafael Kogan, the secretary manager of the Unión Ferroviaria (UF; Railworkers' Union), was responsible for the support that this important union gave to Perón. Kogan was one of the UF's founding members and accumulated considerable power from his administrative position in Argentina's most important union at the time. Considering that railworkers enjoyed strategic negotiating power in an economy that traditionally relied on agricultural exports, they organized (in particular those from La Fraternidad and the UF) the most powerful unions in the country. In the early 1940s, they accounted for a third of all CGT-affiliated union members. During the 1940s, the UF regularly saw changes in its leadership, but Kogan remained in his position until 1948, occupying the highest administrative post in the union's hierarchy. That October, he was replaced by Manuel Palmeiro, who was closer to the incoming secretary general, Pablo Carnero López.

The military government that took power following the June 1943 coup decided to intervene in the railworkers' unions with the aim of weakening the workers' movement. Frigate Captain Raúl A. Puyol, in charge of the intervention, removed from their posts all the members of the board of directors, crafting accusations of "embezzlement" and "violation of the trade union statute." Puyol also fired, without cause, Juan Atilio Bramuglia, the union's legal advisor, and Kogan. These measures provoked a hostile reaction among many railworkers. A flyer titled "One Month of Intervention in the Unión Ferroviaria" voiced "concern and disquiet" regarding these episodes. Those who signed the text omitted their names and were identified only by their section out of fear of the new military government. In that flyer, they protested against the leaders that Puyol had installed at the head of the union, and emphasized that, "it cannot be overlooked that comrades Rafael Kogan and Juan Atilio Bramuglia were removed from their positions … and that no reason was given to even justify such a grave measure. These comrades have had a longstanding and demonstrable participation in the Unión Ferroviaria, and have always acted without betraying the trust placed in them. Nevertheless, the intervention has removed them from their duties, turning a blind eye to the injustice committed and to the moral harm caused."[6]

In the weeks that followed, Perón and Domingo Mercante held a series of talks with the UF leadership. Mercante, a military officer who was close to Perón, had ties with the railworkers through relatives. In late October, Mercante replaced Puyol and accepted the resignation of those officials that Puyol had named, but then decided to return to their posts Managing Secretary Kogan and legal advisor Bramuglia. Thanks to the efforts of Bramuglia and Kogan, from that point on the

UF, in the words of José Domenech, UF past president and former secretary general of the CGT, "provided the most crucial support for Peronism in the country." Domenech added: "Because I have to say in all honesty, telling the plain truth, that 99 percent of the UF's leaders became Peronists."[7]

Kogan was born in 1879 and, along with José Domenech and Luis González, was part of the generation of older railworkers who were Socialist militants. Different UF leaders, from Antonio Tramonti to Domenech, consulted Kogan on a regular basis as his knowledge and experience gave him an important place within the union. The UF had a very centralized structure with a small group of leaders gathered around a small table. Kogan was part of this group for longer than anyone else during the 1930s and 1940s. And it was he who, together with other leaders and Bramuglia, convinced union members to support Peronism in its infancy.

For the Partido Socialista (Socialist Party), Borlenghi, Bramuglia, and Kogan's switch over to Peronism was an example of opportunism and betrayal. As late as August 1943, *La Vanguardia*, in its column "Socialism and Its Men," paid tribute to comrade Rafael Kogan and characterized him as a man "of proven moral strength, and whose will could not be shaken," while singling out his "energy and his dedication to the struggle." The column described the UF founder, "the permanent motor of this powerful organization," as follows:

> Rafael Kogan, worker in the cauldrons of Ferrocarril Sud, responding to the imperatives of solidarity, was left without a job as a consequence of the strike held by railroad workers in 1918. Far from breaking his spirit, this situation led Kogan to join forces with a small group of workers and, having analyzed the causes of the strike's defeat and understanding the need to change the system of organization [of labour], took it upon himself to found what, for two decades, was the pride of the Argentine workers' movement … Rafael Kogan is 64 years old. He has the same material wealth as when he lost his job in Ferrocarril Sud. But his moral and intellectual reserves have been enriched over twenty years of experience at the service of his fellow workers. He is an honest man through and through.[8]

Abraham Krislavin, who became undersecretary in the Ministry of the Interior, and David Diskin – both of them from the Sindicato de Empleados de Comercio (Union of Business Employees) – would come to play an important role in connecting the Peronist administration with various Jewish persons and groups.[9] Diskin became a part of the executive board of the Asociación de Empleados de Comercio de Bahía Blanca (Bahía Blanca Association of Business Employees) as early as 1937. From 1943, he forged ties with Peronism and, in 1945, like several other Jewish union leaders such as Yampolsky, was one of the founding members of the Partido Laborista. A year later he became part of the board of directors of the Caja de Jubilaciones para Empleados de Comercio (Business Employees Retirement Fund), also joining the board of the Confederación General de Empleados de Comercio de la República Argentina (General Confederation of Business Employees of the Republic of Argentina), of which he remained a member until 1955. He was also a member of the council of directors of the CGT during the decade of Peronist administrations.

During that period, Diskin travelled across the nation and to several other Latin American countries as a missionary of the Justicialist doctrine. In 1948, he joined the Argentine delegation representing the CGT at the conference of the International Labour Organization. He occupied this post until 1954. With the support of Borlenghi, he was elected to Congress in 1951 and re-elected in 1954. Diskin participated in the founding congress of the Peronist Asociación de Trabajadores Latinoamericanos Sindicalistas (ATLAS; Association of Latin American Syndicalists) held in Mexico City in 1952. The following year, he was part of President Perón's delegation during his visit to Chile. The public got a sense of Diskin's importance when he shared the stage with Perón and Evita at the stately Teatro Colón and in the Luna Park arena.

Diskin's loyalty to Peronism came at high cost for him. The Revolución Libertadora imprisoned him and accused him of treason against the nation. He was nevertheless freed a few months later and went into exile in Chile. There he joined the Comisión de Resistencia (Resistance Committee), which coalesced in that country in order to mobilize support for the return of Perón to Argentina. In 1958, came back to Buenos Aires under the protection granted by the amnesty that President Arturo Frondizi's administration had declared. During the early 1970s, Diskin was elected secretary general of the Confederación General de Empleados de Comercio and named president of the Banco Sindical de la República Argentina (Union Bank of the Republic of Argentina). He was also a member of the governing council of the "62 Unions" – the group of combative industrial unions that formed part of the Peronist resistance – from 1969 to 1975.

Diskin spoke at an event held in Buenos Aires on 27 October 1998, at which national congressman Alberto Rocamora recalled that while Diskin was president of the Banco Sindical, he granted a monetary loan to each member of the delegation that travelled to Madrid on the charter plane that would bring Juan Domingo Perón back to Argentina from his exile. In 1972, Diskin was a member of the committee tasked with drafting the Law of Work Contracts in collaboration with national lawmakers. In this process, he represented the CGT and the Confederación General de Empleados de Comercio. When democracy returned to Argentina in 1983, Diskin once again involved himself in the municipal politics of Bahía Blanca and he was elected councilman several times during the 1990s.

Union leaders such as Perelman, Yampolsky, Kogan, and Diskin are important in part because their role and significance, though not necessarily tied to their Jewish identity, were nonetheless connected to their condition as Jewish-Argentines. Many of these figures had little connection to their Jewish origins. The close ties that these men forged with Peronism may thus reveal a true opening on the part of the movement toward ethnic groups such as Jews, whom it tasked with broader issues in a shift that was more significant than entrusting a few public servants with specifically Jewish questions.

GELBARD, PERONISM, AND THE NATIONAL BOURGEOISIE

"My father, José Ber Gelbard, was a member of General Perón's cabinet in 1954–55 and in 1973–74, but he was never a Peronist. He was indeed friends with the general and collaborated with him in planning, discussions, and in political and economic action." This is what Fernando Gelbard wrote to me when I told him that I was writing this book.[10]

It is true that up until 1973, José Ber Gelbard was not a Peronist. He confessed to those closest to him that he was a Radical (a supporter of the UCR), but only a few of these friends knew of his ties to Communism and his affiliation with that party up until the start of the 1960s – a party to which he contributed funds and contacts in the utmost secrecy. Nevertheless, his life and work led him to play an important role in Peronism's aim of forging an alliance among socioeconomic classes and in the movement's social and economic policies. His Jewish identity was no secret and he shored up support for Peronism among part of the Jewish-Argentine community, which turned him into the target of several antisemitic manifestations by right-wing elements in 1973–74.

Although joining Peronism would seem like a logical next step for Gelbard given the movement's defence of the interests of both the working class and local industrialists, he did not formally become a Peronist until 1973, when he accepted President Perón's invitation to become minister of the economy and joined his fate to the movement, both in its successes and in its tragic eclipse between the early fifties and the mid-seventies. As Gelbard detested the traditional economic policies dominated by the established elite of Buenos Aires and its British trading partners, he was strongly drawn to the concept of "social justice" and the corporatist vision of an "organized community," as well as to a state that confronted the national and social responsibilities of capitalism. Additionally, the working class's increased purchasing power and the expansion of the internal market benefitted the interests of the Confederación General Económica (CGE; General Economic Confederation), a grouping of small and mid-sized businesses oriented toward the national market. Gelbard began to collaborate with Peronism when he was the head of the CGE, which he himself had founded to organize the nation's business owners. In the words of historian James Brennan:

> A former travelling salesman who originated from a province was the most powerful figure of the CGE for the next two decades and also its first president: José Ber Gelbard. Gelbard was born to Jewish immigrants from Poland and owned a business in Catamarca. He would become the main ideologue of the

Figure 6.1 José Ber Gelbard, president of the Confederación General Económica, delivering a speech at the inauguration of the Confederation's headquarters in the presence of Argentine president Juan Perón, February 1955.

> "national bourgeoisie" and the most staunch advocate of the alliance between businessmen and workers, and of a federalist economic programme … Gelbard made efforts to inculcate a sense of "mission" among members of the CGE. This mission was grounded in the liberating role that the owners of small local businesses (also known as *bolicheros*) across Argentina were destined to play in Argentina, and in the cause of federalism and economic nationalism that would allow small-scale capitalists to achieve national liberation in their crusade to orient capitalism toward the masses.[11]

During the 1950s and 1960s, Gelbard sought to ensure that the CGE was perceived as independent so that it could develop and maintain relations across the political, economic, and military spectra. Gelbard was open to Peronist initiatives within the CGE, but he maintained that this organization had been created precisely in 1952 during Peronism's most difficult year, when the government launched a structural adjustment plan that diverged from the CGE's policies.[12] In fact, long before the CGE was founded, Gelbard had succeeded in establishing himself as the uncontested leader of Argentine business owners – known as "bolicheros" (small businessmen) due to the small scale of their businesses – thanks to decades of activism that began when he was a young man in the province of Catamarca, one of the poorest areas of the marginalized Argentine north. Without ever having completed primary school, Gelbard worked as a "cuentenik" (a salesman who allows his clients to pay in installments) and travelling salesman whose wares included shaving blades, condoms, and combs. He then began to forge a network of businessmen in the northern provinces to enhance their capacity for mutual aid and to pressure the federal government to end discrimination against these provinces in its economic policies.

When Gelbard's parents arrived in the Argentine north on 1 April 1930, José Ber was 13 years old. They were fleeing the misery and pogroms that threatened Radomsko, Poland, where Gelbard was born. Gelbard, along with his father Abraham, a tailor, his mother Sara Tyberg, and his four brothers, settled in the province of Tucumán. Gelbard would return to Radomsko forty years later – as Argentina's minister of the economy and driven in a limousine after being decorated by the Polish prime minister, Stanislav Jerek – to overcome a lingering resentment from his childhood.[13] When the Gelbard family fled Poland, they departed from the port city of Danzig (currently Gdansk). José's uncles awaited them in Argentina: Felipe Cracovsky, a travelling salesman, and Moisés Tyberg, a leatherworker, both established in the province of Tucumán and successfully integrated into its budding local Jewish community, which was beginning to establish associations such as the Casa Israelita de Socorros Mutuos, Préstamo y Ahorro (Jewish House of Mutual Aid, Loans, and Savings) and the Sociedad de Residentes Polacos (Society of Polish Residents), over which Tyberg presided. Zionist institutions were also taking shape in this province: the Centro Cultural Sionista (Zionist Cultural Centre), directed by

Jacobo Farber, whose son would later be involved in the future business undertakings of José Ber (or Iapso, as he was known as a child).[14]

Shortly after the family arrived at San Miguel de Tucumán, they rented a home on the 600 block of San Martín Street and turned it into a boarding house, renting out its rooms to travelling salespersons while also doing door-to-door sales themselves. In 1934, Gelbard began to work at the printing press owned by the Iurcovich family, who were members of Tucumán's Communist Party. A year later, he became active in unions through the Sociedad Israelita de Vendedores Ambulantes (Jewish Society of Travelling Salesmen) that his uncle Wolf Tyberg had founded. In 1936, he left the printing press to join his uncle Cracovsky selling ties and shirts along the road connecting Tucumán and Catamarca, alongside Francisco Murdosky, who was in charge of Catamarca's Communist Party. During those years, Gelbard became good friends with members of the Syrio-Lebanese community in that province, particularly the Saadi family, the future strongmen of Catamarca.

In 1938, José Ber Gelbard married Dina Haskel, the daughter of the founders of the local Jewish community and Gelbard's girlfriend since he was 15 years old. They wedded in Tucumán and moved to San Fernando del Valle de Catamarca shortly after. There, he became the associate of Miguel Behar, and the two opened the Casa Nueva York, a store that sold lingerie and men's clothing. The capital of Catamarca was home to a bustling market of Jewish and Arab travelling salespersons. The local Jewish community was largely comprised of Syrio-Lebanese Jews, which hampered the integration of the newlyweds as they were Ashkenazim. Jewish immigrants and their descendants were well received by Catamarca's elite who acknowledged their considerable commercial activity and even welcomed some into the elite "25 de agosto" club. Gelbard was able to join the club, as his business partner was a member, which allowed him to forge numerous commercial and political ties.

Gelbard's ties with José Iurcovich in Tucumán and with Murdosky in Catamarca led him to become actively involved in the Communist Party. He was in charge of raising funds for the party in the northern provinces, a large part of which came from Jewish business owners.[15]

His political activism increased at the start of the Second World War, as he redoubled his efforts to recruit new members and attract funding for local communism. As part of his fundraising, he imported cars from Paraguay through a clandestine network and sold them in Catamarca, contributing his earnings to the party. Due to his activism in the Communist Party, he was denied Argentine citizenship for over a decade. In spite of this, Gelbard maintained relations with the local Jewish community and also became a founding member of the Cámara de Comercio de Catamarca (Catamarca Chamber of Commerce), which brought him into close contact with other business owners.

Through his activity in these posts and organizations, Gelbard would become the representative of owners of small, modest businesses in the country's interior provinces – the forgotten bolicheros who lacked a political lobby. These small business owners flaunted their identity as bolicheros, opposing it to the interests of the Unión Industrial Argentina (UIA; Argentine Industrial Union), which was run by the longstanding Argentine agrarian oligarchy and which, during the 1930s, had diversified its investments in large industries. These were self-made men, who enthusiastically espoused the "bolicheros" moniker that the porteños had typically used to belittle them, not unlike how the working class had taken pride in reclaiming the identity of "descamisados" (shirtless ones).[16]

In August 1942, Gelbard was elected as a delegate to represent the Cámara de Comercio de Catamarca at the Consejo Central de Comercio de la República Argentina (Central Council of Commerce of the Republic of Argentina). This post allowed him to forge ties with business owners on a national scale. He thus became an important figure, mediating between business owners and politicians, particularly in the north of Argentina. Some months after Perón was elected to the presidency, Gelbard was named president of the Federación Económica de Tucumán (Tucumán Economic Federation), one of the most important such federations in the country. From that platform, he designed a plan to organize those business owners and merchants who had been excluded from the Unión Industrial Argentina and the Sociedad Rural Argentina (Argentine Rural Association).

In keeping with his activism in the Communist Party and his friendship with UCR leader Ricardo Balbín, Gelbard supported the Unión

Democrática in the presidential elections of 24 February 1946. He even participated in some of the protests against Perón's candidacy that linked the Argentine general with fascism. After Perón's victory, Gelbard continued his activities as a business owner and Communist Party militant on a national scale. He was also part of the party's directorship, which aimed to infiltrate the commodities and financial markets. This directorship included business owners such as Gelbard, Simón Duchovsky, and Samuel Sivak; together they were responsible for overseeing the party's funds.

By 1948, Gelbard had organized the Federación Económica de Tucumán and the Federación Económica del Norte Argentino (Economic Federation of Northern Argentina). From the presidency, Juan Perón also took an interest in this group of small industrialists who shared many of Peronism's political notions, such as the need to promote industry, stimulate the domestic market, and forge an alliance between the country's business owners and workers. This interest was related to Perón's ongoing confrontation with the UIA, in which he intervened shortly after his inauguration in 1946. The first such confrontation took place in 1944 while Perón was secretary of labour and welfare, when the UIA opposed the legislation that he promoted to increase employees' retirement funds.

The interests of the large, industry-specific groups represented in the UIA contrasted with Gelbard's concerns and the sort of business owner that he embodied. His organization represented business owners who, in addition to pushing for state support for the country's northern region, supported salaries sufficiently high as to allow workers to consume the products and services of small businesses. As Gelbard would explain decades later:

> Those of us who came up in the country's provinces took action to modify policies that made us dependent upon the large metropolises. We had been trying to stress that urbanization could be done differently from the type of concentrated and anomalous industrialization typical of three or four mini-regions in that country. Another point was that national development did not have to be entrusted to large businesses whose expansion was premised on interests that differ from ours.[17]

Tensions with the upper echelons of the UIA prompted Perón to take steps to reorganize the business sector so that he would have the support of key figures. To that end, his initial attempt consisted in creating the Asociación Argentina de la Producción, Industria y Comercio (Argentine Association of Production, Industry, and Commerce), which included a broader range of business groups than the UIA, focused as it was on industrial groupings. As this project quickly failed, Perón replaced it, in 1948, with the Confederación Económica Argentina (CEA; Argentine Economic Federation). The CEA successfully brought over from the UIA some of the longstanding industrial business owners who were interested in forging ties with the government. This new entity nevertheless had reservations about the participation of business owners from the provinces, who were beginning to apply pressure to be admitted to the confederation as they were at a disadvantage. Gelbard's negotiating skills were showcased in this context. He made efforts to promote the inclusion of some business sectors that had, up until then, been marginalized from power. In that endeavour, his ties with Perón would be crucial.[18]

Their paths crossed for the first time in April 1950, thanks to the intercession of business owner Alberto Dodero and the economy secretary, Alfredo Gómez Morales. Perón summoned Gelbard to encourage him to form "a nationalist UIA." The meeting gave him confidence as he organized a colloquium in which the Acta de Catamarca (Catamarca Act) was drafted to bring into being the Confederación Argentina de la Producción, la Industria y el Comercio (CAPIC; Argentine Confederation for Production, Industry, and Commerce) with the aim of creating a "truly national organization." During that period, Gelbard took part in the meetings of the Consejo Económico Nacional (National Economic Council) and his participation in cabinet meetings was approved by none other than Perón. CAPIC was the true predecessor of the CGE, which Gelbard would found in 1952. James Brennan defined the CGE as "at least in part the response of second- and third-generation immigrants to the resistance of the oligarchic structures of Argentine society," which most prominently combined "anti-liberalism and nationalism."[19] This statement does indeed describe the position of Semitic immigrants in Argentina, both Jewish and Arab, and their descendants: "Perón's anti-oligarchy discourse was particularly appealing in those provinces where even a successful business owner like Gelbard was only one generation removed from the poorest of workers."[20]

The CGE would become the main platform from which Gelbard influenced the national government, as he was this organization's first president. Perón's interests and those of the CGE were complementary, as business owners supported his economic policy, which in turn benefitted their commercial interests. It is worth mentioning that the CGE was able to remain independent from the Peronist movement's corporatist structure. Its support of the national government's policy of economic integration did not entail absolute support of Peronism. In spite of this, Perón and Gelbard had considerable ideological affinities.[21]

The CGE's mission can be summed up in the words that Gelbard spoke to the Congreso de la Productividad (Congress on Productivity) of 1954, when he voiced a formula that satisfied workers and business owners alike: "high salaries and cheap labour."[22] This mission was also palpable in a statement that Gelbard made nearly twenty years later: "to redistribute income across society, but to leave private property untouched" within the framework of a "capitalism that integrated all provinces and that was oriented toward the masses."[23] Thanks to this approach, the CGE became the first business owners' association to collaborate with the CGT in organizing an event, the Congreso Nacional de la Productividad y Bienestar Social (National Conference for Productivity and Welfare), held in 1955, a few months before Perón was ousted.[24]

The 1955 coup would also entail the dissolution and intervention of the CGE, which continued only until 1958. During that period, in the words of Guillermo O'Donnell, a "liberal" alliance coalesced between the agrarian sector's bourgeoisie and the principal industries. This alliance frequently attempted to encroach on the Peronist coalition between the weak urban industrial petite bourgeoisie and the working class, which had joined forces in a strategy to strengthen the internal market and defend the interests of various social classes.[25]

According to Gary Wynia, the UIA, which accounted for six of the nine largest foreign enterprises, adopted a strategy that "welcomed the trend toward denationalization as a blessing, instead of perceiving it as a threat, while attacking vehemently the state's expansion."[26] In contrast, the CGE, which was entirely comprised of Argentine businesses, "continued to lead the crusade in favour of restrictive legislation aimed at hampering the easy access of foreign capital to national industry, particularly through the purchase of existing businesses."[27] In that aspect, the CGE also coincided with the Peronists, as the latter considered that the increasing foreign penetration of the economy was a subtle form of economic domination. When the CGE was declared illegal amid an adverse political climate, Gelbard focused on its relations with business owners, including hotels, businesses, and local newspapers. He associated with two other Jewish-Argentines, Manuel Madanes, the founder of the tire company FATE, and Julio Broner, a future president of the CGE who owned a factory that manufactured gearshifts for Wobron automobiles. Perhaps due to his modest origins, Gelbard had a particular set of goals. His biographer María Seoane described him as follows:

> Gelbard was a paradigm of the Argentine bourgeoisie: he availed himself of corporations' support when he needed to pressure the government, he lobbied to grow his wealth, he evaded fiscal obligations to protect his profits, he also availed himself of privileges from the state and of monopolistic practices to expand his businesses (the Aluar aluminum company and FATE), and had no qualms in accepting commissions when he aided someone. Yet, unlike the powerful Argentine industrial and landowning bourgeoisie, which in the 1960s and 1970s had already converted to the fundamentalism of the market, Gelbard chose to forge alliances with civil society and to forsake the authoritarian vice of resorting to military interventions. He chose to wager on the development of an internal market, to be a vocal critic of the high degree of concentration of wealth and inequality, and to defend a model that would further the nation's industrialization without generating more exclusion. There was no ambiguity or secret around this wager.[28]

As Brennan puts it, Gelbard had successfully built a powerful industrial group. His contacts with the state had been beneficial in the past and would be essential in the future. At the same time, "Gelbard and his economic team were genuinely concerned about elevating the workers' standard of living within the broader project of developing a national capitalism that was also just and that might avoid a socialist revolution in the country. His concerns went well beyond making good deals. He was not pronouncing empty speeches when he spoke of his opposition to a liberalism that was both anti-national and anti-communitarian, and of his desire to establish a humanist model of economic development."[29]

In 1958, the military authorities handed over power in exchange for the continued proscription of the Partido Peronista. The new civilian government, led by President Arturo Frondizi of the UCR, entailed a change in alliances: Gelbard oriented his group toward the newly inaugurated government, and Frondizi decriminalized the CGE. Gelbard, ever conscious of future possibilities, maintained ties with Perón, who was then exiled in Madrid, but did so in such a discrete way that the CGE was able to remain independent from Peronism.

Due to the antisemitism of several public servants, at the time of the Peronist administrations and even more so during the subsequent military government, Gelbard was far more discrete about his ties with Judaism and Zionism. Both topics had been present in his early activism, when, as a teenager, he had been active in the Centro Cultural Sionista, where he sought to unseat those who, in his words, were "old Zionists" interested in Yiddish theatre and sport, and less given to politics and socialism. He also made contacts with the newly launched Comité de la Liga Pro Palestina Obrera (Committee of the Pro-Palestine Workers' League). Zionist ideals also guided his involvement in unions representing business owners – as, for example, in 1935, when he joined the Sociedad Israelita de Vendedores Ambulantes (Jewish Society of Traveling Salesmen). The last position that he officially occupied within a Jewish organization dates from after his marriage to Dina Haskel and their move to Catamarca in 1938, when he became involved in Catamarca's Centro de la Juventud Israelita (Centre for Jewish Youth).

Although Gelbard's political trajectory distanced him from his previous duties in Jewish community organizations, he maintained ties with Jewish activists. He was close to two of the DAIA's presidents, Gregorio Faigón and Isaac Goldenberg, as well as Israel's ambassador, Jacob

Tsur. Beginning in the 1960s, he contributed funds and information to Jewish community organizations in Argentina; María Seoane claims that some of this information helped Israel's Mossad to capture the Nazi war criminal, Adolf Eichmann.[30] During the process that led to the creation of the OIA and the ensuing discord among the community organizations, Gelbard chose to maintain contacts with the veteran established organizations, yet nevertheless had informal ties with the OIA as well. It was at an OIA event held in 1949 that Gelbard met Eva Perón, to whom he would become very close. In 1958, he travelled secretly to Israel to meet with Prime Minister David Ben Gurion and Minister of Foreign Affairs Golda Meir, and also helped to plan Meir's second official visit to Argentina (her first was in April 1951), which took place on 2 May 1959.[31] In another secret trip to Israel in 1969, Gelbard would praise the *kibbutzim*, the farming cooperatives that had been in existence for four decades prior to Israel's creation.

In collaboration with Israel Dujovne, president of the Sociedad Hebraica Argentina during the 1940s, and Gregorio Faigon, who would become president of the DAIA in the late 1960s, Gelbard founded a construction company that would help finance the CGE during the 1970s. He also maintained close ties with Israel's ambassadors in Buenos Aires. Yet, despite these ties and Gelbard's monetary contributions to the Jewish community, he never accepted invitations to join their boards of directors.

In this new phase at the head of the CGE, Gelbard would seek support from a group of business owners that was rather heterogeneous, both in its members' social profiles and their areas of economic activity. Four of these business owners (two of whom were Jewish) should be mentioned here: Julio Broner and Israel Dujovne, as well as Ernesto Paenza (a Catholic married to a Jewish woman) and Ildefonso Recalde. Broner was Gelbard's business partner. Like Gelbard, he was the son of Jewish immigrants from Poland (some sources maintain that he was born in Zaklików in August 1921 and arrived in Argentina during the Second World War, while others argue that, unlike Gelbard, Broner was born in the Chaco region and grew up there with his family). Thanks to the business licence that the Perón government granted in 1955 for the creation of the Wobron plant for manufacture automobile gearshift boxes, Broner was able to develop a genuine monopoly in the sector.

Broner was a notable member of the national bourgeoisie embodied by Gelbard. He played a key role in creating the Cámara Industrial de Fabricantes de Automotores, Repuestos y Afines (Industrial Chamber of Manufacturers of Automobiles, Parts, and Equipment), which aided him in lobbying in favour of national industry. Broner took over the presidency of the CGE when Gelbard stepped down from that post to serve as a minister in Perón's third administration.

Israel Dujovne was the only notable member of the CGE who originated from Buenos Aires. This is congruent with the organization's emphasis on promoting the integration of provinces into the country's industrial fabric. Of the CGE's leadership, Dujovne had the most ties with the Communist Party. He profited from his activities in construction and from his business, Kunar. Dujovne would become president of the CGE in the 1960s. Ildefonso Recalde, originally from Rosario and a notable businessman in the textile industry, played a noteworthy role in transforming the CGE into a forum where nationalist economists could express themselves, particularly through the leadership of the organization's Instituto de Investigaciones Económicas y Financieras (Institute for Economic and Financial Research). Recalde would become Gelbard's righthand man. As he was the leading figure who was most remote from the Communist Party, he had more legitimacy when representing the CGE vis-à-vis the country's elites. Finally, Ernesto Paenza joined the organization as a business owner who focused on importing and exporting. He became secretary of industrial development and president of the Banco Nacional de Desarrollo (National Development Bank) in the 1970s.

Gelbard collaborated with the Frondizi administration in normalizing the CGE. Frondizi had fulfilled his promise to restore to the organization its legal status, but Gelbard opposed this president's welcoming of foreign investment as part of his "developmentalist" policies. In the words of Gelbard, "the technical resources, capital, and other factors of production were oriented toward the creation of wealth that in some cases was of a secondary order of social and economic priority for the development of the nation." Gelbard chose an emblem of developmentalism – the automobile industry – as an example, pointing out that, "even if [this country] didn't have roads, automobile factories continued to saturate the internal market with cars."[32] He nevertheless clarified that "we do not look down upon foreign investments, so long as they are destined toward those sectors that are considered to favour national interests and, obviously, so long as they do not affect our ability to make decisions as a nation."[33]

In a document prepared by its research centre in the early 1970s, the CGE described its own vision of developmentalism. It signalled that the developmentalist model was premised on "a distortion of the productive structure, that it generated unemployment, and heightened problems of vulnerability of the export sector, in addition to increasing economic and technological dependency," as it oriented foreign capital toward the most profit-generating sectors without paying heed to the order or priorities established by the economy's needs," particularly in the new demand for imports, "which worsened the situation of payments to international creditors." According to this analysis, at the end of the developmentalist experiment, debt toward foreign creditors had increased substantially and an essential part of autonomous control over economic decisions had been surrendered. As a result, the high level of development in this model "implied a permanent marginalization of workers and of national production."[34]

In 1962, after Frondizi was overthrown by way of a military coup, Gelbard signed, on behalf of the CGE, a joint platform with the CGT to improve the workers' standard of living. These gradual improvements would come to a halt in 1966 with the beginning of the de facto administration led by General Juan Carlos Onganía. According to Gelbard, from that year on, "the profits of the financial sector had dramatically increased"; Gelbard maintained that the government and those economic sectors that supported it opposed a return to democracy because "an election would force them to come to terms with what they really are: a minority among minorities."[35] He stated further that this administration's policy was premised on recipes for tightening one's belt and that the CGE considered this premise to be immoral, unjust, and ... totally ineffective," as "in our conception of the process, increasing workers' real income is not only just, it is a requisite for the creation of a large internal market that can allow national factories to expand."[36]

The arrival to the presidency of another general, Alejandro Agustín Lanusse, at the start of 1971, seemed again to change the course of relations between the government and the CGE in a way that involved a new role for Gelbard. Lanusse initially chose the CGE as his business interlocutor, privileging it above liberal economic actors. This allowed Gelbard to play an important part in the 1972 pact forged between Perón and Lanusse that would allow the return to the country of the exiled former president. During that period, Gelbard also struck one of his biggest deals: he bribed members of the military government so that they would grant credits and energy for the construction of the aluminium plant Aluar. The army was interested in this initiative for economic and military purposes, and Gelbard's business expertise was a crucial asset in this process. In the meantime, Gelbard continued to visit Perón in Madrid. The former president had no qualms about voicing his support for Gelbard, and he is said to have stated that any attack on Gelbard was tantamount to an attack against him.[37] Perón attempted to convince Gelbard to lead the economic efforts that his government would take once the proscription of the Partido Justicialista had been lifted, ending the eighteen-year ban imposed by the military junta that overthrew him in 1955. In addition to Gelbard's leadership among the nation's business owners, Gelbard offered Perón another advantage: through the CGE, he could contribute the technical economic knowledge that Peronist cadres lacked.[38] Gelbard and the CGE saw in Perón the possibility of finally reaching the height of political power, which in turn would allow them to design Argentina's economic policy.

This state of affairs in the Peronist movement was made public shortly before Gelbard was designated minister. In the summer of 1973, Abrasha Rotenberg's newspaper *La Opinión*, with Jacobo Timerman as its editor-in-chief, was the only newspaper to unequivocally support Gelbard. During that period, Rotenberg ran into Gelbard. The newspaper owner was vacationing at the luxurious resort of Punta del Este and Gelbard accepted his offer to organize a meeting with various acquaintances. Rotenberg recalled that, during that evening, Gelbard "began by referring to the country's economic situation, to the decades of minimal growth, to the perverse policies that benefitted foreign interests and harmed national ones" and "especially to the cruel distribution of wealth in favour of a privileged few at the expense of the masses." These claims he supported with numbers, statistics, and comparisons, which, Rotenberg added, "he handled in a highly competent manner and with impressive precision."[39] Gelbard stated on that occasion that, "at present, we have the support of Peronism, and especially, the good will of General Perón. The logical response would therefore be to vote for Perón."[40] Immediately afterward, he added that, "without seeking to offend anyone, I must warn those who intend to vote for Peronism that they might be making a grave mistake."[41] After this, Rotenberg recalls, "a hush of surprise and dismay quieted the room."[42] Gelbard explained:

> I feel that my duty is to clarify what I know. I fear the Peronism that is coming. The Peronism that is about to triumph is the darkest, most reactionary, and antisemitic sector [of the movement]. I am not referring only to the Right. The Peronist Left, seemingly guided in its actions by revolutionary slogans and seemingly progressive, harbours a background and a substance that are fascist. We should not vote for that Peronism. If it wins the coming elections – a result that it can likely achieve – this must be with a small majority. This Peronism has a deeply rooted thirst for revenge, resentment, and a destructive spirit. What is worse is its unreality. This is why I have asked that we meet: to ask that you not vote for them, and so that you could share my message with your friends. We must demonstrate that many of us will confront them when they show their true colours. This can still be avoided.[43]

As might be expected, members in the audience asked him how he could possibly take part in this Peronism that represented "reactionary and antisemitic fascism."[44] Many Jewish-Argentines shared Gelbard's concern, as they were about to vote in support of Justicialismo in greater numbers than during the 1946 or 1951 elections. As will be seen in this book's final chapter, the Israeli Ministry of Foreign Affairs followed with great concern the events and shifts within the Peronist movement. Peronism return to power in 1973 united Gelbard's path with the movement's fate and trajectory. His undisputed leadership among national business owners, 1,300,000 of whom were affiliated with the CGE according to the organization's own figures, gave Gelbard a key role in the plans sketched out by Perón for his return to power. The now-aged president sought to recreate the alliance between national business owners and workers so as to develop a "national capitalism"[45] in which the Marxist concept of class struggle (i.e., between workers and capitalists) would be replaced by an alliance between classes.

Gelbard resigned from his post as president of the CGE after accepting the position of minister of the economy in Perón's administration. In the goodbye speech that he gave to the CGE's membership, he stated that, "we must take on the commitment of collaborating with the government. We must not lose sight that there is no longer a right-wing force, only an empty symbol to which one can no longer return, and that all the possibilities are to be found at our left. If the commitment that our movement has made to other sectors is not fulfilled, a situation would emerge in the country whose culmination no one can predict."[46] Upon Perón's request, Gelbard was designated economy and treasury minister on 25 May 1973 by the newly sworn-in president, Héctor Cámpora, who won the elections that year as Perón's representative, as the proscription on Perón's participation had not yet been repealed. Cámpora saw in Gelbard a force that was foreign to Peronism but he had to obey Perón's order that Gelbard be designated minister.[47]

A few months prior to Gelbard's swearing-in, the CGE had presented a program that was geared toward the entire political arc, despite knowing that Peronism would almost certainly triumph in the elections. Called "Sugerencias del empresariado nacional para un programa de gobierno" (National Business Owners' Recommendations for a Program of Government), it set the basis for an economic program that attributed a central role to national business owners and workers. These recommendations were ratified shortly after Gelbard was sworn in as minister, in the document "Coincidencias Programáticas del Plenario de Organizaciones Sociales y Partidos Políticos" (Points of Agreement in the Program of the Plenary of Social Organizations and Political Parties), prepared jointly by the CGE and CGT. The document was signed by José Ignacio Rucci on behalf of the CGT, and Gelbard's successor in the CGE, Julio Broner, and it criticized the dominant presence of foreign capital, pointing out that it "had as a consequence the transformation of the economy into one dominated by monopolies and oligopolies." The document then went on to state that "over the last eighteen years, the country has undergone a process of unfair distribution of income, which is why the salaried workers who accounted for over fifty percent of national income during the administration of General Perón now account for only 36.1 percent." They thus agreed in this document that, "the government, the CGT, and CGE commit to joining forces to restore to salaried workers their participation in the nation's income." The final goal expressed in the document was that of bringing salaries closer to 50 percent of the nation's GDP.

The bold economic plan that Gelbard had promoted from the outset included the imposition of strong regulations by the state in the form of twenty economic measures to be legislated by Congress.[48] These measures were aimed at increasing salaries, pension funds, and other social benefits, and also to promote national businesses by increasing the consumption of domestically produced goods and making more public and private credit available. This policy was to be regulated by a social pact between business owners and trade unions and would make possible an increase and subsequent freeze in salaries, as well as a stabilization of prices.[49] For the first time in Argentine history, the workers represented by the CGT and the national business owners represented in the CGE seemed to have the power necessary to design economic policy, thanks to the consensus around Perón.

On 15 June 1973, the leadership of the UIA, the Sociedad Rural Argentina, the Confederaciones Rurales Argentinas (Argentine Rural Confederations), and the Bolsa de Comercio de Buenos Aires (Buenos Aires Stock Market) gathered in the Teatro San Martín together with the leaderships of the CGE and CGT to support this plan. This support was obviously forced by circumstances and not born of any genuine conviction,[50] particularly considering that the plan prescribed measures to finance a shift in production that would give the state and publicly owned businesses a central place in the new economy. One of these measures consisted in opening new commercial channels abroad, a process in which Gelbard's contacts in the countries of the Soviet bloc would play a crucial part. Gelbard answered right-wing criticisms of this plan to forge relations with communist countries by explaining that "the concept of ideological borders is part of the ancient history of international relations."[51]

The agricultural and livestock sector was another perceived source of cash. The plan prescribed the modernization of these areas, requiring that they cease to rely solely on the profits made possible by the favourable conditions of Argentina's soil,[52] but that they seek to increase their exports by augmenting their investments and upgrading their technologies. With this, it would seem that Gelbard and Perón sought to confront the powerful agricultural and livestock sector, which had conducted Argentina's politics for most of the country's history. Gelbard did not hide the fact that the plan would "reduce the relative importance of the agriculture and livestock sector, which in turn would modify the longstanding sources of power in the country."[53] When speaking of the diversification of the oligarchy, he maintained that, "we do not want for Argentina to be a colony, nor for these improvements to always only benefit a select group, generally parasitic to the population."[54] The plan included another law that specifically regulated the presence of foreign capital in Argentina, which it only allowed in those fields where no Argentine competitor existed and as long as foreign capital was not granted any advantage over national investment projects. This was another one of the great struggles taken on by the new government, one that put it in confrontation with multinational companies and with the developmentalist political sector, which, in practice, advocated emphatically for opening the economy to foreign capital. Rogelio Frigerio was the main cadre in the developmentalist sector. Frigerio was an economist and intellectual who also controlled the editorial line of *Clarín*, the highest-circulation daily in Buenos Aires. Gelbard felt that *Clarín* had attacked him, as the newspaper had redoubled its criticisms when Perón chose Gelbard instead of Frigerio to define economic policy.[55] Finding it difficult to confront *Clarín* and its editors directly, Gelbard succeeded in convincing the CGE and the CGT to pressure numerous businesses to withdraw their advertisements from the newspaper; as a result, after several attacks, *Clarín* had to moderate its editorial line.[56]

From the outset, Jacobo Timerman's newspaper *La Opinión* was Gelbard's ally in confronting opposition from the media. Gelbard and Timerman had ideological affinities, both in their interests and in their confrontations with economic elites, and they bonded over their common ethnic roots.[57] Gelbard found in *La Opinión* a media outlet whose interests were not contrary to those of his own project. Timerman, in turn, received the blessing of the businesses affiliated with the CGE as well as assistance from the state such that the paper manufacturer Papel Prensa was transferred to an associate of Gelbard and Timerman, David Graiver. To this end, Gelbard availed himself of his power as economy minister to put pressure on one of the principal shareholders of Papel Prensa, César Civita, so that he would sell his shares, which Graiver then purchased, and also to grant credits and tax breaks so that Graiver could afford to operate Papel Prensa.[58]

When Perón was sworn in as president on 12 October 1973 following Cámpora's resignation, he ratified Gelbard in the post of minister of the economy. One of Gelbard's first measures at this point was to configure his economic goals into a Three-Year Plan for 1974–77. As the plan specified, "the central aegis of this administration's policy to further industrial development is to boost businesses operating on national capital and to revert to the process of transnationalization [of the economy]."[59] He also outlined that, "the plan intended to expand the economy's current dynamism from its present seat in international monopolies to the totality of the nation's private sector, as has been occurring recently, as well as to the state and to national business owners." Gelbard sought to communicate the plan's epic dimension.[60] Accordingly, he observed that it would have been much easier to develop a policy that left the structures of social and economic dependency untouched. His undertaking "was not an intellectual game consisting in finding the neatest packaging to entrench dependency, it was a tireless inquest into the means for us to liberate ourselves as promptly as possible from the nefarious powers of economic, ideological, and cultural colonialism."[61]

Although the administration's confrontation with the agrarian sector, the multinationals, and the highest-circulation newspaper in the country could have been perceived as an excessively ambitious move,[62] the economic outlook was favourable for an improvement in the volume and price of agricultural exports, and the consensus around Perón could yield a new political equilibrium.[63] In fact, the plan's initial results could not have been more promising. At the end of 1973, several successes seemed achievable: worker participation in the GDP had grown from 33 to 42 percent, while consumption had increased by

5.3 percent and unemployment had dropped from 6.1 to 4.5 percent in a context in which the economy grew by 4.8 percent.[64]

This was a powerful social and economic victory for Gelbard, yet he was aware of the fragility of the project, supported in part by the shaky national bourgeoisie.[65] In a speech he gave to business owners affiliated with the CGE, he pointed out that contemporary Argentine industrialists "were a cause of shame, as they only considered that they had achieved something when they were able to purchase a land plot in the humid area of the pampa. They were attached to the nation based on farming and agriculture." He also referred to the longstanding "proliferation of old youths in the leadership" and, in a moment of self-criticism, he stated that, "Argentina would be a different country if those of us who, twenty-five years ago, were fighting for an industrialized and modern nation with national industrialists, had begun to train ourselves and to train a generation of progressive business owners instead of training executives who were derivative and reactionary." He accordingly stated that, "we come here, as young aged persons, without a shred of demagogy, to ask you to participate" in leaving behind "a retrograde past in which we were unfortunately accomplices."[66]

In addition to the opposition of the landowners and multinationals, Gelbard was also attacked by the extreme-right paramilitary organization Alianza Anticomunista Argentina (Argentine Anti-Communist Alliance, also known as Triple A), headed by the minister for social welfare and Perón's righthand man, José López Rega. Through this organization, López Rega orchestrated a campaign against Gelbard.[67] Gelbard also received threats from armed organizations on the extreme Left, which singled him out as an "agent of capitalism." In response to these affronts, Gelbard stated that the "Gran Paritaria Nacional" (National Committee on Wage Negotiations) envisaged in the government's social pact "has, to my judgement, a greater transformative power than an act of terrorism. Yet the material and intellectual terrorists from both extremes refuse to accept this path of National Reconstruction and Liberation."[68] In fact, he frequently included in his speeches references to Perón's "peaceful revolution." Later, Gelbard would say: "General Perón stated that revolutions can be carried out through blood or through time. He chose time. He opened the door to all and showed fists to none. He did not analyze anyone's blood to see what proportion of Peronist blood cells it contained. What mattered to him was individual's desire to forge the nation, and this is the example that we must follow."[69]

By that time, it was no longer an inconvenience for Gelbard to praise Perón publicly. Rather, it had become a necessity, as he relied on Perón as his main source of political support. Aside from the CGE, Gelbard's other source of support was the CGT. In May 1974, he resorted to this confederation to host a conference at its Escuela de Capacitación de Dirigentes Sindicales (Union Leadership Training School). On that occasion, he stated, again in an epic tone: "Like us, you have fought your entire lives for a process of national liberation. We came up with these ideas long before they were adopted by the government, and we were frequently marginalized from society for defending them. It would be difficult to find a better ally than the CGT in this process. Only popular support will allow us to consolidate and deepen the socially oriented economic policy that will lead our country to its fullest fulfilment and liberation."[70]

Crucial to this support, he specified, was the workers' ability to coordinate a mobilization that would include housewives, retired persons, and youth, and march together to the Secretariat of Commerce to demand an end to the to-and-fro on the part of those persons and parties who seemed to lack the maturity to deliver on the price-regulation agreements that they themselves had signed.[71] At that time, the oil crisis of August 1973 was unfolding due to the decision of the Organization of the Petroleum Exporting Countries (OPEC) to unilaterally triple the cost of a barrel of oil on the international market.[72] Simultaneously, European markets began to restrict imports of Argentine beef,[73] and other economic variables also became adverse, which led in turn to violations of the social pact and the price adjustments it prescribed. Increased inflation also made itself felt, as it reached a level of 13 percent over the year.

In the midst of these upheavals, Congress summoned Gelbard to present his vision for the economy. In addressing Congress, he made one of his most politicized and confrontational speeches, stating that, "flaunting their total impunity, some sectors that are outside of the political spectrum are sabotaging our work to bring about change."[74] He then described those sectors as "those who make international monopolies and the lawyers who defend them," and stated that, "as far as one can remember, these same groups were the ones that made it possible for all salaried workers to be substantially divested of their ability to participate in the nation's revenue, and for some adventures to be considered as contributions from foreign capital."[75]

After this introduction, Gelbard pointed out that "such a drastic change in the liberal political and economic traditions, imposed by the employees of the monopolies, could not take place without a few incidents," and then referred to "two real problems, whose magnitude and origin some have been exaggerating to their own ends: shortages and the black market. These deviations are a minor fact in comparison with the context that we have just described."[76] About this, he stated that these problems had also arisen during the first two Peronist administrations, but that this had not prevented "the working classes from participating in half of the nation's revenue, because this is what happens when workers are granted high salaries, simultaneously to the economy's expansion."[77] He also pointed out that "using shortages and the black market as pretexts, some wish to sabotage the policies that were voted into office by the people" and that "liberalism in Argentina has only brought its people misery."[78] He also spoke at length about the unprecedented degree to which Argentina was forging commercial ties and designing investment projects for new trading partners. About this he stated that, "this policy of foreign investments in the metallurgic sector, in naval industry, and in petrochemicals, was not negotiated with colonial powers. Nor did it require the all too familiar currency devaluations or the world tours to find creditors to save the country."[79]

Gelbard also attacked ultra-leftist organizations, referring to them as "agents of anarchy who wish to speed up the [transformation] process and who fail to realize that they are playing the part planned for them by the same old reactionaries."[80] Toward the end of his address, he evaluated the administration's overall performance, emphasizing as one of the most outstanding achievements the fact that "workers' participation in the nation's income increased from 33 percent to 42.5 percent, that unemployment dropped, from 6.6 percent in 1973 to 4.4 percent in October [of that same year], and the yearly inflation rate plummeted from 80 percent when Perón became president to less than 13 percent [at the time of Gelbard's address]."[81]

Political, not economic, issues began to destabilize Gelbard and his project. On 1 July 1974, Juan Perón died at the age of 78 in the midst of a fierce internecine struggle within Peronism between the Peronist armed organization Montoneros and the Triple A, and amid the violent social climate generated by these organizations on the extreme Left and Right, respectively.[82] Perón's death also marked the end of the effort to stimulate the autonomous growth of Argentine society while remaining within the bounds of capitalism by way of the sought-after social pact, which was to moderate and channel confrontations between workers and business owners.

Once Gelbard was bereft of his main political pillar and in the midst of a climate strained by inflation and shortages, his old enemies began to seek revenge. López Rega intensified his antisemitic attacks in a postering campaign in which he "accused" Gelbard of being a "Zionist," a "Bolshevik Jew," and a "traitor Jew"[83] – a continuation of the campaign that he had launched earlier via the lampoon magazines *El Caudillo*, *Las Bases*, and *Patria Peronista*, which he funded from the coffers of the Ministry of Social Development as well as through the nationalist newspaper *Cabildo*, which characterized Gelbard as one of the financiers of the "Jewish-Marxist-Montonero apparatus."[84] Fearing for his life, Gelbard asked the World Jewish Congress to intervene as he did not trust the DAIA's leadership at the time and believed that a reaction from the international Jewish organization might provoke in López Rega fear of being accused of antisemitism. Indeed, this move had its effect, and López Rega met with Jewish community leaders and sought to distance himself from the accusations against him.[85]

Yet it was the intense, ongoing coverage of Gelbard's past acts of corruption in regard to his company Aluar that would hurt him the most. The opposition delved into these facts, which were covered extensively by the press (with the exception of *La Opinión*, in which Timerman again defended Gelbard, claiming that the accusations were motivated by antisemitism).[86]

By September, when the general grief over Perón's death had run its course and powerful factions had begun to operate, *La Nación* managed to publish the draft of an agrarian law that was being discussed in the economic cabinet with the aim of altering the agrarian sector's production structure. After the draft was leaked, the Sociedad Rural Argentina (which represented the landowners' interests) claimed that the legislative draft, prepared by Secretary of Agriculture and Livestock Farming Horacio Giberti, contained "factors that would disrupt Argentina's families" and that it was a direct attack on property that introduced ideas that were foreign to the national sentiment and violated the constitution. The newspaper added that the draft had "a strongly collectivist bent that set the legal basis for an agrarian reform."[87]

Most media outlets began to speak of expropriations even as Giberti took pains to clarify that the project was not in its final form.[88] With a diminished CGE, the potential support of the CGT was crucial, as the two confederations had consistently demanded an agrarian reform. Such unity of purpose was essential both to implement the legislation and to ensure Gelbard's political survival. This is why, to Argentina's great surprise, after some hesitation the leadership of the CGT added their voices to those of the project's critics, leaving Gelbard in complete isolation.[89] All analyses suggest that Gelbard and the CGE had overestimated the unity between the working class and the business owners.

As union leaders began to see their power diminish due to the ongoing two-year freeze in salaries resulting from the social pact, they also began to prioritize their own survival. Many of them had even become allies of public servants in the administration of Isabel Perón, Juan Perón third wife, who had succeeded him in power and who espoused a project for the country that could not be further removed from Gelbard's. Liliana De Riz, in her book *Retorno y derrumbe* (Return and Collapse), posits that without Perón's presence the credibility of the economic model vanished: "The social pact had been a failure and this failure shook the bases of the entire edifice built by Gelbard. It is in this context, that the unions' offensive, with the support of Perón's successors, would defeat him [Gelbard]. To that end, the union leadership would promptly jump ship from the struggle against landowners. The CGT radically changed its stance by refusing to support the draft for an agrarian law. A reformist project thus fell apart under the pressure of the agrarian bourgeoisie and with the consent of the CGT."[90]

A few days before the debate, perhaps realizing that his days were numbered, Gelbard asked to make a speech that would be broadcast on national television, in which he voiced his vision and legacy. He pointed out that economic indicators had substantially improved since his policies were implemented. He also expressed his belief that, "since 1955, the so-called market rules, that exist and must be respected in specific conditions, have always brought misery to the working people," and that "the economic theses implemented by experts trained in the large foreign metropolises have only succeeded at maintaining our dependency."[91] Gelbard insisted that the persistent economic problems "could be solved without reactionary or currency-based surgeries."[92]

But it was too late. By October 1974, Gelbard had lost all political power, as he no longer had even the support of the business owners, who distanced themselves from the CGE, now an outdated project.[93] On the nineteenth of that month, he tendered his irrevocable resignation from his ministerial post and, in his letter of resignation, insisted on the importance of pursuing his project. On that October day, the country lost not just a minister of the economy but an entire political project with nothing to replace it.[94]

Gelbard returned to managing his business group while the country fell apart under a president who was incapable of addressing extreme violence and economic and social chaos. He granted his first (post-resignation) press interview in March 1976, a few days before Isabel Perón was ousted from the presidency. On that occasion he suggested that a campaign had been launched that sought to portray the country's tragic predicament as a result of the economic policy implemented between May 1973 and October 1974. He clarified that, "in fact, we are currently suffering from the consequences of having abandoned that policy. Their strategy is clear: first they forced us to lower the flags of development with social justice and sovereignty, and now they want to ensure that no one will ever dare to raise these flags again."[95] He also defended the lucid actions undertaken by the CGE and Perón. He noted that Perón "stated that while [he] was in government, he would not change that economic policy" and added: "indeed, he did not change it."[96] Gelbard stuck to his views about the project for a social pact, as "class struggle would lead us to destruction."[97]

In the midst of deep social and economic instability, on 24 March 1976 a military junta carried out a coup and instituted what it called the Proceso de Reorganización Nacional (Process of National Reorganization), which was, in fact, a civil-military dictatorship. The

Proceso's short-term aim was to annihilate members of the armed organizations of the extreme Left and, in the long term, to dismantle the remnants of the alliance between national business owners and workers who, as early as the first Peronist administrations, had challenged the oligarchic power of the traditional elites. To that end, one of the first measures taken by the de facto government was intervention into the affairs of the CGE and CGT, as well as implementation of an economic plan consisting of adjustments that reduced workers' salaries so that they accounted for only 25 percent of the GDP by 1977 (down from 43 percent).[98] The military also implemented a policy of state terrorism and persecution that applied not only to armed organizations but to all opponents (perceived or actual) of the junta's project for the nation, a campaign that ultimately was responsible for the murder of between 10,000 and 30,000 people. The proportion of Jewish-Argentines among the victims of this brutal dictatorship was relatively high in comparison to the size of this population.[99] Gelbard decided to go into exile in the United States, knowing that, as an icon and formerly the chief representative of the national bourgeoisie, he would be one of the dictatorship's main targets. By the end of that year, the military centred its investigations on the companies owned by Graiver, as he had been accused of managing the funds that the Montoneros had obtained through kidnappings and subsequent extortion. The investigation expanded to include Gelbard, Madanes, Broner, and Timerman.

Despite Gelbard's warnings, nearly all of the newspapers,[100] including *La Opinión*, had supported the coup and kept silent regarding the kidnappings, tortures, murders, and disappearances of persons by the military.[101] Journalist Rogelio García Lupo clarified that "Gelbard tried to convince Jacobo [Timerman] to keep *La Opinión* out of the game of supporting the coup led by the *good army men* against Isabelita. But Jacobo paid him no heed. For Gelbard, no good military men would come to power from a coup; he saw these military men coming." *Clarín*, Gelbard's old rival, joined forces with *La Nación* and *La Razón* to negotiate with the military the purchase of most of the shares of the paper company Papel Prensa.[102] The editors of *Clarín* also understood the possibility that the military junta could advance mercilessly upon the newspaper's old foe and his organization, the

CGE. Based on this, *Clarín* urged the military to show no mercy toward Gelbard.[103]

A few weeks later, the military junta stripped Gelbard of his Argentine citizenship, leaving him in exile without a homeland, and confiscated his properties, valued at USD $50 million.[104] In April 1976, Rotenberg met with Gelbard at the Plaza Hotel in New York during a visit to the United States. Rotenberg recalled: "this was someone who had been ill: he seemed tired and moved somewhat slowly, although he tried to hide it. This powerful, solid, hard, and rational man who never lost control of the most engaged situations was a fragile and defenceless person."[105] They spoke about the path on which Argentina was embarked and Rotenberg attempted to reassure him by telling him that, as with previous coups, this one would be transitory. But Gelbard warned him: "This military coup is unlike the others. They have very ambitious plans: they want to build another country, a new country with a privileged few and powerless masses. When they step down from power, Argentina will be completely changed. It will take many years to rebuild it."[106]

In October, a brain aneurysm cut his life short. Years ago, when he assumed the post of minister of the economy, he had observed that "we won't be able to live with our conscience if, when action was required of us, we were beaten by the same people as always, those against whom we have struggled all of our lives. This would mean a new defeat that would affect the country that today's youth will inherit."[107]

7

Justicialismo through Israeli Lenses, 1946–76

Juan Perón made considerable efforts to convince critics and opponents, both at home and abroad, that he was not a fascist president. The children's section of the magazine *Mundo Peronista* explained: "We allow you to get angry and to yell when you hear someone say that General Perón is a *dictator* or a *fascist*. General Perón is the leader of [an] extraordinary popular movement. *Dictators* don't take the people into consideration, rather, they enslave it. General Perón is an Argentine who loves his country. 'Fascist' is a *foreign* word that really has no relation to Argentina."[1] In the United States, at least, these efforts were in vain.

Some, like Spruille Braden, the US ambassador to Argentina from May through September 1945 and subsequently undersecretary of state for inter-American affairs until June 1947, considered that Washington should not make efforts to mend fences with governments led by figures such as Perón. In an article published after Perón's 1946 electoral victory, Braden wrote: "With the defeat of Germany, Argentina remains under the bare dictatorship of uniformed men who drink at the fountain where drank Hitler, Mussolini, and Franco. As long as the people of Argentina live under the heel of this dictatorship … none of us can sleep soundly nights."[2] *The Nation*, the progressive liberal weekly magazine published in New York, claimed in early 1946 that Perón had "copied" his political strategy "directly from his Nazi mentor, Adolf Hitler." In another article, the magazine explained to its readers that Perón's regime had made antisemitism an integral part of its platform.[3]

These accusations that swirled around Perón were rooted in the "Germanophile" positions that held sway among the members of the Argentine army since the early 1900s, as well as in Argentina's neutrality during the Second World War (much to the displeasure of the United States), and the entry into the country of Nazi war criminals and Third Reich collaborators. The *Blue Book* published by the US State Department on the eve of the 1946 presidential elections, in an attempt to prevent Perón from winning, alleged that, in contemporary Argentina, Germans dominate "the economic organization – industrial, commercial, and agricultural – which they need to provide a base for the reconstruction of German aggressive power."[4]

Upon taking office in June 1946, Perón therefore took great efforts to enhance his image on the international stage. He clearly understood that improving relations with the United States was a *sine qua non* for the realization of his plan to industrialize and modernize the country. To that end, he did his best to shake off any suspicions of fascism and antisemitism and sought to establish good relations with Argentina's Jewish community and, subsequently, with the new Jewish state. One of the goals of this campaign was to capture the sympathy of US Jews – whose influence Perón had overestimated – in the hope that they could shift the perception of Argentina among the general public and decision makers in Washington. According to Jacob Tsur, Israel's first ambassador to Argentina, Perón "was convinced of the power of world Jewry and its influence on public opinion, especially in North America."[5]

Yet Jewish organizations in the United States also viewed Argentina and its regime with suspicion. As early as July 1945, Louis Lipsky, the chairman of the American Jewish Committee, wrote that "the Fascist state of Argentina had written a shameless record of collaboration with the Axis during all years of the war; even while the conference [in San Francisco at which the UN was established] was being held, it was engaged in proving its enduring friendship for Nazi Germans by providing a haven of refuge for the Nazi criminals and their stolen property."[6]

This view was common in the US media. In contrast, George Messersmith, the US ambassador to Argentina who succeeded Braden, was very concerned by the hostility that the State Department and the US's powerful liberal press had exhibited toward Argentina.[7]

Messersmith developed cordial and friendly relations with Perón. He maintained that "there [was] nothing totalitarian, fascist, or Nazi" in Perón's regime and was convinced of the leader's sincerity in his will to improve relations with the United States and to promote Argentina's participation in the inter-American system. On some occasions he expressed his great sorrow over what he considered as a certain kind of inaccurate, tendentious reporting that continued to be common practice among some of the most prominent US newspapers, especially in their portrayal of Perón's regime as fascist and undemocratic. In a memorandum to the Secretary of State, the ambassador complained: "So far as the American press is concerned, press comment and editorials increasingly are in the direction that the Argentine is a Fascist and totalitarian state, unfriendly to the United States and with sinister designs on its neighbors. Some of our papers and some of our editorial writers speak of the Argentine as though we were in a sort of war with her and she is an enemy country."[8]

Given the generalized hostility, the veteran diplomat sought more effective action. In his attempt to change the perception of Argentina in the United States, Messersmith contacted directly key figures in his country's press. One such example is his forty-three-page letter to Arthur Sulzberger, publisher of the *New York Times*, in which he stated categorically: "I know something about dictatorships, and this is not [one] in the sense we understand the term."[9]

When Messersmith was appointed ambassador to Buenos Aires, the liberal press was delighted and portrayed the diplomat as someone "who knows and hates Nazism from deep and intimate study." One reporter described him as having "an uncanny nose that can smell an S.O.B. as far as the wind can carry the scent," and that this would serve him in confronting the danger inherent in Perón's leadership.[10] A few months later, however, the press began to feature articles focusing on Messersmith's conciliatory attitude toward the "fascist dictator." In August 1946, Messersmith received a threatening message from one of Braden's aides, reminding him that when Nelson Rockefeller had tried to appease Argentina in 1945, the staunch opposition of the *New York Times* and the *Washington Post* led to his removal from the State Department.[11]

Those who succeeded Messersmith in the post of ambassador – James Bruce (1947–49), Stanton Griffis (1949–50), and Albert Nufer

(1953–55) – were also critical of the US media's coverage of events in Perón's Argentina and identified this as a potential obstacle to improving relations between the two countries.[12] Shortly after Bruce was sworn in as ambassador, he praised Juan and Eva Perón for their personalities and promptly earned attacks from several US newspapers.[13] Jacob Tsur characterized this campaign as resulting from the inability of US journalists to understand the particularities of the Argentine case: "The foreign press – and especially the US press – used to paint the president of Argentina in the exotic colors of a typical South American dictator, and some journalists would try to stick him with the label of the well-known dogmas from the old world, communism on this side and fascism on that. That is one of the mistakes of democratic public opinion in the world, it builds molds permanently and then tries to fit any phenomenon it has trouble explaining into these molds."[14]

ISRAEL'S PORTRAYAL OF PERONISM

Surprisingly, the image of Peronism was more complex in the state of Israel, as was reflected in the country's print media during Perón's first two presidencies. I draw this conclusion from an analysis of a selection of contents from seven daily newspapers that reflected the range of ideas in Israeli society at the time, as most of them were supported by or affiliated with political parties: from the right-wing *Herut*, to the more moderate *Maariv*, *Hatzofeh*, *Haaretz*, and *Davar*, and the Socialist-Zionist *Al Hamishmar*, all the way to the Communist Party's newspaper, *Kol Haam*. My analysis focuses on how these newspapers spoke about Peronism in the coverage of key events pertaining to bilateral relations with Argentina or to the development of Peronism. During that period, the most notable such events were the launch of diplomatic relations between the two countries (June–September 1949), the visit to Israel of Diego Luis Molinari, then chair of the Foreign Relations Committee of the Argentine Senate (March 1950), the signing of the first economic agreement between the two countries (April 1950), the visit to Buenos Aires of Yosef Sprinzak, then speaker of the Israeli Knesset (May–June 1950), the presidential elections in Argentina (November 1951), the death of Eva Perón (July 1952), the visit of Israel's minister of foreign affairs,

Moshe Sharett, to Argentina (April 1953), and the overthrow of the Peronist regime (June–September 1955).

An analysis of the coverage of Peronism in the Israeli press during this period needs to begin by discussing the volume of attention given to Argentina. The party magazine *Mundo Peronista*, which was devoted to praising the Peronist regime and argued that people across the world, including the Jewish state, looked up to the actions of the Peronist government, wrote that, "Perón had not only honored the Argentine Jewish community as a part of the Argentine people. The transcendence of his Doctrine and accomplishments is acknowledged across the globe and has had a deep impact on the Israeli nation." Further, the publication traced Perón's popularity to the great sympathy that the "líder" had shown toward the Jewish state, and explained to its readers that, "Perón is as beloved ... by the Israeli people as by our own."[15]

Of course, such statements suppose a degree of exaggeration and distortion. In fact, the volume of news stories and articles on Argentina published in the Israeli press was small. Still, the coverage on Argentina yielded a variety of portrayals of the Peronist regime, unlike the single-minded depictions prevalent in the European and US print media. This diversity of viewpoints reflected Israeli society. A similar complexity and nuance was also evidenced in the opinions of the head of the Israeli legation in Buenos Aires, Jacob Tsur. In his reports to the Ministry of Foreign Affairs in Jerusalem, and in his memoirs, Tsur described the Perón government as having espoused key social reforms that in turn guaranteed the masses' support, but he also characterized the regime as one that limited freedoms and furthered a cult of personality that was not typical in democratic regimes: "From my arrival in this country, I disagreed with the common view that saw only the negative in the regime that rules here. Perón's hazy ideology and his style of leadership also had a positive side. The masses streamed after him for a reason: After decades, the people had finally got a president who cared about their condition and their livelihood. Yet in this regime there was also much that was undefined, turbid, false, and hypocritical."[16]

To illustrate the complexity of the portrayal of Peronism in the Israeli media, I now focus on the Israeli newspapers' coverage of the fall of the Peronist regime. *Haaretz*, a liberal newspaper printed every morning and the oldest of the independent newspapers, generally tried to provide an objective description of the June military rebellion and the self-named Revolución Libertadora that followed in September 1955. It attempted to remain neutral while being respectful to Perón and including the inevitable report that "the Jews in Argentina are safe."[17]

Maariv, the evening newspaper founded in 1948, covered the events much more extensively and prominently, using bold lettering and locating these stories on its front page. The newspaper offered both reports of events and interpretative commentary. The most interesting of these was published on 17 June 1955 and penned by the editor of its international section. Surprisingly, after adopting a condescending tone toward Latin America ("Military revolts are a method exclusive to South America; in Latin America there has never been a true democracy, and few regimes that were truly dedicated to the good of the masses") and enumerating the various shortcomings of Perón's regime (referring to him as a "dictator-president"), the editor also attempted to praise that same regime. He evoked Perón's clash with the Catholic Church and went on to compare Peronism with the French Revolution and with the Republicans in the Spanish Civil War. The editor referred to the Acción Católica as "shock troops" and portrayed in a positive light the social reforms that Perón had implemented. He then compared the "reactionary" opposition to Francisco Franco and his supporters, and described them sardonically and in lugubrious tones. He concluded with a summary: "Since that is the choice, world opinion favours Perón and his regime more, despite its many weaknesses, despite its totalitarian nature, despite the corruption that has impaired many of its components ... *There is no doubt that Perón's regime is one of the best that Latin America has ever known, and the continuation of this regime is one of the conditions required to bring this important part of the world out of the backwardness of generations.*"[18]

Three days after that article, the same newspaper, known for its dedication to high-quality reporting, published another article, which, this time, was largely sympathetic to Perón.[19] While Israeli readers could not agree with quotes in which Perón praised Mussolini as a model to follow – and whose mistakes should be avoided – the article did describe the president as an energetic and talented man, while highlighting how the reforms that he enacted benefitted the country's working class. The author of this column considered that Perón's biggest mistake had been to confront the Church, and that this could seal the fate of his regime.

Within its many news stories on the September coup, *Maariv* included various articles that overall expressed some degree of sympathy and admiration for the Peronist regime. The most notable of those was Philip Ben's "What's next after Perón?" published on 20 September 1955. Ben wrote that although Perón was undoubtedly a tyrant, Peronism was "not a static and conservative tyranny led by a military caste" but that it "represented an idea of social dictatorship that, although not unsullied by fascism, could nevertheless congratulate itself on some accomplishments." Beyond the demagoguery that characterized the regime, Perón had indeed improved the situation of those most disadvantaged, giving them honour and self-respect. Ben further emphasized that no concentration camps had been set up in Argentina, that the country had relatively few political prisoners, and that a measure of freedom of expression had been upheld. The author went on to express pessimism for Argentina's future and added that, independently of what one's opinion of Peronism might be, the clock could not be turned back to before that decade and its achievements should not be erased. Argentines had to build on both the achievements and shortcomings of Peronism.[20]

Davar exhibited the same tendency. This newspaper was founded in 1925 as the press organ of the Histadrut (Israel's General Workers' Confederation), which identified with MAPAI, the social-democratic party that was the predecessor of the Labour Party. An article penned by Shlomo Shafir, *Davar*'s international editor, avoided stark contrasts in his attempt to explain the fall of Perón's regime.[21] He mentioned Perón's "questionable methods," which affected the rule of law and individual freedoms, but also acknowledged his "progressive social policy."

The coverage of the June 1955 failed coup in *Herut* and *Hatzofeh* reveals a slight inclination toward Perón. *Hatzofeh*, which sided with the orthodox religious party, qualified as "uncivilized" the bombing of the Plaza de Mayo (adjacent to the Casa Rosada) by rebel naval aircraft, emphasized Perón's achievements and the support he enjoyed among the general population, and concluded that this ordeal would strengthen the president.[22] Perón's ouster in September of that year was described matter-of-factly, without expressing favour or support for any of the parties involved. These news reports included observations translated from the *New York Times*, which had argued that the only difference between Peronist Argentina and the Soviet purges was that no one in the South American country had been executed after trial. At the most, they faced a lengthy imprisonment.[23]

Herut's political correspondent offered a synthesis of the decade of Peronist administration. In this article, the author highlighted Perón's constructive political program, contrasting it with his rivals' failure to unite around any other cause than their opposition to the regime: "Perón can boast the multi-faceted accomplishment of having transformed Argentina from a semi-colonial country into a diversified and industrial country. Perón can boast the accomplishment of having done a great deal to elevate the masses' standard of living. Independently of the outcome of the current confrontation in Argentina, none of his successors will be able to turn back the clock. The forces awakened in Argentina by the Peronist regime continue to make themselves felt, not only in Argentina but throughout South America."[24]

Of all the Israeli newspapers I examined, *Herut*, the outlet most identified with rightist, revisionist Zionism, expressed most strongly and consistently its sympathy toward the regime for its entire duration, maintaining this stance until the last moment. The newspaper avoided, for example, publishing negative reports about events in Argentina and always wrote about the Peróns respectfully. The regime's nationalist, socially oriented dimension, along with the couple's charismatic leadership, was apparently very attractive to the members of the revisionist party led by Menachem Begin.

The Israeli Left took an overall negative view of Perón's regime. Mordechai Nachumi, writing in *Al Hamishmar*, the newspaper affiliated with MAPAM (the Unified Workers' Party) and founded in 1943, characterized the Peronist administrations as "a period of dictatorial acts and demagoguery."[25] He alleged that Perón's support among the working class had waned during the final years of his presidency due to inflation and the regime's hostility toward the Church. The article concluded that the time had come for "real leftists" to unite the people and to set it on a "true" path, rather than on the road of illusions down which Perón had led them.

Kol Haam, the organ of the Israeli Communist Party, exhibited some perplexity at the events that occurred in Argentina between June and September 1955. This reaction originated, perhaps, in the conflict of interest between Argentine communism and Soviet foreign policy. The newspaper's 19 June edition displayed hostility toward Peronism: "In foreign policy, Perón is following in the footsteps of Mussolini."[26] With some sarcasm, it went on to suggest that Perón had set up governmental organizations and then imposed them upon the working class, and that he had enacted legislation supposedly to "benefit the working class."[27] The newspaper likened Perón's regime to Italian fascism and the Catholic Church, alleging that it attempted to maintain a policy based on harmony between social classes and social peace, and that it "used social demagoguery to attract to its ranks workers who were devoid of class consciousness."[28] The Communist newspaper argued that in fact the Argentine regime was operating against the workers' movement, which "is persecuted beyond endurance."[29] The Argentine Jewish Communist newspaper *Tribuna*, for its part, equated the members of the OIA to the *Judenrat* – that is, to the Jews who collaborated with the Nazis in the ghettos of the German-occupied areas during the Second World War.

Nonetheless, the *Kol Haam* column openly expressed satisfaction at Perón's opposition to "US capital" and to Cardinal Spellman, "an emissary of Wall Street and the Vatican."[30] The author assured his readers that "the Communist Party of Argentina is fighting for the restoration of democratic freedoms and for Argentina's economic independence," and that this party has "great influence among urban and rural workers."[31]

Three months later, the same Communist activist published another column on Argentina that was more favourable to Peronism.[32] He portrayed the military coup as the result of a conspiracy between the State Department and the "Wall Street sharks," and argued that US opposition to Perón's regime was not rooted in the latter's undemocratic nature. Indeed, the author added, politicians in Washington had shown their willingness to support dictatorships when they followed their orders. The real reason for US opposition was Perón's courage in confronting capitalist economic interests and his boldness in cooperating with the Soviet Union. The Communist newspaper favoured this government's adoption of a "third position" in its foreign policy over a government that bowed to US dictates.

Unlike in other countries, this examination of Israeli newspapers during the 1950s therefore does not yield an even or unidimensional portrayal of the Peronist regime. These perceptions were complex, and many of them were uniquely informed by Perón's fight against antisemitism as well as by the close relations between the two countries. Furthermore, as most of the Israeli press was financially supported by the country's political parties, their stances, whether regarding domestic or international issues such as Peronism, were reflected on these newspapers' pages, which were tinged by each party's position vis-à-vis Israeli government policy.

Further, in contrast with the US print media's tendency to portray Peronism as a typical Latin American dictatorship and a megalomaniacal campaign to fulfill the unstoppable desires of Juan Perón and Eva Duarte, Israeli newspapers usually focused on Peronism's ideological facets. Occasional anti-Peronist stances in the Israeli press are often attributable to the fact that none of the Israeli newspapers had permanent correspondents or roving reporters in Latin America's Southern Cone, such that many of these news items were sourced from stories and comments wired from English-language news agencies and the largest US newspapers, above all the *New York Times*. To generalize only slightly, the print-media outlets associated with the Israeli Left generally exhibited expressions of hostility toward Peronism, and sometimes extreme ones, also identifying it with fascism, while the rightist media overall expressed sympathy toward the regime – sometimes unconditionally, as in the case of *Herut*.

Israeli intellectual magazines of the period reveal a more sophisticated approach to Justicialismo, portraying various facets of society, the regime, culture, and ideology in Perón's Argentina. Two articles exemplify this tendency: Y. Toledo's "Perón's Regime: Its Portrait and Its Future," published in the monthly literary and political magazine *Molad* to mark the beginning of Perón's second presidency in 1952; and a piece published in the magazine *Mibifnim*, affiliated with the kibbutz movement, and authored by Yacov Versano (who, under the last name Oved, would later publish specialized studies of Argentina's anarchist movement). Versano's article, titled "The Justicialist Regime in Argentina," was written shortly before the coup in which Perón was ousted and following a stay in Buenos Aires during which Versano served as a delegate of the kibbutz movement. Toledo's and Versano's articles reflected the typical leftist positions but also ventured beyond the traditional Left's hostility to Peronism. In their attempt to understand why the Argentine working class so firmly supported this charismatic leader, these authors allowed themselves to explore criticisms of the positions adopted by the Argentine Socialist and Communist parties.[33]

THE REVERSAL OF AN IMAGE

The return to power of Juan Domingo Perón following a lengthy exile awoke in many Argentines hopes that he would restore political stability in Argentina. After Perón was ousted from power by the military coup of September 1955, successive regimes (whether civil or military, democratic or authoritarian) attempted to maintain and ensure stability and development while excluding Peronism and its supporters from the political system. As Perón had broken the rules of the democratic game during his presidency, gradually limiting opposing views inside his party and out, his political legitimacy was diminished. The same fate awaited the Peronist movement, whose strongly working-class base remained loyal to the ousted general. These administrations' attempts at stability and development failed, however, typically concluding in military uprisings, political violence, and repression. The chasm in Argentine society between Peronists and the various anti-Peronist groupings grew deeper at each phase. As for Perón, he sought refuge in various Latin American republics until the early 1960s, when he crossed the Atlantic and settled in Spain with the consent of its dictator, Generalissimo Francisco Franco.

The continued exclusion from political life of the largest political and social movement in Argentina contributed to a polarization of the postures of some Peronist sectors, which in turn generated stormy working dynamics, protests, and marches, and also gave rise to guerrilla movements. As the Cold War escalated and fears grew about the possible influence of the Cuban Revolution on social struggles across the continent, the military's upper echelons and the governing elites were increasingly concerned that Peronism, too, might become more revolutionary. Within this context, the only possible way to guarantee order and stability in the southern republic was to permit the return from exile of the now elderly general in the hope that the caudillo, at 78 years of age, held the key to salvation. These hopes were obviously exaggerated. Diplomat Jacob Tsur, who had been Israel's ambassador in Buenos Aires during Perón's first mandate, met up with him again shortly before the general's return to Argentina. He expressed surprise at how the physique of the old military man had aged: "I had not seen him in twenty years. I remembered him in his military uniform, his back straight, sure of himself, and with a smile that flaunted his shiny bright teeth. I'll admit it: I was excited and moved prior to our meeting ... Then I saw him facing me, aged, hunched, and shielded in an overcoat. He was 78 years old, but he seemed to me older than an octogenarian, tired and ill ... I chose to keep our conversation short. This man looked ill and broken down. Pathetic."[34]

In the remainder of this chapter, I examine how Perón and the Peronist doctrine were portrayed in the Israeli press between his definitive return to Argentina in June 1973 and the swearing-in of his third wife, María Estela Martínez de Perón (Isabelita), as president in July 1974. The consequences of these events for the Jewish community in Argentina and for relations between Israel and Argentina will also be analyzed from the point of view of contemporary newspapers.

By the early 1970s, Israel's print media offered a portrayal of Peronism far more negative than its earlier, more positive appraisals. Nonetheless, and similarly to their attitudes in the 1950s, the news stories and columns published in Israel in 1973 and 1974 do not portray Peronism unidimensionally. In my view, the doubts that now emerged owed themselves to two factors. On the one hand, from the mid-1960s onward, the right and left wings of Peronism began to exhibit antisemitic and anti-Israel stances, which had also become apparent among some sectors of the CGT. On the other hand, Argentina's foreign policy orientation with regard to the conflict in the Middle East gradually shifted during the first half of the 1970s toward positions more favourable to the Arab countries in general and toward the Palestinians in particular. It is also noteworthy that precisely during this period, many more members of the new generations of Jewish-Argentines joined the ranks of Peronism than had their predecessors during Perón's first two administrations.

The Israeli press did not devote detailed coverage to Perón's brief third presidency (1973–74), perhaps contrary to what would have been typical in a country that had always shown some interest in Argentine matters due to the country's sizable Jewish community and the close ties between the two countries from the late 1940s onward. The reasons for this relatively scant coverage are rather evident. When Perón returned to Argentina in 1973, Israel was still feeling the euphoria of the Six-Day War and its conquest of the West Bank and Gaza Strip. Nevertheless, during the week when Perón was sworn in as president, the outbreak of the Yom Kippur War on 6 October 1973 diverted the Israeli public's attention toward the military campaign and toward what a national commission of inquiry classified as failings in the Israel Defense Forces prior to the joint attack against Israel by Egypt and Syria. International news items, including those covering events in Argentina, were not picked up in the Israeli press during that period.

Changes in Israel's mass media during the early 1970s also accounted for this shift. This was a period of transition in which, in contrast to the conditions in which the country's press was established, privately owned presses began to dominate over the party-affiliated newspapers and their clear ideological stances.[35] Israel was also a much more populous and diversified society, and a new set of social and economic conditions diminished the weight of party newspapers. During this period, the media adopted a more condescending attitude toward Latin America. Israel was a developed country whose growing population and economic development made it more powerful. It was no longer the fledgling nation that had once imposed an austerity plan, whose poor towns paled in comparison to the effervescence of Buenos Aires, and that awaited desperately the shipments of beef from the Río de la Plata. Israel now perceived itself as part of the Western developed world. From this point of view, Argentina looked increasingly like a "Third World" country.

FORCED EXILE AND RETURN TO ARGENTINA

During the nearly two decades of Perón's exile, despite his political isolation and physical distance from his homeland, he continued to play an important part as an arbiter of Argentine politics. From his home on an estate in Madrid's suburbs, he had frequent exchanges with union leaders and with activists from the movement's different branches through emissaries who transmitted messages and instructions to followers. He was apprised of the latest developments thanks to his representatives and proxies, which he replaced often to prevent any individual from accruing too much influence. The aptly named "17 October" estate in Madrid's Puerta de Hierro neighbourhood became the mecca for an ongoing pilgrimage comprising numerous personalities identified with the ousted president's movement. Perón used these channels to kindle the embers of activism among his sympathizers and to stoke the hope that, in a not-too-distant future, he would return to the president's office in the Casa Rosada.

Throughout those years of exile, Perón manoeuvered and manipulated so as to ensure the continuance of his primacy in the movement. His politics typically unfolded in a pendular movement with the aim of dividing and conquering those gathered together in the heterogeneous movement that bore his name. Perón's praise of the revolutionary Left allowed him to gain the support of a large number of radicalized youths, who had been children when the Revolución Libertadora ousted the Peronist regime. The exiled military man refused to condemn the activities of the Montoneros guerrilla organization, a key protagonist during the late 1960s. Instead, he chose to refer to them as "special units" of the movement and, through them, hoped to pressure the military regime to authorize a general election that would return the military men to their barracks.

In July 1972, the government led by General Alejandro A. Lanusse was struggling against dramatically increasing inflation and armed organizations, on both the Right and the Left of the political spectrum, that disseminated terror. In response to these conditions, Lanusse attempted to summon all "democratic forces" to join his Gran Acuerdo Nacional (Great National Accord), a common front to plan for the return of the institutions of governance into the hands of civilians elected in free elections. When the political parties refused to cooperate, Lanusse decided to repeal the proscription of Peronism implemented in 1955. He did not do this out of sympathy for Peronism but because he understood that the military regime needed popular support to solve the nation's problems. Lanusse's decision was also strongly motivated by the hope that Perón's return could contain the growth of the revolutionary Left.[36]

Although Peronism was on the path to becoming part of the mainstream, Perón was not yet allowed to officially re-enter the political arena. The electoral law approved in 1972 required candidates to reside in Argentina for six months prior to election day. As a result, the Peronist ticket for the March 1973 elections put forward Héctor Cámpora, known for his near-absolute loyalty to Perón, as leader of a coalition named Frente Justicialista de Liberación (FREJULI; Justicialist Front for Liberation). Jacob Tsur described Cámpora as a bland and meek person, and Abraham Alón, the representative in Argentina of Israel's General Confederation of Workers, wrote: "Dr. Cámpora possesses a thoroughly meek personality. The main advantage that he offers is his absolute loyalty to Perón during the past decades. He was, after all, Perón's personal delegate in Argentina. The criteria for the former president's choice are still unclear, particularly considering that he could have selected a more visible personality. He may well be motivated by a preference for avoiding that a very independent person lead the list of candidates, as this person could concentrate authority and power beyond what is expected of them."[37]

Cámpora's candidacy made plain to all observers that Perón was the one who, from Madrid, controlled the pawns on the chessboard. The Juventud Peronista (Peronist Youth) cheered on the candidate with their chants of "Qué lindo, qué lindo / que va a ser / el Tío en el gobierno / Perón en el poder" (How nice, how nice / it will be / With the Uncle governing / And Perón in power). The FREJULI, with Cámpora at the head of its ticket, obtained 49 percent of the vote. After Cámpora was sworn in on 25 May, his stay in the presidency lasted a short forty-nine days. During this brief period, all the tensions between the different factions of the Peronist movement came to the fore, as each expressed its loyalty toward the leader and portrayed itself as the "authentic" Peronist tendency, dismissing the others as "traitors" or "infiltrators." The main confrontation was that between the Montoneros and the Peronist Right, organized around the figure of José López Rega. López Rega, Perón's personal secretary during the final years of his exile, who had helped the leader navigate the unions' bureaucratic machinery, was named by Perón as the Cámpora administration's minister of social welfare.

Perón returned to Argentina in June 1973. Hundreds of thousands of supporters – some estimates placed the number at two million – gathered to await their leader on the outskirts of the Ezeiza International Airport in the suburbs of Buenos Aires. This was the largest mass gathering in the country's political history. The site became the stage for a bloody armed confrontation between the Peronist Right and factions from the Left, including the Montoneros. Dozens were killed and hundreds wounded.[38] This altercation demonstrated Cámpora's difficulty in dominating and tempering the rivalry between the Peronist movement's different branches. By mid-July, Cámpora had no choice but to resign from the presidency after Perón made a dramatic announcement in which he withdrew his support from his former delegate. The path was being cleared for the now elderly leader to present his candidacy again and rise to the presidency.

When new elections were held in late September, Perón won with more than 60 percent of the vote. On 12 October 1973, he was sworn in as president of Argentina for a third and final time. Both the Right and the Left viewed his return to power as what could be the nation's last remaining hope. It seemed that Perón was the panacea that would cure all the ills of the republic and put an end to the fracturing of politics, society, and the economy that began two decades ago. Perón was expected to achieve cooperation between different sectors of society, beginning with employers and workers, thus fulfilling his promise to set right the nation.

But violence did not cease after Perón took office. The Trotskyist Ejército Revolucionario del Pueblo, the largest non-Peronist guerrilla movement, renewed its paramilitary campaign. On the Right, the Triple A intensified its activities, which consisted of kidnapping and murdering left-wing militants. Perón made efforts to put an end to the violence and establish a context of national solidarity. Support for Perón grew thanks to an improvement in Argentina's economic situation that manifested in limited inflation and increased exports, which in turn replenished currency reserves.

By that point, the president had the strength necessary to expel from his movement those elements that he had previously supported in the struggle against the military regime but that had since become obstacles to a pragmatic politics, posing a threat to his leadership and endangering the stability of his administration. He gradually marginalized the Juventud Peronista and the Montoneros, and officially announced the movement's divorce from these organizations during the celebrations of 1 May 1974 in a speech that he gave in front of a massive crowd gathered in the Plaza de Mayo – the same public and symbolic stage that had seen the birth of Peronism on 17 October 1945. In this speech, Perón reiterated his government's commitment to liberating the nation not only from the yoke of colonialism but from traitors who had infiltrated the movement and who, acting from within, were far more dangerous than those who acted from the outside. At that point, tens of thousands of sympathizers from the Peronist Left began to walk away from the Plaza, which remained half empty. As this rupture between Perón and the movement's Left was a public one, it was also definitive.

On 1 July 1974, only two months after this episode, Perón, Argentina's most notable political leader of the twentieth century, died from complications related to his many heart issues. The presidency was then transferred to Perón's widow and vice-president, María Estela Martínez de Perón, known by her stage name of Isabel, or Isabelita.

FEARS OF PERONIST ANTISEMITISM

From the time of Perón's four-week visit to Argentina in November 1972, the Israeli press began to cover the situation in Argentina in articles that discussed the country's fractured society, as well as the political leader and his movement. In a lengthy article in *Haaretz*, Abraham Paz wrote about Perón's charismatic leadership and the phases of his trajectory since Perón was first sworn in as president in 1946, but offered no serious discussion of the leader's political doctrine.[39] The next day's newspaper featured two additional articles on this topic, both of which expressed concerns about the fate of the country's 300,000 Jews upon Perón's return to Argentina. One of them wrote of the fears among Buenos Aires Jews of a "new wave of antisemitism," while the other also connected Perón to the possibility of an antisemitic surge in Argentina.[40] Some seven months later,

Haaretz reported that, "Perón promised an Israeli delegation that [his supporters] would adopt a friendly stance," but in the same article added a caveat based on anonymous "sources" that claimed that, "when Perón was in power ... his government did not show a particularly friendly attitude toward Israel and that antisemitism informed his treatment of Jewish Argentines"[41] – two arguments that this book thoroughly refutes. In the same edition, *Haaretz* characterized Peronism as a political movement that was prone to violence and that relied on guerrilla groups. This portrayal of Peronism was, as is plain to see, entirely negative.

Davar, the morning newspaper affiliated with the Labour Party – in power at the time and inheritor of the trailblazing MAPAI – offered contrasting coverage, publishing articles in June 1973 that highlighted the Argentine government's support of Israel in international organizations. One of these articles emphasized that "Argentina rejected a request that Israeli delegates be expelled" from international fora while adopting a balanced stance vis-à-vis the Arab-Israeli conflict and participating in debates with Syrians. Another article mentioned that *Mayoría*, a Peronist weekly, had published an article with the headline "Israel Celebrates Its Twenty-Fifth Year – An Example of Rebirth and Faith in the Nation."[42] *Davar* emphasized that Perón's minister of the economy was Jewish and added some biographical data about José Ber Gelbard, the former longtime leader of the CGE and mediator between Perón and the business owners.[43] Through these articles, the newspaper thus portrayed the Argentine regime as supportive of Israel and therefore as deserving of the sympathies of Israelis, without discussing internal Argentine affairs or even those aspects that affected Argentina's Jewish community.

Shortly before Perón's definitive return to Argentina, Israel's Ministry of Foreign Affairs sent a delegation, led by Jacob Tsur, to meet with him in Madrid. The meeting was set up with the aim of highlighting Perón's positive attitude toward Israel, even in the face of seemingly increasing pressures that the governments of Arab countries placed on the Argentine government and some sectors of Peronism.[44] Officials in Jerusalem had also taken note of the recent visit to Perón's residence of seven ambassadors from Arab countries. The meeting between Perón and the Israeli delegation was widely covered. *Maariv* described the meeting from the point of view of its protagonists: "In Madrid, General Perón gave a friendly hug to the delegate of the Israeli Ministry of Foreign Affairs. The emotional meeting took place."[45] The meeting seemed to confirm Israel's diplomatic success, and Perón was portrayed as expressing his unequivocal support for Israel. "This is a good start for the relations that Israel and the new regime in Argentina are weaving," wrote a journalist at *Maariv*.[46] In the early 1970s, this morning daily boasted the largest circulation in the country and typically focused on Jewish matters, even in its coverage of Argentina.

Davar's report on the meeting between Tsur and Perón also highlighted Perón's positive attitude toward Israel.[47] In an op-ed, it emphasized that the Argentine leader was "one of the most noteworthy figures of the [Latin American] arena over the past thirty years." Although it also described him as "an old man who had made more than a few mistakes during his presidency," this "old man" was portrayed both as capable of strengthening Cámpora's administration and as a supporter of Israel and of Argentina's Jewish community. Nevertheless, as Tsur later attested, the meeting was interrupted when José I. Rucci entered the room. Rucci, secretary general of the CGT, which was hegemonically dominated by Peronists, was rather frosty toward the Israeli guest. "He was part of the antisemitic and anti-Israel wing of the CGT," Tsur wrote in his memoirs. Abraham Alon, the representative in Buenos Aires of Israel's Workers' Confederation, also characterized Rucci as adopting antisemitic stances and as hostile toward Israel, with ties to the reactionaries and the extreme Right.[48]

Al Hamishmar adopted a sympathetic stance toward Peronism and its Leftist currents. Specifically, this newspaper now connected Peronism to socialism. In an article titled "Argentina's Most Beautiful Days," a journalist interviewed Minister Victor Shem Tov, of the MAPAM party, about his experience at the head of the Israeli delegation that travelled to Buenos Aires to attend the ceremony for Cámpora's swearing-in as president.[49] "What I gather from the slogans I heard and the conversations that I had, is that Argentines are using a new word, one that holds the key to people's hearts and wins their trust – this new word is socialism." The article voiced hopes about the conclusion of the military regime and about Cámpora's presidency. Shem Tov was optimistic about the future of the Jewish-Argentine community and bilateral relations between the two states. The newspaper also described how honours were bestowed upon the minister wherever he visited.

One week later, ahead of the presidential elections, *Al Hamishmar* published an article headlined "Perón Wins, but Peronism Is Problematic."[50] The article asked why Peronists needed Perón, and answered that question thusly: "Neo-Peronists also rely on Perón's presence so that he can give his blessing, adopt necessary measures to mediate, and sometimes even decide, among the different sources and currents, all of which mention the Peronist myth."[51] The author of this article also referred to the limits of Cámpora's power and described Perón's vitality as an element that brings cohesion to the heterogeneous coalition united under the movement's banner.

If we compare these positions with the same newspaper's stances during Perón's first mandate, an interesting shift becomes apparent in the attitude toward the leader and his movement. During the late 1940s and early 1950s, *Al Hamishmar* identified with Argentina's Socialists and Communists in their struggle against Peronism, and described the latter as a South American variation on fascism. Nevertheless, during the early 1970s, the same newspaper made a noticeable effort to highlight the social – at times, socialist – facet of the Peronist doctrine, and to shine a positive light on the movement's leader. The MAPAM party, to which the newspaper was linked, had also come a long way since the period of the 1940s and 1950s, when it had expressed admiration for Stalin's Soviet Union. It now looked toward alternative socialist models in Europe and the developing world. The newspaper's reading of the contemporary Peronist Left was selective, similarly to the selective interpretations that diverse strands of Peronism made of the Peronist experience in their efforts to claim for themselves the Peronist myth and to justify their stances.

Out of the five newspapers examined, *Yedioth Ahronoth* adopted the clearest stance. The independent evening daily was founded in 1939 and gradually changed its style to that of a sensationalist tabloid featuring very short stories. In keeping with this orientation, the newspaper's pages adopted a condescending tone in recounting Perón's return and Argentina's social and political fractures as if they were a *telenovela*.

THE EZEIZA MASSACRE

The Ezeiza massacre drew its name from the suburban area that is home to Buenos Aires's Ezeiza International Airport. On the day of Perón's definitive return to Argentina, Ezeiza became the site of a bloody confrontation between the different Peronist factions. *Yedioth Ahronoth* covered the event with the headline: "They Came to Welcome Perón and Were Met with Gunshots." The newspaper described the events as follows: two million were gathered, waiting for the former president, and "Trotskyists" were responsible for the massacre as they began to shoot at the Peronist groups. The following paragraph included a description of the attackers as "Marxists."

Haaretz, on the other hand, supplemented its report of the events with an explanation of the Peronism's internal fragmentation. The newspaper linked the "bloodbath" to the weakness of the president-elect: "At present, it would seem that Perón was elected president and that Cámpora is nothing more than his prime minister."[52] In addition to describing the population's joy at the return of their leader, *Haaretz* wrote with skepticism and in a critical tone about the evolution of the movement: "The activation of the Peronist militia brought back into the fold of politics an armed police force in the service of the party's interests – this police is incapable of ensuring peace even within the ranks of Peronism."[53]

Maariv published on its front page a story titled "Bloodbath," in which it decried the "bloody fight that made a bloodbath and a spectacle of horror out of what should have been Perón's triumphant return to Argentina after 18 years of exile."[54] *Al Hamishmar*, horrified at the events, sustained that "those present began to fire at each other, pitting orthodox Peronists who swear by the Peronist nation against members of an extremist Left supported by former Peronists-cum-urban guerrilleros who want to build a socialist homeland."[55]

PERÓN'S ELECTION TO THE PRESIDENCY

Perón's victory in the presidential elections temporarily generated a clearer situation, even if Argentina's troubles were far from resolved.

Davar, the newspaper affiliated with Israel's Workers' Confederation, enthusiastically applauded the electoral result, portraying the victor as an emissary of the trade unions and his triumph as a promise of democratization, particularly considering the recent military coup in neighbouring Chile. "It is an irony of fate," wrote *Davar*, "that after the democratic regime was taken down in Chile, Argentina has become the Southern Cone's democratic state par excellence."[56] The newspaper recalled that it was Perón who improved the masses' situation by politicizing them and that "the administrations [that succeeded him], whether military or democratically elected, had failed to lessen Peronism's importance among these sectors of society."[57] *Davar* then emphasized that Perón had been elected in free elections and that the working classes and masses were the base of his support.

Other newspapers adopted a different, less enthusiastic approach to Perón's electoral victory. Shaul Ben Haim, head of *Maariv*'s international news bureau, did not portray Perón as the representative of the people's will, or his electoral victory as the outcome of a genuine process of democratization. Rather, he described it as the evident triumph of emotion over reason and common sense. Under the headline "The Trotskyists also Support Perón," *Maariv* made fun of Perón, portraying him as enjoying a patently absurd 100 percent of popular support.[58] Workers and unions were indeed hopeful that the return of Perón would ensure the adoption of an economic policy that protected their interests. Employers' organizations perceived Perón as an Argentine Charles de Gaulle – that is, as a symbol of conservative stability and a barrier against revolutionary currents and anarchy. The Argentine Left viewed Perón as the only leader capable of taking up the fight against imperialism and for the liberation of the nation. In the words of former ambassador Jacob Tsur, who by then was president of the Jewish National Fund's board of directors and had led the Israeli delegation that attended Perón's swearing-in:

> Upon returning to the Argentine capital, it seemed as if this divided nation had miraculously united; conservatives, nationalists, and reactionaries, on one side, and progressives, liberals, and revolutionaries, on the other, all repeated: let's hope it lasts. In his old age, [Perón] appeared on the political scene as a saviour who

> held in his hand the panacea for all of the country's ills. He embodied the wishes of those who wanted order and a firm regime with a strong government, as well as the dreams of the effervescent student youth that pinned its hopes on revolution. No one could explain how such contrasts converged in this complex figure, but the answer to all these difficult questions was: Perón.[59]

In his article in *Maariv*, Ben Haim expressed doubt about whether Perón was capable of effectively dominating the situation in his country, considering his deteriorating health, his ambiguous political platform, and Argentines' lack of discernment in their narrow focus upon the elderly leader's charisma. He closed the article with a zinger: "Perón's return seems like a modern painting: each one sees in it what they wish to find."[60]

Writer Hanoch Bartov voiced sharper criticisms in an article depicting political processes in Latin America in light of the bloody coup that had overthrown the democratically elected president of Chile, the Marxist Salvador Allende.[61] He had some harsh words for Perón, describing him as an "elderly dictator who openly flirted with fascism and was protected by Franco for eighteen years and then returned to his country as a victor who again reached the presidency."[62] Bartov had authored several novels and a biography of the Israeli army's commander-in-chief during the Yom Kippur War. He did not muffle his disappointment at the situation in Argentina and he made light of the arrogance displayed by the country's citizenry, describing them as "these voters, miserable gauchos who seek out charisma, law and order, and who to this day worship Evita."[63] In the two articles that Bartov wrote for *Maariv*, he sought to portray Argentina not as a member of the club of developed nations of the West, whose populations were educated and rational, but as an underdeveloped "Third World" country in which voters were swept away by a charismatic leader and trapped in a nostalgia for a lost golden age that took precedence over the candidate's politics, his electoral platform, or the actual likelihood of him bringing about change.

Despite significant differences between the political views of *Maariv* and *Al Hamishmar*, the latter newspaper wrote about the situation in

Argentina in similar terms: its coverage was also peppered with stereotypes and permeated with arrogance, although, unlike *Maariv*, it attempted to produce a more significant ideological analysis owing to the orientation of the socialist party to which it was affiliated: "Over there [in Argentina], matters are not governed by pure logic and by political reason … Peronism is a fantasy that is unique to Argentina: it combines fascist factors and modes of expression with a non-Marxist socialist ideology known as Justicialismo."[64] *Al Hamishmar* was less hostile toward Peronism but maintained some reservations about its socialist doctrine, considering it to be insufficiently Marxist. The newspaper portrayed Perón's election as inevitable and expressed hopes that his charisma, together with voters' nostalgia, could unify Argentina.

Haaretz also opted for a seemingly objective tone in its coverage of Perón's electoral victory. It emphasized that a higher number of voters than expected participated in the elections despite the antipathy toward Isabelita, Perón's candidate for vice-president and one whom, according to *Haaretz*, most Argentines opposed.[65] Perón, the article continued, was perfectly aware of the dark shadow that the recent military coup in neighbouring Chile cast upon his own country, but this was only one of the challenges that his administration faced. The article analyzed the many troubles that loomed on the horizon and emphasized the old Argentine strongman's ability to solve challenges of this sort: "politicians across the spectrum in Argentina consider that if one person can impose his authority on the Left and on the Right and put an end to terrorism, it's Perón."[66]

Yedioth Ahronoth was the most categorical of the newspapers. Next to a photo of a smiling Perón, an article by Shlomo Shamgar left no doubt about its stance, with the headline: "Perón Is Elected – a tragedy for Argentina."[67] Shamgar explained that the recently elected president "had risen from the ranks of military officers, but he was the most astute of all: wily at praising the masses, he enveloped his regime in an 'opportunist' ideology that he named 'justicialismo.'"[68] Further on, he argued that, "after some shady political maneuvres, he returned to his country and to the seat from which he had been ousted eighteen years ago, before he had fully paid the cost for his failure."[69] Near the end of the article, the aggressive and sensationalist tone typical of this newspaper culminated: "Juan Perón is a scarecrow, an old demagogue that fled his country in 1955 before they could lynch him. Argentina could pay a high price for this omission in the near future."[70]

This reading of Israeli newspapers' coverage of Perón's electoral victory highlights how they refer broadly to the objective hardships that any Argentine president would have faced during that period: tensions between the military and the political parties, fissures within the Peronist movement, confrontations between Left and Right, and, of course, the economy's difficulties and skyrocketing inflation. There were nevertheless differences from one newspaper to the next. While *Davar* typically expressed the hope that Perón could be the right answer for the country's political and economic crisis, *Haaretz* adopted a more neutral stance and *Maariv* began to dramatically foreshadow chaos in the Río de la Plata nation, even before Perón was elected. Although *Al Hamishmar* was somewhat inconsistent in its stance toward Perón, it was more sympathetic than the massively popular *Yedioth Ahronoth* and *Maariv*. All of these newspapers highlighted Perón's charismatic style of leadership and pointed to the fact that, in the chaos in which the country was submerged, he was perhaps the only one capable of guaranteeing "order and stability." This coverage could easily give the Israeli reader the impression that although Perón was not exactly the most democratic of leaders, he had been democratically elected and might yet save his country from its current state of continuous crisis.

THE SHADOW OF LÓPEZ REGA

During the first months of Perón's presidency, Israel's print media devoted little coverage to the situation in faraway Argentina. In light of this, it is noteworthy that, in the middle of a war, Israel sent a delegation to Perón's swearing-in, led by former ambassador Jacob Tsur and the ambassador at the time, Eliezer Doron. Israeli newspapers reported that the commission was well received.[71] Although war had broken out less than a week before, the Ministry of Foreign Relations resolved that Tsur would head to Buenos Aires.

It should be recalled that in the lead-up to the Yom Kippur War, the Jewish-Argentine community was more divided than ever. The Organización Sionista Argentina (Argentine Zionist Organization) faced conflicts ahead of the celebrations of Israel's twenty-fifth anniversary, and Zionist right-wing parties ended up withdrawing from the organization. When celebrations were held in August 1973, at Buenos Aires's Luna Park stadium, the official Israeli representative, Knesset member Yitzhak Navón, was humiliated when young leftist Zionists began to chant slogans denouncing the discrimination against Arab citizens of Israel and the oppression of the Palestinian people in the occupied territories.[72] Although many Jewish young people, especially university students, were primarily concerned with developments in Argentina and were hopeful about the beginning of a new era with the return of Peronism to power, the movement's left wing typically adopted a critical stance toward the United States and its ally in the Middle East, in addition to sympathizing with national liberation movements in the developing world, including the Palestinian cause.[73]

When the war broke out in October 1973, Jewish-Argentines were not particularly concerned with the fate of Israel. Jacob Tsur observed: "Jews believed that in this war, just as six years ago, Israel was not revealing the extent of its victories, so as to prevent the great powers from intervening. [Jewish-Argentine] leaders also spoke in a condescending tone when they received the news that arrived from the capitals of Arab countries, even when that news was true (for example, when the Syrians announced that the Israeli enclave in Mount Hermon had fallen), as they had become used to the Arabs' empty bragging."[74]

But genuine fears began to emerge as the war wore on. On the one hand, relatives of Jewish-Argentines who had immigrated to the fledgling state served in this war (and were thus wounded or killed) in greater numbers than in prior conflicts. Natán Lerner, who had been vice-president of the DAIA during the late 1950s, observed that the war had renewed solidarity among Jews within spheres that had typically set themselves apart from mainstream community activities, particularly within left-leaning circles. These people became involved in organizing public assemblies and promoting the publication in non-Jewish media of open letters in support of Israel.[75] Hundreds of young Jews registered to volunteer to fight on Israel's side, but most of them did not make it to the Middle East. Others organized various educational activities intended for Jewish and non-Jewish audiences.[76]

Those who were hoping that Perón's return to the Casa Rosada would bring about a miracle were disappointed. The leader was in the twilight of his life: elderly, ill, and surrounded by some aides whose conduct was dubious. The most notorious of these was José López Rega, minister of social welfare since May 1973. "Lopecito," as he was known in the political arena, had been an agent of the federal police force and risen to the rank of corporal, which he held until he retired in the early 1960s. While López Rega was still part of the police force he wrote a 740-page treatise titled *Astrología esotérica* (Esoteric Astrology). This work was written in a vague register and included strange theories about "the colours of names and countries" and about how the various musical genres could reveal national idiosyncrasies. As word spread of his propensity toward mysticism, he was nicknamed "El Brujo" (the Warlock). After winning the trust of Isabel Perón, López Rega moved to Spain, where he became the couple's personal assistant. This position allowed him to accumulate power and influence. Many understood that López Rega was the conduit to Perón and that maintaining relations with him worked to their advantage.

Twenty-five years later, Juan Manuel Abal Medina, secretary general of the Partido Justicialista at the time, recounted:

> López Rega's influence grew proportionately to the deterioration of the General's health. In November 1972, López Rega never participated in meetings about political matters. He only walked in on those meetings to serve coffee. By late February 1973, he participated in all such meetings and expressed his opinions to participants. By April, he met with Perón in his office and spoke during meetings similarly to political leaders. López Rega had a hand in everything and Perón allowed him to do so.[77]

Israel's ambassador to Argentina at the time, Eliezer Doron, wrote as follows about López Rega:

> When Perón returned to Argentina, López Rega was officially named to the post of minister of social welfare and, extra-officially, he was the "Rasputin" of President Isabel Perón, the widow of the deceased president. The majority of Argentines accused him of suspected corruption, of being a despot, and of having taken control of Perón when he was elderly and frail,

> and imposing his will upon Mrs. Perón after she became president. He was able to flee back to Madrid before the [March 1976] military coup, leaving behind his reputation as a frivolous and impetuous man, a thief and criminal ... he had also won fame as an antisemite ... he was immersed in astrology and parapsychology and also the Talmud and the Kabbalah and (he said in his defence) it's through these sources that he learned to value the Jewish people and its qualities.[78]

It was also thought that López Rega supported a shift in Argentina's foreign policy in favour of Arab countries and, especially, a rapprochement with Libya. This caused concern, both in the Ministry of Foreign Affairs in Jerusalem and among Jews in Argentina. The closer ties between Argentina and Libya were expressed symbolically in the agreement that the Universidad de Buenos Aires's Instituto del Tercer Mundo (Third World Institute) signed with the Libyan embassy in Argentina to distribute Spanish-language translations of books authored by Muammar Gaddafi and, in exchange, to distribute an anthology of Perón's speeches in Libya.[79] Libya was, at the time, Argentina's main supplier of petroleum. López Rega signed various economic agreements with the government in Tripoli. Afterward he stated that the presence of Jews in Argentina's administration could be an inconvenience in negotiating with Arab countries, a clear allusion to José Ber Gelbard.[80] Through López Rega, Arab-driven antisemitism within the state administration garnered influence in Argentina, encompassing a repertoire of deeply rooted stereotypes that characterized Jews as deicides, as an ethnic group incapable of assimilating, as revolutionary communists, as capitalists who ruined national economies, and as Zionists with dual loyalty.

The minister of economy wasn't the only one singled out by the Peronist Right and López Rega's followers. They also targeted other notable Jewish-Argentines at the time and alleged that these figures obeyed "foreign" interests: the CGE president Julio Broner, influential journalist Jacobo Timerman, and banker David Graiver. A delegation of DAIA leaders asked to meet with Perón and, on that occasion, expressed its concern at the proliferation of antisemitic publications and the aggressive accusations voiced against Jews. Perón rejected the theory that a conspiracy against Argentina was afoot and that Jews had participated in it. The DAIA saw to it that Perón's statements were published in October 1973. Yet, Perón stopped short of condemning or severing ties with those antisemitic elements in his heterogeneous band of supporters. So long as these supporters declared themselves to be Peronist but abstained from portraying their opinions as those of the leader, they could express their numerous, and sometimes divergent, opinions on all topics, including Jews.

Although the four presidents who successively occupied the Casa Rosada in 1973 all spoke out against antisemitism, in practice anti-Jewish activities increased to such an extent that Argentina became the country with the highest incidence of such episodes.[81] The "Andinia Plan" was repeatedly discussed. According to this plan, the "Elders of Zion" joined forces with international Zionism and the state of Israel to bring about the separation from the rest of the country of the provinces of Patagonia, Argentina's southernmost region, aiming to establish a second Jewish state there.[82] In addition, publications like *Ulises* and *Cabildo* agitated against the supposedly vast Jewish influence that made itself felt in Buenos Aires.[83] The concept of "synarchy" became increasingly common in Argentina to describe the international conspiracy against Argentina that was believed to be jointly animated by capitalism, communism, Zionism, and freemasonry. Perón came to use this concept on several occasions and, prior to his return to power, he connected it to Jews and Zionists.[84] These actions were not limited to antisemitic discourse; some actions, carried out by the right-wing and anti-Jewish ALN, also caused physical harm. Among others, the attacks targeted the Sephardi synagogue Shalom in Buenos Aires as well as various community centres across the country, and also included the painting of antisemitic slogans on buildings in various locations. These attacks should nonetheless be framed within the broader context of the generalized violence that shook all of Argentine society in the 1970s.

To ensure that the various Peronist factions treated Jews favourably, even after Perón's death, the DAIA published a compilation that included speeches that the leader had made in the 1940s and 1950s, and transcripts of meetings he held with the Jewish community leadership in 1973–74, all of which documented Perón's sympathies toward his country's Jewish community and his unequivocal condemnations of antisemitism and racism.[85]

PERÓN'S DEATH

Perón's death on 1 July 1974 was an occasion for the Israeli newspapers to publish syntheses and appreciations, which once again expressed these outlets' varied positions, not only with regard to recent events but on the Peronist phenomenon in general. *Yedioth Ahronoth*, the most sensationalist of these newspapers, once again published plenty of photos from Argentina, with descriptions of the hysteria and the tears shed on the streets of Buenos Aires.

Al Hamishmar, which in the 1940s and 1950s had made frequent attempts to decipher the meaning of this social and political movement, published but fleetingly on Argentina and neglected to mention the lavish state funeral organized for Perón, which was reminiscent of the mass grieving that followed Evita's death in July 1952. The day after Perón's passing, *Al Hamishmar* announced the news under the headline "Perón Has Died! Juan Perón, Argentine Strongman in the Forties and Fifties, Who Returned to Government Last Year."[86] It also published a brief note, "The Legend of the Peróns," with a brief historical review and a mention of the "problematic" social origins of Perón's widow Isabel Martínez, who had been a "performer of middle-eastern style dance in Panama" and was now inheriting the presidency.[87] The note highlighted the good relations that the deceased president had forged with Israel, contrasting them to his weak ties with the Arab countries. In general terms, *Al Hamishmar*'s favourable stance toward Perón ahead of his return became somewhat tempered afterward.

This dichotomy was more palpable in other newspapers as they highlighted the close ties that Peronist Argentina had enjoyed with Israel, and also voiced harsh criticisms in its portrayal of contemporary Peronism as a rigid, despotic regime that did not tolerate the opposition's activities.[88] All newspapers highlighted the existing polarization of Argentine society vis-à-vis Perón and his administration. *Maariv* thus stated that many Argentines despised Perón "due to the means through which he stayed in power during his first two presidential mandates during the 1940s and 1950s, when he took advantage of the massive support he had to repress opposition and limit individual freedoms," adding that, "in spite of this, he was loved by many more during his eighteen years of exile, prompted by the military coup that overthrew him."[89] Three days later, *Maariv* published a lengthy column authored by Jacob Tsur, who portrayed Perón in a fully complimentary light.[90] Tsur understood the Peronist phenomenon better than most Israeli public servants and he included his personal point of view as someone who had had many close dealings with the deceased leader. The veteran diplomat sought to shed light on Perón's human qualities and to account for the many contrasts that made up his personality. Tsur seemed to be attempting to decipher the secret of Perón's charisma and success, and, in so doing, to answer the question of why his death left such a gaping void. The column was suffused with Tsur's appreciation of Perón as a powerful head of state endowed with qualities that would have enabled him to reorient the country's situation, had he only been younger.

In an op-ed, *Davar* speculated wrongly that "the downfall of Peronism after Perón's death would be far swifter than that of Gaullism after Charles De Gaulle's retirement" from politics.[91] Yet the French process had not included violent confrontations due, among other reasons, to that country's longstanding democratic tradition, a tradition that had not yet been established in Argentina or within Peronism. In light of this, fears of ensuing dangerous conflicts "and even bloodshed" were justified. *Davar* warned that the new juncture posed a potential danger of antisemitic violence and called upon the leaderships of Jewish community organizations to remain vigilant and to take action equal to this potential threat.

Haaretz also observed that the death of Juan Perón left a void "that Argentines would have trouble filling," adding that "all the political and social forces in the country coalesced around him. His disappearance would cause, sooner or later, a sharpening of parties' ideological postures. His death would also precipitate a fracture between the very different elements that Perón had succeeded at bringing together."[92] Shortly before Perón's passing, the newspaper published the notion that the president's illness was connected to the country's deepest wounds. Perón, who had been exiled in Spain,

> had returned at the request of the military rulers when the social situation in the country was on the verge of exploding … The workers' movement continued to be "Peronist." But within the populism with remnants of fascism that was characteristic of the movement during its first administration, there was a schism between the Right and the Left, and the Left increasingly chose methods of urban terrorism, to such an extent that civil war loomed in Argentina.[93]

Haaretz continued by emphasizing that in Perón's final presidency, his politics had taken a turn toward moderation and conservatism, unlike his stances in the 1940s and 1950s. Of all the newspapers in Israel, *Haaretz* was the only one that continued to update its readers about goings-on in Argentina after Perón's death and during his widow's presidency.

THE DANCER, FROM THE CABARET TO THE CASA ROSADA

Less than two weeks after Perón's death, Abraham Alon, the representative in Buenos Aires of the Israeli Workers' Federation, wrote:

> It is difficult to evaluate the concrete meaning of the disappearance of someone who was, for thirty years, the central aegis of Argentina's political life … The most salient point these days is the fact that, even if [Perón] was the nation's nerve centre, his legacy to future generations seems rather paltry. An objective observer can witness the fact that, in the wake of Perón's death, Argentina is a country riven by internal conflict, devoid of international prestige, lacking a worthy leadership, and sunken in a deep economic crisis. What's worse is the complete absence of indications that in the near future, the country might overcome the shock provoked by the disappearance of its leader. Quite the contrary, a struggle for power seems to be brewing among the different factions of the Peronist movement … The solution that Argentines have known for many generations can come in the form of a new military coup, which would lead the country into another phase of instability and bitterness.[94]

Understandably, the image of Isabel Martínez de Perón, in her new role as president, caught the attention of communications media across the world, including in Israel, because, among other reasons, at 43 years of age she was the first woman in the history of the Western hemisphere to become a head of state.[95] Coverage always reiterated the fact that she was inheriting this position rather than being qualified for it by her experience or skills. *Yedioth Ahronoth* narrated her story as if it were a chapter in a sentimental novel: it described her rise as a dancer who grew up in poverty and omitted any reference to the concrete repercussions that this turn of events might have on the lives and destinies of millions.[96] *Maariv*, which typically had not been sympathetic toward Juan Perón, published a derogatory column criticizing Isabelita for attempting to imitate the style of Evita.[97]

It reviewed the new president's biography in a harsh light: "The slender tan-skinned woman who worked as a dancer in a Panama cabaret, which is where she met Juan Perón, was at first his secretary; then she became his wife and now she was being sworn in as acting president of Argentina."[98] Many newspapers reminded readers that Isabel had not completed primary school and that only thanks to her mother's efforts had she been able to afford dance classes. They also emphasized that Perón had imposed his wife upon the Argentine political sphere by selecting her to run as vice-president. For many weeks, coverage of her presidency was at pains to characterize the widow's approach to government, and doubt and mistrust permeated these articles: "The main question facing Argentina is whether Mrs. Perón will be able to prevent attempts on the part of the Left and the Right to take advantage of this opportunity … as an attempt to take the lead and dominate the country."[99]

During Isabel Perón's brief presidency of less than two years, murderous political violence increased and, with it, the fall into the abyss. During her second week in office, former interior minister Arturo Mor Roig was murdered. Israeli newspapers also highlighted the murder of David Kraiselburd, the Jewish director of the La Plata newspaper *El Día*. A group of armed men kidnapped Kraiselburd during the day in downtown La Plata, capital of the province of Buenos Aires. After a few days, his body was found in a house following an armed confrontation with the police. *Hatzofeh* described Kraiselburd as having "vehemently defended Israel and Jewish matters from the pages of his newspaper."[100]

On the ground, an open war between the Left and the Right had begun. According to reports by Amnesty International, in 1974 alone Argentina experienced 300 politically motivated murders. Statistics published by the *Buenos Aires Herald* indicated that 1,100 killings had stemmed from political violence in 1975. Most of these were attributable to right-wing groups. The scope of the concept of "subversion" was broadened and applied arbitrarily so as to sow fear among the political parties, press, universities, justice system, and unions. In 1975, the practice of kidnapping persons or disappearing them – a method typically identified with the military dictatorship that ousted Isabel from power in 1976 – was already widespread. The new Peronist government, which opted for a right-wing economic policy with authoritarian traits, therefore became synonymous with political and financial crisis, terrorism, and skyrocketing inflation. The Alianza Anticomunista Argentina, overseen by López Rega, chose on several occasions to victimize Jews, regardless of whether they had ties with the Left.

This combination of political violence, spiralling inflation, and the president's lack of political and moral authority became an almost open invitation to a military coup. On 24 March 1976, the army coordinated its actions and took power. The new government immediately began to dismantle the Peronist welfare state in its various manifestations and to liquidate the various factions of the Left. Within that process, Jewish-Argentines paid a high price with their own blood.[101]

To summarize, it may be stated that the coverage of events in Argentina on the part Israel's printed press was relatively substantial and that it paid attention to developments in Buenos Aires. This is all the more notable considering that from October 1973, Israel's political system and society – and with them, its communications media – were dedicated to processing the crisis produced by the Yom Kippur War, including the high number of casualties in which it resulted, and attempting to understand who bore the responsibility for the debacle. Similarly to the portrayal of Perón's first two mandates ending in September 1955, the image of the regime in the Israeli press was neither one-dimensional nor homogeneous, even if each newspaper's emphasis shifted over the course of that period.

During the late 1940s and early 1950s, the Israeli press's portrayal of Peronism was more complex. Perón was largely characterized as a friend of Israel, particularly as he had offered assistance to the young state in its struggle to secure its existence and helped it through great economic difficulties so that it could accommodate the massive contingents of migrants that landed on its shores. This positive portrayal was less frequent in coverage during the 1970s. Expressions of antisemitism on the part of some members of the Peronist Right and some figures in the CGT generated an exaggerated and distorted image of an anti-Jewish Peronism. This portrayal persists to this day, and typically it does not differentiate between Perón's first two presidencies and his third, which was framed within an entirely different national and international context.

Davar expressed satisfaction that Peronism was back in power. As this newspaper was the organ of the Workers' Confederation, it made sure to emphasize that the movement had the support of the masses and the workers. In light of its ties with the party in power, *Davar* also noted how the Israeli government and its foreign policy might benefit directly from this presidency. *Al Hamishmar*'s affiliation with the MAPAM party led it to revise its typically hostile stance toward Peronism and to show some enthusiasm at the strengthening of the left wing within the Peronist movement. Specifically, it voiced satisfaction at Cámpora's electoral triumph and Perón's return. This enthusiasm gradually decreased due in part to Perón's shift to the right. *Maariv* and *Haaretz* had the broadest and most varied coverage of events in Argentina, and the perspective of *Maariv* was condescending and critical toward Argentine politics in general and Peronism in particular.

THE ETHNIC INCLUSIVITY OF PERONIST POPULISM

Returning to the starting point for this book, I would like to insist on the importance of re-evaluating the attitudes of Jewish-Argentines toward Peronism as well as the relations that Perón, his movement, and his administrations cultivated with Jews and the state of Israel during the 1940s and 1950s. The emergence and rise of Peronism during the 1940s is viewed as a critical turning point in Argentina's modern history, one that has left a lasting impact on present-day society. Most scholars have focused on processes of economic development and social modernization in Peronist Argentina, but little attention has been devoted to the inclusion of various ethnic immigrant communities and their descendants born in Argentina.

During the Peronist decade, the meanings and the contours of citizenship in Argentina were transformed. The country witnessed deep changes, and the government's actions contributed to promoting a debate on how citizenship was conceptualized and understood. Political representation in Argentina also changed during that period as the country embarked on a path to become simultaneously a participatory democracy and a multicultural society. Ethnic identities came to be less threatening to understandings of Argentine identity. Instead of furthering the traditional racial melting pot, the Peronist regime increasingly recognized hyphenated identities and multiple identities, emphasizing the broad variety of cultural sources from which Argentine society drew its strength. In doing this, authorities took unprecedented steps toward the recognition of multicultural differences.

This book has closely examined the efforts Peronism undertook to mobilize support among the Jewish-Argentine population, particularly through the Jewish section of the Peronist movement, the OIA. The OIA leadership advocated in favour of the social integration of Jews while also defining and asserting an identity that highlighted their Argentine identity component without rejecting their Jewish ethnic identity component, their Zionism, or their affective ties to their imagined motherland, Israel. With the support of the government, this complex view of identity challenged the existing vision of the racial melting pot.

The concept of citizenship can function as both a lens and a framework for analyzing and understanding the transformations in how Jewish-Argentines related to the Argentine state's institutions and symbols. Any discussion of citizenship must also involve questions of belonging to and integrating into a political community. Prior to Peronism, Argentina offered little space for non-Catholics, whether in society, politics, or public discourse. From its first day as an independent nation-state, Argentina's intellectuals and statesmen concerned themselves with the country's demographic composition. Although many agreed on the necessity of encouraging immigration so as to "whiten" the population and ensure the country's development and progress, there was disagreement on who could be considered an

Argentine. Among liberal elites, even the most fervent promotors of immigration welcomed the idea of a racial melting pot in the hope that newcomers, particularly those who were not Catholic and/or European, would abandon the customs and idiosyncrasies imported from their countries of origin to adopt the new culture that was taking shape in the new society of immigrants. Argentine debates on national identity were dominated by the idea of an Argentina that was essentially white, Christian, and European-descended. This attitude, along with the pressure to achieve cultural homogeneity and to assimilate, became a stronger concern among those who had ties to nationalist Catholic and xenophobic sectors.

As Peronism was a populist movement, it adopted an anti-liberal stance. Interestingly, this allowed Peronism to challenge long-held ideas about the racial melting pot. Innovative points of view emerged to broaden the meaning of politics and citizenship alike. In light of this, what did Peronism change in the relation between ethnicity, citizenship, Argentine identity, and the state? The straightforward answer is that: a) Peronism went beyond the legal rights granted to Jews as Argentine citizens by offering them political rights as well; and b) it legitimated the desire among many Jewish-Argentines to proudly display their ethnic identity. In Peronist Argentina, political representation became somewhat corporatist, in keeping with Perón's vision of "organized community," which instituted the state as a mediator between different sectors or groups organized around social, economic, and professional interests. It is interesting that Peronism granted recognition to ethnic communities as it did to powerful organizations such as the workers' movement represented in the CGT, the CGE, the Confederación General de Profesionales (CGP; General Federation of Professionals), the Confederación General Universitaria (CGU; General Federation of University Students), and even the Unión de Estudiantes Secundarios (UES; High School Students' Union). Perón met frequently with the leaders of Jewish, Spanish, Italian, and Arab community organizations, and through these meetings reconfigured the criteria according to which one could belong to and be an actor in Argentina's political community. He thus opened the door to what would, decades later, become contemporary multicultural Argentina.

Epilogue

The recent death of Héctor Timerman (1953–2018) sparked a debate in Argentina. Timerman had been minister of foreign affairs in Cristina Fernández de Kirchner's administration (2010–15) and was the son of journalist Jacobo Timerman, the founder of the reputed newspaper *La Opinión*, who became the military dictatorship's most renowned opponent during the 1970s.

In 2013, Héctor Timerman had been charged with treason for his role in negotiating an agreement with Iran pertaining to the 1994 bombing of the largest Jewish community centre in Buenos Aires.[1] The deal with Iran was part of an effort to obtain answers from the Iranians, who were accused of carrying out a suicide attack of the Asociación Mutual Israelita Argentina in which eighty-five people were killed and some 300 injured. The two countries had agreed to establish a joint commission to investigate the bombing. Although the agreement was approved by the Argentine Congress, it was later declared unconstitutional.

During the last phase of the Fernández de Kirchner administration, the Jewish-Argentine federal prosecutor, Alberto Nisman, claimed that the agreement with Iran was part of a cover-up designed to make sure that no Iranian official would face justice, that Interpol fugitive notices affecting any of these officials would be cancelled, and that, as a result, the officials suspected of having committed a crime in Argentina would be allowed to travel freely.[2]

In January 2015, shortly after Nisman made these claims against President Fernández de Kirchner and Minister Timerman, and just a day before he was to have appeared before an Argentine congressional committee, the prosecutor was found dead in his Buenos Aires apartment from a gunshot wound to the head. The circumstances leading to his death remain unsolved. While opponents of President Fernández de Kirchner, who now support Argentina's current president, Mauricio Macri, are convinced that Nisman was murdered to protect the Kirchner government, the Kirchneristas insist that Nisman committed suicide.

But the controversy around these two Jewish-Argentine figures, Timerman and Nisman, extended well beyond the memorandum of understanding signed with the Iranian government. To a large extent, it is rooted in Jewish-Argentines' support of, or opposition to, the Peronist movement in its various manifestations. It is also rooted in the differences between the Jewish community institutions and unaffiliated Jews, as well as in relations between the diaspora and the homeland, involving in this case the Argentine Jewish community and the state of Israel, which strongly opposed the Iran deal. The organized Jewish community and Israel have transformed Nisman into a hero and Timerman into a villain.[3]

In Nisman's politicized afterlife, the federal prosecutor seems to have become more Jewish, at least in the eyes of Jewish community institutions. As David Sheinin has emphasized, "though non-observant, Nisman was buried in a religious ceremony at the La Tablada Jewish cemetery, in front of the monument to those who had fallen in defence of Israel."[4] This juxtaposition of the figures of Timerman and Nisman as representatives of longstanding ideas on what it means to be Jewish in Argentina illuminates the issues discussed in this book. The controversy of late 2018/early 2019 highlights the contemporary relevance of my arguments.

Following Timerman's death from liver cancer at the age of 65, former president Fernández de Kirchner was quick to issue a statement. "Argentine, Peronist, and Jewish" was the title she gave to the lengthy letter, which she published in a Facebook post. The letter begins by clarifying that Timerman did not die as a result of "the misfortunes brought on by life itself. Héctor fell ill from the pain and suffering provoked by the irrational and unfair attack that we both suffered because we signed the memorandum of understanding with Iran in the hope that it could shed light on the terrorist attack against the Jewish mutual aid society and, in doing so, move forward the AMIA's court case that is still paralyzed twenty-five years after the fact, with no one found guilty.[5] The former president also characterizes Timerman as "Jewish through and through," and remembers how he organized her first visit to Israel and Palestine in 2005. She added that, "he was, above all, an Argentine and a Peronist.[6]

The strongest defence of Timerman was offered by members of the Corriente Judía Nacional y Popular (the Jewish National and Popular Tendency, previously known as the Jewish Kirchnerista Tendency) and the Llamamiento Judío Argentino (Jewish-Argentine Calling). On their website, the members of the latter identify themselves as follows:

> We are an institution that harbours men and women who are Jewish and Argentine and who aspire to contribute to strengthening democracy, social equality, and sovereignty for all of this country's inhabitants. We are politically committed to the traditions of the Argentine republic that enhance the nation, the people, and democracy. We represent those progressive sectors within the Jewish community; in function of this, we fight for a plural Judaism, one that welcomes, without imposing any other requisite, those who identify with any element linking them with the Jewish culture and traditions. We feel that we are a part of the Patria Grande and strongly identify with the perspectives of gender-related issue.[7]

In an article that I wrote in 2015 for the high-circulation Argentine daily *Clarín*, I tried to point to continuities between the OIA, endorsed by the first Perón administration, and the more recent Jewish-Argentine groups promoted by both Kirchner governments. I described the Llamamiento as a direct descendent of the OIA and added that the deeply rooted myth according to which only a handful of Jews supported Peronism during the 1940s and 1950s was incorrect. There was a large gap between the unsupportive positions and attitudes of the DAIA leadership toward the Peronist regime and those of many

Jewish-Argentines, particularly those who were not affiliated to community institutions.

The OIA is often portrayed as a group of marginal figures in the community, eagerly awaiting an opportunity to occupy centre-stage. While some of the OIA's members could be described that way, many others joined the organization because they identified with the concept of social justice, with the economic and social policies of the Peronist government, or because they supported and were part of a movement that was backed by a majority of Argentines.

Just as Peronism divided society at large between its supporters and opponents, it caused similar reactions among Jews (although it enjoyed the support of only a minority). Some Jewish-Argentine union leaders supported the new party and played a crucial role in the mobilization of popular support for Perón. A similar phenomenon occurred among businesspersons and business owners who benefitted from the Peronist government's protectionism toward Argentine industries.

These Jewish supporters of Perón challenged the DAIA. Most notably, they had the support of reputed intellectuals such as Israel Zeitlin (known by his pseudonym, César Tiempo), Bernardo Ezequiel Koremblit, León Benarós, and Julia Prilutzky Farny. The support of Peronism during the 1940s and 1950s among these members of the Jewish community is crucial to understanding Jews' broad support of Peronism during the 1960s and 1970s, as well as the recent defence of the Kirchners' project by the new organization Llamamiento.

My brief article provoked hostile comments from several Jewish-Argentines who supported Kirchnerismo, who insisted that we meet during one of my visits to Buenos Aires. We did indeed meet, in a traditional café at the intersection of Corrientes and Scalabrini Ortiz, the heart of the supposedly Jewish neighbourhood of Villa Crespo. These activists were amazed when I pointed to similarities in the manifestos of the OIA and their own texts.

While supporters of *Kirchnerismo*, including the Jewish-Argentine members of the Corriente Judía Nacional y Popular, defended Timerman after his death, none of the leaders of the longstanding Jewish community organizations sent even the briefest of messages to the Timerman family to express their condolences. This came as no surprise considering that the leaderships of the AMIA and the DAIA were part of the offensive that culminated in the house arrest of Héctor Timerman and in his being charged with treason – a charge that the court subsequently threw out. Interestingly, Abraham Foxman, the former national director of the US-based Anti-Defamation League (ADL), did convey his respects and condolences to the Timerman family.[8]

Foxman was one of the few who intervened during the military dictatorship in Argentina in the 1970s. When the regime imprisoned and tortured Héctor's father Jacobo Timerman, some say that the leadership of the Jewish community organizations turned a blind eye. Foxman, who had been the ADL's national director for twenty-nine years, launched a campaign that succeeded in obtaining a permit for Héctor to leave Argentina, thus saving his life, and later for Jacobo to follow and write, from exile, his landmark book *Prisoner without a Name, Cell without a Number* about his illegal imprisonment.[9]

In 1981, Columbia University awarded Jacobo the prestigious Maria Moors Cabot Prize. A fierce lobby was undertaken to deny him this award, motivated by pressure from the Argentine dictatorship. Various sources suggest that the leaderships of the Jewish community organizations also opposed the decision to grant this award to Timerman. When Timerman passed away in November 1999, the leaders of the AMIA and the DAIA did not show up at the burial. Curiously, Foxman was the only dignitary who attended, as it coincided with a visit to Argentina.

As the title of this book indicates, however, my scholarly interest goes beyond the specific case of the Peronist movement and its attitudes toward and ties with the local Jewish community. My interest lies in issues related to Latin American populism and ethnicity. By focusing on groups that are not Afro-descendant, indigenous, or mestizo, my research project intends to complicate discussions about race and ethnicity in Argentina. Binary categories such as blackness and whiteness fall short when accounting for the experiences of Jewish-, Arab-, or Asian-Argentines, which some might consider, at least for the first generation of immigrants, as groups that are "in between."

As many scholars have studied the Peronist regime as a static entity, they have paid little attention to the dynamics and changes that occurred during those years. Thus historian Eduardo Elena claims that, "the regime's ideologues highlighted the nation's white, Catholic, and Hispanic character in the design of propaganda, tourism material, and school texts.[10] This was true in the earlier phase of Peronism, as we have seen. By the early 1950s, however, the Argentine populist movement had adopted a more inclusive approach whereby respect for all religions became a defining feature of Peronism. The Peronist ambition of protecting the rights of minorities and weak, marginal groups from the encroachments of the privileged now extended to the ethnic and religious spheres. Peronism was presented as a conglomerate that welcomed every Argentine who supported the Justicialist project. This book is devoted to Jewish-Argentines in Peronist Argentina, but other studies of mine look at Arab-Argentines and Japanese-Argentines as well.[11]

Following the election of Donald Trump in the United States and the rise of extreme right-wing movements in Europe, much has been published on populism, both in media outlets and in scholarly works, claiming that populism is a global, transnational phenomenon and that its discussion should not be reduced to a particular country or region. Statements such as "Populism is as American as it is Argentine" tend, however, to blur several important differences between distinct populist movements and leaderships.[12] Thus, while most Western European populist movements, and the current US administration, are notable for their xenophobia and anti-immigrant rhetoric, Latin American populism, broadly speaking, has been characterized by an inclusive approach.[13] At the same time, while post-Second World War populisms in Western Europe have frequently been backward-looking and reactionary, Latin American populism has often displayed progressive stripes. The Peronist movement discussed in this book is the prime example of this trait of Latin American populism.

Notes

INTRODUCTION

1 Abramovich, "Perón y los judíos."
2 Rein, *Argentina, Israel.*
3 *Mundo Israelita*, 21 August 1948, 29 August 1948; DAIA, *Pensamiento*, 15; DAIA, *Perón*, 11; *American Jewish Year Book* (henceforth AJYB), vol. 50 (1948–49), 270.
4 DAIA, "Medio siglo," 10; Sebreli, *Cuestión judía*, 156.
5 Rein and Panella, eds, *Cultura para todos.*

CHAPTER ONE

1 See: Scobie, *Buenos Aires*; Walter, *Politics*; Gorelik, *Grilla.*
2 For a general overview of immigration to Argentina, see: Solberg, *Immigration*; Moya, *Cousins and Strangers*; Baily, *Immigrants.*
3 On Jewish immigration to Argentina, see Avni, *Argentina and the Jews*; Mirelman, *Jewish Buenos Aires.*
4 See, for example: Hourani and Shedhadi, eds, *Lebanese in the World*; Kabchi, ed., *El mundo árabe*; Rein, ed., *Árabes y judíos*; Rein, ed., *Más allá.*
5 Gerchunoff, *Gauchos judíos.*
6 Feierstein, ed., *Mejores relatos.* On representations in Argentine cinema of the symbolic importance of these agricultural settlements, see: Tal, "Other Becomes Mainstream."
7 These agricultural settlements have attracted lively interest among researchers. They have been examined most exhaustively in Avni, *Argentina*, *"Promised Land."* For new approaches, see: Freidenberg, *Invention.* Numerous memoirs of life in the settlements have also been published. See, for example: Zimerman de Faingold, *Memorias*; Gutkowski, *Rescate.*

8 Quoted in Klich, "Criollos," 266.
9 Quoted in Solberg, *Immigration*, 88–9.
10 Aráoz, *Inmigración*, 48.
11 On antisemitism in Argentina, see, among others: Lvovich, *Nacionalismo y antisemitismo*; Senkman, ed., *Antisemitismo*.
12 Recent studies can be found in Jmelnizky and Erdei, *Población judía*; Rubel, *Población judía*; Della Pergola, "Jewish Autonomy."
13 Erdei, "Demografía e identidad."
14 On Jews originating from Syria, see: Brauner, *Ortodoxia religiosa*.
15 Huberman, *Pasajeros del Weser*.
16 Rosenswaike, "Jewish Population," 205.
17 On Jewish social life in Buenos Aires during that period, see: Sofer, *From Pale to Pampa*; Nouwen, *"Oy, My Buenos Aires."*
18 See the important work by Federico Finchelstein, *Ideological Origins*.
19 Senkman, *Argentina, la segunda guerra*.
20 Argentine nationalist discourse echoed at least in part the traditional religious antisemitism of Catholicism. See: Ben-Dror, *Catholic Church*.
21 On this measure, see: Senkman, "Etnicidad"; Sassone, "Migraciones ilegales."
22 Wilde, *Obras completas*, 29–30.
23 Sofer, *From Pale to Pampa*.
24 On the prostitution of Jewish women in Argentina, see, among others: Yarfitz, *Impure Migration*; Avni, *"Clients"*; Levy, *Mancha*.
25 On the importance of Yiddish in twentieth-century Jewish culture, see: Eliahu Toker, *Ídish*; Sneh, ed., *Buenos Aires*.
26 Moya, "Jewish Experience," 17.
27 About the Tragic Week, see: Dizgun, "Immigrants," ch. 1; Dimenstein, "En busca"; Bilsky, *Semana trágica*; Godio, *Semana trágica*.
28 Vaccarezza, *Conventillo de La Paloma*.
29 Rein, *Fútbol, Jews*.
30 Avni, "Antisemitismo."
31 See: Rein, *Argentina, Israel*, ch. 7. About Tacuara, see: Gutman, *Tacuara*; Bardini, *Tacuara*.
32 On antisemitism during the most recent military dictatorship and the high percentage of Jews among the disappeared, see: Kaufman, "Jewish Victims"; Goldman and Dobry, *Ser judío*.
33 Rein, *Argentine Jews*, ch. 7.
34 See: Potash, *Perón*, passim.
35 The situation of Jews during that military regime is addressed in Senkman, "El 4 de junio"; Ben-Dror, "La Argentina católica."
36 *Mundo Israelita*, 18 September 1943, 23 October 1943, 6 November 1943.
37 For a comparative perspective, see: McGee Deutsch, *Derechas*.
38 See: Rein, *In the Shadow*, on how Spain contributed to saving Jews during World War II.

39 Page, *Perón*, 90.
40 For analysis of the "Revolution of October 1945" as the event that gave birth to Peronism as a movement and set the base for the unique and enduring bond between Perón and the Argentine working class, see: Torre, ed., *17 de octubre*.
41 *La Nación*, 23 December 1945.
42 *New York Times*, 26 November 1945, 28 November 1945; *New Republic*, 22 November 1945. For more on the pressures that US correspondents in Buenos Aires faced in 1945, including death threats, see: *Foreign Relations of the United States* (henceforth FRUS), 1945, vol. IX, 505–26; and Bosoer, *Braden o Perón*.
43 Quoted in Avni, *Emancipation*, 98. Authorities attempted to quell the concerns of the Jewish community and reassured its leadership that the government condemned all expressions of antisemitism or of racial persecution. See, for example, the statements made by General Felipe Urdapilleta, Minister of Interior, *Buenos Aires Herald*, 2 November 1945.
44 AJYB, vol. 48 (1946–47) (Philadelphia: 1946), 246; M. Yagupsky to Segal, 24 December 1945, Archive of the American Jewish Committee Files (henceforth AJC), box 1.
45 Joseph Proskauer to James F. Byrnes and Spruille Braden, 28 November 1945, AJC, boxes 1 and 3.
46 Quoted in Avni, *Emancipation*. The Partido Laborista's firm opposition to antisemitism between 1945 and 1947 was confirmed to the author by Cipriano Reyes (interviews by the author, Quilmes, 15 September 1989; La Plata, May 3, 1996).
47 Avni, *Emancipation*; *La Época*, 29 November 1945; *La Prensa*, 12 December1945; Cabot to the Secretary of State, National Archives, Documents of the Department of State, Record Group 59, College Park, MD (hereafter NA), 835.00/12-445, 4 December1945; Potash, *Army and Politics*, 27–8.
48 *El Laborista*, 12 January 1946; *Democracia*, 14 January 1946.
49 See Avni, *Argentina and the Jews*; Yagupsky to Segal, AJC, box 1. An example of the perspective of a Jewish-Argentine who considered that Perón was not an antisemite can be found in Temkin, "Choice Before Perón."
50 Schmelz and Della Pergola, *Demografía*, 111–14; Laikin Elkin, *Jews of Latin America*, 149–52; Horovitz, "Jewish Community," 205–7.

CHAPTER TWO

1 Bascomb, *Hunting Eichmann*; Rein, "Reconsiderando."
2 Allison, "White Evil."
3 *New York Times*, 22 March 1997, 23.
4 For the explanation that Perón gave to the US ambassador and his comparison of Argentina's attitude during the war with that of Sweden, see: "Memorandum of a Conversation with President Perón," 5 February 1953, NA 611.35/2-553.

5 Numerous studies have analyzed Argentina's relations with the United States and Great Britain during that period. See, among others: Sheinin, *Argentina*; Tulchin, *Argentina,* ch. 6; Escudé, *Gran Bretaña*; Rapoport, *Gran Bretaña.*
6 On the confrontations between the United States and Argentina in the context of pan-American conferences, see: Sheinin, *Searching for Authority*; McGann, *Argentina, the U.S.*
7 On the nationalist movements of the 1930s and 1940s, see: Finchelstein, *Ideological Origins*; McGee Deutsch, *Derechas*; Rock, *Authoritarian Argentina*; Zuleta Álvarez, *Nacionalismo argentino.*
8 On the German influences on the Army, see: White, *German Influence*; Atkins and Thompson, "German Military Influence."
9 See: Welles, *Time for Decision*, 228–32; Humphreys, *Latin America*, 1:165–81.
10 On Great Britain's attitude toward Argentina's neutrality, see, among others: Rapoport, *Gran Bretaña*, particularly ch. 3, as well as the memoirs of the British ambassador to Buenos Aires, David Kelly, *Ruling Few*, 287–314.
11 The June 1943 Revolution and its precedents are explained in Potash, *Army and Politics*, ch. 7; Díaz Araujo, *Conspiración del 43.*
12 On relations between Argentina and Bolivia, see: Figallo, "Bolivia y la Argentina."
13 USA, Department of State, *Consultation*, 6–17; Potash, *Army and Politics*, 169–73, 222–3; Figallo, "Argentina y España"; Quijada and Peralta Ruiz, "Triángulo."
14 Hull, *Memoirs*, 2:100–1; Newton, *"Nazi Menace"*, pt. II.
15 Hull, *Memoirs*, 2:1405–8.
16 On the espionage and propaganda undertaken by German agents in Argentina, see: Rout and Bratzel, *Shadow War*, chs 7–8.
17 MacDonald, "Politics of Intervention," 386; Tulchin, *Argentina*, 92; Kelly, *Ruling Few*, 307.
18 USA, Department of State, *Consultation.* The official, detailed response to these accusations was published approximately one month after the elections. See: Ministerio de Relaciones Exteriores y Culto, *República.* See also: Frank, *Juan Perón*; Braden, *Diplomats.*
19 Quoted in Potash, *Army and Politics*, 41. It seems that the Argentine government considered severing diplomatic relations with the US as a result of the publication of the *Blue Book.* See: Vannucci, "Elected," 62.
20 Tulchin, *Argentina*, 63.
21 Cabot to Department of State, 25 February 1946, in FRUS, 1946, vol. XI, 221–2, 233–4.
22 Avni, *Argentina y las migraciones judías*, 523–4.
23 Senkman, "Etnicidad."
24 Peralta, *Acción*, 110–11.
25 Ibid., 116–17.
26 Ibid.

27 República Argentina, Dirección de Migraciones, *Conceptos*, 3.
28 Lightman to JDC, 17 July 1944, AJC, box 2; Zanatta, *Perón*, 115–21.
29 Quoted in Avni, *Emancipation*, 95.
30 This is precisely what would happen after the decree became law during the second half of the 1940s. See: AJYB, vol. 51 (1950), 265.
31 On this "Pastoral letter" and the Church's stance during the electoral campaign, see: *Criterio* (Buenos Aires), 22 November 1945; Caimari, *Perón*, 94–100; Zanatta, *Perón*, 400–38.
32 The links between Peronism and the Church's social doctrine are detailed in Buchrucker, *Nacionalismo*, 305–8.
33 The author has documented this process in interviews he conducted with Joaquín Díaz de Vivar, leader of the majority bloc in the National Congress (Buenos Aires, 22 June 1989), Rodolfo Decker, the president of the Peronist bloc (Buenos Aires, 31 August 1989), and Cipriano Reyes, who had abandoned Peronism prior to the congressional debate and opposed that law (Quilmes, 15 September 1989).
34 Quoted in Confaloneri, *Perón*.
35 Confalonieri, *Perón*, 254–5.
36 The memorandum is reproduced in its entirety in Avni, *Emancipation*, app. B, doc. 4, 186–7.
37 On the Ley de Educación (Education Law) and its passing, see: República Argentina, *Diario*, 9:568–879; Leonard, *Politicians*, 82–90; Bianchi, "Iglesia Católica."
38 Quoted in Avni, *Emancipation*, 84.
39 Interview with the father of Hernán Benítez by the author, Buenos Aires, 29 June 1989; and letter from Perón to Pius XII, 28 March 1947, a copy of which was obtained from Benítez's father.
40 Lila Caimari outlines this thesis in "Peronist Christianity."
41 Wiesenthal, *Justice*, 76.
42 Some newspaper reports dating from the end of the war speculated that the IV Reich would be formed in Argentina and that "concentration camps" had been set up following orders of the military regime. See, for example: Josephs, *Argentine Diary*, 193.
43 Ignacio Klich, "Nazis in Argentina," 55, n4.
44 Page, "Prólogo," in Klich and Buchrucker, *Argentina*, 7.
45 Hunt, *Secret Agenda*; Bower, *Paperclip Conspiracy*; Simpson, *Blowback*. Within Latin America, Argentina and Brazil made the most notable efforts to attract these scientists. See: De Nápoli, *Científicos nazis*.
46 Luca de Tena et al., *Yo, Juan Domingo Perón*, 86; Rom, *Así hablaba*, 107–8.
47 Meding, "Refugio seguro," 254–5; Meding, *Ruta*.
48 At the beginning of the 1950s, Perón announced Argentina's impressive achievements in the production of nuclear energy and hailed the country as a superpower in this field. He announced, among other things, that Argentina

had developed the capacity to sell atomic energy in 1.5-litre bottles intended "for the use of families and in industry." These statements were promptly disproved, to the glee of members of the opposition. See: Confalonieri, *Perón*, 214; Page, *Perón*, 225–7; Newton, *"Nazi Menace"*, 378–9; Mariscotti, *Secreto atómico*. Richter was secretly arrested in late 1952 and was only released from prison after Perón's regime was overthrown.

49 On Tank's professional trajectory, see: Wagner, *Kurt Tank*; Conradis, *Design for Flight*.

50 Burzaco, "Científicos alemanes," 14–15; Klich, "Pericia científica."

51 Rudel returned to Germany in 1952 and subsequently participated in neo-Nazi activities. Rudel was grateful to Perón, whose "sympathy for Germany and everything German [was] genuine." See: Newton, *"Nazi Menace"*, 381.

52 See Aarons and Loftus, *Unholy Trinity*, ch. 2; Devoto, "Inmigrantes." A report that ambassador Conrado Traverso sent to the Argentine Ministry of Foreign Affairs in 1947 mentions that Pope Pius XII was pleased at the readiness of the Argentine government and people to take in those refugees that were forced to leave Europe after the defeat of fascism. See the prologue by Beatriz Gurevich in DAIA, *Proyecto testimonio*, 1:55.

53 In February 1947, General John Hildring, the US assistant secretary of state for occupied areas of Europe, explained to one of Argentina's representatives in Washington that "the US government believed that every American nation should have complete freedom of action and independence to resolve the question of the refugees in the way that it considered to be most appropriate to its interests." Quoted in Senkman, "Relaciones," 91.

54 See: Solberg, *Immigration*.

55 See: Newton, *German Buenos Aires*.

56 Sutin, "Impact of Nazism"; Jackisch, *Nazismo*.

57 Posner and Ware, *Mengele*, particularly chs 5–7; Astor, *The "Last" Nazi*, ch. 10.

58 Freiwald and Mendelsohn, *The Last Nazi*, particularly chs 9–10.

59 Bower, *Klaus Barbie*.

60 Bohne was the first Nazi war criminal to be extradited by Argentina (to West Germany) in 1966. Kutschmann, whose residence in Argentina was kept secret until the mid-1970s, died in 1986 before he could be deported to West Germany to stand trial for his involvment in the murder of Jews in 1941. The Federal Republic of Germany also requested the extradition of Schwammberger in 1973, but he was only sent to stand trial in Germany after two decades of a lengthy court battle. Priebke was extradited to Italy fifty years after the crimes he had committed. For further details, see: DAIA, *Proyecto testimonio*.

61 "Actividades de los fascistas europeos en la Argentina" (in Hebrew), 24 May 1951, Israel State Archives, Jerusalem (hereafter ISA), 2575/3.

62 Pávelic lived in Argentina for nearly a decade, and then moved to Franco's Spain, where he was wounded in an attempt to murder him, and died of his injuries two years later. See: Ignacio Klich, "Ingreso"; Montes de Oca, *Ustashas*.
63 Luca de Tena, *Yo, Juan Domingo Perón*, 85–6.
64 Newton, *"Nazi Menace"*, 375.
65 Klich and Buchrucker, "Tercer Reich," 263.
66 Charles Hamilton, *The Hitler Diaries* (Lexington, KY: University Press of Kentucky, 1991).
67 Ibid., 271.

CHAPTER THREE

1 Claudio Bajraj (Krislavin's nephew), interviews by the author, Buenos Aires, May–June 2017.
2 Sebreli, *Cuestión judía*, 147–8.
3 *Mundo Israelita*, 22 February 1947.
4 Central Zionist Archives, Jerusalem (hereafter CZA), Z6/22; *Di Idishe Tzaitung*, 16 February 1947, 18 February 1947; *Di Presse*, 13 February 1947; *Mundo Israelita*, 22 February 1947.
5 *El Argentino*, 18 February 1947, 4.
6 Bell, "Jews and Perón," 164; see also: *Di Presse*, 18 February 1947. Woscoff seems to have been motivated by, among other factors, the "pressure" that Borlenghi put on him in threatening to hamper the operations of Laboratorios Woscoff, the business that he owned. Alberto Woscoff, interview by the author, Buenos Aires, 1 December 2008.
7 Perla Cortés, interview by the author, Buenos Aires, 5 August 2008; and Rosalía Cortés, interview by the author, Rio de Janeiro, 12 August 2009.
8 Lewin, *Inmigración judía*, 273; Bell, "Jews and Perón," 164–5.
9 Romina Manguel, "Abuelo Pablo."
10 Enrique Scheinsohn, interview by the author, Buenos Aires, December 2008.
11 Quoted in Feierstein, *Historia*, 349.
12 For previous studies of this Jewish Peronist organization, see: Senkman, "Peronismo," 115–36; Marder, "Organización Israelita Argentina."
13 Pablo Manguel's files, Comisión Nacional de Investigación, Archivo General de La Nación, Buenos Aires (hereafter AGN).
14 Acha, *Muchachos peronistas*, 57.
15 *Di Idishe Tzaitung*, 26 February 1947; *Mundo Israelita*, 8 March 1947, 26 June 1948.
16 *Mundo Israelita*, 21 August 1948, 29 August 1948; DAIA, *Pensamiento*, 15; DAIA, *Perón*, 11; AJYB, vol. 50 (1948–49), 270.
17 *Mundo Israelita*, 1 March 1947, 4 April 1947, 11 October 1947.

18 Alberto Woscoff, interview by the author, Buenos Aires, 1 December 2008.
19 *La Nación*, 10 June 1949; *La Prensa*, 9 July 1949.
20 *Constitución de la Nación Argentina de 1949*, art. 28, 29–30; Tov to Eytan, 7 March 1950, ISA, 2574/17; *Mundo Israelita*, 19 March 1949; AJYB, vol. 51 (1950), 266; AJYB, vol. 52 (1951), 214.
21 DAIA, "Medio siglo," 10; Sebreli, *Cuestión judía*, 156. Some interpreted Evita's positive attitudes toward Jews as a way of showing her gratitude to the owner of Radio Belgrano, the platform from which she was catapulted to fame. It was from the airwaves of Radio Belgrano that, in 1943, Eva Perón began to broadcast a program on famous women in history.
22 DAIA, *Pensamiento*, 23, 27–9; DAIA, "Medio siglo," 14–15; Perón, *Historia*, 58.
23 *El Día*, 21 July 1954, 5 September 1954.
24 Visacovsky, "Herencias."
25 McGee Deutsch, *Crossing Borders*.
26 "Eva Perón," Organización Sionista Femenina Argentina (hereafter OSFA), no. 138, year XIV (August 1952), 1.
27 Eshel to the Ministry of External Relations, 20 July 1950, ISA, 2571/9.
28 *Di Idishe Tzaitung*, 8 April 1951; Segal to Hochstein, 15 May 1951, AJC, box 3.
29 Schneersohn to the Ministry of External Relations, 1 August 1951, ISA 2574/3; *Mundo Israelita*, 7 July 1951; AJYB, vol. 54 (1951), 203. On the diverging opinions that the DAIA's leadership held about the OIA, see: Actas del Consejo Directivo de la DAIA, 1948–52. I am grateful to Beatriz Gurevich for sharing this documentation with me.
30 See: *Di Presse*, 7 October 1951, 19 October 1951; *Mundo Israelita*, 10 November 1951.
31 Senkman, "Peronismo," 116–18.
32 Darom to Tov, 27 November 1951, and Tsur to the Ministry of Foreign Relations, 29 November 1951, ISA 2579/16; Senkman, "Peronismo," 118.
33 Tsur to the Ministry of External Relations, 11 June 1952, 23 June 1952, 24 August 1952, ISA 2579/16; Aznar to the Ministerio de Asuntos Exteriores (MAE), 30 June 1952, Archivo del Ministerio de Asuntos Exteriores, Madrid (henceforth AMAE), R. 3177/49; Torrehermosa to the MAE, 31 March 1952, AMAE, R. 3177/49.
34 Kubovy to Darom, 23 November 1953, ISA 2573/14; *La Prensa*, 27 February 1954, 20 March 1954, 15 April 1954; *Di Idishe Tzaitung*, 29 June 1952; *Di Presse*, 28 June 1952.
35 DAIA, *Pensamiento*, 33–5; Arazi to the Ministry of External Relations, 19 November 1953, ISA, 4701/1.
36 *El Día*, 21 December 1954; *La Prensa*, 21 December 1954; Bejar, "Entrevista Dickmann-Perón."
37 Corbière, *Estaban*, 159–63. An even greater exaggeration of the influence wielded by the Jewish Peronist organization can be found in the report filed in

January 1950 by the Spanish ambassador to Argentina, José María de Areilza, from January 1950. See the archive of the Fundación Francisco Franco, Madrid, leg. 121, fol. 56.

38 Riegner, "Argentina," 51.

39 Chávez, *Eva Perón*, 158–9.

40 Tsur, *Credential no.* 4, 42, 45; Bell, "Jews and Perón," 175.

41 Quoted in Bell, "Jews and Perón," 171.

42 Quoted in Bell, "Jews and Perón," 172.

43 Vicepresidencia de la Nación, *Libro negro*.

44 Vicepresidencia de la Nación, *Libro negro*, vol. 3.

45 For press coverage on Sojit, see the articles "Luis Elías! Qué personaje!", in the magazine *Gente* (n.d., 1970), and "Un ilusionado del micrófono," by Carlos Marcelo Thiery, in the newspaper *Clarín* (n.d., 1985). See also: Diario Olé, *Diccionario*, 522. Although Sojit's son emphasizes that his father did not have a marked Jewish identity, he was buried in 1982 in the Jewish cemetery of Liniers. Eduardo Isidoro Sojit, interview by the author, Buenos Aires, 4 December 2008.

46 *Di Presse*, 24 March 1949, 28 August 1949.

47 Klich, " First Trade Accord."

48 Marcos Korenhendler, interview by the author, Tel Aviv, 21 August 2000; and David Hurovitz, interview by the author, Tel Aviv, July 2004.

49 *Di Idishe Tzaitung*, 29 June 1954, 29 December 1954; *La Luz*, 14 January 1955, 15, quoted in Bell, "Jews and Perón," 263.

50 Bell, "Jews and Perón," 263.

51 Eliachar, *Living*, 287.

52 *Mundo Israelita*, 19 July 1952.

53 Yagupsky to Segal, 30 August 1953, AJC, box 1.

54 This interview was conducted by journalists Shlomo Slutzky and Julián Blejmar (Buenos Aires, August 2014). I am grateful to them for sharing the recording with me.

55 Ibid.

56 Ibid.

57 Ibid.

58 Dobry, *Rabinos*.

59 *Mundo Israelita*, 11 July 1953; Sergio Groisman, emails with author, November 2018; Weisbrot, *Jews*, 233–6.

60 *Mundo Israelita*, 20 November 1954.

61 On the relations between Perón and the Catholic Church, see: Caimari, *Perón*; Zanatta, *Perón*; Lida, "Catolicismo"; Adamovsky, "Bendita medianía."

62 Aznar to Artajo, 1 August 1952, Archivo de la Presidencia del Gobierno, Madrid (henceforth APG), leg. 14; Oficina de Información Diplomática, "Se pide la beatificación de Eva Duarte de Perón. Comentarios de prensa," 23 August 1952, APG, leg. 14. On the expropriation of *La Prensa*, see: Panella, "*La Prensa*."

63 Martindale to Department of State, 22 October 1952, in NA 735.00\10-2252.
64 On indoctrination in the educational system between 1952 and 1955, see: Rein, *Politics and Education*, ch. 3; Bernetti and Puiggrós, *Peronismo*; Gvirtz, "Politización"; Somoza Rodríguez, "Educación."
65 "Review of Church-State Developments," 5 May 1955, NA, 835.413\5-555; Potash, *Army and Politics*, ch. 6; Stack, "Avoiding"; *Primera Plana*, 24 December 1968, 31 December 1968, 14 November 1969. The versions upheld by the Church and Juan Perón can be consulted respectively in *Criterio*, 25 November 1954, 28 July 1955, and Boizard, *Esa noche*; Perón, *Poder*, ch. 5.
66 For an analysis of the various possible motives for overthrowing Perón, see: Memorandum of the Deputy Assistant Secretary of State for Inter-American Affairs (Lyon) to the Secretary of State, *Foreign Relations of the United States, 1955–57*, vol. 7: 381–2.
67 The text of the speech can be consulted in *La Prensa* and *Democracia*, 11 November 1954; *Hechos e Ideas* (October–November 1954), 387–97.
68 Lila Caimari, "Peronist Christianity."
69 For examples of this in second-grade textbooks, see: Gómez Reynoso, *Hada buena*, 54; Lerdo de Tejeda, *Un año más*, 12.
70 These arrests were not, however, part of a policy of mass detentions. Between October 1954 and May 1955, twenty-five priests were arrested and were, in their majority, released shortly thereafter. See: "Review of Church-State Developments," 5 May 1955, NA, 835.413/5-555.
71 Castiella to the MAE, 23 December 1954, APG, leg. 21.
72 Siracusa to the Department of State, 12 April 1955, NA, 735.00/4-1255; Siracusa to the Department of State, 15 April 1955, NA, 735.00/4-1555. This US diplomat did not characterize negatively the government's measures against priests but rather the authoritarian manner in which the government applied these measures.
73 República Argentina, *Diario*, 1955, 1:213–43.
74 Rein, "Nationalism, Education."
75 Fordham to the Foreign Office, Public Record Office, Foreign Office Papers (henceforth FO), London, 7 January 1955, FO 371/114066.
76 Alberto Woscoff, interview by the author, Buenos Aires, 1 December 2008.
77 Potash, *Army and Politics*, 175–6; Lafiandra, ed., *Panfletos*, 227–8; Paz, *Memorias*, 208–9; and Clara Borlenghi, interview by the author, Buenos Aires, 9 September 1997. Borlenghi was forced to publicly emphasize his Christian faith despite his criticisms of the Catholic Church's leadership. See: Kubovy to Tov, 10 June 1955, ISA 2571/10.
78 Kubovy to Tov, 12 May 1955, ISA 2571/10; Yagupsky to Segal, 2 May 1955, AJC, box 1. Yagupsky mentions that some of these pamphlets likely originated in pro-Nazi or in Arab groups, and not necessarily in Catholic initiatives.
79 Yagupsky to Segal, 8 December 1954, AJC, box 1.
80 See the Memorandum by S.A. Fineberg, 14 June 1955, AJC, box 3.

81 República Argentina, *Diario*, 1955, 1:35.
82 Kubovy to Tov, 18 April 1955, and Tov to Kubovy, 3 May 1955, F, 2571/10; *Mundo Israelita*, 26 February 1955; Yagupsky to Segal, 8 December 1954 and 26 July 1955, AJC, box 1.
83 *La Razón*, 13 January 1955, quoted in Confalonieri, *Perón*, 280.
84 Yagupsky to Segal, 8 December 1954, 2 May 1955, and 26 July 1955, AJC, box 1.
85 Ibid.
86 On the Argentine Army, particularly its stance vis-à-vis Perón and its role in the Revolución Libertadora, see: Potash, *Army and Politics*, 188 and ff. In a trial by martial court where Perón's minister of the navy was judged for participating in the events of 16 June, the minister declared that he had supported Peronism up until it began its attack on the Church. See: Olivieri, *Dos veces*, 139.
87 It was only during his exile in Spain, in the 1960s, that Perón managed to mend fences with the Vatican.
88 On the failed rebellion of 16 June, see: US embassy in Buenos Aires to the Department of State, 22 June 1955, NA, 735.00/62255; Potash, *Army and Politics*, ch. 6; Rouquié, *Poder militar*, vol. 2, ch. 3; Godio, *Caída*. Members of the Instituto Judío Argentino de Cultura e Información accompanied Cardinal Caggiano on his visit to many of the churches that had been damaged. See: Yagupsky to Segal, 27 July 1955, AJC, box 1.
89 Tov to Kubovy, "Las actividades de Manguel," 18 July 1955, ISA, 2388/11; Tov to Kubovy, 2 August 1955, and World Jewish Congress to Tov, 4 August 1955, ISA, 2574/4; interview with Rosalía Manguel (Manguel's spouse), Instituto Nacional de Investigaciones Históricas Eva Perón, Programme in Oral History, 8. The positions to which Manguel was assigned indicate that Perón continued to support the OIA and maintained policies that were supportive of Jews. See: Hevesi to Hochstein, 8 July 1955, and Liskofsky to Danzig, 30 June 1955, AJC, box 3.
90 See report dated 4 August 1955, ISA, 2574/4.
91 See Goldstein, "Influence," 309; *Di Presse*, 18 June 1955; *Di Idishe Tzaitung*, 7 July 1955, 1 September 1955.
92 On the period between June and September of 1955, see: Sáenz Quesada, *La Libertadora*; Potash, *Army and Politics*, 180–213; Rouquié, *Poder militar*, vol. 2, ch. 3; Page, *Perón*, ch. 35; del Carril, *Crónica interna*; Godio, *Caída*.
93 DAIA, "Medio siglo," 14.
94 ABC (Madrid), 30 November 1946; Newton, *"Nazi Menace"*, 240–1; Goyeneche, *Ensayos*.
95 Newton, *"Nazi Menace"*, 120; Page, *Perón*, 302, 306, 307; Amadeo, *Ayer*.
96 See Turkow's memorandum dated 30 September 1955, and Heymann to Nahum Goldman, CZA Z6/926.
97 Yagupsky to Segal, 28 September 1955, AJC, box 1.

98 Quoted in Bell, "Jews and Perón," 283.
99 *Idishe Tzaitung*, 13 October 1955.
100 *Mundo Israelita*, 29 October 1955.
101 A copy of the DAIA's telegram to Lonardi dated 25 September 1955 can be consulted in the ISA 474/23; Bernstein to Pratto, 20 November 1955, ISA 2574/4; Kubovy to Pratto, 20 October 1955, ISA 2579/18.
102 Interview with Rosalía Manguel, 9.
103 *La Razón*, 9 November 1956; *La Nación*, 11 February 1957.
104 Claudio Bajraj (Krislavin's nephew), interviews by the author, Buenos Aires, May–June 2017.
105 Bell, "Jews and Perón," 286.
106 On the scandal caused by the removal of Woscoff from his functions, see: *Di Idishe Tzaitung*, 20 October 1955; *Di Presse*, 20 October 1955; *Mundo Israelita*, 22 and 29 October 1955.
107 Eliav to the Ministry of External Relations, 23 November 1955, ISA 477/10; AJYB, vol. 57 (1956), 524; AJYB, vol. 58 (1957), 405; Yagupsky to Segal, 28 September 1955, AJC, box 1; memoranda submitted by Heymanm, 22 November 1955 and 29 November 1955, CZA.
108 *La Luz*, 26 November 1954, 24 December 1954.
109 *La Luz*, 7 October 1955.
110 *La Luz*, 7 October and 25 November 1955; *Mundo Israelita*, 26 November 1955.
111 Weisbrot, *Jews*, 127.
112 Interview conducted by journalists Shlomo Slutzky and Julián Blejmar, Buenos Aires, August 2014.
113 Ibid.
114 See, for example, 11 June 1955.

CHAPTER FOUR

1 See the memoirs of Guatemala's delegate to the United Nations Jorge García Granados, *Birth of Israel*; and Rodríguez Fabregat, *Sión*.
2 On the participation of Latin American countries in the UN during that period, see: Houston, *Latin America*.
3 On Argentina's international relations at the time and its difficulties with the US, see, among others: Sheinin, *Argentina*; Lanús, *Chapultepec*; Rapoport and Spiguel, *Relaciones*.
4 Tov, *Murmullo*, 87. On the Peronist administrations' policy toward the Middle East, see: Klich, "Equidistance"; Paulo Botta, "Diplomacia."
5 Benno Weiser Varon, *Professions*, 132.
6 "Secreto – Para agregar a las instrucciones que posee actualmente la delegación argentina ante asamblea general de las Naciones Unidas" (emphasis in the original), Juan Atilio Bramuglia Papers, Hoover Institution Archives, Stanford University (henceforth JAB), 10 October 1946.

7 Rein and Noyjovich, *Muchachos peronistas árabes.*
8 See: memorandum from Tov to Sharett, October 1947, CZA, S25/7502; Weiser Varon, *Professions*, 133; *Democracia*, 28 December 1945, 4.
9 Viquendi, "Sirio-libaneses," 31.
10 16 October 1945, CZA, Z5/373; 2 November 1945, Z5/1087; 17 February 1947, 5 March 1947, Z5/3469; AJYB, vol. 48 (1946–47), 255.
11 5 March 1944, CZA, Z5/737; 15 March 1946, S25/2037; 13 February 1946, 18 February 1946, and 7 August 1946, Z5/1087. On Benítez Piriz, see: Tov, *Murmullo*, 83–4.
12 On this initiative, see: Cipriano Reyes (dissident Peronist delegate), interviews by the author, Quilmes, 15 September 1989; La Plata, 3 May 1996; República Argentina, *Diario*, 1946, 4 September 1946 and 23 September 1946; *La Nación*, 5 September 1946; Klich, "Failure."
13 *El Estado Judío*, 19 September 1947; Tov, *Murmullo*, 77–9.
14 The correspondence between A. Mibashán and Nahum Goldmann can be consulted in the CZA, Z5/1087. On Tov's visit, see: 21–22 August 1946, Z5/1087; correspondence between Tov and Mibashán throughout 1947, Z5/3468, Z5/3469; Tov, *Murmullo*, 77–102. On Bramuglia's supportive stance vis-à-vis the Jewish question and Zionism, see the firsthand account of Moisés Goldman, Oral History Project, Institute of Contemporary Jewry, Hebrew University of Jerusalem, 25–6.
15 Copies of telegrams to Truman, Perón, and Corominas, CZA, Z5/3468; DAIA, "Medio siglo," 10.
16 Tov to Mibashán, 12 October 1947; Mibashán to Tov, 17 October 1947; Tov to Mibashán, 18 October 1947; Mibashán to Tov, 20 October 1947, CZA, Z5/3468.
17 *Haaretz*, 4 November 1947; *Davar*, 3 November 1947; *Hamishmar*, 3 November 1947; *Kol Haam*, 3 November 1947; *Hatzofe*, 3 November 1947.
18 *El Mundo* and *La Nación*, 23 May 1946.
19 Corominas to Bramuglia, 22 September 1947, JAB; Areilza to the Ministerio de Asuntos Exteriores, 31 October 1947, AMAE, R. 1453/1.
20 Klich, "Árabes, judíos."
21 Hipólito Jesús Paz (Minister of Foreign Affairs, 1949–51, and Argentine ambassador to Washington, 1951–55), interview by the author, Buenos Aires, 29 April 1996.
22 Tov, *Murmullo*, 98.
23 On Bramuglia's political career, see: Rein, *Bramuglia.*
24 Rein, *Entre el abismo.*
25 "Consultas formuladas por el embajador Arce," 12 October 1947, JAB.
26 Corominas to Bramuglia, 21 November 1947, JAB.
27 Quoted in Glick, *Latin America*, 86.
28 Lorch, *Seven Chapters*, 48; Schenkolewsky-Kroll, *Zionist Movement*, 356–7; Mibashán to Tov, 20 March 1947; Tov to Mibashán, 24 March 1947, CZA, Z5/3469; "El delegado argentino ante la UN reiteró el apoyo del país a las demandas sionistas," *El Estado Judío*, 4 April 1947.

29 Corominas to Bramuglia, 17 October 1947, JAB.
30 Corominas to Bramuglia, 22 September 1947, JAB.
31 Corominas to Bramuglia, 7 November 1947, JAB.
32 Corominas to Bramuglia, 25 November 1947, JAB.
33 Ibid.
34 Ibid.
35 Elath, *Struggle*, 679; Tov, *Murmullo*, 95–6; Arce, *Mi vida*, 145–6; *La Nación*, 14 April 1949.
36 See: *La Prensa*, 10 May 1949; *La Nación*, 12 May 1949; Tsur to Irigoyen, 12 May 1949, Archivo del Ministerio de Relaciones Exteriores y Culto, Buenos Aires (hereafter AMREC), Political Division, Israel 1949, box 53, exp. 8.
37 *La Prensa*, 4 May 1949; Tov, *Murmullo*, 77–102; Shertok to Bramuglia, 27 February 1949, AMREC, Israel 1949, box 53, exp. 8.
38 DAIA, *Perón*, 16; *Mundo Israelita*, 19 March 1949; Sebreli, *Cuestión judía*, 149.
39 *La Prensa*, 23, 26, and 31 May 1949; República Argentina, *Diario*, 1949, 1:500–1, 2:1917–9; Baltiérrez, "Creación"; Navasqües to the MAE, 1 June 1951, AMAE, 2829/68. See also: Tsur to Eytan, 4 April 1949, ISA 2574/3.
40 *La Prensa*, 1 September 1949; Tsur to Eytan, 4 April 1949, ISA 2574/3. On the reception that Manguel received in Israel, see: Manguel to MREC, 2 September 1949, AMREC, Israel 1949, box 53, exp. 6.
41 *La Nación*, 14 June 1949, 2 August 1949; *La Prensa*, 23 May 1949. See also Tsur's memoirs: *Credential No. 4*, 100–4, 107.
42 *Haaretz*, 8 June 1949; *Maariv*, 14–15 September 1949; *Davar*, 3 August 1949. On the formal ceremony, see also: Tsur, *Credential No. 4*, 48–51.
43 See: AJYB, vol. 58 (1957), 408.
44 Tsur, *Credential No. 4*, 46.
45 Argentine officials wanted representatives from each country to bear the title of ambassador, but Israel turned down their request due to budgetary and political reasons. Manguel and Tsur therefore fulfilled their duties as ministers, in Tel Aviv and Buenos Aires respectively. See: Tsur to Tov, 18 May 1949, ISA 2571/9.
46 Eshel to Ministry of Foreign Affairs, 8 September 1949, ISA 2574/3.
47 DAIA, *Perón*, 16; Sebreli, *Cuestión judía*, 149.
48 Tsur, *Credential No. 4*, 64; Tsur to Darom, 13 March 1950, ISA 4701/1.
49 See: Eytan to Tsur, 11 September 1949; Tsur to Ministry of Foreign Affairs, 12 September 1949; Darom to Tsur, 18 September 1949; Tsur to Eytan, 22 December 1949, ISA 2571/9.
50 Tsur to Eytan, 3 January 1950, ISA 2574/3. See also: Tsur, *Credential No. 4*, 124–5.
51 Abraham Darom, interview by the author, Tel Aviv, 16 June 1986.
52 Tov to Eytan, 7 March 1950, ISA 2574/3. The memorandum is titled "What is the O.I.A." and can be consulted in CZA Z6/326.
53 Tsur to Eytan, 19 August 1949, ISA 2572/7.

54 Tsur to Ministry of Foreign Affairs, 6 March 1950, ISA 2574/3.
55 Ibid.
56 Tsur to Darom, 18 April 1950, ISA 2574/3.
57 Tsur, *Credential No.* 4, 45, 134–5.
58 Ibid.
59 Sebreli, *Cuestión judía*, 150–1.
60 In 1950, the newspaper *Crítica* published excerpts of Weizmann's autobiography, which was subsequently published as a book and made available to a broad readership. See AJYB, vol. 51 (1950), 266.
61 Tsur to Ministry of Foreign Affairs, 16 December 1952, ISA 463/12; Amir to Ministry of Foreign Affairs, 1 October 1952; Tsur to Ministry of Foreign Affairs, 15 December 1952; Pratto to Ministry of Foreign Affairs, 9 January 1953, 16 January 1953, ISA 469/6.
62 See the report by Tuvia Arazi, 30 January 1953, ISA 2578/22; *Di Idishe Tzaitung*, 28 January 1953.
63 Nufer to Department of State, 28 January 1953, NA 835.413/1-2853; Martindale to Department of State, 29 January 1953, NA 835.413/1-2953; Lockhart to Foreign Office, 6 February 1953, FO 371/103211.
64 See the report of the Israeli legation in Buenos Aires, 4 February 1953, and the memorandum by Tsur, "Perón, los judíos e Israel," 23 March 1953, ISA 2578/22; "Debe facilitarse la salida de los judíos amenazados hacia Israel y el mundo libre. Audiencia del General Perón a una delegación judía," *Mundo Israelita*, 24 January 1953; DAIA, *Perón*, 11–12; *La Prensa*, 29 and 30 January 1953; *La Nación*, 30 January 1953; *Clarín*, 30 January 1953; *El Mundo*, 30 January 1953.
65 See: Tsur to Ministry of Foreign Affairs, 19 December 1952, ISA 4701/1; Goldstein, "Influence," 274–5; E. Hervesi, confidential memo, AJC, box 3.
66 Tsur to Ministry of Foreign Affairs, 26 January 1953, ISA 4701/1.
67 Israel State Archives, *Documents on the Foreign Policy of Israel*, vol. 8 (Jerusalem, 1953), 76–7.
68 See: Tsur to Ministry of Foreign Affairs, 8 May 1953, ISA 2381/2.
69 On the warm welcome that Jewish-Argentines gave to Kubovy and his first impressions of the community and its institutions and leaders, see: Kubovy to Ministry of Foreign Affairs, 1 December 1953, ISA 2573/20.
70 ISA 471/15; Goldstein, "Influence," 292; Siracusa to Department of State, 10 November 1953, NA 635.84[a]/11-1053; *Democracia*, 8 November 1953.
71 Levavi to Kubovy, 11 January 1954, ISA 2573/20.
72 República Argentina, *Diario*, 1954, 2:1561–78.
73 *La Prensa*, 23 May 1949 and 29 May 1949; AJYB, vol. 48 (1946–47), 255.
74 Gitter, *Story*, 171.
75 Ibid., 191–2.
76 *Haaretz*, 5 March 1950, 20 March 1950, 20 April 1950, 23–24 April 1950; *Maariv*, 19 April 1950; *Davar*, 23 April 1950; *Al Hamishmar*, 20 April 1950,

23 April 1950; *Hatzofe*, 20 April 1950, 23 April 1950; *Herut*, 20 April 1950, 23–24 April 1950.

77 Minister plenipotentiary Manguel also told Minister of Foreign Affairs Sharett that Perón saw in Israel a possible hub through which to distribute Argentine commodities in the Mediterranean area. See: Drapkin to Buenos Aires legation, 6 September 1949, *Documents on the Foreign Policy*, vol. 4 (1949), 440.

78 On the agreement, see: Tsur to Tov, 13 January 1950, ISA 2571/9; AMREC, Departamento de Política, Israel, 1950, box 3, file 8; Ministerio de Finanzas de la Nación, Banco Central de la República Argentina, *Memoria anual* [henceforth *Memoria anual*] *1950* (Buenos Aires, 1951), 47–8; Klich, "First Trade Accord."

79 Gitter, *Story*, 148–9.

80 See, for example: "Memorandum of Conversation," 11 December 1948, in FRUS, 1948, vol. IX, 307–8; Ray to Department of State, 24 February 1949, FRUS, vol. II, 481; Acheson to US embassy in Argentina, 24 February 1949, FRUS, vol. II, 482–3; Nufer to Department of State, 5 February 1953, NA 611.35/2-553.

81 On the policy of boycott toward Argentina adopted by the administrators of the Marshall Plan, see: Escudé, *Argentina*, ch. 1.

82 FRUS, 1950, vol. II, 691ff.

83 Gitter, *Story*, 150.

84 Statistics on these fundraisers in Argentina between 1948 and 1958 can be consulted in Goldstein, "Influence," 320–1.

85 *Memoria anual 1951* (Buenos Aires, 1952), 40–1; *Memoria anual 1953* (Buenos Aires, 1954), 46; *Memoria anual 1954* (Buenos Aires, 1955), 66–7; *Memoria anual 1955* (Buenos Aires, 1956), 53–4.

86 On this topic, see: Kubovy to Ministry of Foreign Affairs, 5 September 1954, ISA 4701/1. Statistics in Israeli currency on the trade between the two countries can be consulted in Israel's Central Bureau of Statistics, *Statistical Abstract of Israel 1949–1950*, 79; *Statistical Abstract of Israel 1951–1952*, 83; *Statistical Abstract of Israel 1953–1954*; *Statistical Abstract of Israel 1955–1956*, 177.

87 Tsur, *Credential No. 4*, 135.

88 On the Fundación Eva Perón, see: Plotkin, *Mañana*, 215–55, 335–48; Stawski, *Asistencia social*. On assistance to Israel, see: AJYB, vol. 52 (1951), 218; AJYB, vol. 54 (1953), 205; Report of the Tel Aviv Legation, 20 July 1950, AMREC, Israel 1950, box 3, exp. 1; *Davar*, 4 July 1950; *Herut*, 1 and 4 August 1950; *Haboker*, 1 August 1950; *Al Hamishmar*, 4 August 1950.

89 Tsur, *Credential No. 4*, 54.

90 See: Report of the Israel Legation in Buenos Aires, 4 February 1953, ISA 2578/22.

91 DAIA, "Medio siglo," 10. See: Arazi to the Ministerio, 19 November 1953, ISA 47.1/1.

CHAPTER FIVE

1 Tiempo was invited to attend Mario Satanowaski's talk "El pueblo 'joven' de Israel: impresiones de un reciente viaje" (see the letter signed by the president, Guillermo Cracovski, and the secretary, Bernardo Mayantz, 29 June 1954, Archivo César Tiempo, Biblioteca Nacional, Buenos Aires). In the mid-1960s, under the presidency of Jacobo Kovadloff and with Bernardo Ezequiel Koremblit as director of cultural activities, the Sociedad hebraica begins anew to invite Tiempo to events and, in January 1964, they also invite him to contribute to the literary journal *Davar* (see the letter from Bernardo Ezequiel Koremblit, 31 January 1964).

2 Tiempo, *Campaña antisemita*. See also: Ben-Dror, *Católicos*, 108–15.

3 Fiorucci, "Neither Warriors Nor Prophets," 49.

4 Fiorucci, "Marginados de la Revolución." See also Fiorucci's "Aliados o enemigos?", as well as her doctoral thesis "Neither Warriors Nor Prophets."

5 Rein, *Entre el abismo*, ch. 4; Goldar, *Peronismo en la literatura*. The US embassy in Buenos Aires also shared that vision. See the report on the meeting that Perón held with nationalist intellectuals in November 1947: Buenos Aires Embassy to State Department, 18 November 1947, NA, 835.42/11-1847.

6 Sitman, *Victoria Ocampo*; King, *"Sur."*

7 Fiorucci, "Neither Warriors Nor Prophets," 49.

8 On the journal "Hechos e Ideas," see: Cattaruzza, "Empresa cultural," and Persello, "Diversidad."

9 Herrera, "Socialismo." In the April 1954 elections, the Partido Socialista de la Revolución Nacional (Socialist Party for National Revolution) presented its candidates in the federal capital district. Saúl Groisman was on this slate.

10 Rein and Panella, eds, *Cultura para todos*.

11 Galasso, *Scalabrini Ortiz*, 99.

12 César Tiempo to Máximo Yagupsky, 27 April 1954, Archivo Máximo Yagupsky in the Archivo de la Fundación IWO, Buenos Aires.

13 Toker, ed., *Buenos Aires*, 17.

14 This is drawn from the LP *César Tiempo por él mismo, cancionero del judío errante*, recorded by the poet in Buenos Aires in August 1967 for the company AMB. A CD version is included in the book compiled by Toker, *Buenos Aires esquina Sábado*. See also: "Tiempo, César," in Galasso, ed., *"Malditos"*, 360–5.

15 For information on and interpretations of Tiempo's life and work, see: Toker, *Buenos Aires*; Senkman, *Identidad judía*, 153–95; Lindstrom, *Jewish Issues*; Feierstein, "César Tiempo." Tiempo's own autobiography can be consulted; it was published under the title *Capturas recomendadas*.

16 On the literary groups of Boedo and Florida, see: Méndez, "Argentine Intellectuals."

17 Fingueret, "César Tiempo," 44–5.

18 The lives of Jewish prostitutes in Argentina continue to be illuminated by historians. Recent such publications include: Yarfitz, *Impure Migration*; Glickman, *Jewish White*; Vincent, *Bodies and Souls*; Avni, *"Clients."*
19 Beter, *Versos de una....* It is significant that this first book by Tiempo was published by Antonio Zamora's publishing house, Claridad, known for its overtly socialist stances.
20 Gleizer published the works of Argentine intellectuals such as Scalabrini Ortiz, Vicente Cutiño, and Arturo Cacela. See: Delgado and Espósito, "Emergencia del editor," esp. 76–8; Buonocore, *Libreros*, ch. 5, esp. 102–5.
21 Senkman, *Identidad judía.*
22 Rotenberg quoted in Fingueret, "César Tiempo," 51.
23 Tiempo, "Alberto Gerchunoff," 38.
24 *La Opinión* (Buenos Aires), Sección Cultural, 10 December 1972, 9.
25 Fingueret, "César Tiempo," 49.
26 Tiempo, "Alberto Gerchunoff."
27 Weinstein and Gover de Nasatsky, eds, *Escritores judeo-argentinos*, 65–74; Bertazza, "Cuestión de ponerse," *Página/12*, Radar Libros, 27 July 2008.
28 Rein, *Politics and Education*, ch. 3.
29 My thanks to Alejandro Dujovne for sharing this interview of Alejandra Prilutzky.
30 Sosa de Newton, *Diccionario biográfico.*
31 Korin, "Intelectual." *Crítica* combined features of sensationalist media with intellectual expression. See: Saitta, *Regueros de tinta.*
32 On FORJA, see, among others: Scenna, *F.O.R.J.A.*; Jauretche, *FORJA*; Falcoff, "Argentine Nationalism"; Buchrucker, *Nacionalismo y peronismo*, 258–78; Spektorowski, *Autoritarios y populistas*, passim.
33 Quadraccia, *Koremblit.*
34 Koremblit, "Bohemia cultural," 51–6.
35 Fingueret, "César Tiempo," 25.
36 Ibid., 50.
37 César Tiempo to Máximo Yagupsky, 27 April 1954, Archivo Máximo Yagupsky.
38 A 1955 brochure titled *Epitafios*, quoted in Galasso, *"Malditos"*, 364.
39 Quoted in Galasso, *"Malditos"*, 364.
40 Ibid., 365.
41 Letter from the president of the Sociedad Hebraica, David Fleischer, and its secretary, Saúl Bermann, to César Tiempo, 31 July 1973, Archivo César Tiempo.
42 Matallana, *Jaime Yankelevich*; Matallana, "Inventando la Radio."
43 Karush, *Cultura de clase*; Matallana, *Locos por la radio.*
44 Acosta, "Radio."
45 Arribá, "Peronismo y la política," 22.
46 Matallana, *Jaime Yankelevich*, 89.

47 Matallana, *Imágenes y representación*, 149–51.

48 Healey, *Peronismo entre las ruinas*.

49 Matallana, *Jaime Yankelevich*, 110.

50 Ibid., 88.

51 Matallana, *Imágenes y representación*, 155.

52 Matallana, *Jaime Yankelevich*, 128–9.

53 Varela, "Peronismo y medios."

54 Rein and Panella, eds, *Peronismo y prensa*.

55 Varela, "Peronismo y medios."

56 Arribá, "Peronismo y la política," 21; Mercado, *Inventor del peronismo*.

57 Varela, "Peronismo y medios," 6.

58 Acosta, "Radio."

59 Varela, "Peronismo y medios," 8.

60 Arribá, "Peronismo y la política," 33.

61 García, "Peronismo y su relación," 145, 150.

62 Matallana, *Imágenes y representación*, 167.

63 Girbal-Blacha, "Industria invisible"; Orozco Gómez et al., *Historias*, 23–63.

64 Ulanovsky, Itkin, and Sirvén, *Estamos en el aire*. On the uses and abuses of fútbol at that time, see: Rein and Frydenberg, eds, *Cancha peronista*.

65 Arribá, "Peronismo y la política."

66 Matallana, *Jaime Yankelevich*, 127.

67 García, "Peronismo y su relación," 152.

68 This is the argument, for example, of Pablo Sirvén in his *El Rey de la TV* (Buenos Aires: Sudamericana, 2013).

CHAPTER SIX

1 See Perelman's memoir *Cómo hicimos el 17 de octubre*. On 17 October, see, among others: *Torre, ed., El 17 de octubre; Senén González and Lerman, eds, El 17 de octubre.*

2 Perelman, *Cómo hicimos*, 41.

3 Ibid., 63.

4 Di Tella, *Perón*, 335, 343; Reyes, *Yo hice*, vol. 2: 111 and vol. 3: 199, 213, 226.

5 Gay, *Partido Laborista*, 56; Senén González, *Laborismo*, 27–8.

6 JAB, box 15/1.

7 Interview with J. Domenech, Proyecto de Historia Oral, Instituto Di Tella, Buenos Aires, II, 177. See also: Del Campo, *Sindicalismo*, part II.

8 *La Vanguardia*, 29 August 1943.

9 See Rein, *Bramuglia*, 57–8. Diskin was a member of the CGT's Board of Directors from 1946 to 1955 and member of the National Congress from 1952 to 1955. See: David, *Perón*, 9–32; Diskin, *Borlenghi*.

10 Fernando Gelbard, correspondence with the author, April 2014.

11 Brennan, "Industriales," 119, 130.

12 "La rebelión de los empresarios," *Primera Plana*, no. 470, 17.
13 Seoane, *Burgués*, 351.
14 Ibid., 29–32. On Tucumán's Jewish community, see: Cohen de Chervonagura, *Comunidad judía.*
15 Gilbert, *Oro*, ch. 12.
16 Basualdo, *Estudios*, 27; Schvarzer, *Empresarios*; Brennan, "Industriales," 116.
17 "El ministro de Economía presidió en Catamarca la clausura de una reunión de jóvenes empresarios," *Boletín del Ministerio de Economía*, no. 36, 28 June 1974, 7.
18 See: Brennan and Rougier, "José B. Gelbard."
19 Brennan, "Industriales," 118–19.
20 Rougier and Fiszbein, *Frustración*, 55.
21 Brennan and Rougier, *Politics*, 86–8; David Selser, interview by the author, Buenos Aires, July 2014. Selser was at the time treasurer of the CGE.
22 Rougier and Fiszbein, *Frustración*, 56. See also: Bitrán, *Congreso*.
23 Gelbard made these statements after the signing of the Acta de Compromiso Nacional (Act for National Commitment).
24 "La rebelión de los empresarios," *Primera Plana*, no. 470, 16, 19.
25 *O'Donnell*, "*Estado* y *alianzas*," 523, 534, 546–7.
26 Wynia, *Argentina*, 301.
27 Ibid.
28 Seoane, *Burgués*, 14; Duilio Brunello, interview by the author, Buenos Aires, July 2014. Brunello worked with Gelbard in the FATE and collaborated with him in the CGE.
29 Brennan, "Industriales," 133, 137.
30 Seoane, *Burgués*, 84, 65, 122. On the kidnapping of Eichmann by Mossad agents, see: Rein, "Reconsiderando."
31 Seoane, *Burgués*, 107.
32 "Reportaje polémico a Gelbard," *Revista Cuestionario*, March 1976, 14.
33 *Boletín del Ministerio de Economía*, no. 13, 18 January 1974, 5.
34 Confederación General Económica, "Nueva política económica, su sentido y sus metas para 1974," in *Estudios sobre la Economía Argentina*, no. 17 (Buenos Aires: Instituto de Investigaciones Económicas y Financieras, 1973), 37, 40.
35 "La rebelión de los empresarios," *Primera Plana*, no. 470, 16. See also: Broner and Larriqueta, *Revolución industrial.*
36 *Boletín del ministerio de Economía*, no. 1, 18 January 1974, 6–7.
37 Alejandro Horowicz, *Cuatro peronismos*, 3.
38 Wynia, *Argentina*, 305.
39 Rotenberg, *Historia confidencial*, 146–9.
40 Ibid.
41 Ibid.
42 Ibid.

43 Ibid.
44 Ibid.
45 De Riz, *Retorno y derrumbe*, 60. Perón was referring to the "creation" of a "capitalism that was primarily oriented toward social questions and sought to temper the sacrifice of peoples."
46 Seoane, *Burgués*, 256.
47 Brennan, "Industriales," 135.
48 De Riz, *Retorno y derrumbe*, 86.
49 Vitto, "Plan económico"; Horowicz, *Cuatro peronismos*.
50 Leyba, *Economía y política*, 23.
51 "Reportaje polémico a Gelbard," 14.
52 Wynia, *Argentina*, 294.
53 Ibid.
54 "Reportaje polémico a Gelbard," 14.
55 Mochkofsky, *Pecado original*, 43.
56 Ramos, *Cerrojos*, 155.
57 Mochkofsky, *Timerman*, 165, 201.
58 Sivak, "*Clarín*", 248.
59 See the section "Para qué y para quiénes se produce" in *Plan Trienal 1974–1977*, Ed. Ministerio de Economía, 1973.
60 Ibid.
61 *Boletín del ministerio de Economía*, no. 11, 2 January 1974, 2.
62 Basualdo, *Estudios*, 115.
63 Wynia, *Argentina*, 314.
64 *Boletín del ministerio de Economía*, no. 26, 19 April 1974, 8; and no. 21, 21 March 1974, 3.
65 De Riz, *Retorno y derrumbe*, 91.
66 "El ministro de Economía presidio en Catamarca la clausura de una reunión de jóvenes empresarios," *Boletín del ministerio de Economía*, no. 36, 28 June 1974, 7.
67 Seoane, *Burgués*, 363. About the Triple A, see: González Janzen, *Triple A*; Larraquy, *López Rega*, passim.
68 *Boletín del ministerio de Economía*, no. 26, 19 April 1974, 11.
69 *Boletín del ministerio de Economía*, no. 50, 4 October 1974, 2.
70 "Los trabajadores y el gobierno combatirán a los enemigos de la liberación nacional," *Boletín del ministerio de Economía*, no. 31, 24 May 1974, 2.
71 Ibid.
72 Leyba, *Economía y política*, 51. Leyba states that, in October 1973, shipments of petroleum accounted for only 3.1 percent of exports, but soared to 15 percent shortly after.
73 Leyba quotes statistics prepared by multilateral organizations that demonstrate that, after an initial phase during which commodities appreciated, in late 1973, the European market would restrict the purchase of meat by 60 to 70 percent in order to stem the flight of currency from the area's countries.

74 Ministerio de Economía, "Exposición del ministro de Economía de la Nación, José Ber Gelbard, ante la sesión realizada hoy por la Honorable Cámara de Senadores de la Nación, 19 de junio de 1974," 24 June 1974.
75 Ibid.
76 Ibid.
77 Ibid.
78 Ibid.
79 Ibid.
80 Ibid.
81 Ibid.
82 Horowicz, *Cuatro peronismos*, 3.
83 Seoane, *Burgués*, 363.
84 Mochkofsky, *Timerman*, 333.
85 Seoane, *Burgués*, 375, 377.
86 Mochkofsky, *Timerman*, 201.
87 Sociedad Rural Argentina, *Memoria y Balance*, 1974, 48.
88 Torre, *Gigante invertebrado*, 90.
89 Torre, *Gigante invertebrado*, 91; Brennan, "Industriales," 137.
90 De Riz, *Retorno y derrumbe*, 104.
91 *Boletín del ministerio de Economía*, no. 45 (annex), 30 August 1974, 6; Abalo, *Derrumbe del peronismo*, 94.
92 Ibid.
93 Abalo, *Derrumbe del peronismo*, 88.
94 Horowicz, *Cuatro peronismos*.
95 "Habla Gelbard," *Revista Cuestionario*, no. 1324, March 1976.
96 Ibid.
97 Ibid.
98 Basualdo, *Estudios*, 122.
99 See: Kaufman, "Jewish Victims"; Goldman and Dobry, *Ser judío*.
100 Blaustein and Zubieta, *Decíamos ayer*; Brennan, "Industriales," 139. After publicly supporting Gelbard for a period, the large capitalist groups launched their own offensives against Gelbard and the CGE, which included a harsh campaign of media coverage and defamation. See: Sivak, "*Clarín*", 292.
101 Mochkofsky, *Timerman*, 230.
102 Mochkofsky, *Pecado original*, 75.
103 Sivak, "*Clarín*", 287.
104 Seoane, *Burgués*, 411.
105 Rotenberg, *Historia confidencial*, 276.
106 Ibid.
107 "El ministro de Economía presidió en Catamarca la clausura de una reunión de jóvenes empresarios," *Boletín del ministerio de Economía*, no. 36, 28 June 1974, 7.

CHAPTER SEVEN

1 *Mundo Peronista* 21, no. 15 (May 1952), 50 (emphasis in the original).
2 Braden, "Germans in Argentina," 43. On Braden and his fight against Perón, see: Braden, *Diplomats and Demagogues*; Frank, *Juan Perón*; Vannucci, "Elected"; Bosoer, *Braden o Perón.*
3 Quoted in Klich, "Background," 202.
4 Quoted in Bruce, *Perplexing Argentines*, 10.
5 Tsur, *Credential No* 4, 45.
6 See: Lipsky, *Memoirs*, 579–80.
7 J.H. Stiller, *George S. Messersmith*, ch. 7. On portrayals of Perón in the printed press across the Western world, see the second section of Rein and Panella, eds, *Peronismo y prensa escrita.*
8 "Inter-American Collaboration" (secret memorandum for the Secretary), 10 December 1946, 14; private letter to Little, 12 March 1947, and confidential report from 29 April 1947, George S. Messersmith Papers (henceforth GSM), University of Delaware.
9 See, for example: private and confidential letters to Sulzberger, 25 September 1946, 3 April 1947, GSM.
10 *U.S. News and World Report*, 19 April 1946; *Time*, 15 April 1946.
11 Stiller, *George S. Messersmith*, 245.
12 Nufer to State Department, 5 February 1953, NA, 611.35/2-553.
13 See press clippings from November 1947, James Bruce Papers, University of Maryland Libraries, College Park, MD.
14 Tsur, *Credential No* 4, 119.
15 "Por la felicidad y la grandeza de todos los pueblos," *Mundo Peronista* 80, no. 1 (February 1955): 12–14; "Un periodista extranjero," *Mundo Peronista* 61, no. 15 (March 1954): 15–16.
16 Tsur, *Credential No* 4, 62. See also pages 115, 124–5.
17 *Haaretz*, 17 June 1955, 19 September 1955, and 20 September 1955.
18 *Maariv*, 17 June 1955.
19 Sh. Ner, "Perón and the 'Descamisados'" (in Hebrew), *Maariv*, 20 June 1955.
20 *Maariv*, 20 September 1955.
21 Sh. Shafir, "The Military Coup in Argentina" (in Hebrew), *Davar*, 21 September 1955.
22 M. B., "The Uprising in Argentina and Its Lessons" (in Hebrew), *Hatzofeh*, 20 June1955.
23 *Hatzofeh*, 20 September 1955 and 22 September 1955.
24 "The Civil War in Argentina" (in Hebrew), *Herut*, 20 September 1955. See also the positive note included in the section "Names in the news – Juan Perón," published on the same day.
25 M. Nachumi, "How They Overthrew Perón" (in Hebrew), *Al Hamishmar*, 22 September 1955.

26 B. B., "What Is Happening in Argentina?" (in Hebrew), *Kol Haam*, 19 June 1955.
27 Ibid.
28 Ibid.
29 Ibid.
30 Ibid.
31 Ibid.
32 B. B., "What Is Happening in Argentina?" (in Hebrew), *Kol Haam*, 20 September 1955.
33 Y. Toledo, "Perón's Regime: Its Portrait and Its Future" (in Hebrew), *Molad*, no. 51 (July 1952), 143–51; Y. Versano, "The Justicialist Regime in Argentina" (in Hebrew), *Mibifnim* (May 1956), 411–24.
34 Tsur, *Credential No* 4, 212.
35 Caspi and Limor, *Intermediaries*.
36 Lanusse, *Mi testimonio*; Lanusse, *Protagonista*.
37 See: Tsur, *Credential No* 4, 210; A. Alón to M. Hatzor, 21 December 1972, P. Lavon Archive of the Labour Party, Tel Aviv, div. 208 IV, file 6007; and Shaul Ben Haim (international news editor at *Maariv*), "A Peronism without Charisma" (in Hebrew), *Maariv*, 24 May 1973.
38 Verbitsky, *Ezeiza*; Feinmann, *López Rega*.
39 "From Overthrow to Return" (in Hebrew), *Haaretz*, 20 November 1972.
40 *Haaretz*, 21 November 1972.
41 *Haaretz*, 14 June 1973.
42 *Davar*, 5 June 1973, 15 June 1973.
43 Egon Friedler, "A Jewish Minister in Argentina" (in Hebrew), *Davar*, 18 June 1973.
44 Joel Barromi, interview by the author, Jerusalem, 2 December 1986.
45 Yehoshua Bitzur, column, *Maariv*, 18 June 1973.
46 Ibid.
47 "Perón Returns to Argentina" (in Hebrew), *Davar*, 21 June 1973.
48 Tsur, *Credential No* 4, 213; Alón to M. Hatzor, 20 August 1973, Lavon Archive, div. 219-4, file 10A.
49 Dalia Shjori, column, *Al Hamishmar*, 17 June 1973.
50 *Al Hamishmar*, 24 June 1973.
51 Ibid.
52 *Haaretz*, 22 June 1973.
53 Ibid.
54 *Maariv*, 21 June 1973.
55 *Al Hamishmar*, 22 June 1973. See also: *Hatzofeh*, 22 June 1973.
56 *Davar*, 25 September 1973.
57 Ibid.
58 *Maariv*, 23 September 1973.
59 Tsur, *Credential No* 4, 216.

60 *Maariv*, 23 September 1973.
61 Hanoch Bartov, "Viva Zapata," *Maariv*, 25 September 1973, 5.
62 Ibid.
63 Ibid.
64 *Al Hamishmar*, 25 July 1973.
65 *Haaretz*, 24 September 1973.
66 Ibid.
67 *Yedioth Ahronoth*, 25 September 1973.
68 Ibid.
69 Ibid.
70 Ibid.
71 *Haaretz* and *Davar*, 23 October 1973; *Aurora*, 17 October 1973. See also: Tsur, *Credential No* 4.
72 See: Lerner, "Latin America: Its Origins," and the testimony of Jacob Tsur, both in Davis, ed., *Identification*.
73 See: Avni, *Jewish University*.
74 Jacob Tsur's testimony in Davis, ed., *Identification*, 237–8.
75 Natán Lerner, "Overview."
76 On the various reactions within Argentina's Jewish community, see: Informativo DAIA, "Desde la agresión a Israel y al pueblo judío en Iom Kipur al cese del fuego," 6–10.
77 *Página/12*, 20 June 2003.
78 Doron, *Observing*, 293; Tsur, *Credential No* 4, 211–12.
79 *Aurora*, 28 January 1974.
80 Lerner, "Latin America: Its Origins," 112; *Aurora*, 7 February 1974, 29 May 1974.
81 Jewish American Comittee, *Comunidades judías de Latinoamérica*, 36–47; Naomi F. Meyer, "Argentina," AJYB, vols 74 (1973) and 75 (1974–75).
82 "El Plan Andinia," appendix in Sallairai, *Los Protocolos*, 269–74. An analysis and rebuttal of this plan can be consulted in DAIA, *Versión argentina*.
83 On *Cabildo* and its antisemitic stances, see: Waisman, "Capitalism, Socialism."
84 *Primera Plana*, 23 June 1971; *La Razón*, 13 December 1972; Juan D. Perón, "Prólogo," in Pavón Pereyra, *Coloquios*, 9.
85 DAIA, *Perón y el pueblo judío*.
86 *Al Hamishmar*, 2 July 1974.
87 *Al Hamishmar*, 3 July 1974.
88 *Davar*, 3 July 1974; *Hatzofeh*, 3 July 1974. In fact, from 1973, Argentina's foreign policy positions were more favourable to the Arab countries when topics pertaining to these countries were debated in international organizations. See: Sharif, "Latin America."
89 "Juan Perón Has Died – The President was Argentina's Biggest Hope" (in Hebrew), *Maariv*, 2 July 1974.
90 Tsur, "The Return and Death of Juan Perón" (in Hebrew), *Maariv*, 5 July 1974.

91 *Davar*, "A Peronism without Perón" (in Hebrew), 3 July 1974.
92 *Haaretz*, 5 July 1974.
93 *Haaretz*, 1 July 1974.
94 Alón to M. Hatzor, 12 July 1974, Lavon Archive, div. 219-4 IV, file 10A.
95 Sáenz Quesada, *Isabel Perón*.
96 "A Former Cabaret Dancer – President of Argentina" (in Hebrew), *Yedioth Ahronoth*, 1 July 1974.
97 "Isabelita Perón Tries to Imitate Evita's Style" (in Hebrew), *Maariv*, 1 July 1974.
98 Ibid.
99 Ibid.
100 *Hatzofeh*, 19 July 1974, 21 July 1974.
101 On the high proportion of Jewish victims during the dictatorship, see: Centro de Investigaciones Sociales de la DAIA, *Informe*; Goldman and Dobry, *Ser judío*.

EPILOGUE

1 On the history and memory of the AMIA bombing, see: Levine and Zaretsky, eds, *Landscapes of Memory*.
2 Daniel Politi, "Héctor Timerman, 65, Argentine Ex-Foreign Minister Indicted in Iran Deal, Dies," *New York Times*, 31 December 2018.
3 On the controversy over Nisman, see: Sheinin, "Centesimal Nisman"; Budassi and Fidanza, "Nisman's Puzzle."
4 Sheinin, "Centesimal Nisman," 188. See also: Mochkofsky, "Alberto Nisman."
5 "'Argentino, peronista y judío': la despedida de Cristina Kirchner a Héctor Timerman," *Clarín*, 30 December 2018.
6 Ibid.
7 http://llamamiento.net/quienes-somos/.
8 Kollmann, "Vereda de enfrente."
9 On Timerman, see Mochkofsky's biography, *Timerman: el periodista que quiso ser parte del poder*; Rein and Davidi, "'Exile of the World.'"
10 Elena, "Argentina in Black and White," 186–7.
11 Rein and Noyjovich, *Muchachos peronistas árabes*; Rein and Udagawa, "Muchachos peronistas japoneses."
12 Finchelstein, *Fascism*, xii; Semán, "Comparing Trump"; Moses, Finchelstein, and Piccato, "Juan Perón"; Schwartz, "Donald Trump."
13 There is a vast bibliography on populism in Latin America. For two useful collection of essays, see: Arnson and de la Torre, eds, *Latin American Populism*; and Conniff, ed., *Populism in Latin America*.

Bibliography

ARCHIVES

American Jewish Committee Files, YIVO Institute for Jewish Research, New York
Archive of the Gelbard Family, Los Angeles
Archive of the Manguel Family, Buenos Aires
Archivo César Tiempo, Biblioteca Nacional, Buenos Aires
Archivo de la Fundación Francisco Franco, Madrid
Archivo de la Presidencia del Gobierno, Madrid
Archivo del Ministerio de Asuntos Exteriores, Madrid
Archivo del Ministerio de Relaciones Exteriores y Culto, Buenos Aires
Archivo General de la Nación, Buenos Aires
Archivo Máximo Yagupsky, IWO, Buenos Aires
Beit Hatefutsot Photo Archive, Tel Aviv
Central Zionist Arhives, Jerusalem
Israel State Archives, Jerusalem
Government Press Office, Jerusalem
Juan Atilio Bramuglia Papers, Hoover Institution Archives, Stanford University
National Archives, Washington, DC, and College Park, Maryland
Oral History Project, Institute of Contemporary Jewry, Hebrew University of Jerusalem
Pinchas Lavon Archive of the Labour Party, Tel Aviv
Proyecto de Historia Oral, Instituto Di Tella, Buenos Aires

Aarons, Mark, and John Loftus. *Unholy Trinity*. New York: St. Martin's, 1991.

Abalo, Carlos. *El derrumbe del peronismo y la política económica del gobierno militar*. Buenos Aires: IDES, 1976.

Abramovich, Ariel. "Perón y los judíos." *Nueva Sión*, 13 August 2014.

Acha, Omar. *Los muchachos peronistas: Orígenes olvidados de la Juventud Peronista (1945–1955)*. Buenos Aires: Planeta, 2011.

Acosta, Diego. "La radio: de los pañales a los pantalones largos." *Todo es Historia* 258 (1988): 58–69.

Adamovsky, Ezequiel. "La bendita medianía: Los católicos argentinos y sus apelaciones a la 'clase media,' c. 1930–1955." *Anuario IEHS* 22 (2007): 301–24.

Allison, Victoria. "White Evil: Peronist Argentina in the US Popular Imagination Since 1955." *American Studies International* 42, no. 1 (February 2004): 4–48.

Amadeo, Mario. *Ayer, hoy, mañana*. Buenos Aires: Ediciones Gure, 1956.

Aráoz, Ernesto M. *La inmigración en la Argentina y sus vinculaciones con la cuestión social*. Salta, Argentina: Imprenta de las Llanas, 1919.

Arce, José. *Mi vida*. Vol. 2. Madrid: Editoriales Reunidas, 1958.

Arnson, Cynthia J., and Carlos de la Torre, eds. *Latin American Populism in the Twenty-First Century*. Baltimore: Johns Hopkins University Press, 2013.

Arribá, Sergio. "El Peronismo y la política de radiodifusión." Paper presented at the VI Encuentro Panamericano de Comunicación, Universidad Nacional de Córdoba, 2013.

Astor, Gerald. *The "Last" Nazi: The Life and Times of Dr. Joseph Mengele*. New York: Donald I. Fine, 1985.

Atkins, G.P., and L.V. Thompson. "German Military Influence in Argentina, 1921–1940." *Journal of Latin American Studies* 4, no. 2 (1972): 257–84.

Avni, Haim. "Antisemitismo en Argentina: las dimensiones del peligro." In *El legado del autoritarismo*, edited by Leonardo Senkman and Mario Sznajder, 197–216. Buenos Aires: GEL, 1995.

– *Argentina and the Jews: A History of Jewish Immigration*. Tuscaloosa, AL. University of Alabama Press, 1991.

– *Argentina, "The Promised Land": Baron de Hirsch's Colonization Project in the Argentine Republic* (in Hebrew). Jerusalem: Magnes, 1973.

– *Argentina y las migraciones judías: de la Inquisición al Holocausto y después*. Buenos Aires: Milá, 2005.

– *"Clients," Prostitutes and White Slavers in Argentina and Israel* (in Hebrew). Tel Aviv: Yedioth Ahronoth, 2009.

– *Emancipation and Jewish Education: A Century of Argentinian Jewry's Experiences, 1884–1984* (in Hebrew). Jerusalem: Shazar, 1985.

– *Jewish University Students in Argentina and the Organized Public* (in Hebrew). Jerusalem: Office of the President of Israel, 1971.

Baily, Samuel. *Immigrants in the Land of Promise: Italians in Buenos Aires and New York City, 1870–1914*. Ithaca, NY: Cornell University Press, 1999.

Baltiérrez, Rodolfo. "La creación del Estado de Israel." *Todo es Historia* 252 (June 1988): 36–9.

Bardini, Roberto. *Tacuara*. Mexico City: Oceáno, 2002.

Bascomb, Neal. *Hunting Eichmann*. New York: Houghton Mifflin Harcourt, 2009.

Basualdo, Eduardo. *Estudios de historia económica argentina. Desde mediados del siglo XX a la actualidad*. Buenos Aires: FLACSO/Siglo XXI, 2006.

Bejar, M.D. "La entrevista Dickmann-Perón." *Todo es Historia* 143 (1979): 83–93.

Bell, Lawrence. "The Jews and Perón: Communal Politics and National Identities in Peronist Argentina, 1946–1955." PhD diss., Ohio State University, 2002.

Ben-Dror, Graciela. *The Catholic Church and the Jews: Argentina 1933–1945*. Lincoln, NE, and Jerusalem: Nebraska University Press with the Vidal Sassoon International Center for the Study of Antisemitism, Hebrew University of Jerusalem, 2008.

– "La Argentina Católica y los judíos, 1943–1945." *Proceedings of the Eleventh World Congress of Jewish Studies* 3 (1994): 345–52.

– *Católicos, nazis y judíos: la Iglesia argentina en los tiempos del Tercer Reich*. Buenos Aires: Lumiere, 2003.

Bernetti, Jorge Luis, and Adriana Puiggrós. *Peronismo: cultura política y educación (1945–1955)*. Buenos Aires: Galerna, 1993.

Beter, Clara. *Versos de una....* Rosario: Ameghino, 1998.

Bianchi, Susana. "Iglesia Católica y peronismo: la cuestión de la enseñanza religiosa (1946–1955)." *Estudios Interdisciplinarios de América Latina* 3, no. 2 (1992): 89–103.

Bilsky, Edgardo. *La semana trágica*. Buenos Aires: Centro Editor de América Latina, 1984.

Bitrán, Rafael. *El congreso de la productividad. La reconversión económica durante el segundo gobierno peronista*. Buenos Aires: El Bloque, 1994.

Blanksten, George I. *Perón's Argentina*. New York: Russell & Russell, 1967.

Blaustein, Eduardo, and Martín Zubieta. *Decíamos ayer: la prensa argentina bajo el Proceso*. Buenos Aires: Colihue, 1998.

Boizard, Ricardo. *Esa noche de Perón*. Buenos Aires: Siruela, 1955.

Bosoer, Fabián. *Braden o Perón: La historia oculta*. Buenos Aires: El Ateneo, 2011.

Botta, Paulo. "La diplomacia argentina y la partición de Palestina desde el punto de vista de sus protagonistas." ANMO 1, no. 1 (2011): 5–27.

Bower, Tom. *Klaus Barbie – The Butcher of Lyons*. New York: Pantheon Books, 1984.

– *The Paperclip Conspiracy: The Hunt for Nazi Scientists*. Boston: Little, Brown, 1987.

Braden, Spruille. *Diplomats and Demagogues*. New Rochelle, NY: Arlington House, 1971.

– "The Germans in Argentina." *Atlantic Monthly*, 17 (April 1946): 43.

Brauner, Susana. *Ortodoxia religiosa y pragmatismo político: los judíos de origen sirio*. Buenos Aires: Lumiere, 2009.

Brennan, James P. "Industriales y bolicheros: la actividad económica y la alianza populista peronista, 1943–1976." *Boletín del Instituto Dr. Emilio Ravignani*, 15 (1997): 101–41.

Brennan, James P., and Marcelo Rougier. "José B. Gelbard. Líder empresarial y emblema de la 'burguesía nacional.'" In *La segunda línea. Liderazgo peronista, 1945–1955*, edited by Raanan Rein and Claudio Panella, 195–213. Buenos Aires: EDUNTREF/Pueblo Heredero, 2014.

– *The Politics of National Capitalism: Peronism and the Argentine Bourgeoisie, 1946–1976*. University Park, PA: Pennsylvania State University Press, 2012.

Brodsky, Adriana, and Raanan Rein, *The New Jewish Argentina: Facets of Jewish Experiences in the Southern Cone*. Boston: Brill, 2013.

Broner, Julio, and Daniel Larriqueta. *La revolución industrial argentina*. Buenos Aires: Sudamericana, 1969.

Bruce, James. *Those Perplexing Argentines*. New York: Longmans, Green, 1953.

Buchrucker, Christian. *Nacionalismo y peronismo: la Argentina en la crisis ideológica mundial (1927–1955)*. Buenos Aires: Sudamericana, 1987.

Budassi, Sonia, and Andrés Fidanza. "Nisman's Puzzle." *Anfibia*. http://revistaanfibia.com/cronica/nismans-puzzle/ (accessed 1 March 2009).

Buonocore, Domingo. *Libreros, editores e impresores de Buenos Aires*. Buenos Aires: Bowker, 1974.

Burzaco, Ricardo. "Los científicos alemanes y Perón." *Todo es Historia* 29, no. 334 (May 1995): 8–25.

Caimari, Lila. *Perón y la iglesia católica*. Buenos Aires: Ariel, 1994.

– "Peronist Christianity and Non-Catholic Religions: Politics and Ecumenism (1943–1955)." *Canadian Journal of Latin American and Caribbean Studies* 20, nos 39–40 (1995): 105–24.

Caspi, D., and I. Limor. *The Mediators: The Mass Media in Israel, 1948–1990* (in Hebrew). Jerusalem: Am Oved, 1992.

Cattaruzza, Alejandro. "Una empresa cultural del primer peronismo: la Revista 'Hechos e Ideas' (1947–1955)." *Revista Complutense de Historia de América* 19 (1993): 269–89.

Chávez, Fermín. *Eva Perón sin mitos*. Buenos Aires: Fraterna, 1990.

Cohen de Chervonagura, Elisa B. *La comunidad judía de Tucumán*. Tucumán, Argentina: Sociedad Unión Israelita Tucumana, 2010.

Confalonieri, Orestes D. *Perón contra Perón*. Buenos Aires: Antigua, 1956.

Conniff, Michael L., ed. *Populism in Latin America*. Second Edition. Tuscaloosa, AB: University of Alabama Press, 2012.

Conradis, Heinz. *Design for Flight: The Kurt Tank Story*. London: Macdonald, 1960.

Constitución de la Nación Argentina de 1949. Buenos Aires: Ediciones Realidad Política, 1983.

Corbière, Emilio J. *Estaban entre nosotros*. Buenos Aires: Letra Buena, 1992.

DAIA (Delegatión de Asociaciones Israelitas Argentinas). "Medio siglo de lucha por una Argentina sin discriminaciones." *Todo es Historia* (supplement), 1985.

– *El pensamiento del presidente Perón sobre el pueblo judío*. Buenos Aires: DAIA, 1954.

– *Perón y el pueblo judío*. Buenos Aires: DAIA, 1974.

– *Proyecto Testimonio*. Buenos Aires: Planeta, 1998.

– *Versión argentina de la mayor superchería del siglo*. Buenos Aires: DAIA, 1972.

DAIA, Centro de Investigaciones Sociales. *Informe sobre la situación de los detenidos-desaparecidos judíos durante el genocidio perpetrado en Argentina*. Buenos Aires: DAIA, 1999.

David, Guillermo. *Perón en la chacra asfaltada: figuras del peronismo bahiense*. Punta Alta, Argentina: Ediciones de la Barricada, 2006.

Davis, Moshe, ed. *The Identification of the Nation with the State in the Wake of the Yom Kippur War* (in Hebrew). Jerusalem: Institute of Contemporary Jewry, 1975.

– *The Yom Kippur War: Israel and the Jewish People*. New York: Arno Press, 1974.

De Nápoli, Carlos. *Los científicos nazis en la Argentina*. Buenos Aires: EDHASA, 2008.

De Riz, Liliana. *Retorno y derrumbe: el último gobierno peronista*. Mexico City: Fs. Ediciones, 1981.

Del Campo, Hugo. *Sindicalismo y peronismo: los comienzos de un vínculo perdurable*. Buenos Aires: CLACSO, 1983.

Del Carril, Bonifacio. *Crónica interna de la Revolución Libertadora*. Buenos Aires: Emecé, 1959.

Delgado, Verónica, and Fabio Espósito. "La emergencia del editor moderno." In *Editores y políticas editoriales en Argentina, 1880–2000*, edited by José Luis de Diego, 59–88. Buenos Aires: Fondo de Cultura Económica, 2006.

Della Pergola, Sergio. "Jewish Autonomy and Dependency: Latin America in Global Perspective." In *Identities in an Era of Globalization and Multiculturalism: Latin America in the Jewish World*, edited by Judit Bokser Liweran, Eliezer Ben-Rafael, Yossi Gorny, and Raanan Rein, 47–80. Leiden: Brill, 2008.

Devoto, Fernando. "Inmigrantes, refugiados y criminales en la 'vía italiana' hacia la Argentina en la segunda posguerra." *Ciclos*, 19 (2000): 151–75.

Di Tella, Torcuato. *Perón y los sindicatos*. Buenos Aires: Ariel, 2003.

Diario Olé. *Diccionario enciclopédico del fútbol*. Buenos Aires: Diario Olé, 1997.

Díaz Araujo, Enrique. *La conspiración del 43*. Buenos Aires: La Bastilla, 1971.

Dimenstein, Marcelo. "En busca de un pogrom perdido: memoria en torno de la semana trágica de 1919." In *Marginados y consagrados*, edited by Emmanuel Kahan et al., 121–41. Buenos Aires: Lumiere, 2011.

Diskin, David. *El compañero Borlenghi: su trayectoria, su integridad, su temple*. Buenos Aires: no publisher, 1979.

Dizgun, John. "Immigrants of a Different Religion: Jewish Argentines and the Boundaries of Argentinidad, 1919–2009." PhD diss., Rutgers University, 2010.

Dobry, Hernán. *Los rabinos de Malvinas*. Buenos Aires: Vergara, 2012.

Doron, Eliezer. *In Observing and Confronting: From the Diary of an Israeli Ambassador* (in Hebrew). Jerusalem: Mabat, 1978.

Elath, Eliahu. *The Struggle for Statehood* (in Hebrew). Tel Aviv: Am Oved, 1982.

Elena, Eduardo. "Argentina in Black and White: Race, Peronism, and the Color of Politics, 1940 to the Present." In *Rethinking Race in Modern Argentina*, edited by Paulina L. Alberto and Eduardo Elena, 184–210. Cambridge: Cambridge University Press, 2016.

Eliachar, Elie. *Living with Jews* (in Hebrew). Jerusalem: Marcus, 1980.

Erdei, Ezequiel. "Demografía e identidad: A propósito del estudio de la población judía en Buenos Aires." In *Pertenencia y alteridad. Judíos en/de América Latina: cuarenta años de cambios*, edited by Haim Avni et al., 341–63. Madrid: Iberoamericana, 2011.

Escudé, Carlos. *Gran Bretaña, Estados Unidos y la declinación argentina, 1942–1949*. Buenos Aires: Belgrano, 1983.

– *La Argentina vs. las grandes potencias. El precio del desafío*. Buenos Aires: Belgrano, 1986.

Falcoff, Mark. "Argentine Nationalism on the Eve of Perón: Force of Radical Orientation of Young Argentina and Its Rivals." Phd diss., Princeton University, 1970.

Feierstein, Ricardo. "César Tiempo, un hombre de dos mundos." In *Crecer en el gueto, crecer en el mundo*, edited by Ricardo Feierstein and Stephen A. Sadow, 304–17. Buenos Aires: Milá, 2005.

– *Historia de los judíos argentinos*. Buenos Aires: Planeta, 1993.

Feierstein, Ricardo, ed. *Los mejores relatos con gauchos judíos*. Buenos Aires: Ameghino Editora, 1998.

Feierstein, Ricardo, and Stephen A. Sadow, eds. *Recreando la cultura judeoargentina*. Buenos Aires: Milá, 2004.

Feinmann, José Pablo. *López Rega, la cara oscura de Perón*. Buenos Aires: Legasa, 1987.

Figallo, Beatriz J. "Bolivia y la Argentina: los conflictos regionales durante la Segunda Guerra Mundial." *Estudios Interdisciplinarios de América Latina* 7, no. 1 (1996): 107–25.

– "La Argentina y España durante la Segunda Guerra Mundial." *Res Gesta* (January–June 1988): 69–83.

Finchelstein, Federico. *La Argentina fascista: Los orígenes de la dictadura*. Buenos Aires: Sudamericana, 2008.

– *From Fascism to Populism in History*. Oakland: University of California Press, 2017.

– *The Ideological Origins of the Dirty War: Fascism, Populism, and Dictatorship in Twentieth Century Argentina*. New York: Oxford University Press, 2014.

Fingueret, Manuela. "César Tiempo: El poeta de los tres nombres." Unpublished manuscript.

Fiorucci, Flavia. "¿Aliados o enemigos? Los intelectuales en los gobiernos de Vargas y Perón." In *El primer peronismo: de regreso a los comienzos*, edited by Raanan Rein and Rosalie Sitman, 83–108. Buenos Aires: Lumiere, 2005.

– "Los marginados de la Revolución: los intelectuales peronistas (1945–1955)." *La Memoria de Nuestro Pueblo*, Year 5 (February 2009): 17–21.

– "Neither Warriors Nor Prophets: Peronist and Anti-Peronist Intellectuals, 1945–1956." PhD diss., Institute of Latin American Studies, University of London, 2002.

Frank, Gary. *Juan Perón vs. Spruille Braden: The Story Behind the Blue Book*. Lanham, MD: University Press of America, 1980.

Freidenberg, Judith Noemí. *The Invention of the Jewish Gaucho*. Austin, TX: University of Texas Press, 2009.

Freiwald, Aaron, and Martin Mendelsohn. *The Last Nazi: Josef Schwammberger and the Nazi Past*. New York: W.W. Norton, 1994.

Furman, Rubén. *Puños y pistolas*. Buenos Aires: Sudamericana, 2014.

Galasso, Norberto, ed., *"Los Malditos": hombres y mujeres excluidos de la historia oficial de los argentinos*. Buenos Aires: Ediciones Madres de Plaza de Mayo, 2005.

– *Vida de Scalabrini Ortiz*. Buenos Aires: Ediciones del Mar Dulce, 1970.

García, Martín. "El peronismo y su relación con los medios de comunicación." *Revista Peronistas*, no. 5 (2004): 145–65.

García Granados, Jorge. *The Birth of Israel – The Drama as I Saw It*. New York: A.A. Knopf, 1948.

Gay, Luis. *El Partido Laborista en la Argentina*. Buenos Aires: Biblos, 1999.

Gerchunoff, Alberto. *Los gauchos judíos*. La Plata, Argentina: Talleres Gráficos Joaquín Sesé, 1910.

Gilbert, Isidoro. *El oro de Moscú*. Buenos Aires: Planeta, 1999.

Girbal-Blacha, Noemí María. "La industria invisible. Entre las finanzas y la política. Empresas de cultura popular en la Argentina peronista (1946–1955)." *H-industri@* 6, no. 11 (2012). http://bibliotecadigital.econ.uba.ar/download/hindustria/hindustria_v6_n11_05.pdf

Gitter, Benno. *The Story of My Life*. London: Weinfeld & Nicolson, 1999.

Glick, Edward B. *Latin America and the Palestine Problem*. New York: Theodor Herzl Foundation, 1958.

Glickman, Nora. *The Jewish White Slave Trade and the Untold Story of Raquel Liberman*. Nueva York: Taylor & Francis, 2000.

Godio, Julio. *La caída de Perón*. Buenos Aires: CEAL, 1985.

– *La semana trágica de enero de 1919*. Buenos Aires: Granica, 1985.

Goldar, Ernesto. *El peronismo en la literatura argentina*. Buenos Aires: Freeland, 1971.

Goldman, Daniel, and Hernán Dobry. *Ser judío en los años setenta: testimonios del horror y la resistencia durante la última dictadura*. Buenos Aires: Siglo XXI, 2014.

Goldstein, Yosef (Jorge). "The Influence of the State of Israel and the Jewish Agency on Jewish Life in Argentina and Uruguay, 1948–1953" (in Hebrew). PhD diss., Hebrew University of Jerusalem, 1993.

Gómez Reynoso, Celia. *El hada buena*. Buenos Aires: Luis Lesserre, 1953.
González Janzen, Ignacio. *La Triple A*. Buenos Aires: Contrapunto, 1986.
Gorelik, Adrián. *La grilla y el parque: espacio público y cultura urbana en Buenos Aires, 1887–1936*. Buenos Aires: Universidad Nacional de Quilmes, 2010.
Goyeneche, Juan Carlos. *Ensayos, artículos, discursos*. Buenos Aires: Dictio, 1976.
Gutkowski, Helene. *Rescate de la herencia cultural. Vidas … en las colonias*. Buenos Aires: Editorial Contexto, 1991.
Gutman, Daniel. *Tacuara – Historia de la primera guerrilla urbana argentina*. Buenos Aires, 2003.
Gvirtz, Silvina. "La politización de los contenidos escolares y la respuesta de los docentes primarios, 1949–1955." In *El primer peronismo: de regreso a los comienzos*, edited by Raanan Rein and Rosalie Sitman, 37–49. Buenos Aires: Lumiere, 2005.
Hamilton, Charles. *The Hitler Diaries*. Lexington, KY: University Press of Kentucky, 1991.
Healey, Mark. *El peronismo entre las ruinas: el terremoto y la reconstrucción de San Juan*. Buenos Aires: Siglo XXI Argentina, 2012.
Herrera, Carlos Miguel. "Socialismo y 'revolución nacional' en el primer peronismo." *Estudios Interdisciplinarios de América Latina* 20, no. 2 (2009): 89–114.
Horovitz, Irving Louis. "The Jewish Community of Buenos Aires." *Jewish Social Studies* 24, no. 4 (October 1962): 195–222.
Horowicz, Alejandro. *Los cuatro peronismos. Historia de una metamorfosis trágica*. Buenos Aires: La Biblioteca de Tiempo, 2010.
Hourani, Albert, and Nadim Shedhadi, eds. *The Lebanese in the World: A Century of Emigration*. London: I.B. Tauris, 1992.
Houston, John A. *Latin America in the United Nations*. New York: Carnegie Endowment for International Peace, 1956.
Huberman, Silvio. *Los pasajeros del Weser: la conmovedora travesía de los primeros migrantes judíos a la Argentina*. Buenos Aires: Sudamericana, 2014.
Hull, Cordell. *The Memoirs*. Vol. 2. New York: Macmillan, 1948.
Humphreys, R.A. *Latin America and the Second World War*. Vol. 1. London: Athlone Press, 1981.
Hunt, Linda. *Secret Agenda: The United States Government, Nazi Scientists, and Project Paperclip, 1945 to 1990*. New York: St Martin's, 1991.
Israel. Central Bureau of Statistics. *Statistical Abstract of Israel 1949–1950*.
– *Statistical Abstract of Israel 1951–1952*.
– *Statistical Abstract of Israel 1953–1954*.
– *Statistical Abstract of Israel 1955–1956*.
Israel. Israel State Archives. *Documents on the Foreign Policy of Israel*. Vol. 8. Jerusalem, 1953.
Jackisch, Carlota. *El nazismo y los refugiados alemanes en la Argentina, 1933–1945*. Buenos Aires: Editorial de Belgrano, 1997.

Jauretche, Arturo. *FORJA y la década infame*. Buenos Aires: Peña Lillo, 1974.
Jmelnizky, Adrián, and Ezequiel Erdei. *La población judía de Buenos Aires: estudio sociodemográfico*. Buenos Aires: AMIA, Centro de Documentación e Información sobre Judaismo Argentino Marc Turkow, 2005.
Josephs, Ray. *Argentine Diary: The Inside Story of the Coming of Fascism*. London: Victor Gollancz, 1945.
Kabchi, Raymundo, ed. *El mundo árabe y América Latina*. Madrid: UNESCO, Prodhufi, 1997.
Karush, Matthew. *Cultura de clase: Radio y cine en la creación de una Argentina dividida, 1920–1946*. Buenos Aires: Ariel Historia, 2013.
Kaufman, Edy. "Jewish Victims of Repression in Argentina under Military Rule (1976–1983)." *Holocaust and Genocide Studies* 4 (1989): 479–99.
Kelly, David. *The Ruling Few*. London: Hollis & Carter, 1952.
King, John. *"Sur": Estudios de la revista argentina y de su papel en el desarrollo de una cultura, 1931–1970*. México City: Fondo de Cultura Económica, 1989.
Klich, Ignacio. "Árabes, judíos y árabes judíos en la Argentina de la primera mitad del novecientos." *Estudios Interdisciplinarios de América Latina* 6, no. 2 (1995): 109–43.
– "A Background to Perón's Discovery of Jewish National Aspirations." *Judaica Latinoamericana* 1 (1988): 192–223.
– "Criollos and Arabic Speakers in Argentina: An Uneasy Pas de Deux, 1888–1914." In Hourani and Shehadi, eds, *The Lebanese in the World*, 177–205.
– "Equidistance and Gradualism in Argentine Foreign Policy towards Israel and the Arab World, 1949–1955." In *The Jewish Diaspora in Latin America*, edited by David Sheinin and Lois Baer Barr, 219–37. New York: Taylor & Francis, 1996.
– "Failure in Argentina: The Jewish Agency's Search for Congressional Backing for Zionist Aims in Palestine." *Judaica Latinoamericana* 2 (1993): 245–64.
– "El ingreso a la Argentina de nazis y colaboracionistas." In *Discriminación y racismo en América Latina*, edited by Ignacio Klich and Mario Rapoport, 401–28. Buenos Aires: Grupo Editor Latinoamericano, 1997.
– "La pericia científica alemana en el amanecer del proyecto nuclear argentino y el papel de los inmigrantes judío." *Boletín del Instituto de Historia Argentina y Americana Dr. Emilio Ravignani* 10 (1994): 61–89.
– "The First Argentine-Israeli Trade Accord: Political and Economic Considerations." *Canadian Journal of Latin American and Caribbean Studies* 20, nos 39–40 (1995): 177–205.
– "The Nazis in Argentina: Deconstructing Some Myths." *Patterns of Prejudice* 29, no. 4 (1995): 53–66.
Klich, Ignacio, and Cristian Buchrucker. *Argentina y la Europa del nazismo. Sus secuelas*. Buenos Aires: Siglo XXI, 2009.
– "El fin del Tercer Reich y la 'conexión argentina' en la bibliografía revisionista." In Klich and Buchrucker, *Argentina y la Europa del nazismo. Sus secuelas*.

Klich, Ignacio, and Efraim Davidi. "'Exile of the World': Israeli Perceptions of Jacobo Timerman." *Jewish Social Studies* 16, no. 3 (2010): 1–31.

Kollmann, Raúl. "En la vereda de enfrente de la DAIA y la AMIA." *Página/12*, 10 January 2019.

Koremblit, Bernardo Ezequiel. "La bohemia cultural judeoargentina de las décadas del '30, '40 y '50." In Feierstein and Sadow, eds, *Recreando la cultura judeoargentina*, vol. 2, 51–6.

Korin, Moshé. "Intelectual, escritor y ensayista de las letras judeoargentinas. Homenaje a Bernardo Ezequiel Koremblit." *La voz y la opinión*. https://www.delacole.com/cgi-perl/medios/vernota.cgi?medio=lavoz&numero=agosto2005&nota=agosto2005-8

Lafiandra, Félix, ed. *Los panfletos – su aporte a la Revolución Libertadora*. Buenos Aires: Itinerarium, 1955.

Laikin Elkin, Judith. *The Jews of Latin America*. Ann Arbor, MI: Scholarly Publishing Office, University of Michigan Library, 2011.

Lanús, Juan Archibaldo. *De Chapultepec al Beagle: Política exterior argentina, 1945–1980*. Buenos Aires: Emecé, 1984.

Lanusse, Alejandro A. *Mi testimonio*. Buenos Aires: Lasserre, 1977.

– *Protagonista y testigo*. Buenos Aires: Marcelo Lugones, 1988.

Larraquy, Marcelo. *López Rega*. Buenos Aires: Sudamericana, 2004.

Leonard, Virginia. *Politicians, Pupils and Priests: Argentine Education since 1943*. New York: P. Lang, 1989.

Lerdo de Tejeda, Ana. *Un año más*. Buenos Aires: Luis Lesserre, 1953.

Lerner, Natán. "Latin America: Its Origins." In Davis, ed., *Identification*, 110–24.

– "Overview." In Davis, ed., *Yom Kippur War*, 125–37.

Levine, Annette H., and Natasha Zaretsky, eds. *Landscapes of Memory and Impunity: The Aftermath of the AMIA Bombing in Jewish Argentina*. Boston: Brill, 2015.

Levy, Larry. *La mancha de la Migdal*. Buenos Aires: Norma, 2007.

Lewin, Boleslao. *Cómo fue la inmigración judía en la Argentina*. Buenos Aires: Plus Ultra, 1983.

Leyba, Carlos. *Economía y política en el tercer gobierno de Perón*. Buenos Aires: Biblos, 2003.

Lida, Miranda. "Catolicismo y peronismo: debates, problemas, preguntas." *Boletín del Instituto de Historia Argentina y Americana Dr. Emilio Ravignani* 27 (2005): 139–48.

Lindstrom, Naomi. *Jewish Issues in Argentine Literature*. Columbia, MO: University of Missouri Press, 1989.

Lipsky, Louis. *Memoirs in Profile*. Philadelphia: Jewish Publication Society of America, 1975.

Lorch, Netanel. *Seven Chapters in Relations between Israel and Iberian America* (in Hebrew). Jerusalem: Institute of Cultural Relations Israel-Ibero-America, 1977.

Luca de Tena, Torcuato, Luis Calvo, and Esteban Peicovich. *Yo, Juan Domingo Perón*. Barcelona: Planeta, 1976.
Lvovich, Daniel. *Nacionalismo y antisemitismo en la Argentina*. Buenos Aires: Vergara, 2003.
MacDonald, C.A. "The Politics of Intervention: The U.S. and Argentina, 1941–1946." *Journal of Latin American Studies* 12, no. 2 (1980): 365–96.
Manguel, Romina. "El abuelo Pablo." *Veintitrés Internacional*, May 2008.
Marder, Jeffrey. "The Organización Israelita Argentina: Between Perón and the Jews." *Canadian Journal of Latin American and Caribbean Studies* 20, nos 39–40 (1995): 125–52.
Mariscotti, Mario. *El secreto atómico de Huemul*. Buenos Aires: Sudamericana/Planeta, 1985.
Matallana, Andrea. *Imágenes y representación*. Buenos Aires: Aurelia, 2010.
– "Inventando la Radio Comercial: Apuntes para una biografía de Jaime Yankelevich." *Revista de Instituciones, Ideas y Mercados* 58 (May 2013): 147–66.
– *Jaime Yankelevich: la oportunidad y la audacia*. Buenos Aires: Capital Intelectual, 2013.
– *Locos por la radio. Una historia social de la radiofonía en la Argentina, 1923–1947*. Buenos Aires: Prometeo, 2006.
McGann, Thomas F. *Argentina, the U.S., and the Inter-American System, 1880–1914*. Cambridge, MA: Harvard University Press, 1957.
McGee Deutsch, Sandra. *Las Derechas: The Extreme Right in Argentina, Brazil, and Chile, 1890–1939*. Stanford: Stanford University Press, 1999.
– *Crossing Borders, Claiming a Nation: A History of Argentine Jewish Women, 1880–1955*. Durham, NC: Duke University Press, 2010.
Meding, Holger M. "Refugio seguro. La emigración alemana de la posguerra al Río de la Plata." In *El genocidio ante la historia y la naturaleza humana*, edited by Beatriz Gurevich and Carlos Escudé, 249–61. Buenos Aires: GEL, 1994.
– *La ruta de los nazis en tiempos de Perón*. Buenos Aires: Emecé, 1999.
Méndez, Jesús. "Argentine Intellectuals in the Twentieth Century, 1930–1943." PhD diss., University of Texas at Austin, 1980.
Mercado, Silvia. *El inventor del peronismo: Raúl Apold, el cerebro oculto que cambió la política argentina*. Buenos Aires: Planeta, 2013.
Meyer, Naomi F. "Argentina." *American Jewish Yearbook*, vols 74 (1973) and 75 (1974–75).
Ministerio de Finanzas de la Nación. Banco Central de la República Argentina. *Memoria anual 1950*. Buenos Aires, 1951.
– *Memoria anual 1951*. Buenos Aires, 1952.
– *Memoria anual 1953*. Buenos Aires, 1954.
– *Memoria anual 1954*. Buenos Aires, 1955.
– *Memoria anual 1955*. Buenos Aires, 1956.
Mirelman, Victor A. *Jewish Buenos Aires, 1890–1939*. Detroit: Wayne State University Press, 1990.

Mochkofsky, Graciela. *Pecado original: Clarín, los Kirchner y la lucha por el poder*. Buenos Aires: Planeta, 2011.
– *Timerman. El periodista que quiso ser parte del poder (1923–1999)*. Buenos Aires: Sudamericana, 2003.
– "Why Alberto Nisman Is No Hero for Argentina – or the Jews." *Forward*, 10 March 2015. https://forward.com/news/216076/why-alberto-nisman-is-no-hero-for-argentina-or-t/
Montes de Oca, Ignacio. *Ustashas: el ejército nazi de Perón y el Vaticano*. Buenos Aires: Sudamericana, 2013.
Moses, A. Dirk, Federico Finchelstein, and Pablo Piccato. "Juan Perón shows how Trump could destroy our democracy without tearing it down." *Washington Post*, 22 March 2017. https://www.washingtonpost.com/posteverything/wp/2017/03/22/juan-peron-shows-how-trump-could-destroy-our-democracy-without-tearing-it-down/
Moya, José C. *Cousins and Strangers*. Berkeley: University of California Press, 1998.
– "The Jewish Experience in Argentina in a Diasporic Comparative Perspective." In Brodsky and Rein, eds, *The New Jewish Argentina*, 7–29.
Newton, Ronald C. *German Buenos Aires, 1900–1930: Social Change and Cultural Crisis*. Austin, TX: University of Texas Press, 1977.
– *The "Nazi Menace" in Argentina, 1931–1947*. Stanford: Stanford University Press, 1992.
Nouwen, Mollie Lewis. *"Oy, My Buenos Aires": Jewish Immigrants and the Creation of Argentine National Identity, 1905–1930*. Albuquerque: University of New Mexico Press, 2013.
O'Donnell, Guillermo. "*Estado y Alianzas* en la Argentina, 1956–1976." *Desarrollo Económico* 16, no. 64 (1977): 523–54.
Olivieri, Aníbal O. *Dos veces rebelde*. Buenos Aires: Sigla, 1958.
Orozco Gómez, Guillermo. *Historias de la televisión en América Latina*. Barcelona: Gedisa, 2012.
Page, Joseph A. *Perón – A Biography*. New York: Random House, 1983.
Panella, Claudio. *"La Prensa" y el peronismo: Crítica, conflicto, expropiación*. La Plata: Universidad Nacional de La Plata, 1999.
Pavón Pereyra, Enrique. *Coloquios con Perón*. Madrid: Editores Internacionales, 1973.
Paz, Hipólito. *Memorias*. Buenos Aires: Planeta, 1999.
Peralta, Santiago. *La acción del pueblo judío en la Argentina*. Buenos Aires: n.p., 1943.
Perelman, Ángel. *Cómo hicimos el 17 de octubre*. Buenos Aires: Coyoacán, 1962.
Perón, Eva. *Historia del peronismo*. Buenos Aires: Volver, 1987.
Perón, Juan D. *Del poder al exilio*. Buenos Aires: Ediciones Argentina, 1982.
Persello, Ana Virginia. "De la diversidad a la unidad: 'Hechos e Ideas': 1935–1955." In *Cuando opinar es actuar. Revistas argentinas del siglo XX*, edited by

Noemi Girbal-Blacha and Diana Quatrocchi-Woisson, 273–302. Buenos Aires: Academia Nacional de la Historia, 1999.

Plotkin, Mariano. *Mañana es San Perón*. Buenos Aires: Ariel, 1993.

Posner, Gerald L., and John Ware. *Mengele – The Complete Story*. New York: Cooper Square Press, 1986.

Potash, Robert A. *Perón y el GOU*. Buenos Aires: Sudamericana, 1984.

– *The Army and Politics in Argentina, 1945–1962*. Stanford: Stanford University Press, 1980.

Quadraccia, Haydée Marta. *Koremblit: pensamiento y lenguaje de un humanista*. Buenos Aires: Dunken, 2005.

Quijada, Mónica, and Víctor Peralta Ruiz. "El triángulo Madrid-Berlín-Buenos Aires y el tránsito de bienes vinculados al Tercer Reich desde España a la Argentina." *Ciclos* 10, no. 19 (2000): 129–48.

Ramos, Julio. *Los cerrojos a la prensa*. Buenos Aires: Amfin, 1993.

Rapoport, Mario. *Gran Bretaña, Estados Unidos y las clases dirigentes argentinas, 1940–1945*. Buenos Aires: Belgrano, 1980.

Rapoport, Mario, and Claudio Spiguel. *Relaciones tumultuosas: Estados Unidos y el primer peronismo*. Buenos Aires: Emecé, 2009.

Rein, Mónica Esti. *Politics and Education in Argentina, 1946–1962*. Armonk, NY: Sharpe, 1998.

Rein, Raanan, ed. *Árabes y judíos en Iberoamérica: Similitudes, diferencia y tensiones*. Seville: Fundación Tres Culturas, 2008.

– *Argentina, Israel, and the Jews*. College Park: University Press of Maryland, 2003.

– *Argentine Jews or Jewish Argentines?* Boston: Brill, 2010.

– *Entre el abismo y la salvación: El pacto Franco-Perón*. Buenos Aires: Lumiere, 2003.

– *Fútbol, Jews, and the Making of Argentina*. Translated by Martha Grenzeback. Stanford: Stanford University Press, 2008. A brief version of this was previously published as: *Los bohemios de Villa Crespo: judíos y fútbol en la Argentina* (Buenos Aires: Sudamericana, 2012).

– *In the Shadow of the Holocaust and the Inquisition*. Second edition. London: Routledge, 2013.

– *Juan Atilio Bramuglia. Bajo la sombra del líder: la segunda línea del liderazgo peronista*. Buenos Aires: Lumiere, 2006. Translated by Martha Grenzeback as: *In the Shadow of Perón: Juan Atilio Bramuglia and the Second Line of Argentina's Populist Movement* (Stanford: Stanford University Press, 2008).

– ed. *Más allá del Medio Oriente: las diásporas judía y árabe en América Latina*. Granada: Editorial de la Universidad de Granada, 2012.

– "Nationalism, Education, and Identity: Argentine Jews and Catholic Religious Instruction, 1943–1955." In *Memory, Oblivion and Jewish Culture in Latin America*, edited by Marjorie Agosin, 163–75. Austin, TX: University of Texas Press, 2005.

– "Reconsiderando el caso Eichmann: El presidente Frondizi en la encrucijada." *Todo es Historia* (February 2014): 6–26.

Rein, Raanan, and Julio Frydenberg, eds. *La cancha peronista: fútbol y política, 1946–1955*. Buenos Aires: Universidad Nacional de San Martín, 2015.

Rein, Raanan, and Ariel Noyjovich. *Los muchachos peronistas árabes: los argentines árabes y el apoyo al Justicialismo*. Buenos Aires: Sudamericana, 2018.

Rein, Raanan, and Claudio Panella, eds. *Cultura para todos: el suplemento cultural de "La Prensa" cegetista (1951–1955)*. Buenos Aires: Biblioteca Nacional, 2013.

– *Peronismo y prensa escrita*. La Plata: UNLP, 2008.

Rein, Raanan, and Aya Udagawa. "Los muchachos peronistas japoneses." Paper delivered at the conference Migrants, Refugees, and Asylum seekers in Latin America, Tel Aviv University, June 2019.

República Argentina. *Diario de Sesiones de la Cámara de Diputados*. 1946–55.

República Argentina, Dirección de Migraciones. *Conceptos sobre inmigración*. Buenos Aires 1946.

República Argentina, Ministerio de Relaciones Exteriores y Culto. *La República Argentina y el "Libro Azul."* Buenos Aires, 1946.

República Argentina, Vicepresidencia de la Nación. *Libro negro de la segunda tiranía*. Buenos Aires, 1958.

Reyes, Cipriano. *Yo hice el 17 de octubre*. Buenos Aires: CEAL, 1984.

Riegner, Kurt J. "Argentina's Jewry under Perón." *Wiener Library Bulletin* 9, no. 5 (1955): 51.

Rock, David. *Authoritarian Argentina – The Nationalist Movement, Its History and Its Impact*. Berkeley: University of California Press, 1993.

Rodríguez Fabregat, Enrique. *Sión: Rebelión y cumplimiento*. Jerusalem: Institute of Cultural Relations Israel-Ibero-America, 1982.

Rom, Eugenio P. *Así hablaba Juan Perón*. Buenos Aires: A. Peña Lillo, 1980.

Rosenswaike, Ira. "The Jewish Population of Argentina: Census and Estimate, 1887–1947." *Jewish Social Studies* 22, no. 4 (October 1960): 195–214.

Rotenberg, Abrasha. *Historia confidencial. "La Opinión" y otros olvidos*. Buenos Aires: Sudamericana, 1999.

Rougier, Marcelo, and Martín Fiszbein. *La frustración de un proyecto económico. El gobierno peronista de 1973–1976*. Buenos Aires: Manantial, 2006.

Rouquié, Alain. *Poder militar y sociedad política en la Argentina*. Buenos Aires: Emecé, 1998.

Rout, Leslie B., and John F. Bratzel. *The Shadow War: German Espionage and United States Counterespionage in Latin America during World War II*. Frederick, MD: University Publications of America, 1986.

Rubel, Yaacov. *La población judía de la Ciudad de Buenos Aires. Perfil sociodemográfico*. Buenos Aires: Agencia Judía para Israel, Iniciativa de Demografía Judía, 2005.

Sáenz Quesada, María. *Isabel Perón*. Buenos Aires: Planeta, 2003.

– *La Libertadora: de Péron a Frondizi, 1955–1958*. Buenos Aires: Sudamericana, 2007.

Saitta, Silvia. *Regueros de tinta: el diario "Crítica" en la década de 1920*. Buenos Aires: Sudamericana, 1998.

Sallairai, Aurelio. *Los Protocolos de los Sabios de Sión y la subversión mundial*. Buenos Aires: n.p., 1972.

Sassone, Susana M. "Migraciones ilegales y amnistías en la República Argentina." *Estudios Migratorios Latinoamericanos* 6–7 (1987): 249–89.

Scenna, Miguel Angel. *F.O.R.J.A., una aventura argentina (de Yrigoyen a Perón)*. Buenos Aires: Belgrano, 1983.

Schenkolewsky-Kroll, Silvia. *The Zionist Movement and the Zionist Parties in Argentina, 1935–1948* (in Hebrew). Jerusalem: Magnes Press, 1996.

Schmelz, U.O., and Sergio Della Pergola. *La demografía de los judíos en la Argentina*. Tel Aviv: Tel Aviv University, 1974.

Schvarzer, Jorge. *Empresarios del pasado. La Unión Industrial Argentina*. Buenos Aires: Imago Mundi, 1991.

Schwartz, Jack. "Will Donald Trump Be America's Own Juan Perón?" *Daily Beast*, 23 January 2017. https://www.thedailybeast.com/will-donald-trump-be-americas-own-juan-peron

Scobie, James. *Buenos Aires: Plaza to Suburb, 1870–1910*. New York: Oxford University Press, 1974.

Sebreli, Juan José. *La cuestión judía en la Argentina*. Buenos Aires: Tiempo Contemporáneo, 1973.

Semán, Ernesto. "Comparing Trump to South American Authoritarians Reveals a Dangerous Misunderstanding of Democracy." *Washington Post*, 20 February 2018. https://www.washingtonpost.com/news/made-by-history/wp/2018/02/20/stop-comparing-trump-to-south-american-dictators-hes-actually-far-worse/?utm_term=.fea533930doe

Senén González, Santiago. *Laborismo. El partido de los trabajadores*. Buenos Aires: Capital Intelectual, 2014.

Senén González, Santiago, *and Gabriel D. Lerman, eds. El 17 de octubre de 1945: antes, durante y después*. Buenos Aires: Lumiere, 2005.

Senkman, Leonardo, ed. *El antisemitismo en la Argentina*. Second edition. Buenos Aires: CEAL, 1989.

– *Argentina, la segunda guerra mundial y los refugiados indeseables, 1933–1945*. Buenos Aires: Grupo Editor Latinoamericano, 1991.

– "Etnicidad e inmigración durante el primer peronismo." *Estudios Interdisciplinarios de América Latina* 3, no. 2 (1992): 5–38.

– *La identidad judía en la literatura argentina*. Buenos Aires: Pardés, 1983.

– "El peronismo visto desde la legación israelí en Buenos Aires: sus relaciones con la OIA, 1949–1955." *Judaica Latinoamericana* 2 (1993): 115–36.

– "El 4 de junio de 1943 y los judíos." *Todo es Historia* 193 (1983): 67–78.

– "Las relaciones EE.UU.-Argentina y la cuestión de los refugiados de la post-guerra, 1945–1948." *Judaica Latinoamericana* 1 (1988): 90–114.

Seoane, María. *El burgués maldito*. Buenos Aires: Planeta, 1998.

Sharif, Regina. "Latin America and the Arab-Israeli Conflict." *Journal of Palestine Studies* 7, no. 1 (1977): 98–122.

Sheinin, David. *Argentina and the United States: An Alliance Contained*. Athens, GA: University of Georgia Press, 2006.

– "Epilogue: The Centesimal Nisman." In *The New Ethnic Studies in Latin America*, edited by Raanan Rein, Stefan Rinke, and Nadia Zysman, 185–200. Brill: Boston, 2017.

– *Searching for Authority: Pan-Americanism, Diplomacy and Politics in United States-Argentine Relations, 1910–1930*. New Orleans: University Press of the South, 1998.

Simpson, Christopher. *Blowback: America's Recruitment of Nazis and Its Effects on the Cold War*. New York: Weidenfeld & Nicolson, 1988.

Sirvén, Pablo. *El Rey de la TV*. Buenos Aires: Sudamericana, 2013.

Sitman, Rosalie. *Victoria Ocampo y "Sur": entre Europa y América*. Buenos Aires: Lumiere, 2003.

Sivak, Martín. *"Clarín," el gran diario argentino. Una historia*. Buenos Aires: Planeta, 2013.

Sneh, Perla, ed. *Buenos Aires idish*. Buenos Aires: CPPHC, 2006.

Sofer, Eugene F. *From Pale to Pampa: A Social History of the Jews of Buenos Aires*. New York: Holmes & Meier, 1982.

Solberg, Carl. *Immigration and Nationalism, Argentina and Chile, 1890–1914*. Austin, TX: University of Texas Press, 1970.

Somoza Rodríguez, José Miguel. "Educación y política en Argentina. Creación de identidades y resocialización de sujetos (1943–1955)." PhD diss., Universidad Nacional de Educación a Distancia, Madrid, 2002.

Sosa de Newton, Lily. *Diccionario biográfico de mujeres argentinas*. Buenos Aires: Plus Ultra, 1986.

Spektorowski, Alberto. *Autoritarios y populistas. Los orígenes del fascismo argentino*. Buenos Aires: Lumiere, 2013.

Stack, Noreen Frances. "Avoiding the Greater Evil: The Response of the Argentine Catholic Church to Juan Perón." PhD diss., Rutgers University, 1976.

Stawski, Martin. *Asistencia social y buenos negocios: política de la Fundación Eva Perón, 1948–1955*. Buenos Aires: Imago Mundi, 2009.

Stiller, J.H. *George S. Messersmith – Diplomat of Democracy*. Chapel Hill: University of North Carolina Press, 1987.

Sutin, Stewart Edward. "The Impact of Nazism on the Germans of Argentina." PhD diss., University of Texas, 1975.

Tal, Tzvi. "The Other Becomes Mainstream: Jews in Contemporary Argentine Cinema." In Brodsky and Rein, eds, *The New Jewish Argentina: Facets of Jewish Experiences in the Southern Cone*, 365–91.

Temkin, Alfred. "Argentina, The Choice Before Perón." *Commentary* (June 1946): 14–21.

Tiempo, César. "Alberto Gerchunoff: vida y manos." *Hispania* 35, no. 1 (February 1952): 37–41.

– *La campaña antisemita y el director de la Biblioteca Nacional*. Buenos Aires: Mundo Israelita, 1935.

– *Capturas recomendadas*. Buenos Aires: Librería del Jurista, 1978.

Toker, Eliahu, ed. *Buenos Aires esquina Sábado. Antología de César Tiempo*. Buenos Aires: Archivo General de la Nación, 1997.

– *El ídish es también Latinoamérica*. Buenos Aires: Instituto Movilizador de Fondos Cooperativos, 2003.

Torre, Juan Carlos. *El gigante invertebrado. Los sindicatos en el gobierno, Argentina 1973–1976. Buenos Aires: Siglo XXI, 2004.*

– *ed. El 17 de octubre de 1945. Buenos Aires: Ariel, 1995.*

Tov, Moshé. *El murmullo de Israel – Historial diplomático. Jerusalem: La Semana, 1983.*

Tsur, Jacob. *Credential No.* 4 (in Hebrew). Tel Aviv: Maariv, 1981.

Tulchin, Joseph S. *Argentina and the United States: A Conflicted Relationship*. Boston: Twayne, 1990.

Ulanovsky, Carlos, Silvia Itkin, and Pablo Sirvén. *Estamos en el aire*. Buenos Aires: Emecé, 1999.

USA. Department of State. *Consultation Among the American Republics with Respect to the Argentine Situation*. Washington, DC, 1946.

Vaccarezza, Alberto. *El Conventillo de La Paloma*. Buenos Aires: Ediciones del Carro de Tespis, 1965.

Vannucci, Alberto P. "Elected by Providence: Spruille Braden in Argentina in 1945." In *Ambassadors in Foreign Policy: The Influence of Individuals on U.S.-Latin American Relations*, edited by C.N. Ronning and A.P. Vannucci, 49–67. New York: Praeger, 1987.

Varela, Mirta. "Peronismo y medios: control político, industria nacional y gusto popular." *Red de historia de los medios*. http://www.rehime.com.ar/escritos/documentos/idexalfa/v/varela/Mirta%20Varela%20-%20Peronismo%20y%20medios.pdf

Verbitsky, Horacio. *Ezeiza*. Buenos Aires: Planeta, 1995.

Vincent, Isabel. *Bodies and Souls: The Tragic Plight of Three Jewish Women Forced into Prostitution in the Americas*. New York: Harper Perennial, 2005.

Viquendi, Marcos A. "Los sirio-libaneses frente a la política nacional en el marco del primer peronismo (1946–1955)." Master's thesis, Universidad Nacional de Tres de Febrero (Buenos Aires), 2017.

Visacovsky, Nerina. "Herencias de 1947: Di ídische froi y el sufragio femenino." In *Sufragio femenino: Prácticas y debates políticos y culturales en Argentina y América Latina*, edited by Carolina Barry, 91–111. Buenos Aires: Eduntref, 2011.

Vitto, Cecilia. "Plan económico del tercer gobierno peronista. Gestión de Gelbard (1973–1974)." *Problemas del Desarrollo* 43, no. 171 (2012): 111–34.

Wagner, Wolfgang. *Kurt Tank: Focke Wulf's Designer and Test Pilot.* Atglen, PA: Schiffer, 1999.

Waisman, Carlos. "Capitalism, Socialism, and the Jews: The View from *Cabildo*." In *The Jewish Presence in Latin America*, edited by J.L. Elkin and G.W. Merks, 233–52. Boston: Allen & Unwin, 1987.

Walter, Richard. *Politics and Urban Growth in Buenos Aires, 1910–1943.* New York: Cambridge University Press, 1994.

Weinstein, Ana E., and Miryam E. Gover de Nasatsky, eds. *Escritores judeo-argentinos: bibliografía 1900–1987.* Buenos Aires: Milá, 1994.

Weisbrot, Robert. *The Jews of Argentina: From the Inquisition to Perón.* Philadelphia: Jewish Publication Society of America, 1979.

Weiser Varon, Benno. *Professions of a Lucky Jew.* New York: Cornwall, 1992.

Welles, Sumner. *The Time for Decision.* New York: Harper and Brothers, 1944.

White, Elizabeth B. *German Influence on the Argentine Army, 1900–1945.* New York: Garland, 1991.

Wiesenthal, Simon. *Justice Not Vengeance: Recollections.* New York: Grove Press, 1990.

Wilde, Eduardo. *Obras completas.* Buenos Aires: Talleres Peuser, 1917.

Wynia, Gary. *La Argentina de posguerra.* Buenos Aires: Belgrano, 1986.

Yarfitz, Mir. *Impure Migration: Jews and Sex Work in Golden Age Argentina.* Rutgers, NJ: Rutgers University Press, 2019.

Zanatta, Loris. *Perón y el mito de la nación Católica: Iglesia y Ejército en los orígenes del peronismo (1943–1946).* Buenos Aires: Sudamericana, 1999.

Zimerman de Faingold, Raquel. *Memorias.* Buenos Aires: n.p., 1987.

Zuleta Álvarez, Enrique. *El nacionalismo argentino.* Buenos Aires: La Bastilla, 1975.

Index

Acción Católica (Catholic Action), 37, 58–9, 99, 100, 175, 228
Alberdi, Juan Bautista, 15
Alianza Anticomunista Argentina (AAA), 215, 256
Alianza Libertadora Nacionalista, 7, 36, 41, 106, 191, 251
Allies (Second World War), 4, 47–9, 53, 69, 72, 188, 219
Aloé, Carlos, 81
Amadeo, Mario, 108, 110, 154
American Jewish Committee, 41, 43, 95, 104, 140–1, 224
AMIA. *See* Asociación Mutual Israelita Argentina (AMIA)
Andrea, Monsignor Miguel de, 104
anti-Israel. *See* Israel
Antisemitism: Arab antisemitism, 250; in Argentina, 8, 17, 35–9, 55, 79, 80, 91, 127, 140–1, 205, 218; Nazi antisemitism, 42; in the Soviet Union, 139, 140, 156; struggle against, 4–5, 7, 40, 79, 84, 86–7, 108, 138, 141, 232, 251–2; under Perón, 41–2, 223–4, 239–40, 257
anti-Zionism. *See* Israel
Arab League, 117, 120–1, 126
Arabs: Arab-Israeli conflict, 122, 240; Arab nationalism, 18; Arab countries, 114, 116–17, 120, 126, 129, 131, 150, 234, 240, 248, 250, 252; in Argentina, 10, 13, 118, 121, 125–8, 202, 259, 264–5; Arab immigration to the Americas, 18, 22
Aramburu, Pedro Eugenio, 110
Arce, José, 122–8
Argentina, 3, 12–15, 18, 38, 59, 102, 110–11, 155–7, 165, 167, 171, 175, 179, 186, 197–8, 200, 213, 222, 237, 251, 257–65; and Catholic Church, 98, 107; education in, 57; as haven for Nazi war criminals, 45, 64–73; in First World War, 4; liberalism in, 217; as melting pot, 16; national library, 153; neutrality in Second World War, 45–54, 116; portrayal in Israel, 226–33, 235, 239–42, 244–7, 252–7; portrayal in United States, 223–6; pro-Arab policy, 127; relations with Arab countries, 116, 117, 120, 250; relations with Israel, 81–2, 86, 117, 122, 129–31, 133, 138–45, 148–52, 234, 240–1, 247; relations with Palestine, 119, 121–2; relations with United Nations, 5, 115, 117, 120, 122; relations with United States, 45, 51, 115–16, 130, 134, 143, 146–7, 247; television and radio in

Argentina, 10, 169–70, 175, 177, 180, 182–4; in UN General Assembly, 128–30; Zionism in, 118–21
Asociación Mutual Israelita Argentina (AMIA), 32, 84, 94, 97, 111, 112, 260, 262–4
Auschwitz, 67
Austria, 26, 66–7, 85
Axis powers, 7, 40, 46, 48–50, 53, 67–8, 72, 107, 224

Baldrich, Alberto, 60
Balfour Declaration, 117, 120
Bard, Leopoldo, 93
Bartov, Hanoch, 245
Basavilbaso, 89
Begin, Menachem, 230
Belnicoff, Manuel, 85
Ben Gurion, David, 142, 206
Bercovich Rodríguez, Raúl, 11
Benarós, León, 11, 163, 164
Benítez Piriz, Leonardo, 119–20, 126
Ber Gelbard, José, 7, 10, 178, 184, 195–222, 240, 250
Bioy Casares, Adolfo, 41, 164
Blum, Amram, 11–12, 95–7, 103, 110, 112, 179
Bolivia, 50, 67–8
Bolsheviks, 26, 39, 218
Borges, Jorge Luis, 41, 163–5
Borlenghi, Ángel, 74, 81, 86, 88, 96, 103, 110, 193–4
Braden, Spruille, 52–3, 72, 190, 223–5
Bramuglia, Juan Atilio, 79, 119–23, 125–8, 147, 192–3
Brazil, 15, 19, 24, 28, 38, 48, 50, 75, 111, 118, 150
Britain, 4, 19, 46–7, 49, 55, 71, 114, 116, 131, 143, 146
Broner, Julio, 10, 204, 206–7, 211, 221, 250
Bruce, James, 147, 225–6
Brunello, Duilo, 7
Buerdman, Samuel, 76

Cabildo (newspaper), 107, 218, 251
Caggiano, Antonio, 104
Campana (ship), 75
Carrillo, Ramón, 78
casteidish (language), 30
Castillo, Ramón, 48–9, 176, 189
Catholic Action. *See* Acción Católica
Catholic Church, 7, 19, 38, 46, 66, 95, 97, 105, 154, 175, 228, 231; social doctrine of, 4
Catholic Maronite Christians, 18
caudillo, 164, 218, 234
CEANA. *See* Commission of Enquiry into the Activities of Nazism in Argentina (CEANA)
CGE. *See* Confederación General Económica (CGE)
CGT. *See* Confederación General del Trabajo (CGT)
Chacarita Juniors (football club) 34–5
Chapultepec Conference, 51
Chile, 34, 49, 67, 104, 115, 161, 194, 244–6
Club Atlético Atlanta (football club), 35, 93
Cold War, 63, 69, 127, 139, 233
Commission of Enquiry into the Activities of Nazism in Argentina (CEANA), 64, 67
Confederación General de Empleados de Comercio, 10, 86, 194–5
Confederación General del Trabajo (CGT), 11, 98, 101, 154–5, 160, 188, 190, 192–5, 203, 208, 211–13, 216, 219, 221, 234, 241, 257, 259
Confederación General Económica (CGE), 7, 10, 196–8, 202–16, 219–22, 240, 250, 259
Congregación Israelita, 31
conventillos, 28

Copello, Santiago Luis, 61, 104, 107
Corominas, Enrique, 122–9
Cortés (Shejtman), Eduardo, 76, 84, 91
Cortesi, Arnaldo, 41
Croatia, 68–9
Cucciti, Carlos, 104
Czechoslovakia, 139

DAIA. *See* Delegación de Asociaciones Israelitas Argentinas (DAIA)
Darom, Abraham, 136, 140
De Gaulle, Charles, 244, 253
De la Torre, Lisandro, 60
Decker, Rodolfo, 7
Delegación de Asociaciones Israelitas Argentinas (DAIA), 8–9, 32, 38, 40–1, 43–4, 59, 62, 75–6, 78–9, 84, 86–7, 91, 94, 97, 103–5, 107–12, 118–19, 130, 136, 151, 205–6, 218, 248, 250–1, 262–4
Dell'Oro Maini, Atilio, 108
Democracia (newspaper), 42, 118
Democratic Progressive Party, 60
Democratic Union. *See* Unión Democrática
de-Peronization, 110, 113
Di Idishe Tzaitung (newspaper), 32, 38, 107
diaspora, 33, 149, 261
Dickmann, Enrique, 88, 130
Diskin, David, 9, 86, 194–5
Doron, Eliezer, 247, 249
Dual Loyalty, 135, 250
Dubrovsky, Ricardo, 9, 76–7
Dujovne, Israel, 10, 206–7

Eastern Europe, 7–8, 15–16, 18–19, 22, 24, 32–3, 39, 91, 121, 141
Egypt, 28, 116, 235
Eichmann, Adolf, 35, 45, 64–5, 67–8, 73, 135, 206
Ejército Revolucionario del Pueblo (ERP), 238
Eliachar, Eliahu, 95
Entre Ríos (province), 11, 20, 26, 43, 89–90, 161, 170–2
ERP. *See* Ejército Revolucionario del Pueblo (ERP)
Espejo, José, 98
Ethnicity, 32, 259, 264
Evian Conference, 26
Eximbank, 142, 147
Eytan, Walter, 136–7
Ezeiza Massacre, 243
Ezrah Jewish Hospital, 9, 76, 179

Falklands/Malvinas War, 97
Farrell, Edelmiro J., 41, 50–2, 120, 177, 180, 190
fascism, 4, 28, 41, 45, 52, 96, 107, 136, 159, 201, 210, 224, 226, 229, 231–2, 242, 245, 254
First World War, 16, 24–5
Foxman, Abraham, 264
France, 19, 26, 28, 32, 68, 89, 124, 131, 172, 175
Franco, Francisco, 26, 39–40, 50, 69, 107–8, 122, 223, 228, 233, 245
Frente Justicialista de Liberación (FREJULI), 237
Frondizi, Arturo, 183, 194, 205, 207–8
Fundación Eva Perón, 12, 81, 89–90, 148, 150–2

Gainza Paz, Alberto, 160
Gerchunoff, Alberto, 19, 89, 92, 156, 159, 162, 167
Germany, 4, 26, 38, 41, 45–7, 50–1, 56, 64–8, 70–2, 108, 116, 172, 223
Gilbert, Alberto, 38
Goldman, Moisés, 43, 62, 78, 109–11, 119
Goldstein, Joseph, 91
Goyeneche, Juan Carlos, 107–8
Graiver, David, 214, 221, 250
Gran Acuerdo Nacional, 236

Grandi, Dino, 69
Great Britain. *See* Britain
Great National Accord. *See* Gran Acuerdo Nacional
Griffis, Stanton, 225
Grinstein, Manuel, 76
Grünberg, Carlos M., 143, 162, 167
Grupo de Oficiales Unidos, 36, 177
Guardia Restauradora Nacionalista (GRN), 35
Guardo, Ricardo, 62

Herzl, Theodor, 18, 81
Hirsch, Maurice de, 19, 25, 43
Histadrut (Israeli labour federation), 82, 229
Hitler, Adolf, 45, 64–7, 70–2, 107, 113, 172, 223
Hudal, Alois, 66
Hull, Cordell, 47–8, 50–2
Hungary, 28, 95

immigration, 14, 17–8, 22, 24–5, 28, 31, 36, 54–7, 66–8, 79, 86, 151, 158, 258–9
Instituto Judío Argentino, 104
Integration of Jews into Argentine society, 159
Israel, 6, 28, 34, 68, 82, 84, 139–42, 227, 228, 231–2, 235, 238, 255–7; anti-Israel or anti-Zionism, 36, 234, 241; Argentine embassy in, 6, 11; and Argentine Jewish community, 6, 8, 54, 74, 78, 86–7, 91, 94, 110, 132, 258, 261–2; creation of, 11, 115, 119, 130–1; Eichmann kidnapping and, 68, 73, 206; migration to, 24; Peronist administration and, 12; relations with Argentina, 5, 7, 36, 76, 80–2, 85–6, 90–1, 93–4, 104–5, 108–9, 113, 117, 123, 129–31, 133–45, 148–52, 206, 224, 226, 234, 240–1, 244, 247–9, 251–4, 257; shipments to, 82, 145; and Six-Day War, 235
Italy, 4, 16, 28, 41, 50, 68, 76, 135, 152

Jabbaz, Israel, 11, 190
Japan, 10, 18, 48, 50–1, 116, 265
JCA. *See* Jewish Colonization Association (JCA)
Jewish Agency, 94, 118, 125–6
Jewish-Argentines, 5, 8, 10–12, 14, 17, 19, 22–8, 30–1, 35–6, 40, 43, 54–5, 57, 60, 62, 77, 80, 82, 84–5, 87–93, 96, 100, 106, 109, 113, 130–1, 135–8, 142, 149, 155, 162, 167, 170, 175, 179, 186, 190, 204, 210, 221, 234, 240, 248, 250, 256–9, 261–3
Jewish Colonization Association (JCA), 25
Jewish Community, 3, 5–7, 9, 12, 16–17, 31, 33, 36–7, 39, 44, 54, 57, 59, 61–2, 74, 75, 78–9, 84–6, 88, 90–2, 95–7, 103–4, 106–7, 109–12, 118–19, 121, 130–3, 135–8, 140, 144, 148, 155, 160, 179, 186, 198–200, 205–6, 218, 224, 227, 231, 234–5, 240–1, 251–3, 260–4
Jewish gauchos, 19–20, 162, 175, 245
Jewish immigration to Argentina, 14, 24, 28, 54–7, 75, 86, 89, 95
Jewish National Fund (Keren Kayemeth), 86, 142, 148, 244
Judenstaat (book), 19
Justicialismo, 3, 58, 81, 85, 160, 211, 223, 232, 246
Justicialist Party, 11
Justo, Agustín P., 60, 208
Juventud Peronista, 237, 239

Kafia, José, 76
Kaplan, Nelly, 162
Katz, Jevel, 30
Keren Hayesod (United Israel Appeal), 84, 87

Keren Kayemeth. *See* Jewish National Fund
Kessler, Ana, 7
Kirchner, Cristina Fernández de, 260–3
Kismer de Olmos, Raquel Cecilia (Kelly), 7
Klement, Ricardo. *See* Eichmann, Adolf
Kogan, Rafael, 9, 191–3, 195
Kordón, Bernardo, 11, 162
Koremblit, Bernardo Ezequiel, 11, 155, 162–6, 263
Kovadloff, Jacobo, 153
Kraiselburd, David, 255
Krasbutch, John, 76
Krislavin, Abraham, 84–6, 110–11, 133, 194
Kubovy, Arieh (León), 106, 110, 142

Lanusse, General Alejandro, 208–9, 236–7
Latin America, 51, 118, 120, 135, 137, 170, 186, 228, 245
League of Nations, 26, 117
Lebanon, 116, 120–1, 152
Lend-Lease program, 48
Leo XIII (pope), 60
Levavi, Arye, 142
Liberating Revolution, 9, 91
Lipsky, Louis, 224
Lithuania, 24
Llamamiento Judío Argentino, 262–3
Lokman, Carlos, 76
Lonardi, Eduardo, 107–10
López Rega, José ("El Brujo"), 215, 218, 247, 249–50

Madanes, Manuel, 204, 221
Maguidovich, Clara, 81
Manguel, Pablo: appointed ambassador to Israel, 11, 77, 94, 106, 132, 133; in OIA, 6, 76–7, 80, 82, 89, 93; relations with Juan and Eva Perón, 6, 82, 85–6, 89, 91; response to antisemitism, 106; victim of anti-Peronist campaign, 110
MAPAI (Mifleget Poalei Eretz Yisrael), 144, 229, 240
MAPAM (Mifleget Poalim Meuhedet), 230, 241–2, 257
Martel, Julián, 39
Martínez Zuviría, Gustavo, 37, 57, 60, 153–4, 156
Matrajt, Sujer, 8, 76, 80, 91–2, 94, 131, 148
Mauricio (colony), 24
Maurras, Charles, 39, 107
Meir, Golda, 12, 82–3, 139, 206
Menem, Carlos Saúl, 64
Menéndez, Benjamín, 88
Mengele, Josef, 67–8
Mercante, Domingo, 88, 192
Messersmith, George, 224–5
Mibashan, Abraham, 94, 118–20, 126
Middle East, 16, 81, 86, 114, 122, 129, 131, 144, 150, 234, 248
Midgal, Zwi, 31
Minorities, 13, 15–16, 18–19, 23, 31, 33, 42, 46, 63, 100, 118, 124, 154, 170, 179, 208, 263, 265
Minyevsky, Adolfo, 91
Moisesville (colony), 24
Molinari, Diego Luis, 120, 144, 226
Montoneros, 218, 221, 236–9
Mor Roig, Arturo, 25
Morocco, 24, 144
Mosca, Enrique, 54
Mossad, 35, 45, 68, 73, 206
Mu Mu (candy factory), 97
Mundo Israelita (newspaper), 89, 107, 113
Mundo Peronista (magazine), 223
Muslims, 15, 18, 22, 116, 121

Nasser, Gamal Abdel, 28

nationalists (Argentine), 15, 38, 41, 50, 53, 102, 110, 133, 135, 154, 158, 244
National-Socialist Party, 67
Nazi agents, 52
Nazi fugitives, 51, 64, 69
Nazi Germany, 26, 38, 50
Nazi war criminals, 35, 45, 64, 72–3, 206, 224
Neruda, Pablo, 161, 163
Nikiprovesky, Mauricio, 76, 78
Nisman, Alberto, 260–1
Novoa, Ramón, 105
Nudelman, Santiago L., 85
Nufer, Albert, 225

Ocampo, Victoria, 155, 163–4
Once (neighbourhood), 17, 32–4, 43, 85
Organización Israelita Argentina (OIA): and DAIA, 86, 130–1, 133; foundation of, 8, 75–6; opposing views of OIA, 88–94, 136–7, 231, 262–3; and Pablo Manguel, 6, 85, 109, 131, 134; relations with Perón, 76, 78–86, 90, 94–5, 113, 135–7, 142, 144, 152, 206, 258
Ortiz, Roberto M., 47–9, 176, 189
Ottoman Empire, 18, 24
Oved. *See* Versano, Yaacov

Palestine, 5, 11, 18, 19, 94, 114–15, 117, 119, 120, 124, 126–7, 130, 143, 205, 262
Pan-American Defense Agreement, 48
Paraguay, 68, 200
Partido Laborista, 9, 42, 191, 194
Pavelic, Ante, 69
Pearl Harbor, 48, 69
Peralta, Santiago, 55–7
Perelman, Ángel, 9, 186–90, 196
Perlinger, Luis, 37
Perlmuter, Gregorio, 76
Perón, Eva Duarte ("Evita"), 4, 10–11, 77, 82, 84, 89–90, 97, 105, 144, 148, 151–2, 165, 177–8, 183, 206, 226, 232
Perón, Juan Domingo, 4–6, 8–11, 40, 42, 45, 50, 52–4, 57–8, 60, 63, 69, 71–2, 81, 88–9, 98–9, 100–2, 105–7, 113, 115, 131, 154–5, 161, 177, 181, 183, 188–90, 192, 194–5, 201, 206, 209, 220, 223–4, 228–33, 236–9, 249, 252, 255, 259, 262; and antiemitism, 3–4, 80, 96, 140, 251; and Argentine Catholic Church, 62, 105; and Argentine Jews, 77–8, 82, 85–6, 92–6, 102, 104, 112, 133–4, 138, 156, 168, 170, 177–9, 200, 202–3, 209, 213–14, 216–18, 228, 250–1; death, 252; decline and overthrow, 6, 52, 92, 112; and immigration, 28; and Jewish community organizations, 2, 7–8, 11–12, 43–4, 74, 79, 83–4, 86, 131, 136–7, 227, 263; and military coup d'état, 91; and Nazi war criminals, 64; and Palestine policy, 115; relations with Great Britain, 143, 146; relations with Israel, 78, 86, 94, 117, 119–20, 129, 131, 132–3, 135–8, 140, 142–3, 151–2; relations with United States, 51, 86, 141, 143, 147, 182, 224; return to Argentina, 194–5, 234–5, 238–9, 243
Perón, María Estela Martínez de ("Isabel" or "Isabelita"), 219–20, 234, 239, 249, 252, 255–6
Peronism, 4–6, 8–13, 17, 23, 41, 62–3, 73, 76, 78, 88, 90, 92–3, 98–101, 110, 114, 130, 137, 154, 156–7, 160, 163–4, 166–7, 179–80, 184–7, 193–4, 196, 201–11, 218, 226–9, 232–7, 239–42, 246, 248, 252–3, 256–9, 262–3, 265

Peronist doctrine, 60, 234
Peronist Party, 76, 89, 102, 126, 136, 161
Pius XII (pope), 60, 62, 94
Plaza Lavalle, 31–2, 34
Poland, 10, 18, 24, 34, 48, 196, 206
porteños, 34, 37, 156–8, 200
Prilutzky Farny, Julia, 11, 162–5, 263
Primo de Rivera, Miguel, 39, 107

Quijano, Hortensio, 53, 12, 183

Rabinovich, José, 162
Railworkers' Union. *See* Unión Ferroviaria
Ramírez, Pedro Pablo, 50, 59, 177
Red Army, 66–7
Red Cross, 66, 72–3
Revisionist Zionism, 230
Revolución Libertadora, 9, 91–2, 107–8, 110, 168, 194, 228, 236
Richter, Ronald, 66
Rinsky, Benjamin, 62
Roatta, General Mario, 69
Rockefeller, Nelson, 51, 225
Rojas, Isaac, 108
Roosevelt, Franklin D., 38, 47, 52, 176
Rozovsky, Jaime, 76
Rudel, Hans Ulrich, 66

San Martín, José de, 136
Sánchez Sorondo, Marcelo, 159
Scheinsohn, Manuel, 76, 80, 92
Schlesinger, Guillermo, 104
Schneider, Julio Jorge, 76
Scorza, Carlo, 69
Second World War, 4–5, 7, 24, 27, 34–5, 40, 43, 45–6, 52, 56, 66–7, 69, 107, 108, 116, 121, 145, 147, 176, 188, 200, 206, 224, 231, 265
Sharett, Moshe, 139–40, 142, 227
Shem Tov, Victor, 241
Six-Day War, 235
Slinin, Moisés, 84
Sociedad Hebraica Argentina, 153, 165–6, 169, 206
Sojit (Shoijet), Luis Elías, 91, 111
Soviet Union, 92, 139, 231, 242
Spain, 28, 50, 150, 233
Spellman, Cardinal Francis, 231
Sprinzak, Yosef, 226
Stettinius, Edward, 51
Storni, Admiral Segundo, 50
Sulzberger, Arthur, 225
synagogue, 12, 24, 31–2, 40–1, 90, 95–6, 103, 139, 251
Syria, 116, 120–1, 235, 240, 248
Syrian-Lebanese migration, 18, 22, 33, 79, 95–6, 118, 121, 199

Tacuara, 35
Tamborini, José, 43, 54
Tank, Kurt, 66, 72
Tarnopolsky, Samuel, 162
Tato, Manuel, 105
Teitelbaum, Miguel, 95–7, 112
Third Reich, 64, 67, 69, 222
Tiempo, César. *See* Zeitlin, Israel
Timerman, Héctor, 260–4
Timerman, Jacobo, 167, 209, 213, 218
Tov, Moshe, 104, 117, 119–20, 123, 126, 135–7, 241
Tragic Week, 33, 39
Trujillo, Rafael Leonidas, 27
Truman, Harry, 52, 119
Tsur, Yaacov, 90–1, 131–3, 135–8, 141–2, 144, 150–1, 206, 224, 226–7, 234, 237, 241, 244, 247–8, 253
Turkow, Marc, 106

Ukraine, 156–7, 165
Unión de Estudiantes Secundarios (UES), 99, 259
Unión Democrática, 3, 43
Unión Ferroviaria, 191–2

Unión Obrera Metalúrgica (UOM), 9, 186
United Israel Appeal. *See* Keren Hayesod
United Jewish Appeal (UJA), 139, 144, 148–9, 152
United Nations (UN), 5, 11, 51–2, 114, 116, 119, 122, 125–6, 131, 145
United States (US), 15, 24–5, 38, 46–52, 54, 71–2, 80, 112, 115–16, 120, 127, 139, 141, 143, 146–9, 176, 224–5, 248, 265
Uriburu, José Félix, 36–7, 159
Uruguay, 15, 70, 85, 110, 112, 131, 150

Vaccarezza, Alberto, 34
Valentín, Fernando, 11
Vargas, Getúlio, 50
Velazco, Juan Filomeno, 79
Ventura, José, 84
Versano, Yaacov ("Oved"), 232–3
Villa Clara (colony), 24–5
Villa Crespo (neighbourhood), 17, 33–4, 93, 130, 171, 263
Villa Lynch (neighbourhood), 34
Villada Achával, Clemente, 108
Viñas, David, 168

Weidman, Rodolfo, 85
Weiser Varon, Benno, 117
Weizmann, Chaim, 81, 94, 131–2, 138–9
Wesser (ship), 24
Wiesenthal, Simon, 64, 70–2
World Jewish Congress, 75, 90, 106, 119, 141, 218
World War I. *See* First World War
World War II. *See* Second World War
Woscoff, Alberto, 75
Woscoff, Salvador, 76, 78, 81, 91, 111–12

xenophobia, 158–9, 259

Yagupsky, Máximo, 43, 95, 104–5, 109, 111, 156, 168
Yampolsky, Ángel, 9, 190–1, 194–5
Yankelevich, Jaime, 10, 92, 169–85
Yiddish, 30, 32–3, 38, 156, 158, 170, 205
Yom Kippur War, 235, 245, 247, 256
Yrigoyen, Hipólito, 58, 93, 175

Zabotinsky, Ezequiel, 11, 77, 85–6, 91, 94, 110
Zeitlin, Israel ("César Tiempo"), 11, 77, 85–6, 91, 94, 110, 153–6, 163, 165–8, 263
Zionism, 6, 8, 81, 86, 91, 123, 129, 132, 135, 205, 230, 251, 258